Shifting Gears
Tales of pistons, paint cans and personalities

Shifting Gears
Tales of pistons, paint cans and personalities

As experienced by "World Famous"
Tony Vickio

Preston Woods Publishing Co. • Los Gatos, Calif.

Shifting Gears: Tales of pistons, paint cans and personalities
By Tony Vickio

Preston Woods Publishing Co.
Los Gatos, CA 95032 USA

© 2014 by Tony Vickio
All rights reserved. Published 2014
Printed in the United States of America

Second Printing 2024

10 9 8 7 6 5 4 3 2

No portion of this publication may be reproduced in whole or in part, or stored in a retrieval system, or transmitted in any form or by any means, electronic, mechanical, photocopying, recording, or otherwise, without written permission of the publisher.

Library of Congress Control Number: 2014950166

ISBN 978-0-9725571-6-0

Contents

Pit Row ix
Pace Lap xi
Lap 01: The Beginning 1
Lap 02: Drag racing 7
Lap 03: My Dream Car 12
Lap 04: Building a Race Car 16
Lap 05: My First Race 27
Lap 06: Learning to Win 36
Lap 07: A New Direction 42
Lap 08: Memorable Dirt Races 49
Lap 09: I Learn a Hard Lesson 58
Lap 10: A Love of Painting 68
Lap 11: Applying Life's Lessons 72
Lap 12: My First Asphalt Race 78
Lap 13: From Hobby To Career 86
Lap 14: Dark Side of Racing 89
Lap 15: The Superspeedway 94
Lap 16: The Bombshell 102
Lap 17: Preparing to Paint 108
Lap 18: Painting the Grass 115
Lap 19: Back to My New Job 124
Lap 20: Midgets Speed 131
Lap 21: Risking a Grassy Death 139
Lap 22: Not Again! 145
Lap 23: Back to School 149
Lap 24: Back With Friends 156
Lap 25: Getting Started 161
Lap 26: Here We Go. . . Painting 181
Lap 27: Major Problem 187
Lap 28: The Bar Brawl 192
Lap 29: Saturday Excitement 195
Lap 30: Talladega Race Day 199
Lap 31: The Road to Daytona 205
Lap 32: Teaching Class 212
Lap 33: Speed Week 218
Lap 34: We Face the Walls 227
Lap 35: High Wallers 235
Lap 36: Talladega Race Time 244
Lap 37: Pace Car Rides 250

Lap 38: Back to Work 255
Lap 39: Painting and Repainting 259
Lap 40: How Many Hits? 264
Lap 41: Under Attack 269
Lap 42: Highwaller Shoes .274
Lap 43: Painting Big. 282
Lap 44: We Paint the Asphalt 287
Lap 45: This Bud's for You 294
Lap 46: Startling Sights 297
Lap 47: We Play the Game 303
Lap 48: Racing Southern Style 311
Lap 49: We Paint for Dale. 317
Lap 50: Painting New Walls 324
Lap 51: The Inaugural Race 329
Lap 52: Work and Play 332
Lap 53: Chicagoland Race Day 336
Lap 54: Peeling Vinyl 339
Lap 55: Stepping into History. 343
Lap 56: Wild Ride. 349
Lap 57: Déjà Vu. 352
Victory Lap 361
Index 363

For my "Pretty Lady"

I am proud to dedicate *Shifting Gears* to my wonderful wife, Harriett. Without her love, inspiration, support, and understanding, the tales from 1982 to the present would never have happened. Harriett saved my life. She was always there for me and somehow understood the crazy life of a sign painter whose business was intertwined in the exciting world of auto racing.

Don Romeo (left) changing spark plugs while I wait for him to finish.

Some of my fellow painters. From left to right: Gary Kerbein, Steve Hughey, me, John Nicholson, Larry Orr, Bob Timmerman.

Pit Row

I learned very early that if you want to be successful in auto racing, you have to surround yourself with people who have the same values, drive and enthusiasm about winning as you do. I was lucky! Not only was I surrounded by talented people, but they were also great friends. The same was true when I started doing large paintings at race tracks around the country. I was always surrounded by one or two "sign guys" that had the same talent I had. This made the work fun. I'm not saying it was not hard work. It was, but at the same time it was fun. You will meet many of these friends in this book.

From Don Romeo: It's been my pleasure to be a good friend of Tony's for well over 40 years. During that time I have watched Tony accomplish many things, from race car crew member to owner and driver, from pin striping vehicles to a full service sign shop to an author. Tony is one of those rare people that when you meet him you become friends. I am proud to be part of this trip through time and included in Tony's Book. So sit back and enjoy the book, because with Tony you never know what is going to happen next.

From Larry Orr: I remember thinking after a trip or two helping the "Famous" a.k.a. Tony Vickio, "How good is this for a small town sign painter and lifelong race fan? Big-time work at big-time venues and garage passes for race day." After a few more road jobs I thought, you know, there's enough adventure and humor in these jobs, Tony could write a book—and Famous being Famous, he's done it!

From Steve Hughey: Tony (or "Famous" as his sign buddies call him) seems to be a magnet for interesting happenings that make great stories. This book is no exaggeration of the events I was privileged to be part of. I will always be grateful to Tony for all the adventures he has shared with me, except maybe the time we spent all day on top of the high bank (34-degree slope) in Talladega. Afterwards I could not bend my ankles and had to do the shuffle-along instead of a normal walk. Ten years later my ankles still hurt. Seriously, these are memories I will always treasure. Thanks Famous!

From Steve Tinker: I have known Tony since around 1970 when we worked at Shepard Niles, Montour Falls, New York together. We became good friends, because of our mutual hobbies, racing cars, snowmobiling, and just being young and usually out of control. I really don't know what has been written in this book, but I am positive some stories are best not to be told, EVER… Tony has accomplished two life times of CRAZINESS, and I am very proud to have been sucked into some of Tony and my memories. God Bless and a treasured FRIEND FOREVER.

My first race car. Back then my hair was black.

Pace Lap

In the 1990s I was mostly working at Watkins Glen International. Whenever I came back from one of my trips to another racetrack where I had done some sign work, I'd sit down in Michelle LaDue Benjamin's office—she was our administrative assistant—and tell her, and anyone that would listen, the tales from the latest trip and the amazing people I had met.

Michelle would always tell me, "Toneman" (that is what she called me), "you have to write this stuff down! This is amazing!"

Well, twenty-five years later, I wrote this stuff down. In my wildest dreams, I never thought I'd write a book—but once I started writing (and reliving some of the unbelievable experiences I've had), I couldn't stop. I found myself laughing, tearing up, frowning, swearing, breathing faster, and just staring off at nothing, lost in memory. One tale led to another and then to another, shifting gears between the racing world and the world of a sign man. I hope that you will enjoy reading this book as much as I did writing it. It will give you a look into what goes on behind the scenes at major racetracks, and perhaps give you a newfound appreciation for the sign business.

I jumped into two careers at the same time, with hardly any training in either one, and went full throttle with both. Is that determination? Stupidity? I'm not sure . . . but it worked! Through auto racing and through sign painting, I have unique tales to tell.

Thank you Michelle!

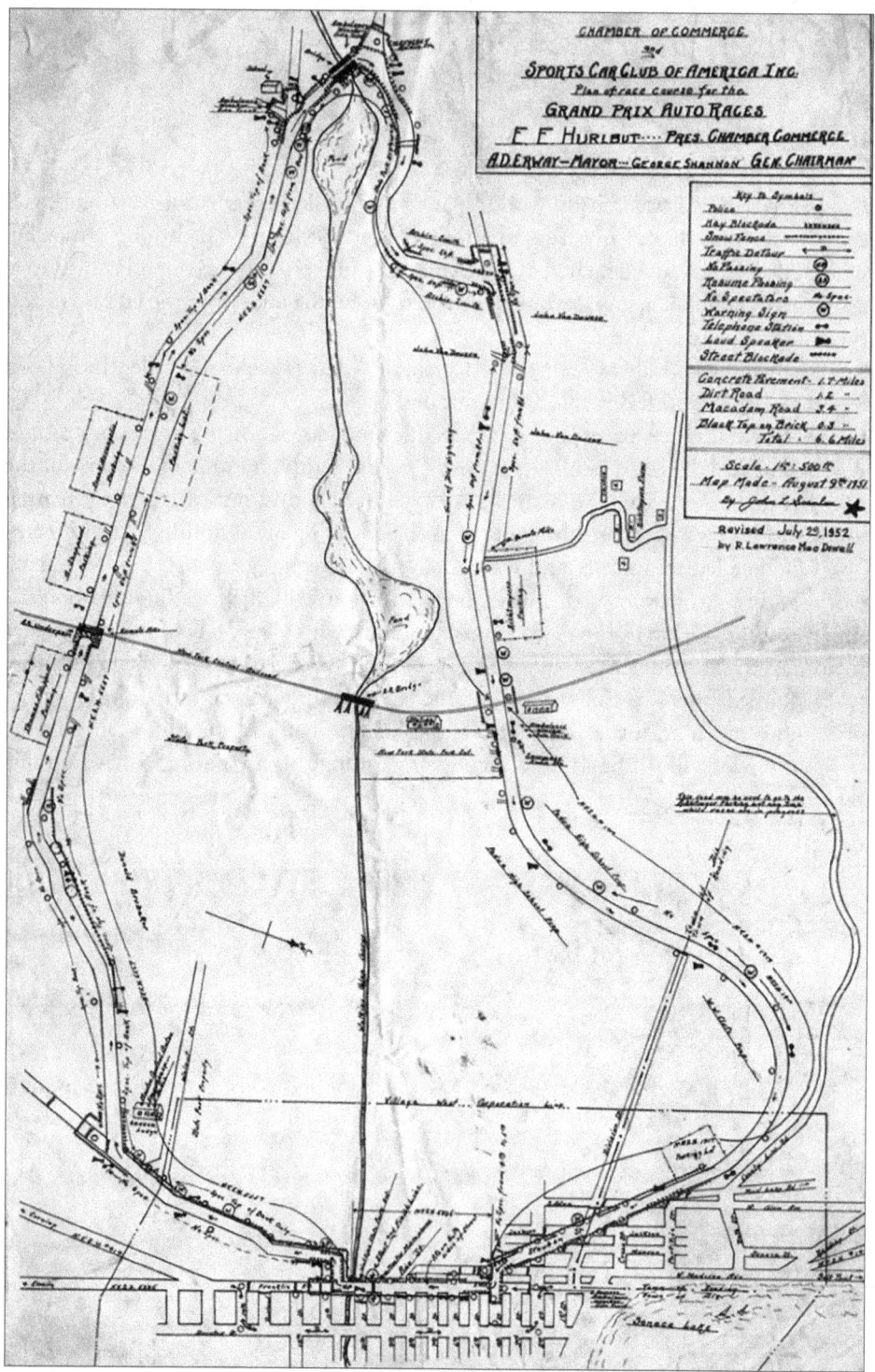

An original map of the Watkins Glen track, ink drawing on linen/Mylar. This course was used from 1948 to 1952.

The Beginning

I was exposed to the excitement of auto racing when I was just two years old. For that, I have my parents and a man named Cameron Argetsinger to thank.

My parents, Nick and Rachel, were the children of immigrants who'd come from northern Italy in the early 1900s looking for a better life. They grew up in Watkins Glen, New York, met in school, fell in love and married. With the help of a retired barber from Reynoldsville, New York, a man who could also lay bricks, my father built a house in 1946. It was on land that my mother's father owned on State Route 329, just above Seneca Lodge in Watkins Glen. I grew up there with my parents and my younger brother—named Nick, but we all called him "Chip" instead. When my parents started building their home on my grandfather's land, little did they know that their road would become a part of road racing history.

Cameron Argetsinger came home from World War II with a vision of road racing in the United States. Using European road racing as a model, in 1948 he plotted the road course through the village of Watkins Glen and into the countryside on existing village, town, county, and park roads.

Race day, 1948. I am two years old (standing on the left in this photo of my front lawn on race day).

Before the races came to town, my family lived in an isolated area. We never thought of the road as a race course—it was just the way to go to town to get ice cream. I was two years old when the first race was run on that road, so I don't remember much about it. What I do remember was the activity—crowds of people and cars in our lawn, which was turned into a parking lot. It was chaos, and I didn't know why. And it was *loud!* That race car noise. It burned into my young, mushy brain.

Argetsinger chose a start/finish line in the center of Watkins Glen, right in front of the village's historic courthouse. From there, the course passed in front of the famous Watkins Glen gorge, took a 90-degree right turn, and then proceeded up a steep, winding road. At the top of the hill, the road straightened out—that's where it ran past my house. The course ran under the old New York Central Railroad underpass, built in 1902, and on for another mile before another sharp right turn that dropped the racers onto a twisting, winding road that crossed a picturesque stone bridge. (This became a famous site for photos.) Right after the bridge, the road again turned 90 degrees to the right. After winding through the woods at the bottom of the gorge, it headed steeply up the other side of Hidden Valley (which we called White's Hollow) and through some narrow "S" turns. On the left, next to the road and not two feet from the asphalt surface, was a stone wall. On the right was a drop-off into the water of the gorge, protected only by some steel posts with a steel cable attached to them. At the top of the hill was a sharp, off-camber left turn. After a short straightaway, there was yet another sharp right turn.

The road—to this point asphalt—turned to dirt. It was now a high-speed run,

The view from my driveway (with a race official standing guard).

dust flying and swirling in the air, on a fairly straight section along the top rim of the gorge. The dirt road lasted for about a mile. At the end of the dirt road a pair of railroad tracks crossed the road at a 90-degree angle. Here the cars were at full speed, going fast enough to get airborne as they went over the railroad tracks. Fifty feet along, when the wheels finally made contact with the road again, they were back on asphalt. Now came the scary part.

The road started down a long straightaway. As it began its descent off the top of the mountain, it also started a sweeping mile-and-a-half right turn back into the village. As Seneca Lake came into sight, drivers got an awesome view—although, at the speed their cars were going down this hill, I don't think the drivers had much time to admire it. The long turn then finally straightened out and the road dropped down steeply into the village. At the bottom of the hill was a 90-degree left turn—now named Milliken's Corner in honor of racer Bill Milliken who rolled his car on this turn in 1948 (and walked away uninjured). Those cars didn't have the brakes race cars have today. That downhill section took a tremendous amount of courage and trust in the car. If a driver lost his brakes there, it was *not* going to be good when he reached the bottom of the hill. Milliken could vouch for that!

After Milliken's Corner, it was straight for a block and then a 90-degree right turn took the drivers back down Franklin Street, the main street through the village of Watkins Glen. Back then, the road was a brick surface for a quarter mile to the finish line. The complete course ran 6.6 miles and included almost any possible surface. That was racing. With the creation of that road course in 1948, Watkins Glen became a true piece of racing history.

The railroad bridge near my house was a favorite spot for spectators to watch these early races. During the race weekends, my parents parked cars in our lawn and kept an eye on me. My uncle Ed Menio set up a food stand on our front lawn and sold food all day. On that one day the people came to our house and that was a big deal.

I watched from my front lawn. The cars racing past, the roar of the open exhausts, and all the exhaust fumes as the race cars sped by my house when I was two years old certainly had their effects. I have not been quite right ever since! I'm convinced it was the speed of those cars that seeped into my blood. From that point on, racing was a part of me, and speed a part of my soul.

In 1956, my brother Chip and I built my first race car. I was ten years old. We used wood that we found around the house for the body. The rear wheels were off an old baby carriage. They had chunks of rubber missing in a few spots around the old steel rims, making the car bump up and down as Chip pushed me down the dirt driveway and around the yard. The front wheels were a lot better than the rear ones. I don't remember where we found those, but they were the best pieces we had on the whole car. The front axle, a two-by-four board, swiveled on a single bolt in the center of the wood floorboard. Two ropes were tied at the outer ends of the front axle, and that was my steering. I used the single-loop-wrap method (a rope wrapped once around my hands) to steer. I figured I had better control with this ingenious method

My brother Chip pushing me in my first race car in the yard.

as it would be harder to rip the rope out of my hands that way.

My car number was 11. It was the only number I could make with the black electrical tape that my father had.

When Chip finally got tired of pushing me around, I started in on my father to take me up to the new racetrack and let me coast down the Big Hill.

The Watkins Glen road races no longer ran through the streets of village. After a spectator, a young boy, was killed in 1952, the track relocated about four miles from town. After racing on two temporary courses using county roads, a new track was being constructed (which would become Watkins Glen International). On Sunday rides we would go past the new racetrack and watch it being built. I always looked at the Big Hill and dreamed of coasting down that hill. The Big Hill was the part of the track that is now called the Esses. No matter how many times I asked, my dad always had the same answer: "No, don't be stupid."

I was relentless. For weeks I begged and begged for my dad to take me to the racetrack. "Come on, Dad. Take me to the Big Hill. Pleeease?"

One day he must have had enough. Out of the clear blue he said, "OK. Let's load it up and get it out of your system." I couldn't believe it. I felt like Christmas had come early.

Around noon on that fateful summer day, my dad, Chip, and I loaded my race car into the back of our 1950 Ford woodie station wagon and headed for the new racetrack. The track was not open yet, and on that day it looked deserted. Workers were still putting the finishing touches on it, but apparently they were not working on Sunday.

We drove up the Big Hill. Dad stopped the car about three-quarters of the way up the hill. I think he had second thoughts after seeing how steep that hill was, but nothing could've stopped me at that point—though I admit that when I got out of the car and looked back down the hill, I had some second thoughts, too. We unloaded my race car and pointed it down the hill. My dad stood in front of it while I got in.

Chip handed me my white plastic football helmet with the red stripe over it, and I put it on. I grabbed the rope, twisted my hands in unison to apply my single-loop method, and pulled tight. I looked at my dad and didn't say a word, just quickly jerked my head to the right a couple of times to signal him to get out of the way!

The car started to roll slowly at first, and then Chip ran up behind me and started to push me as fast as he could. I was quickly going faster than he could run. I don't know if he fell down or not. I didn't look back. It was now too late for second thoughts. It was too late to jump out.

The rear wheels with the missing chunks of rubber vibrated so badly that my vision blurred. Little chunks of rubber flew off the almost-bare metal rims and hit me behind the elbows. I wanted to slow down—but the one thing we hadn't built into this high-tech racing machine was a brake. Yup. Down the Big Hill with no damned brakes. Midway down the hill I was really moving. The wind was howling around inside my football helmet and I could feel it escaping past my ears and out the ear holes in the helmet. The chin strap was tight under my chin as the wind was trying to lift the helmet off my head!

I had almost reached the bottom when I crashed.

A single stone had been peacefully sitting in the middle of the track bothering no one. It must have come off one of the dump trucks that had been working at the new track. With the severe vibrations blurring my vision, I didn't see the stone until it was too late.

Just as I had achieved maximum velocity, the right front wheel hit the stone. The wheel skidded behind the stone, ripping the single-loop rope through my left hand so fast I could smell the skin on my palm burning. The stone stuck under the front of my wheel stopping it dead. But not me. And not the car. The axle spun back so far that the right front wheel went under the floorboard. This all happened in a millisecond. The wheel under the floor caused my race car to flip upside down. I had time to suck in a breath before impact.

Before I knew what the hell happened, I noticed the wind was no longer blowing past my ears. Then I noticed I was on the track looking straight up at the sky. I don't know how fast I'd been going, but thank God I had that football helmet on. My wooden race car had disintegrated on impact. It was weird. One second I was flying down the Big Hill, high in a dream of winning the Indy 500. The next second, all I had left was a rope in my right hand with a two-by-four tied to the end of it. On the far end of the two-by-four one wheel was still spinning.

When Chip and my dad got down the hill, I was sitting in the middle of a pile of kindling. I just sat there too scared to cry. The helmet had taken most of the damage; it had deep scrapes down the left side, and small black stones were stuck into the white plastic. My left shoulder was bleeding from road rash, but it didn't hurt until I stood up. My left hand had a hell of a rope burn on the palm and my elbows were bleeding.

Thinking about it now, that accident was historic. Not only was it my first race car accident, it was also the first racing accident at the new Watkins Glen International track. I can honestly say that on that eventful day, my blood became part of the track and Watkins Glen International became part of my blood. Dad, Chip, and I left the pile of wood that used to be my race car in Turn 2 at Watkins Glen and went home. My dream had been fulfilled—but instead of giving me satisfaction, it only ended up making me dream more.

When we got home my mother made it clear that my racing days were over. "Yeah. All right, Mom," I said—then wandered around the rest of the day with the biggest smile on my face you could imagine.

That night, when the pain in my shoulder started to subside, I began thinking about the hill. I didn't think about the crash. I was thinking about the speed. *The speed!* That had been my first real taste of adrenaline. I didn't know what it was at the time, but man, it felt good! I couldn't wait to feel that feeling again.

Kings Dragway

Drag racing

I graduated from high school in 1964, right smack dab in the middle of the muscle car era. The dictionary defines muscle cars as "any of a group of American-made 2-door sports coupes with powerful engines designed for high-performance driving." In Watkins Glen and the surrounding area—Montour Falls, Odessa, Millport, and so on—there were a lot of muscle cars! There were Dodge Charger Hemis, Corvettes, Camaros, El Caminos, GTOs, and every other type of high-horsepower car that you could imagine. Drag racing on the street was a nightly event. When I was in school and while everyone else was going to the school dances, I was reading about cars or working on one of my friends' cars. From my junior year in high school onward, I wanted a muscle car! There was just one major problem. *Money!*

In 1965, I got a good job at Shepard Niles Crane & Hoist Corporation in Montour Falls, working in the stockroom. With my job came a paycheck! I still lived at home and was driving my father's 1964 Chevy Nova, but I was always looking for my own car. Of course I wanted it to be a muscle car. I had been saving some money for a car of my own when, in 1966, I found a beautiful 1965 Oldsmobile 442 for sale in Odessa. It was yellow with a black interior and—being a true muscle car—it had a 400 cubic inch engine hooked to a four-speed transmission. The little money I had saved wasn't even enough for a down payment. My parents did not have money to lend me and the bank sure as hell was not going to give a loan to some kid that just started his first job. I had to find a way to get this car! One of my uncles had recently moved to Watkins Glen, and he'd owned a large construction business in Ohio. I got up the courage to ask him for a loan. To my surprise he said yes!

Although it took a while to get used to, I really enjoyed the horsepower of my Olds 442. I was spinning tires every chance I got. I couldn't stop! That not only felt good, the burning rubber also smelled good to me! After a while, I had a stack of six or eight tires behind my father's garage that I had burned off the car.

Several friends and I discovered that we could drive around the Wedgewood Road gate at Watkins Glen International and onto the Back Straight. A real racetrack! Late at night, around 2 a.m., we would drag race as long as we could before being interrupted by the sheriff. We raced and we raced and we raced! Back then, we raced for bragging rights—very rarely did money change hands. I had no money at the time as it all went to pay for my car and to keep tires on it! In this type of racing—at night and on private property—everyone raced everyone! There was no time to figure out what class a car would be in based on model and engine size as would be done at a real drag strip. We simply lined up against whoever was in the opposite lane and raced. On any racetrack there are no friends. You might be friends with someone before and after the race, but not during the race. I won more races than I lost.

Some nights, a set of headlights would appear and the sheriff would chase one of the cars as we all scattered from the track in different directions. One night while we were standing around waiting for a couple of cars to race, someone hollered, "We got company!" We all looked back toward the Wedgewood gate and saw two sets of headlights turning onto the racetrack! The Schuyler County sheriff was getting serious!

My girlfriend (and future wife) Kathy jumped in our car and said, "Hurry up! Let's get out of here before they chase us!"

Everyone ran and jumped in their cars and took off down the track heading for the gate on the other side from where the sheriff came in. Once out of the track we all split up and took off down different roads. I went east down County Route 16 and then turned left onto Meads Hill Road. Mead's Hill ran for about three-quarters of a mile across flat pasture land and then dropped off—like going over a cliff—down a steep grade.

Going down Meads Hill Road I slowed up. "We're clear," I said to Kathy, laughing out loud. "Wonder who's getting chased?"

We were halfway down the steep grade when over the ridge behind us came a pair of headlights. It had to be one of the guys from the drag racing, I thought. Then against the moonlit sky I saw the silhouette of the light bar on top of the roof. "Shit! It's the sheriff! He's got his lights off!" I said as I shifted into second gear and stepped on the gas.

As I got to the bottom of the hill, I shut my lights off. I made sure no cars were coming and blew through the stop sign. I crossed Route 329, the road I lived on, and continued down into White's Hollow. We were now driving on a section of the old 1948 racetrack. It was beautiful down there, but I had no time to look around. We crossed the old stone bridge and wound up the steep hill on the other side of the gully. After a couple of sharp turns the paved highway turned to dirt. High speed on dirt makes dust! Lots of dust. I found out it also kicks up stones! I saw the driver's side headlight go out on the sheriff's car. I instantly started weaving the car left to right, back and forth. More dust and stones! In a few seconds the other light went out. Kathy and I drove home to race another night!

☙

One day one of my friends went to a real drag strip and came home with a trophy. That changed everything. Now, every Sunday, instead of going up to the track at 2 a.m., my friends and I headed up to Kings Dragway, west of Syracuse, New York, and tried to win our own trophy to claim bragging rights for that week. King's

Dragway had opened as Jackson's Dragway in 1958—named for Paul Jackson, the businessman who built it and then sold it to the King family in 1966. Although King's Dragway was located in South Butler, everyone called the racetrack Savannah. The track consisted of two lanes separated by a grassy median. Each lane was a quarter mile of asphalt for racing followed by an eighth of a mile of asphalt for shutdown and a final eighth of a mile of dirt. A dirt return lane brought racers back to the start.

South Butler had a population of about four hundred at the time. On any given Sunday, three hundred entries would race in several different classes, and about three thousand spectators would be there to watch. Some nights it didn't get over until 11 p.m. The track lighting was so bad they had spectators shine their headlights up the track so the racers could see the surface.

Winners returning with a trophy to Watkins Glen—or wherever they came from—were like Wild West gunslingers. In the West, the more men a gunslinger killed, the more someone wanted to call him out and challenge him. During the week, late at night on some long straight highway, someone would challenge the preceding week's trophy winner! I managed to win several trophies, and I loved this custom. Each win only increased my need for speed which fed on the midweek action.

One afternoon, a strange thing happened while I was racing at Kings Dragway. My Olds 442 had a competition Hurst shifter—a standard item in the 442s with four-speed transmission—which allowed for super-fast shifting (a must in drag racing) and was designed to be bulletproof. I had just started a run and was shifting from first to second when my so-called bulletproof competition Hurst shifter broke off in my hand! After I got back to the pits, in second gear, no one could believe I had broken a Hurst shifter. Of course I couldn't drive all the way back to Watkins Glen in second gear. Luckily a fellow racer knew the farmer across the road from the track. "Jim has a welder over there," he said. "Maybe he can weld the shifter back on well enough to get you home."

I drove off looking for Jim, the welding farmer. He was home and willing to help me out. He hooked up the welder and tried to weld the shifter on. Because he was lying across the seat, he could not hold the shifter and weld at the same time. "Get around the other side," he said to me, "and hold it where you want it."

"I'm not going to get a shock, am I?" I said.

He just mumbled something as he reached up and pulled his helmet down. I turned my head. *Zzzzzzit!*

The shield on a welder's helmet is really dark (to keep the arc from blinding him), and in the tight space Jim couldn't see me. He'd accidentally laid that welding rod right on my thumb! I jumped so hard I thought I had broken the steering wheel off. We finally got the shifter welded on and I was able to drive home, still feeling the effects of one hell of a jolt to the end of my thumb. It left a perfectly round burn mark as a signature, too.

☙

I drag raced my Olds 442 for a few years before I had a chance to drive an even faster car. My friend Chris Franzese had been working for Roger Penske on the Trans Am Camaro team. When he moved back to Watkins Glen, he brought a used 305 cubic inch TRACO racing engine that had been pulled out of one of the Penske Trans-Am Camaros that Mark Donohue drove. At the time, TRACO—located in California—was one of the best racing engine builders in the country. Chris put that TRACO engine in his 1964 convertible Corvette. He stripped out the Corvette's interior, took off the windshield, had a roll bar put in it, and turned it into a real Corvette dragster.

I helped Chris with the work. It was a hectic time, so I named the Corvette "Acid Indigestion."

"Acid Indigestion," the Corvette dragster I raced.

Chris didn't feel he had the experience at first to drag race, so he asked me to drive his Corvette. I raced it about twenty times. I loved Corvettes! Since I was a young boy, I had always thought there was nothing more beautiful than a Corvette. Driving this Corvette dragster was awesome! Where my Olds was turning times in the low thirteen-second bracket, the Corvette was turning times in the mid ten-second bracket. My best time in the car was 10:29 seconds at 123 mph! It was a rocket!

One day at Kings Dragway, I was in Chris's Corvette in the staging lane waiting to go to the line. The two cars ahead of me took off and disappeared down the track. The starter motioned my competitor and me to the line. When the starting lights lit, we took off. I glanced down at the tachometer, located on the steering column, as it is critical to shift at the precise rpm. As I shifted into fourth gear, I looked up. I couldn't believe my eyes. The car that had just raced ahead of me was coming back down the track in my lane—right at me! I made the choice in a split second to turn! I missed the oncoming car, but hit the grass going 120 mph. The Corvette flew straight across a pasture so fast it was like I was skimming over the blades of grass! The ride wasn't rough at all. I crossed the small field and blew through a hedgerow, collecting leaves and small branches in the car. (Had there been a big tree in that hedgerow, this book would not have been written!) The car slowed down as I crossed the second field and came to rest sideways in another hedgerow at the far side—a long way from where I

"Acid Indigestion" at Savannah Dragway.

started. It took a while for anyone to find me.

I found out later the guy driving toward me didn't want to get his car dusty so he decided to drive back to the pits on the track instead of using the dirt return road that ran parallel with the drag strip. Word got back to the pits before I did that I was going to kill him when I got back—so when I reached the pits, he was long gone! For what it had gone through, the Corvette had very little damage. I, on the other hand, had the crap scared out of me!

Finally Chris took over driving, and it was hard to go back to racing my 442 after that. I needed to find another outlet for my speed addiction.

My Dream Car

It was 1967 when I first saw it.

Driving past the Gulf gas station in Watkins Glen, I glanced to my right and there it was. No one was with me, but I screamed out loud, "Holy Christ!"

I turned left, raced around the block and pulled into the gas station. I got out of my yellow 1965 Olds 442 and walked toward the most beautiful Corvette I had ever seen.

When I saw John "Shiny" Lurcock, the guy who ran the gas station, I hollered, "Shiny! Who the hell owns that car? It's damned awesome."

I had never seen a car so beautiful.

Shiny was short and stocky and about thirty-five years old. He wore a T-shirt and jeans held up with the red suspenders he wore all the time. A pack of unfiltered Camels was rolled up in the left sleeve of the T-shirt.

"She's mine," Shiny said in his normal high-pitched, squeaky voice. "Just drove her home."

"Holy shit! I love it."

The car had been repossessed and Shiny managed to buy it. When I first saw that car, I was in *love*. It was all I could think about. I was overcome by its beauty. It was so beautiful it was sinful!

I slowly walked a circle around the Corvette, taking in every curve and detail. This Vette was a 1965 Sting Ray coupe. It had knock-off wheels—an option on 1963 to 1965 Corvettes that provided quick removal or installation of the aluminum wheels, which was good for a race car. The side exhaust had the most incredible sound I could imagine, powered by the rarest thing of all, a 327 cubic inch engine with the Rochester fuel injection that gave it an incredible 375 HP. They only made 771 of these cars in '65.

In the 1960s, General Motors named some of their Corvette paint colors after racetracks like Daytona Blue and Riverside Red. This Corvette was Glen Green. Yes, named after the Watkins Glen track. Glen Green with a tan leather interior. Owning that car became my dream.

Shiny never let me drive his Corvette, but one day I was at the gas station and he said, "Get in. We're goin' for a ride."

"A ride? Where?"

Well, Cameron Argetsinger, the man who started racing in Watkins Glen in 1948, was president of the Sports Car Club of America (the SCCA) that year, and Ford Motor Company had given him a car to drive for the year. And no normal car— a 1965 Ford GT-40, which was rarely seen on the street as it was a full-blown race car.

Argetsinger had taken it to the local body shop where Junior DeSarno, the body shop owner, was repairing a damaged fender. Junior and Shiny were friends. Junior had called Shiny and said the GT-40 was done and ready for a test drive. This had all the earmarks of a race.

As Shiny and I drove down Main Street, he told me we were going to run the Corvette and the GT-40 up Corning Hill (Route 414), a two-mile hill that headed south out of Watkins Glen and toward Corning, New York.

Just as we started up the hill, Junior, in the GT-40, came out of a side street. Shiny slammed the shifter into first gear and floored the throttle. The Corvette turned into an animal, and suddenly I was pinned back in the seat. Second gear . . . third gear . . . Just as the tach hit 7,000 rpm, an ungodly noise went by Shiny's open window. It was the GT-40. The set of Webber carburetors on that 351 engine were suckin' in so much air it was hard to breathe for a second. We were flying, but as the GT-40 went by it suddenly felt like we were stopped. In a few seconds the rear end of that GT-40 was almost out of sight. The GT-40 blew our doors off—which was no surprise given the kind of car it was.

I still loved that Corvette. I would stop at the gas station every once in a while to wash and wax the car for Shiny.

❦

The ride in Shiny's Glen Green beauty, added to the time I'd spent driving "Acid Indigestion"—my friend Chris's Vette—at Kings Dragway, made me want to own my own Corvette even more. "Acid Indigestion" was a dragster and could not be driven on the street. The gearing in the rear end, the tires, the tuned racing exhaust headers—and the lack of headlights or taillights—kept this car from being street legal. Shiny's Corvette, on the other hand, was street legal. Even though it was not as fast as the dragster, it was still fast for a street legal car. The one thing they shared was looks! The C2 Corvette (built from 1963 to 1967) was unmistakably a Corvette. In my opinion, it was one of the most beautiful American cars ever made.

Two years passed and I was driving down the Montour Falls highway (Rt. 14) at 6:45 a.m. on an overcast day that was threatening rain. I was on my way to work at Shepard Niles Crane & Hoist. Halfway between Watkins Glen and Montour Falls I passed Bovaird's used car lot at about 65 mph, half asleep at the wheel. Out of the corner of my eye I caught a glimpse of something that shouldn't be there. It was so out of place that at first my mind could not comprehend what I had just seen. My head spun to the left and didn't stop until I was looking straight out the back window. I pulled off the right side of the road and stopped. I looked in the mirror to see if what

I saw was real but I couldn't see from that angle. No one was coming so I made a U-turn while mumbling to myself, "No, no, no. It can't be. Oh my God. It can't be." I pulled along the side of the road in front of Bovaird's and came to a stop at the middle of the front row of used cars and just stared. There it was. As I was opening the door to get out, I was mumbling to myself, "Oh my God. Oh my God."

In the middle of the front row, flanked by used Buicks, Chevys, and a couple of Mopars (custom Chryslers), was the car of my dreams. Shiny's 1965 Fuel Injected Corvette Sting Ray.

Leaving my car along the side of the road, still running, I walked to the Corvette and gently touched the front fender. I quietly said, "It's OK. I'll take care of you. Don't worry."

I walked between the rows of cars to the office door. The sign said they opened at 9:00. I ran back to my car, made a U-turn, and headed to work, speeding all the way. I punched in and ran to find my boss, Jimmy Root. I told him I had an appointment and that I had to leave. Two minutes later, I punched out. I flew back down the highway toward Bovaird's, thinking somehow the Vette would be gone when I got back. I practically slid into the parking lot. "There. It's still here."

I pulled up, parking sideways behind the Corvette, and turned my engine off. I had it blocked in. It was nine minutes after 7:00. I sat there for two hours waiting for Ed Bovaird to open. No one but me was getting this car, no matter what. By noon, I had swapped my 442 Olds and some money and I was driving my dream car down the road. It was my dream came true.

Owning a car like this in your early twenties is dangerous. I was racing someone all the time. Drag racing was fun, but what I really liked was road racing. I would road race whenever I found a victim. One night a guy with a yellow Boss Mustang took the challenge. We were going to race from Clute Park, at the end of Seneca Lake, to the Empire Phone building, three miles north up Route 414.

We started the race side by side on the flat part of the road that runs in front of Seneca Lake, with me on the right. It was just as a drag race would start. A friend, I can't remember who it was, stood in the middle of the road in front of us. He raised his hand, held it up for a second, and then slammed it down. That was the signal to GO. The Mustang got the lead right at the start.

The road took a long left turn up Burdett Hill. A quarter mile up the hill, there was a Y in the road. We took the left fork, which dropped off at a sharp angle. There, we both went airborne with me right on his bumper. Down the two-lane road we reached 120 mph. The road was narrow—on the right a rock cliff ran straight up, not two feet from the road, and on the left a single guardrail and the trees were all that separated us from Seneca Lake many feet below. The road wound its way along the cliffs—not at all a straight shot.

There were two other roads where a car could turn onto our raceway, so along our route, we had placed two cars that would flash their lights at us if another car was approaching. Starting out at three in the morning also helped avoid traffic.

We passed the first lookout car. No lights. We were clear for the next mile.

When we started, I had no worries about beating the Mustang. At this point, it had become a different story. This guy was fast. Just before Hector Falls bridge there was a downhill right turn. The Mustang went a little wide and lifted off the throttle a split second. I didn't. I passed him on his right just as we crossed the bridge.

The second lookout car was a blur. No lights.

We went flat out on a short straight then took a right turn up a hill. The Mustang's headlights were a foot off of my bumper. Up the hill, the finish line was in sight. I knew the Mustang could not get the speed to pass. *I had won!*

What did I win? Nothing. We raced for the fun of it. Looking back on it now, it scares me. One slip, a blown tire, even a deer, and it would have been all over.

Street racing was risky and my speeding tickets were starting to add up. I realized that I had to find another way to go fast.

Washing my Corvette in front of the Watkins Glen Fire Department (I was a volunteer fireman at the time).

 Building a Race Car

Chuck Ciprich, the guy who married my cousin Faith Vickio, was older than me, but he was possessed by the same demon. *Speed!* I remember when Chuck was racing a '49 Ford at the Dundee Speedway—a 4/10 mile clay oval about twelve miles north of Watkins Glen. One night, I rode with Chuck and his crew to the speedway to see my first oval track race. He stopped about a half mile from the speedway and let me out. I had no money, so Chuck said, "Just walk down that field to the far right side of that hedgerow. Wait in there till it's dark and sneak across the little field and find us in the pits."

I waited until dark and hunched down, then sneaked across the field and into the pits. I wasn't in the grandstands, but in the pits! I was surrounded by race cars,

Chuck Ciprich in his Dirt Modified "Ole Yeller." I am on the right standing behind the car.

people, the smell of oil and gas, all in the dimly lit pit area at Dundee Speedway. From that night on, I started to work on Chuck's race car. My friend Don Romeo, from Montour Falls, would also help out. We did everything from washing the car to changing engines and any repair that was needed. We ended up going to three dirt tracks a week. We spent a lot of time working on the car to get it through three nights of racing.

I worked on Chuck's crew for a couple of years, and we won a ton of races. I remember watching Chuck race his "Dirt Modified" around the super-fast dirt tracks in the area. Keeping a Dirt Modified car running was a full-time job. A Dirt Modified, back then, was made from a car frame that had a tubular roll cage welded together. They used old coupe bodies. Chuck's started life as a '36 Olds Coupe. The front axle was a straight I-Beam axle out of a '30s model car. The rear end was a racing Franklin Quick Change—allowing the gear ratios for different tracks and conditions to be changed more quickly than a conventional car rear end. The engine we used was a 427 cubic inch model built by Baldwin Chevrolet. The tires were 22-inch Goodyear dirt tires. These cars were fast and furious.

In 1972, I was watching Chuck running a qualifying race and thinking of the many hours of hard work and money that went into that car. Working with Chuck, I learned a whole lot about the mechanics of setting up a car, how to run on various tracks, and what it took mentally to win races.

I vividly remember one specific night. I was standing in the pits at Rolling Wheels Raceway in Auburn, New York, near the inside of Turn 1, watching Chuck and a group of three Modifieds power-slide side by side through the turn. Just as they went by me, it happened.

It was just like a scene from the movie *The Blues Brothers*. In the movie, John Belushi was standing at the back of a church in the aisle. The choir was singing and the sun rose outside the church and suddenly a bright ray of light shone through the stained glass window and onto Jake's head. He suddenly had a revelation. He then proceeded to do back flips down the aisle to the music of Little Richard. Well, minus the sun and the back flips, it was just the same for me. Right out of the warm night sky, and with the same force as being struck by lightning, I was engulfed by a wave of heat—pure energy and a divine wind. Just then, straight into my head on the end of a red-hot pitchfork, came the thought: *I can do this. What the hell am I doing standing here? I should be out there!* I'm *going to race.*

Just like that, my whole life changed—my attitude, my ambitions, my thoughts and aspirations. I was married to Kathy at the time, and we had a son, Mark, who was five years old. We lived in an apartment in Watkins Glen and, as I mentioned before, I worked at Shepard Niles Crane & Hoist—those days as a structural steel draftsman. I was pretty much drivin' a straight line down the road of life. Then, in that moment of inspiration, I suddenly turned a sharp left at the "Y" in the road of life and onto a new highway full of new adventures. The rest of the night I could not think of anything else. I *was going to race.*

It was hard to explain why I wanted to race. I just had to go fast. And I wanted to win. The prize money was a factor—but only to afford new tires and parts to race more. Adrenaline feeds on danger, and this natural drug the body produces was damn addicting. A good adrenaline rush was hard to explain if you had never experienced it. It was a part of racing. As Chris Economaki (publisher of *Speed Sport News*) said when he was a track announcer in the 1950s at short tracks in New Jersey, "Come see the drivers cheat death at every turn. Come see racing tonight for the young and old alike." Back to the race, it was almost impossible to concentrate on the job of setting up Chuck's Modified to go after a win that night.

The next day, I got busy planning to build a race car. I decided to build a Late Model stock car, as this class was between the Street Stock (lowest class) and the Modifieds (the highest class). Many of the Late Model drivers started in the Street Stock class then moved up to the Late Models. Street Stock was the easiest form of dirt track racing to get into, but I didn't want to do that. In this lowest class of cars, a driver could build his own car, take it to a track, pay $10 for a pit pass, and race. I knew from watching the lower-class races while working with Chuck that this practice of paying $10 and racing was not a good idea. Nobody screened the drivers, and some of those guys out there were just plain dangerous.

I decided to start in the Late Model class because the drivers were experienced and the cars were much faster than the Street Stocks. Why waste time? I figured I could learn from these drivers. The Late Model class was mostly made up of Chevelles, Ford Fairlanes, Camaros, Mustangs, and Dodge Chargers. To build one, a driver started with a street legal model and then stripped out the interior, the glass, and everything that was not necessary. Then he had a full roll cage welded in and installed a racing-style rear end, along with aluminum racing hubs, larger brakes, and racing tires and rims. With a 400 HP engine thrown in, a driver had himself a Late Model.

Many fans considered the Late Models their favorite class of racing at any of the tracks they raced at. At any Late Model race, fans couldn't pick a winner. The competition was very close and the drivers put on a fantastic show.

I decided to help Chuck through the end of the season in October and then, over the winter, go full bore on building my own car for the next season. There were things I had to do before I could actually start building a Late Model dirt car.

First, I needed a place to work. The next night I went up to my father's house and took over his garage. My dad came out and stood there shaking his head and mumbling something. OK, I have my dad's garage now, I thought, as I proudly looked around. It wasn't much, but to me it was my new race car shop.

The place was small—and I mean small! It was a 10'×24' one-car garage made from the wood of an old building torn down at a local salt plant in the 1960s. Most of the boards were soaked with creosote. You could still smell it. The garage had no interior walls or ceiling, just the heavy plank boards. There was a small door on the south side of the garage and one on the north side, both toward the rear of the garage, and two small windows on the north wall. It didn't have an overhead door. As a matter of fact, there was no door of any type on the front. Oh, and it had a dirt floor. I figured the dirt floor was all right for now as I was building a dirt track car anyway. My car would feel right at home.

Since dad's garage had no insulation—and I had no money to buy insulation—I got an old coal stove from a friend. One Saturday my friend and I hauled the stove up to the garage in the back of his 1966 Chevy pickup. At the rear of the garage I placed four cinder blocks on the dirt floor. We struggled to get the heavy cast-iron stove up onto the cinder blocks. The cinder blocks sitting on the dirt floor were not quite level, so I found some paint stir sticks and I put two of them under the two front legs, making the stove somewhat level. At least it didn't wobble anymore.

My new stove was high-tech: it burned wood or coal! I was a volunteer fireman at the time and had seen many stove fires, so I put a lot of effort into installing the used stovepipe that came with the stove. I cut a hole in the back wall and ran the pipe outside, where it turned upward and ended with a rusty cone-shaped cap to keep the rain out. I stockpiled coal—from a small coal yard in Burdett, New York—in five old metal buckets that I stacked up in a lean-to off to the left of the garage. (The lean-to was about the same size as the shop but full of junk. My '65 Corvette Sting Ray eventually spent twenty years in that lean-to.)

I had to enclose the garage if I wanted to keep the heat in when winter hit, so I built front doors out of plywood and two-by-fours. My new doors swung open from the center in two sections. On the left side door I cut out a 6"×12" rectangle at eye level and screwed a piece of scratched-up clear Plexiglas that I found someplace over the hole. I wanted to be able to see whoever drove up to my new race car shop.

The lighting in the shop wasn't great. I only had four 4-foot fluorescent light fixtures that I scrounged somewhere, and they were mounted to the roof beams—since there was no ceiling. Despite the challenges, I was happy how my new race car shop had turned out. Most important, it was mine to work in.

The second thing I would need to start building a car was tools. I looked around my dad's shop. Christ. Not a damned tool in sight. Wait, I had seen something over in the corner. I walked over and looked at the tool leaning up against a beam in the far corner of the shop. It was an old pipe threader with a T-handle. Not much use for a pipe threader in my new race car shop! I walked back to the bench and leaned back against it. Where was I going to get some tools? I had no extra money.

I started to save money from week to week to buy a cutting torch and welder. Chuck had an old cutting torch and hoses that he sold to me cheap. Eventually, I saved enough money to buy a brand new Lincoln welder. It came in a large cardboard box and it had to be put together. Its small wheels were designed for a concrete floor—they didn't work for crap on my dirt floor. When I moved it, I had to skid it along behind me or carry it by the handle.

I eventually collected used tools from friends who were interested in helping with my new race car. Along the right side of the wall in the back of the shop I built a six-foot workbench for my tools. For the top, I used a piece of 24"×72" steel from a scrap bin at Shepard Niles. Luckily, the front and rear edges of the steel were bent just right to fit my bench. It sat perfectly over the plywood top.

After a garage and tools, I needed a car. That fall, Steve Tinker and I located a 1965 Chevrolet Chevelle that I managed to get for next to nothing. If I'd had to pay a premium for a car, my racing would have been over before it started. I had very little money to spend on a race car. Kathy, my wife at the time, felt for some strange reason that we needed food and rent money more than I needed to race. I had to haul the Chevelle—as it wouldn't run—back to my new race car shop. The next step was to strip the car of everything except the body, frame, and tires.

With the car inside, I realized how damned *small* the shop was. I could hardly walk around the Chevelle. Oh well, it was all I had. It would have to work. Often, when I worked on my car in my dad's garage, I had to jack the car up, set it on jack stands, and take the tires off—so I could walk around it.

I started by stripping off the inside body panels. The interior, lights, glass, and everything unessential had to go. I stripped it down to the sheet metal skin. With the help of friends, I lifted the body off the frame and set it outside. Now all that was left in the shop was the bare frame.

When friends and neighbors found out I was building a race car, I had a lot of volunteers to help. My neighbor, a car nut named Bob Olevnik, lived just up the road. He would drive by and slow down and look to see what car I had in the garage. (I mean race car shop!) Finally, he stopped in and got hooked. I couldn't keep him away. Don Romeo stopped working on Chuck's car and helped me on my new project. Then Bill Meehan, John Cherock, Jeff Williams, Denny Snow, Kirk Williams, Jay Smith, Robbie DeDominick, Mike Wood, and a few others volunteered to help with every aspect of building my race car from cleaning parts to building engines.

With the car stripped down to its frame, I got to work on the roll cage.

∾

When building a race car, either you or someone you know must have certain skills. For one, someone has to know how to weld. I had done some welding, so I had some the knowledge—but not enough to bet my life on at that point, and my life really could depend on the welding of the roll cage. Fortunately, I knew "Holley" DeMunn, a hunched-over older guy who worked at Seneca Engineering in Montour Falls as a welder. I'd always joked, "Holley, you're so good you could weld water." He taught me all the secrets of welding, and after much practice and him teaching me, I could weld water, too. It was friends like Holley that helped me reach my goal.

Another guy who became a major player in my racing was Bill Meehan. Bill, a lifelong friend, was taking a machinist class at the time, and he was just starting to do machine work in the empty Town of Dix Grange building near his father's farm. In this little wood building he had a pipe bender, an old Bridgeport milling machine, and a small 1930s lathe. It was so dark in there I had to watch where I walked or risk breaking my shin on a piece of steel. The place smelled of oil from the machines, and the wood floors squeaked as we walked around. (Today, Bill owns BMS Manufacturing Co., one of the largest employers in Schuyler County.)

I worked like crazy on that race car. I would take a measurement for a pipe for the roll cage at my shop, drive three miles to Bill's to bend the pipe, and drive back to the shop. Then I would notch the pipe and weld it in place. A roll cage has a lot of pipes, which meant a lot of trips.

When I worked for Chuck, I saw a few center-steer Late Models on the circuit. I

Welding on my new car in my shop with my son Mark watching.

liked the idea. Instead of the driver's seat on the traditional left side, these cars had the seat in the middle. It was safer to sit there, farther from a side impact. The Modifieds, like the one Chuck drove, were center-steer cars. The driver sat a little higher (being over the driveshaft), but it still seemed safer. I had decided my first race car would be a center-steer car.

I needed a bucket seat for my center steer race car. I saw some in a racing magazine, but I didn't have enough money for one of those fancy fiberglass seats. Instead I thought of Smalley's Garage, which was just down the road in Watkins Glen. Lester Smalley would have a bucket seat.

Lester was one of the founding fathers of the original road race in the U.S. in 1948. His garage, a combination gas station and workshop with the classic Art Deco look, was where they held the tech inspections for the first road races held at Watkins Glen; it is now a registered Historic Site. Since Lester worked on foreign cars, he had many junk MGs and Triumphs out behind his garage. *There has to be a bucket seat in one of the old cars out there,* I thought.

I walked through the double glass doors and over to the glass counter where Lester was taking care of someone who had just purchased gas. Twenty or thirty cans of motor oil were stacked along the wall and about twenty Gates fan belts, in varying lengths, hung from the light green pegboard wall behind the counter. Neon signs and old parts were all over the office.

The counter looked out of place—like it belonged in a dairy store. It had a chrome frame with glass front panels and a glass top that was all scratched up from years of use as a parts counter. Inside it Lester kept all types of candy, gum, and headlight bulbs. I spotted a pack of Juicy Fruit gum, but then I opted for the bubble gum machine in the corner off to the right of the counter. Besides, it was only a penny. The large glass globe was half-filled with all sorts of bright-colored balls of gum. It sat on top of a chrome stand with a large round chrome base.

I reached in my pocket and found a shiny penny. I slipped the penny in the slot and turned the chrome handle. "Clink." I heard the gum ball hit against the chrome door. I pulled the chrome flap open as I placed my other hand under it, and a yellow gumball fell onto my hand. It immediately rolled off of my palm and dropped to the floor. It bounced about a foot in the air. After several bounces halfway across the floor, I finally caught it. Looking around to see if anyone was looking, I wiped it on my dirty pants and plopped it into my mouth. Just then I saw Lester standing behind the counter with both hands resting on the glass top. He was glaring at me. I looked away.

A pile of New York State road maps filled an old cardboard antifreeze box on the end of the glass countertop. Over by the large window were a couple of chrome chairs with thick, deep burgundy leather pads. The leather was dry and cracked and the horsehair padding was sticking out of the cracks in a couple of spots. The place even had its own smell, a distinct one I can recall just by thinking about it—that intoxicating garage smell: a mixture of gas, rubber, oil, and antifreeze. I liked that smell.

"Hey, Lester," I said. "Got a bucket seat in one of those MGs out back you wanna sell?"

"Yeah, I guess I got one here someplace," he said. "Ya only want one? Ya don't want a matchin' set?"

I had known Lester for a while. He was a tall, lanky guy but he never moved too fast, just sort of in slow motion. He always wore a French beret sideways on his head (almost covering his left eye)—probably because he was also a Citroën dealer. Those French-built cars were noted for their air suspension. Even if one of the wheels came off, the suspension adjusted and the car would run on three wheels. Lester had a

Citroën sitting in front of his station on three wheels for a while, which sure had gotten a lot of attention. One day, he gave me a ride in that Citroën at about 60 mph up the road to where I lived—driving on only three wheels! He even drove into the ditch and back out and the car never wavered. Lester might have moved slowly, but he sure could drive fast. (I think Lester was eighty-eight years old when he drove his last race at Dundee Speedway, in Dundee, New York, in the 4-cylinder class.)

Lester disappeared into the back room to look for the MG bucket seat. The back room was filled with half-torn-apart cars and parts strewn all over the place. It was dark in there, with only a bare light bulb hanging on a cord from the ceiling. After a few minutes he walked out of the back room with a well-used, two-tone green bucket seat. The brackets were fairly rusty and bent up at one corner. The seat cover was tattered and dirty and I could see a spring sticking through a four-inch rip right where my left ass cheek would be.

It was perfect!

Lester set the seat on the glass countertop with a clink that I thought was going to break the glass. "Can't be fussy with the color," he said. "That'll be five bucks."

I slid five ones across the glass.

"You gotta MG to put that in?" Lester asked. "I didn't know you had an MG. Where did you get it?"

I excitedly reached over the glass counter and pulled my first race car bucket seat toward me. "Nope. Don't have an MG. I'm using this in my Chevelle," I said, proudly. "I'm building a stock car."

I didn't get the word *car* out of my mouth before Lester, moving faster than I had ever seen him move, reached right across the glass counter and in one swooping motion grabbed the seat right from my grip. Lester pulled the seat away so fast the momentum spun him halfway around.

"The hell you are," he hollered. "You can build any car you want, but you ain't usin' one of my seats in a stock car." He stormed off and disappeared with my seat into the dark room where it came from. When it came to sports cars, Lester was a purist. He did not want to see any part of them used for something they were not intended. Some race car drivers are like that. They will race one type of car: a dirt car, a sports car, or an asphalt car. A lot of other drivers will race anything for the pure thrill of racing. I fit that category.

I waited for a minute but he never came back out. I took my money off the counter and put it back in my pocket, waited for a few seconds, and then turned and left.

"Why the hell didn't I hold onto it tighter," I thought.

Eventually, I saved enough money to get a fiberglass race car seat. That seat was my first real—purpose-built—race car part. Of course I couldn't afford the padding that was an option for the seat. With almost no money, I had little choice. I would have to ride it bare. Two bolts were at the bottom of the seat and two more on the back, just below the shoulder blades. Those four bolts held the seat to the metal frame that was attached to the roll cage. I covered the bolt heads with about eight layers of gray duct tape.

I was doing small jobs here and there to get enough money to buy some of the parts I needed. When I was starting, local racers would give me or sell me for next to nothing used parts for my car. I had an old open-face helmet from my snowmobile days. Not a full-face helmet yet, as I couldn't afford it. My seat belts came from the army surplus store in Ithaca, New York. My army surplus goggles were the rubber type that WWII pilots wore. They were army green and along with the clear lens that was in the goggle came an extra amber lens and a green one wrapped in white tissue paper. What a deal!

Back then, a fire suit wasn't mandatory, even though the top drivers wore them. I was afraid of fire as I had seen some burning wrecks while working on Chuck's Modified. I had a J.C. Whitney catalog, and I ordered a fire suit from page 108. I got the best one I could afford, but what I could afford was really just an imitation fire suit. It was gold with black stripes running down the arms and legs. I even had "Tony Vickio" embroidered, in black, on the right chest area. This suit, in a fully engulfed car fire, would give me protection for about . . . two seconds. Then the stitching would burn before the suit material melted, causing the suit to fall apart—leaving me nude in a fire.

Another area of concern, especially in a wreck, was the gas tank. I had no money for an aircraft-style fuel cell—a square metal container with a rubber bladder inside, filled with spongy stuff that would keep the fuel from pouring out if the case got cracked. Fuel cells were not mandatory at the time in the Late Model class. For my gas tank, I found myself an aluminum beer keg. The half keg held 15.5 gallons instead of the 22 gallons in a fuel cell, and was probably one I had emptied myself (I don't remember). My friend Holley TIG welded an aluminum screw-on cap on top and an outlet on the bottom for the fuel line. (I couldn't weld aluminum yet.) When he was done, I had a gas tank. I spent hours polishing my beer keg. I had the best-looking beer keg gas tank around.

Late Model races were only twenty laps long so the keg would hold plenty of gas to run a full race. I strapped it in the trunk with two 1.5-inch steel bands and from that point on I was basically a human bomb. (I didn't know it at the time, but I think I inadvertently invented the first suicide car bomb!)

Instead of seat padding, a fuel cell, or the best fire suit, I spent all my money on *horsepower*. For all the things the car lacked, it did not lack a good motor. Don Romeo built it for me: a Chevrolet 327 cubic inch engine bored .030 inches oversize, making it 331 cubic inches. It had 12.5 compression TRW forged pistons, a Reed solid lifter cam, Crane roller rockers, Z28 aluminum intake, a 650 Holley carb, and Hedman Headers. The cylinder heads were the high-performance "Fuelie" heads with the 2.02-inch valves. Horsepower was between 400 and 450.

While working at Shepard Niles Crane & Hoist, I fell in love with the color orange, which is what the company painted some of its cranes. My employers didn't know it at the time, but they supplied the paint for my car. My friend Denny Snow, who owned a body shop in Montour Falls, painted my car Shepard Niles Orange. When people asked me why the hell I painted it orange, I would say, "Because nothing rhymes with orange." I knew that was a stupid answer, but it shut people up. They would wander off, mumbling to themselves, trying to come up with a rhyme for orange. After Denny Snow painted it, I lettered it, choosing the number 16. I don't know why I chose the number 16. I guess it just sounded good (and I didn't have to use electrical tape anymore).

I worked on that race car all winter. For months, I worked seven nights a week. My wife, Kathy, somehow put up with the madness. There were many late nights, cases of beer, and buckets and buckets of coal. I can remember going home after those long winter nights working in the shop with my mouth tasting like I just came out of a West Virginia coal mine.

Finally, in the early spring of 1973, the car was finished. I was the proud owner of a Late Model race car and I was anxious to put it to the test. There was a race that Friday night at Rolling Wheels Raceway in Auburn. That was the racetrack where I first got my supreme inspiration to go racing, so I had it in my head that Rolling Wheels Raceway should be where I had my first racing experience. Some of the other racers told me, "Man, you gotta have a lotta balls or no brains to start your first race at the Wheels." The Wheels was their nickname for Rolling Wheels Raceway. "Maybe you should wait till next week and start off at Dundee Speedway." Dundee was a short 4/10-mile track, which meant the speeds were much slower. Rolling Wheels was a 5/8-mile track, the second-fastest dirt track in New York State after the one-mile dirt track at the New York State Fair Grounds in Syracuse.

"I ain't waitin'," I said. That's all there was to it. "I worked my ass off all winter and like I had said all winter, 'The day the car is done is the day I race.'" It just hap-

Me and my son Mark in the front yard the day of my first race. Notice my dream car parked by the hedge in the background.

pened to be a Friday.

Truth was both Dundee and Rolling Wheels had races on Friday night. Dundee was closer to home (about twelve miles instead of sixty), but I chose the Wheels because of the caliber of cars running there. They were the best of the best. That was where I wanted to be. I wanted to be one of the best. I figured the only way to be the best was to get my ass beat over and over by the best. I would learn from it. It would also inspire me to do better. This theory applies to anything you may want to do; you can apply racing to anything.

Before we left for Rolling Wheels, my friends (the crew) came over to my race car shop and were shining the car up and checking everything. Don Romeo fired the motor up and set the timing on the engine. I was so anxious to race that I never gave myself time to drive or test the car. I hadn't even given much thought to how I was going to get my car to the track. Luckily, Denny had his 1972 black, four-wheel-drive Chevy pickup (which he still has to this day) and a car trailer. Loading the car was a classic clusterfuck. We had to put street tires and rims on the front wheels for transport, since with the large racing tires on, the car wouldn't fit between the fenders of the trailer. I didn't have room for extra tires, which was OK since I didn't have the money for any spares either. As we loaded, we were running into each other, trying to remember everything. Bob Olevnik brought his tool box from his house and loaded it in.

"I think we're ready," I said.

"Got yer helmet?" Bob asked.

"No." I ran to the garage to get it.

"Goddamned fool," I heard Bob mumble.

I ran to the truck carrying my gleaming, virgin, gold fire suit and pure white helmet. I figured that if I didn't run well, I sure as hell would look good.

Gathered at the garage was my wife, Kathy, along with Denny Snow, John Cherock, Bob Haight, and Jeff Williams. All of us were nervous. It didn't matter. Tonight was the night. My father, who'd watched me build the car from the ground up, surely thought we'd all lost it. Mom was in the house, I'm sure wringing her hands and holding her rosary beads while at the same time lighting a couple of candles in front of a picture of St. Anthony! My dad, who was always in the garage while I worked on the car, would mumble at times. I think he was saying, "What the hell's the matter with you, wasting all this time and money on this junk?" But he was always in the shop. My mother didn't want me to get hurt. I don't think she was ever in the garage once.

Our caravan of cars, trucks, and a race car pulled out onto Route 329. Denny was towing the race car with Jeff riding along. John was driving his car. Bob was with him, and Kathy and I were driving behind them all. It was quite a sight looking at what was in front of me. Almost unbelievable. Looking forward to a new adventure, I got that strong feeling of excitement I had when I first went down the Big Hill.

 # My First Race

We drove through the gates of Rolling Wheels Raceway around 6 p.m. I'd done this many times when I was riding with Chuck, but never following a truck towing my own race car. The excitement was so great I could hardly stand it. Denny and Jeff drove the truck and car trailer through the pit gate and went down the gravel road to the pit sign-in shed. John and I parked our cars in the field next to the pit entrance, paid at the sign-in shed, and then walked in. The woman had stamped a big blue star on the top of our hands and we were good to go.

As we unloaded the car, the drivers and crew members from some of the other cars started to crowd around my car. Any new car that showed up at a racetrack drew attention, and mine was no exception. I was the new guy with a brand new car and the competition wanted to check it out. I had done the exact same thing to other drivers when I was working on Chuck's car.

My friends and I proudly rolled the car backward off the trailer, and the people gathered around had to step back to make room. Denny and Bob slid the ramps back on the trailer with a loud, squeaking sound. *Argh!* I shivered. That squeak had that same effect on me as fingernails on a chalkboard. We pushed the car toward the trailer. The guys took the hood off after unhooking the hood pins and set it on the trailer. Don Romeo instantly huddled over the motor making last-minute adjustments before firing it up. I reached inside the car, wiggling the shifter back and forth to make sure it wasn't in gear. I looked up at Don and he gave the nod, so I flipped the black plastic ignition toggle switch up and hit the chrome starter button.

Vroommm!

The engine came to life with a roar. It was idling with a thumpity-thump. Man, did it sound good. I stood back behind the crowd as they strained to get a look into the engine compartment. Some of the guys were on their tiptoes, necks stretched out. It was awesome! Knowing how hard we had worked to get the car ready, I was proud of all the attention it was getting.

Once the engine was warmed up, Don set the timing. I loved the sound of that motor.

I was walking around trying to look cool in my new gold fire suit. I must have

First race at Rolling Wheels Speedway. From left: John Cherock, Jeff Williams, me, Denny Snow, and Bob Haight.

looked like a guy in one of those discos, walking around under the black lights with a white shirt on. That brand new fire suit had a glow that must have been hard to look at directly. By the end of the night, I was certain that my suit would be as dirty as the other drivers' suits. Then I would blend right in.

Inside I was one big knot. I was pacing around, sure my nervousness was starting to show. I talked to a few of the other drivers that I knew. One second I couldn't wait to get out there, but the next second I wanted to go home. I looked at the right rear tire of my car, a brand new Firestone, thinking everything was ready—then I got hammered with that, *What the hell am I doing?* I was having serious second thoughts.

Needing something to get my mind away from thoughts of disaster, I turned and nervously walked to the food stand near the center of the pits. I stood there a second staring at the menu board, then turned and walked away. I'd thought I wanted a hot dog, but when I got there I was too nervous and had lost my appetite. Then I remembered what Chuck used to say when we offered him a hot dog at the track. "Don't eat anything before you race," he said, "because if you get in a bad wreck you don't want to get knocked out while you're getting sick and choking on your own puke. You could choke to death." Not like a bad wreck couldn't kill me, anyway, but I didn't get the hot dog.

Suddenly the speakers blared out a message making me jump. "Late Models to the track. Late Models to the track."

My stomach tightened and a shot of fear went through me. At the dirt tracks, the three classes of cars—the Street Stocks, the Late Models, and the Modifieds—each had three or four qualifying heat races depending on the number of cars that night. Each heat usually had eight to ten cars and ran from eight to ten laps. The first few cars in each heat would qualify for the feature event (four, five, or six, depending on the size; tonight it was five). All the cars that failed to qualify in a heat race would have one more chance to qualify for the feature event. It was an eight-lap race called the consolation race, or "consi" as it was known by the drivers. That word *consi* put fear into any race car driver. It was a last-chance, slam-bang race where only three cars qualified. And as many as fifteen or twenty cars could be in the consi, as it was open to all the cars in all the heat races that did not qualify. The feature event is the money race. Normally twenty to twenty-four cars started the feature race, which lasted twenty laps.

Before the race, the maintenance people drove a huge old water tank truck around the dirt track to wet it down. The truck usually had a three-inch galvanized pipe mounted across the lower back side of the tank, drilled full of holes to spray out the water to soak the track. When they finished watering the track, they had the Late Models with their bigger tires go out and do very slow laps to pack the track in so it wouldn't be too muddy to race. If the track got too dry, they would water it again after the heat races.

I was nervous just getting ready to pack down the track! At the same time, I was anxious to see what the track looked like from out there. Until now, I had only watched Chuck go around a track. I had never seen a track from inside a race car.

I climbed through the window and plopped myself into the fiberglass seat. I was so nervous I didn't even notice the bolts that were sticking in each ass cheek and the other two that were jammed on either side of my spinal column. I buckled up with the help of about three guys all trying to reach through both sides of the car at once with hands flailing around. There were hands on my seat belts, shoulder harness, helmet, and goggles. I couldn't touch anything with my own hands even if I wanted to. I felt like an astronaut getting buckled into an Apollo space capsule.

Finally, with me secured inside the car, I fired the motor and drove out Pit Lane and onto the track for the first time. The darkness of the pits gave way to the bright lights that illuminated the racetrack, and I slowly drove out to Turn 1 looking at the track from a perspective that I had only dreamed of. Slowly, I drove round and round counterclockwise until, halfway down the Front Straight, I noticed the flagman who stood on a platform about fifteen feet above the track. The flagman waved a rolled-up red flag toward the pits, signaling us to pull in on the next lap.

I went down the backstretch in second gear just puttering along, when I got an urge to hit the throttle. *No one will do anything,* I thought. I hit the throttle—just for a second! "Holy Christ Almighty!" The power and noise was absolutely frightening. I had never felt anything like it before. I instantly let off the throttle. That was damned scary. Not only scary, I had just about blown out both car drums.

I pulled into my pit, with the mud making the car weigh double what it did when I went out. My crew and I spent the next fifteen minutes cleaning huge chunks of the stuff off the car and from under the wheel wells. That was one disadvantage of dirt racing. My once perfectly clean brand-new car was now muddy and broken in. The PA system blared to life again. "Late Model warm-ups. Late Model warm-ups in ten minutes."

Jeff yelled, "Get in and get ready."

Goose bumps instantly spread from the back of my neck straight down my spine. At exactly the same time, they started at my ankles and came up the back of my legs—meeting right at my ass! That is what fear did. I don't remember the walk to the car. I was in a trance, like I was walking to the gallows. Was I going to die? When I reached the front of the car I raised my right leg up and stuck it through the driver's side window. Part of me wanted to pull my leg right back out, but it was as if something inside the car was pulling me in. I turned and put my body through the window and slid into the car plopping down hard onto the fiberglass seat. My left leg followed me in. Once again in my unpadded seat, things were a blur. Everyone was shouting, "Tighten the belts and check the brakes."

"Listen, you idiot!" Don hollered as he leaned in the left side of the car. "Make sure you look at the oil pressure and water temperature gauges when you are out

On the left, my ex-wife wife Kathy and Kirk Williams. On the right, Bob Olevnik (standing) and John Cherock looking in.

there. Don't forget. Fire it up!"

This was just the warm-ups. What the hell would the race be like? The next thing I knew, bright lights were shining into the car as I drove onto the track.

Better pull my goggles down, I thought. There. Now I felt like a race car driver. I drove slowly around Turn 2 and got a good look down the Back Straight. *Why am I out here?* I didn't have a clue as to what to expect. Deep inside, I did want to feel that power again.

The Modifieds had warmed up just before the Late Mods. The track was fairly smooth and packed down, with not much mud left. It was dark brown and even had a slight shine to it.

Down the Back Straight the track was not well lit, and it felt like a long way from Turn 2 to Turn 3. On my left I saw a single row of guardrail held up by six-by-six wood posts. On my right, just off the track, was about fifty feet of grass and then woods. No guardrail. Man, I did not want to go off into the woods. They'd never find me. I puttered around Turn 4 and could see the grandstands full of people. It was much brighter on the Front Straight as the lights shone from the grandstands to the track—lots more lights. Because of the safety fence and the way the lights were shining, I couldn't see faces in the grandstands very well. It was just a colorful blur. Just then I looked up and noticed the flagman, who, with no warning, twirled the rolled-up green flag above his head signaling the start of hot laps. (Hot laps were eight to ten warm-up or practice laps run at full speed.)

Ignoring the possibility of death waiting for me in the first turn, I mashed the gas pedal hard against the floor. For the first time, my mighty steed leaped ahead with its 400 horsepower motor creating a noise that was indescribable. With the tires spinning and the engine revving, I found myself sawing the wheel back and forth as the huge racing tires dug in for traction going down the Front Straight. *Hang on*, I told myself. This thing was flying.

I thought I was really haulin' ass as I shifted to fourth until a car went by my passenger side window so fast I couldn't even tell what color it was. A blue one went by on the inside just as fast and not two inches from my door. The sound of those two engines mixed with mine did a strange harmonizing thing. It was weird. The two cars came together in front of me and went into Turn 1 side by side sliding sideways. A thirty-foot stream of dark brown dirt spit out from their rear wheels. I slid around the turn right into that spray of dirt and stones. Chunks of mud and stones bounced off my helmet.

The cars had no windshields—a windshield would collect too much mud. In place of glass we had put a wire screen, more like chicken wire than door screening. The theory behind the 2"×3" openings was to let the little stuff go through and catch the big stuff that would take my head off. Well, that was fine, but when some of that little stuff smacks home at 100 mph . . . it hurts! Especially without a full-face helmet.

I followed the cars into Turn 1 and, using my throttle, did a power slide through Turn 1 and Turn 2. I came onto the Back Straight only to see the two cars that had passed me going into Turn 3. I guessed I wasn't moving as fast as I thought. As I reached the end of the Back Straight, my eardrums were getting battered by the noise generated by my engine spinning about 7,000 rpm. It hurt. Imagine pushing pencils into each ear and shoving them in until they touched each other. Though the pain, I thought, *Man, does my engine sound good!* Reaching Turn 3, I felt a vibration at about 6,500 rpm. Oh no, the motor! I was worried now. Suddenly I saw a yellow flag. Someone had spun out at the start of the second lap.

I eased off and went through Turn 3 slowly, then kicked my car out of gear and coasted down the Front Straight slowing even more. Watching the tach, I revved the motor up to 6,500 and held it there for a second. Smooth as glass. That meant it was the drive shaft or a tire that was causing the vibration, not the motor. We went back to green and I finished the eight-lap warm-up feeling better about being out there. I had accomplished two major things: my car was in one piece and I wasn't dead!

I returned to the pits, found my spot, pulled in behind the trailer, and shut off the motor.

Wow. My hands dropped from the wheel and hung straight down. They were shaking. I took a deep breath. The guys were jumping around like I had won a race. *Hell,* I thought to myself, *what would they do when I really did win a race?* I guess I had the right attitude since I thought *when I win,* not *if I win.* The guys were just happy I didn't wreck the car in the warm-up, I guess. I got out, took off my goggles and helmet. My hair was wet with sweat. If I sweat this hard after eight laps, how was I going to last twenty laps in a feature race?

Don ran up shouting, "How was the oil pressure? What was it? How was the water temperature?"

I looked at him for a second with a puzzled look. "I don't know," I said. "I forgot to look."

"Christ," Don said. "Ya gotta look at that stuff, man. How many times did you tell Chuck to always look at his gauges?"

☙

It was different being out there. I knew I had to learn to look at the gauges. Don reached in the car and fired up the engine so he could check them. Oil pressure was OK, but the water gauge was pegged at 250 degrees. We looked and found the radiator was packed with mud. I went over to Chuck's car and got some fine screen to put in front of my radiator for the heat race. When I worked for him, we always carried new screen. I couldn't believe I had forgotten it. I had so much to learn. Going fast alone was one thing, but adding about twenty-five more cars made it exciting. The Modified warm-ups were going on. I didn't have time to watch but I could hear the engines screaming and wished I was out there with them. After cleaning the radiator, we put water in and just checked everything else to make sure I could run in the heat race. I noticed the track grow quiet—the Modifieds' warm-up had finished.

The PA system boomed to life. "Late Models. First heat. Late Models. Line up for the first heat. Five minutes." My heart started racing. I was scheduled for the second heat. It was hard to wait. I got into my car before the first heat even went out. As I strapped in, I turned the steering wheel and pushed on the pedals. Everything felt OK. The car now had that smell—the smell of a race car: Wolf's Head rear-end lube and hot engine oil plus hot brakes and tire rubber. Ahhh, the smell of racing.

I saw an official holding a clipboard approach. Without slowing down he hollered into my passenger side window, "You're behind the 24. Fourth row. Outside." I gave him the thumbs-up.

The bolts of my seat pressed into me. *I've got to get a pad for this seat,* I thought to myself.

The official came walking through the pits again holding one finger over his head and twirling it while leaning down a little looking at me through the screen. I could see his lips moving and it looked like he was saying, "Fire it up." Don Romeo slapped the hood and sort of waved. I pulled out onto the track with about ten other cars and looked up in the stands. The crowd was standing up, waving and cheering. This was it, I thought. Let's see what we got. We lined up into a double file along the back straight. I got behind car 24, Walt Mitchell, about three-quarters of the way back in the field. I realized that my first dirt track race was only two corners away! My heart started racing out of control. I was on the verge of hyperventilating.

I looked at all the shiny, different colored cars ahead of me as the Back Straight lights reflected off their roofs. *I'm here. I'm actually here*, I thought to myself. So much work to get here and it was finally happening. Driving slowly, our cars bounced down the Back Straight. (On a dirt track, the slower you went, the more bumps you felt, but at speed it felt smoother.) The sound of the engine, the smell of racing fuel from the cars ahead of me, and the darkness just past the track increased my anticipation. The double line of cars slowly rounded Turn 4. From watching Chuck's races, I knew to watch the starter, not the guy ahead of me. I looked over the roofs of the cars ahead of me. As we came through Turn 4, the starter waved the green flag frantically over his head. My first race had started!

As the green flag waved, the relative silence gave way to ear-splitting sound. All my senses and all my muscles hit 100 percent output at the same instant. I felt like I was hooked to an IV of pure adrenaline with the knob turned wide open. I was mainlining the body's most powerful and addicting drug straight through a tube the size of a garden hose. I was amazed at how fast I went from fear and apprehension to total concentration and aggression in a split second.

I went into the first turn, not wanting to fall too far behind. The car slid up the banking, and I cranked the wheel to the right to catch the slide while feathering the throttle. I had no dirt track racing experience. I was driving totally on instinct and from what had I learned watching Chuck race. Looking back, instinct was the key factor. Everyone is born with certain traits. For me, it seemed racing was one of mine.

It was a good thing that I started on the outside row or I would have taken someone out as I took Turn 1 wide. A blue and white car shot past on my left, not four inches from my door. The sound of his engine and mine harmonized for a second and then he was twenty yards ahead of me. I was now riding the rim—up on the outside of the groove and almost in no-man's-land. *Man*, I thought, *it's dark out here. Better get back down on the track.* My car finally stuck to the track. I hadn't lifted off the throttle while I was in no-man's-land trying not to fall too far behind.

Down the Back Straight, my engine pulled with awesome power. The sound of that Chevy small block turning 7,000 rpm was like an orchestra—I was playing a tune on the exhaust pipes. What a feeling. There wasn't a car out there with more power than I had. Although I lost some ground at the start, I was slowly gaining it back. By Turn 3, I caught up to the blue and white car that had passed me in Turn 1. Through Turns 3 and 4, I slid up the track again. The cars ahead of me once again pulled away a little. "Slow down," I said out loud as I entered Turn 1. "Take the damned corner smooth. Slow down a little. Take it smooth."

I caught up to the blue and white car again. I found he was faster in the corners because he was smart enough to slow down to take them. I slowed my pace through the next corner and then pushed hard on the throttle about three-quarters through the turn. What a difference. The car shot out of that corner so fast that I actually scared myself. I learned that you had to develop a rhythm when racing on an oval track. I passed two cars before I knew what was happening. Every lap, no, every corner I tried to learn something. Racing with the best actually helped. I learned by watching—following a faster car and trying to drive the line he was using. My learning adventure went on all eight laps of the heat. As I came around the fourth turn, I caught a flash of something out of my windscreen. *Was that the checkered flag? I don't know.*

I was so focused on the race that I forgot to look at the starter when I came off Turn 4. I kept going through Turns 1 and 2 and down the Back Straight where I suddenly ran up on two cars slowing down. I hit the brakes hard and turned the car to the outside of the track to avoid a collision. I drove past the slowing cars way too fast on the outside. Embarrassing. I had almost rear-ended two cars after the race was over. It *had* been the checkered flag. I learned you have to watch the starter every lap. He controls the race.

As the adrenaline started to drain from my body, I couldn't help but smile. I had done it. I was gonna drive race cars! I was hooked. You couldn't have removed that smile from my face with a sandblaster.

I pulled into the pits and Don, Denny, Bob, and Jeff all ran to the car. In my first race I had finished fifth in a field of ten. Not only that, but I did it on the fastest 5/8-mile track in the state. A couple other drivers came over and congratulated me on a good run. (I would get to know them better the more I raced. One of them, Dennis Taney, died years later in a racing accident at Canandaigua Speedway.)

"The car looked real strong down the straight," Don said. "How'd it sound?"

"Man," I said. "It just pulled right up to seven grand like nothing." In my excitement, I forgot to tell Don that the vibration had returned.

"That water gauge is pegged again," he told me. "Make damn sure you watch it out there, or you will cook the motor for sure. We might have to gear it up a hair for this track. I don't want it to run over 6,800."

Before the feature event, we had work to do on my car. We were oblivious to the races going on around us as we prepared. The radiator was the only thing really causing trouble that night. I was worried about it. We borrowed more screen to put in front of it and with a wire brush cleaned out the dirt from the radiator core as best we could. We checked the whole car over. It was ready. I was so excited. I couldn't wait for the feature race. I finished fifth in the heat, so what the hell! I figured I could finish fifth in the feature. That was simple logic.

Above the roar of the engines, I heard the loudspeaker: "Late Models, Late Models. Feature to the line. Feature to the line."

My heart jumped with a new jolt of adrenaline. I got in my car and started to get buckled in. Don handed me my helmet through the window. "You're behind car 12 on the inside," he said. "You're about eighteenth." I nodded and put my helmet on, then goggles, then gloves. My goggles were already getting scratched up from wiping mud off them. I pushed the clutch in, flipped up the ignition switch, and pushed the chrome starter button. The engine fired with a thunderous sound. I was about to run my first feature race.

I thought I heard the national anthem playing as we waited at the exit of the pits.

My heart was really beating as I drove onto the track. I was way back in the double line of brightly colored cars making their way to the field of battle. I found car 12 and got in line behind him. I was ready. We drove slowly down the Back Straight on the pace lap. I tightened the belts once more. I could hear Don's voice in my head, "Look at the damned gauges, you idiot." I looked down. Oil, OK. Water, OK so far. The only other gauge was the tachometer. Drivers don't need a speedometer. It's simple: if you're not in the lead, you're not going fast enough.

Out of Turn 4, I looked for the flagman. Green flag! The garden hose started pumping adrenaline. I drove into the first turn with a sight in front of me that I'll never forget—seventeen cars bouncing off of each other, sliding through Turn 1 and Turn 2 with tires throwing mud back at 100 mph. The cars ahead flew up the Back Straight, zigzagging back and forth. Up ahead I caught a flash—a reflection of the track lights off the roof of a car as it spun sideways down the track. Instinctively I turned to the left and drove past. The caution lights came on, and we slowed as the pace car came out of the pits. Once the disabled car was towed from the track, we restarted.

I only ran about six more laps before my race ended—almost for all time.

When things happen in racing, they usually happen fast. I was going down the Front Straight under full throttle. My mouth was open, sucking in air when a chunk of mud flew through the wind screen. You guessed it. Right in my mouth. It wasn't big, maybe the size of a marble, but it was going so fast that it stuck in my throat. I was *choking*! Down the Back Straight I went, gagging, with my foot to the floor and cars all around me. I didn't want to lose a spot but I couldn't cough it up. Panic time! I was almost to the point of pulling over and stopping when I did the only thing I could do. I swallowed it. "Holy shit," I said out loud. I thought I was going to die in my first race, not from a crash but from a chunk of mud. Pushing the thought aside, I continued to drive. To my credit, I never slowed down.

But then, heading down the Front Straight where the lights were brighter, I glanced through my watering eyes at the gauges and sure enough, the water gauge was up to 250. "Shit!" I hollered out loud, hitting the steering wheel with my fist. I had to stop. I had moved up from eighteenth to tenth, but I couldn't afford to hurt that engine. I had no choice. I reluctantly pulled to the inside of Turn 3 and started to slow down. I was devastated. I watched as the cars went flying past on my right and disappeared into Turn 1 as I pulled into the pits. I pulled in behind the trailer and the guys looked as dejected as I was. Don stuck his head in and looked at the water temperature gauge. "Damn good thing you looked at the gauge this time," he said.

We headed home that night pleased with our first race. I was in one piece and the car was strong. And I could half-ass drive! I didn't tell anyone about the clod in my throat at the time. It was too embarrassing to be a macho race car driver who almost choked to death on a chunk of dirt. (It wasn't until years later that I spilled my guts about that incident.)

 # Learning to Win

This racing thing was harder than I had thought. By the halfway point of the season, I had not come close to winning a race. I'd thought for sure that it would not take so long to win. I'd chosen to run most of my races at the big tracks—Canandaigua, Rolling Wheels, and Weedsport—and the level of competition was so intense that it was very rare to have the same car win a feature race at a particular track two weeks in a row. Those guys ran hard from the green to the checker—and, to make things worse, they were good. To win a Late Model race at one of these tracks was quite an accomplishment. I guess winning a feature race my rookie year was a lot to expect.

I raced three nights a week—on Friday, Saturday, and Sunday—which was a tremendous undertaking. I raced either at Dundee (twelve miles away) or Rolling Wheels Raceway (sixty miles away) on Friday night, depending on the event held at each track. Saturday night I raced at Canandaigua Speedway (sixty miles away) or Five Mile Point Speedway (also sixty miles away). Sunday night was Weedsport Speedway (fifty miles away). My weekends were full of driving.

Besides all that driving to and from races, after each race the car had to be gone over before the next event. Monday through Thursday was nonstop work on the car as it tended to get pretty beat-up.

I knew we had a car that could win. Roy Evans, who owned a radiator shop one road over from me on County Route 16, solved the radiator problem. He took a fork lift radiator core and made me a custom radiator with four rows of tubes, and that cured my overheating problems. (From that day on, I bought custom radiators from Roy for all my race cars. He really knew what he was doing.)

After so many races, I was getting more used to the car and the guys I raced against. Whether I was at Weedsport, Rolling Wheels, Canandaigua, or Dundee, I raced against 70 percent of the same guys at every track. It was important to learn how each of my competitors drove. Knowing the competition allowed me to make the right decisions. Now I knew who I could pass on the outside and who I should stay away from. If I knew I could shake a guy by tapping on his bumper, then I kept on tapping his bumper. Chances are he would get nervous and drive into the corner too fast and I could slip under him.

At Dundee Speedway one Friday night, I was running in a qualifying heat race. The track was a 4/10-mile oval, almost a circle—hardly any straightaway. Instead it had long sweeping corners that added up to *speed*. Dundee was one fast short track.

I was racing in a ten-lap qualifying race and had worked my way up to third—about where I had been qualifying lately. With four laps to go, the car ahead of me went into Turn 1 a little too hot and slid about four feet up the track. It was just enough to give me the chance to give it a little more throttle and get a fender under him. We bumped but I was not going to back off. Through Turn 1 and Turn 2 we were side by side. We bumped side to side probably three more times in the corner. I could smell the rubber from my right front tire as it rubbed on his door, but I wasn't going to let off. Down the Back Straight and into Turn 3 we were still side by side. The two engines side by side made a sound that I can't describe. It was awesome.

I slowed down a little more than normal going into Turn 3. I was being a little smarter now. *Stay on the bottom*, I told myself. He went into the turn a little fast, trying to out power me, and slid up the track even more. As I came off of Turn 4, I was ahead of him. I let the car slide up to the retaining wall, directly in front of him. I was now in second with three laps to go! All of a sudden I realized—*I can win* this race! "Slow up a little going into the turns and be smooth," I kept telling myself. "Don't get excited and screw up." With two laps to go I was on the leader's bumper. He was really slowing for the corners, protecting the inside. I decided to try the inside one more time in Turn 3—but if he kept slowing, I'd try to pass him going into Turn 1 on the outside. There weren't many laps left.

Going into Turn 3 he slowed again, way slower than he needed to. I dropped back slightly, anticipating him doing the same thing in Turn 1. I'd raced against this guy before and I knew he would *never* run the outside. He would slow up so as to stick to the bottom of the track no matter what. Sure enough, knowing I was right behind him, he slowed even more so as not to slide up out of the groove and give me a chance to pass him on the inside. As he hit the brakes in the turn, I jerked the wheel to the right and with my momentum and running the higher line, I shot up to his right front fender. He couldn't get back on the gas as soon as I could because I was now on the outside of him blocking his exit line off the corner. I pulled him off the corner and down the Back Straight. Going into Turn 3, I was ahead of him. I brought the car to the bottom of the track knowing he would not try to pass me on the outside. I saw the checkered flag! I'd *won* my first race!

Even though it was only a qualifying race, it was still a race and I *won*. MY *first win*. I felt like I'd won the Indy 500. Now I knew how to win and how it felt to win. I was sitting on the Front Straight holding the checkered flag out the window of the car and getting my picture taken. If I thought I was hooked on racing before, now I was *addicted!*

I didn't win the feature that night. (As a matter of fact, I think I crashed, but it's all a blur.)

During my second year of dirt track racing, my friend Gary Hurd decided he wanted to race. He purchased a Late Model Sportsman Chevelle, #2X, from a local and started racing at Dundee Speedway. Gary had never driven anything with any amount of power before, and when he told me he wanted to go to Canandaigua Speedway on a Saturday, I instantly felt he was not ready for this super-fast half mile. But I couldn't talk him out of it.

Gary, to my surprise and his, made it into the feature at Canandaigua. This was his first time here so he started on the pole as he had no points. (On regular race nights, cars with the lower points started up front.) I was starting about sixteenth. After looking at the lineup for the feature event I had to figure out a plan. With Gary on the pole (the inside row) I knew that not having experience at starting in front of the field he would slow up the entire inside row at the start of the race. Canandaigua was a wide and fast track. I felt I was getting closer to a feature win and I wanted a good start. Since I was also starting on the inside row, I had to formulate a plan to get from the inside row to the outside row as soon as I could. As we went down the Back Straight, I would look for a hole to open up so I could get to the outside. If I could get to the outside, I felt I could pass a lot of cars in the first five laps. As we rounded Turn 4 on the pace lap, I looked down the Front Straight to see the starter waving the green flag.

My plan never had a chance to work.

As the green flag waved, the field of cars surged forward but Gary didn't get a good start. Someone hit him in the rear and spun him sideways in front of the entire field of twenty-four cars. The rest of the cars flew down the Front Straight with the outside row going to the right around Gary and my inside row having no choice but to squeeze between Gary and the inside grass. Several cars made it through, but the car ahead of me slowed. I hit the brakes and bumped him in the rear fender. The car

Gary standing with his hands on his hips and looking at my overturned race car. (Photo by Gater News staff photographer Dick Tanner)

behind me hit my right rear fender sending me into Gary's car. When I hit, my car did a slow roll and I found myself hanging upside down. There were twenty-four cars on the track, and I was the one that ended up with my hood on the trunk of Gary's car. Holley DeMunn had taught me well! The welds held and that roll cage did not budge! Actually, the only damage was a few dents in the fender and hood. Gary sold his car shortly after that race.

The next night I won a heat race at Weedsport Speedway.

On another warm Sunday night at Weedsport Speedway, I was racing in the first warm-up session when for some unknown reason my car's four-speed transmission broke a gear and locked up. I didn't even make it through the warm-ups. "Get the damned thing out," Bob Olevnik (my neighbor and crew man) said, meaning my car's transmission. "While you're getting the transmission out, I'll go back to the shop and get the spare."

"You idiot," I said. "No way you can drive a hundred miles" (to the shop and back) "before the race." Bob got in his Dodge Coronet and took off. I shouldn't have doubted him! He made it back early enough for us to replace the transmission in time to race. Bob should have been the one racing. (To this day, I don't know how he did it. I accused him of having the spare in his trunk all along, but he swore that he made the run.)

The following night we went to Canandaigua Speedway. I could tell my whole crew was feeling good about racing that night. We were pumped up from winning a qualifying race at Weedsport the week before, and we unloaded the car in record time—anxious to race as our recent heat wins gave us the feeling a feature win was not far away. Canandaigua had the smoothest clay oval in the state, and that clay was tacky like a sponge that night. For a dirt track, smooth plus tacky equals *speed!* It was just right. Dominic Tantallo, the track owner, sure knew how to prepare a clay track for racing.

When I went out for the hot laps, I thought, *This track is so sticky tonight, I wonder if I can run an entire lap without lifting off the throttle?* Going all the way around without ever lifting off the throttle is what we call a flat lap. In the warm-up laps, I got up the courage to try it. I went into Turn 1 full throttle. It took a lot of guts not to let off the throttle. The G-force was incredible. I couldn't imagine a car being able to go around a corner that fast on dirt. I kept the throttle glued to the floor down the Back Straight and pulled way to the outside, my right side tires clipping the grass, and waited for a second before turning into Turn 3. I wanted to hit the apex a little later than normal to get a lower line when I came out of Turn 4. If I missed the turn, I'd run into the Front Straight's concrete wall which came up fast. Keeping the throttle down through Turn 4, I let the car slide right up to the wall. With throttle down, I crossed the finish line and completed my flat lap. It was incredible. But I don't think I could have done two in a row! Two reasons: first—I would be carrying too much speed into Turn 1 on the start of the second lap, and second—I couldn't hold my breath that long!

That night the track was perfect, the car was perfect and I felt good. I finished third in the qualifying race and got ready to start the feature event—twenty laps of balls-out dirt track racing. I was in the middle of the twenty-four-car field as we took the green. This race turned out to be caution free (which was rare), meaning it went by fast. With no cautions, twenty laps don't take long.

With four laps to go, I had worked my way up to second place and my arms were tired. This was a tough nonstop race. I found myself right behind Walt Mitchell, the leader. Walt was a hell of a competitor, a track champion, and a friend off the track. (It is a strange thing and I don't think it's just me, but when drivers are seriously racing, they have *no* friends on the track. All of that is gone.) The only thing on my mind was how get by that car. Walt was not going to let me get by him without earning it.

Into Turn 1 on lap 16, I pushed, more like mentally willed my orange Chevelle under Walt's blue and white Dodge Coronet. I made the pass down the Back Straight. I was ecstatic! I knew he could not get back by. I did a flat lap earlier and if I had to I would do it again. *He was not getting back by me.*

I knew that if I made no mistakes the next couple of laps, I would have my first feature win. We flew around the track and as I came out of Turn 4, I looked up at the starter, "Wee" Willie Allen (an ex-Modified driver). He was waving the white flag. One more lap to go. I suddenly got a panicked feeling. *Oh my God. What do I do?* Concentrate. That's what I needed do. Even though I could hear Walt's engine right behind me, I was not going to screw this up! Through Turn 1 and Turn 2, I held a good line on the inside. Where I normally let the car slide up high on the Back Straight, I held it down to the center of the track. Down the Back Straight, the motor was pulling like a team of four hundred sweating horses, nostrils flaring while being whipped silly by an insane cowboy. All those horses were screaming at the same time.

Coming into Turn 3 one last time, I used up the whole track. Sliding around the

After my first feature win, at Canandaigua Speedway. (Gater News photo)

smooth clay surface, I let the car drift out of Turn 4 right up to the concrete wall for maximum speed. The motor was under full throttle and running as smooth as a Swiss watch. I looked down the straightaway and there was Willie waving the checkered flag. What a sight. I was hollering and beating my fist on the steering wheel as I went under the Starter's Stand. My first feature win! (As I'm writing this, my breathing is a little faster and after all these years I can still feel it.) *What do I do now?* I had seen Chuck pull up to the flagman and get his picture taken with the flag many times. Now it was my turn. I had real tears in my eyes. I took off my goggles and wiped my eyes as I went down the Back Straight. Walt pulled up on my right side, gave a quick thumbs-up, and then sped off toward the pits. Holy shit! My first win.

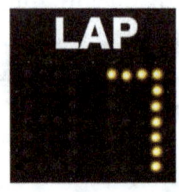

A New Direction

I had a passion for racing, but I found another passion when I was twenty-six years old. In 1972—within a few months of building my first race car—Don Romeo told me he was going to have his car pinstriped. I didn't care about going with him until he said, "You might want to go with me. I got some beer."

"Beer? I'll go."

It was Wednesday night and I found myself sitting on some old tires in the dimly lit wash bay of Frank Smalley's Esso gas station in Watkins Glen, drinking beer and watching Bob Shaw (from Dundee, New York), paint freehand pinstripes on Don's new '72 Corvette. Between sips of my Genesee Cream Ale, I finally paid some attention to what this guy was doing. *This is so cool,* I thought to myself.

I actually stopped drinking my beer as I didn't want to miss a single stroke of the striping brush. Bob had a long, thin brush, and he would carefully dip it in some paint and stroke the brush back and forth on a palette to get the paint to the right consistency. Then he would gently place his hand on the fender of the car. While holding the brush between two fingers, he would pull a clean, straight stripe over the rear fender. I watched in total amazement.

I remember thinking, *Man, I wish I could do that.* I was mesmerized. After he finished pinstriping the Corvette and started cleaning the brush, I walked over to him and started asking him all kinds of questions. "How did you learn this? How long have you been doing it? How do you do it?" I must have been a pain in the ass.

To my surprise he turned to me. "Here ya go," he said, handing me the brush he had just finished cleaning. "Practice." I slowly reached out. When I touched that brush, I had the strangest feeling that I somehow knew how to pinstripe. Of course I didn't, but that was how I felt. The brush felt right at home between my fingers—almost like I'd held it before. That was how I first started painting. Bob Shaw started me on a new road that would take me to more places and allow me to meet more people than I could ever have dreamed of.

That night Bob let me keep one Mack pinstriping brush. I took care of that brush like it was gold. I practiced by pinstriping everything in sight. The pinstriping naturally led me to trying some lettering. I went to the Hobby Shop in Watkins Glen and bought a couple of small brushes that were meant for painting models. Then I just started to letter things, like my mother's vacuum cleaner (no kidding). I remember pinstriping it and then painting her name, Rachel, on the side.

I was having trouble with the letters O, S, R, and G. Anything curved was a chore for me. To be honest, every letter was a chore. To practice, I pinstriped and lettered

One of the first helmets I painted was for Steve Ely. Photo was taken in my shop where his helmet is now on display.

a couple of snowmobile helmets for my friends. One of the first helmets I pinstriped and lettered was for Steve Ely. At that time I had absolutely no real lettering experience and the pinstriping and lettering I was doing was simply a hobby. I painted the numbers on my own race cars, of course, but as time went on, I wound up painting and lettering many, many others.

One night in 1973, at about 9 p.m., someone knocked on my door. Kathy and I were living in an apartment above Bill's Taxi and Hobby Shop on Franklin Street in Watkins Glen at the time. We were watching TV. "Who the hell is that?" I muttered to Kathy, as I reluctantly got up from my too comfortable recliner. Only a few of my crazy friends would come up at that time of night. I opened the door expecting Larry Hurd or Al Waugh. Instead, two guys I'd never seen before were standing at the top of the stairs in the narrow, dark hallway. (The hallway light had been blown for about a year. I was going to fix it at some point but hadn't gotten to it yet.)

The two were dressed in strange-looking uniforms and holding a large (about two feet by four feet) white Thing. At first, with them standing in the darkness and in uniforms, I thought they were the police. Looking closer I realized it wasn't the police. *Who the hell are these guys and what the hell do they want?* I thought to myself. As it turned out, that night, those men and that Thing would change my life forever.

I stood there looking at the Thing. "Hello buddy," the man on the left asked in a thick English accent. "Are you Tony the sign writer? Some good sport from the track sent us trucking down here to see you. Sorry 'bout the hour. He told us you are the only sign writer around and you may be able to help us out as we are in a bit of a bind."

With a puzzled look, I stared at him and then back to the Thing they were holding. I couldn't talk. Finally, I snapped out of my trance. "That's me," I said. "I'm Tony." At the same time I was thinking, *What the hell is a sign writer?*

The taller of the two Englishmen then said something that actually put fear in me. I felt myself turn cold, like I had a sudden chill. (Have you ever had someone tell you they were so afraid at one time or another, they felt the blood drain from their head? My hair started to turn cold and from there, the chill went all the way to my toes.) "We are from the racetrack and we spilled some bloody fuel on the rear wing of the car and it seems to have removed most of the bloody writing. We were told you are the only chap around that can replace it," he said.

As I said, I had never done any real lettering, just fooling around with a couple of snowmobile helmets for my friends and such. Other than lettering my own race car I had never painted a sign. Apparently I must have lettered a helmet or snowmobile for someone that worked at the racetrack and when this race team started asking around about a sign painter someone must have given them my name. These guys didn't have a snowmobile; they had a real race car and it needed real lettering. *I can't do it,* I told myself.

"Well I don't know who would have sent you down here," I said, being totally honest with them. "I'm just getting started at sign painting, I'm really new at this. I'm sorry, but I don't think I can do this for ya. As a matter of fact, I can't do it."

"It can't be that bloody hard." He wasn't going to take no for an answer. "The sign writers in Europe just splash it right on there. Can you come to the track and do it tomorrow? We really don't want to leave the wing behind. It's sort of important," he said while lifting it up in front of me.

Before I could stop myself, the words just came out. I didn't want to say it, but it was like my damned mouth was out of control. My jaw was moving and I couldn't stop it. "I, I guess so. I'll be there," I stammered. Yet one more occasion when I just decided to do something and then actually thought about it later!

The taller of the two said, "We are in the front part of the garage, car number 24, Graham Hill's car." I tried to keep my jaw from dropping. Graham Hill was the Formula 1 World Champion. My *first* actual paying lettering job would be for a Formula 1 World Champion Grand Prix driver. I was stunned. I recognized the Thing as the rear wing of a race car. The two men turned and waved as they slowly walked down the dark steps carrying the Thing. Halfway down, one of them looked back at me. "See you tomorrow, sport."

I went back inside and fell back into my overstuffed easy chair. My arms stretched out on the armrests and my fingers clutching the padding. I tipped my head back, stared at the ceiling, and groaned out loud. "Who was that?" Kathy asked.

"You won't believe it. I can't believe it. What the hell did I just do?"

I told her the story.

"Are you going?"

"I told them I would be up in the morning. I don't know what to do. I can't letter that wing. I don't know how to do that kind of painting. I'm going to look like a fool. Why the hell did I tell them I'd do it? That was really stupid."

"What are you painting on it?" Kathy asked. I suddenly realized I didn't know. I hadn't asked. I guess it didn't really matter. If I couldn't letter, it didn't matter what it needed to say. I didn't sleep much that night. I was a wreck.

I arrived at the track at 7:30 a.m. The two guys recognized me and one of them whistled, waving a hand up in the air and motioning me over. *Oh no. They found me*, I thought. I was hoping that maybe they wouldn't be there and I could just leave. "Shit," I mumbled out loud as I walked over with my brand new brown metal Craftsman toolbox, which I used to carry some paint and two brushes, and I put it on the workbench that was off to the left of the beautiful Formula 1 race car. They brought the rear wing over and put down some clean gray shop rags on the metal workbench and then gently laid the wing on the rags.

The tall guy proceeded to tell me what they wanted. One word, no outline (thank God because I didn't really know how to letter so how the hell did they think I was going to outline something). They wanted a big red "Embassy." Looking at the wing, I could still see the ghost shadow of the old lettering. I didn't like the idea of having to paint two Ss, though, especially not side by side. I found that it was going to take a lot of practice to master painting Os and Ss. The way a paintbrush twists and flattens out as you make a turn takes a lot of skill to get it right. Also the right brush for the job is a must. A cheap brush will give cheap results. I didn't have that skill — yet. I also didn't have the best brushes. The few brushes I had were not the cheapest, but they were not

My first paint kit in a brown metal Craftsman toolbox. I still use it!

the best either. Thank God for that ghost shadow; *maybe I can pull this off*, I thought. Man, I was nervous. I felt sick to my stomach.

The garage at the racetrack was packed with people as it was Formula 1 Weekend at The Glen. *Can't I just go hide someplace and do this?* I thought to myself. I must have had the saddest look on my face one can imagine. *I do not want to be here. Why did I agree to do this?*

I jumped as the tall guy suddenly said, "Here, I'll clean the wing for ya, sport. You can do your sign writing right here." Oh God, it was getting worse. I looked around to my left, then to the right. Everybody was watching me. They all wanted to see what I was going to do. There were hundreds of people lined up at the fence looking at the World Champion's car and *me*. Without question, this was the worst day of my young life. How the hell did I get into this damned mess? I knew how. It was obvious. It was *my big mouth*. Little did I know that this day was going to be another turning point in my life.

Man, was I nervous. I never felt so alone in my life. I was feeling a bit ill and wished I could just puke and get it over with. If there is such a thing as a panic attack, I had it! Oh well, I didn't think they had a gun. They couldn't shoot me for screwing this up. What could they do? Not pay me? Oh God. I hadn't even thought about money.

I struggled with the layout, even with the ghost shadow to go by. The letter S is hard enough to paint, but two of them side by side? The pencil layout looked close, so I broke out the #4 Dick Blick Camel Hair brush and a 4 oz. can of Bright Red One-Shot lettering paint.

I was halfway through the letter A when a tall, lanky man from the team walked over. I could see him out of the corner of my eye. He was dressed in expensive-looking dark slacks, a tan sports jacket, and a dark green turtleneck sweater. He was a very classy Englishman. His hands were clasped behind his back, and he moved really slow as each movement was calculated and deliberate. He slowly leaned over my left shoulder. *He must be the team manager,* I thought to myself. *Why is he stand-*

Graham Hill's car that I lettered years early at Watkins Glen. The guy with me is Chris Melon, crew chief on the vintage F1 car.

ing there, looking over my shoulder? After quietly studying my progress, he bent down lower and close to the side of my head. Then, in a low (so no one else could hear) English-accented voice, he said, "You know, there's a sign writer in Europe that uses just the tip of the brush, in a sideward motion to square off the corners of the letters. It seems to make them crispy looking. I think the team owner just might like that a little better. Let me try to show you what I mean." Holding his hand out, he said in a real low voice, "The brush please."

I handed him the brush and moved aside. He stepped closer to the bench and bent over the wing. I sheepishly looked around him to see if anyone was watching. Man, was this embarrassing. On the letter A, he tried to show me the technique of how to square the corners of a letter. After making the stroke to form the side of the letter, he would move the brush in a sideward motion to make a sharp corner at the end of the brush stroke.

"I'm not a sign writer," he said, "but in Europe, I watch them do this all the time. Do you see what I'm trying to do?" As he straightened up, I straightened up at the same time. I looked at the letter A. It did look better. He handed the brush back.

"I'll try it. Thank you for the lesson, man."

He didn't stay to watch me. He just smiled, turned and walked away. I tried to do what he showed me and to my amazement, it worked. As a matter of fact, it looked great. I learned something from a guy that was not a sign writer. That showed me how much I didn't know. *I have to practice this when I get home*, I thought.

Finally, I finished my first paying lettering job. I stood back and looked at the finished product and, to my amazement, I could actually read it. Then I realized my back hurt. The two men from Graham Hill's crew that were in my apartment were happy, or at least they acted that way. I went home totally exhausted. I was mentally drained. The good part was I had a crisp $20 bill in my pocket and I learned a new (to me) lettering technique.

When I got home, Kathy asked, "Well? How did it go?"

Smiling, I held up that crisp $20 bill and said, "Holy Christ, it was scary. But look. I can make money. Twenty bucks!"

I look back on that day and I am sure the guy that showed me how the sign writers in Europe squared off a letter realized that I was a total amateur. He was politely trying to help me. He was a real gentleman. I wish I knew his name.

Memorable Dirt Races

After my two years of racing, seeing how some of the faster cars I had raced against were built, I decided to build a new car. As soon as the season ended, Joe Matwiejow and I poured a concrete floor in the garage. My race car shop was still small, but the new floor was a big morale booster. I now had a real shop. I could actually roll a jack around without getting stones jammed in the wheels!

My new car started as a '69 Chevelle. Steve Tinker and I acquired it one afternoon and towed it to his father's barn where we stripped it to the bare skin.

At the time, Late Model dirt cars sat very high, but I had been watching the Formula 1 and Indy Cars at Watkins Glen. With their lower center of gravity, they were faster around the corners. So I built my Chevelle low, turning it into the best race car I ever had.

My new car (16) is noticeably lower than the rest of the cars. Visibility was fine when I was in front, but when I was behind the taller cars, it was hard to see ahead.

Unfortunately, until other drivers started to build lower cars, I had a definite *dis*advantage. Was it fast? *Very.* Did it handle well? *Awesome.* Then what was wrong? When you are racing in a pack of cars, you actually look through the windshields of three to four cars ahead of you while racing. You want to see things happening before you get there. Well, now that I had this low car, I was looking right at the trunks of the higher cars—not what I wanted to see. I learned to compensate, by peeking around cars and darting back and forth, but it really bothered me.

My new car had a new Don Romeo–built 331 cubic inch Chevy engine. It started life as a four-speed, but I removed second and third gears to reduce friction and heat. In dirt racing you don't shift once you reach race speed—everybody stays in fourth gear. Also I had a homemade full-floating Oldsmobile rear end. A full floating rear end is rather complicated to explain, but it would be stronger and have less friction than a factory rear end. Also, with a floater, the wheel and brake drum wouldn't fly off the car if the axle broke during a race!

At work on the new Chevelle with my dad in my now-concrete-floored shop.

A lot of the guys were using Olds rear ends as they were tough, but nobody had a floater like mine. I got the idea from a retired GM engineer named John Camden, who'd worked on the crew of the '58 Corvettes that raced at Sebring, Florida. To build a floater, I needed a three-quarter-ton Ford truck axle, which was a problem: the axle spline was different from the Olds.

John showed me how to take the center section of the rear apart and weld—with a high-nickel rod—the three-quarter-ton Ford spider gears into the Olds differential. Welding the axle gears together tied the rear tires together, meaning the rear was what we called *locked* and both wheels would turn all the time. Now, with both wheels turning at the same time, it was best to have the inside tire smaller around than the outside tire so I could drive through a corner without the car sliding so much. (This difference in tire circumference is called *stagger*, and the right amount of stagger is critical in the set-up of the car at each track.)

With the extra money I made painting, I added a racing fuel cell to my car—no more converted beer kegs for me! Just as well I could afford it, as it was mandatory at that time. With the extra money, I could also afford spare tires.

All in all, this car was going to make us one of the top Late Model competitors in New York State.

After Joe Matwiejow helped me put the concrete floor in my garage, we became good friends. I soon found out that this guy could work on race cars. Being an ex-racer himself, he knew what was going on—and if there was a problem, he knew how to fix it. He lived on the Wedgwood road, which was not too far from me, or from the Watkins Glen track.

One day, while working on my new Chevelle, Joe came up with a fabulous idea to mess with the guys at the track who analyzed every new car that showed up. Joe pulled into the driveway at the shop and got out of his truck with a big, shit-eatin' grin on his face. *What the hell is he up to now?* I thought to myself. Joe's facial expressions give him away every time he has something up his sleeve. He walked over to where I was, not saying a word, just smiling. From behind his back he held out his right hand. I stood up and said, "What the hell is that?"

He just kept that grin on his face and finally said, "It's our new top secret invention." What Joe had and what he wanted to do with it was pure genius.

"You sly bastard," I said out loud.

What Joe had was a broken pressure gauge off a brine tank at the Watkins Salt Company. It was four inches in diameter and made of brass. Fittings stuck out of the gauge at the nine o'clock and three o'clock positions. The thick glass had a crack across it and the white face of the gauge had black numbers placed around the arc of the dial. The interesting part was that the black pointer was stuck at 322 pounds—about three-quarters of the way across the 500-pound gauge, putting it in the four o'clock position. Joe put copper tubing out of each end of the gauge at the fittings on each side. The tubing on each side was about a foot long.

My dad (left) and me at Rolling Wheels.

Right in front of the engine is the cross member of the frame of the race car. It holds the right and left side frame rails together and bends down under the front of the engine. It's in plain sight if you look into the compartment, and it has factory holes that do nothing but lighten it or strengthen it. Joe slid one tube in a hole on the right and then put the other tube in a hole on the left. The gauge was in the center of the cross member facing up. The tubes went far enough into the frame so you could not see the ends.

When we unloaded the car at Weedsport Speedway, it took about three minutes for the word to get around the pits. I have never seen such a commotion around a car. There was loud mumbling among the guys looking into the engine compartment that we had, accidentally, left open. Some of the guys were lying on the ground trying to see where the tubes went. We had to retreat to the back of the car hauler so they wouldn't see us laughing. Joe's idea was fantastic. We never did tell anyone what it really did. To this day, no one knows that it did absolutely nothing. That was one of the fun parts of racing.

We had some feature wins at Canandaigua and Dundee, but the track where drivers were set apart, if they could win there, was Rolling Wheels. Weedsport too. These two places were *the* tracks. The competition at these two tracks was so great that only the best of the best could win. I had won qualifying races at both of these tracks but no feature wins. I wanted to win at Rolling Wheels. I liked my chances during the Memorial Day Special races. Along with the Modifieds and Late Models, Rolling Wheels was also going to run a Sprint Car event. The pits at Rolling Wheels were on the inside of the track. With those three classes of cars racing that night, it was a prob-

In my mud covered Late Model 1969 Chevelle at Canandaigua.

lem finding room for all the cars and haulers. We were pitted facing the Back Straight, right along the guardrail, about halfway up the straightaway. While working on the car I noticed a truck and trailer with a yellow Sprint Car on the back slowly driving by. He drove around twice trying to find a spot to pit but the place was packed with race cars. I said to Joe, "Why don't you move our truck over that way tighter to the other hauler and I'll get the guy next to us to move the other way and when he comes around again, point him in here." That's what we did, and the guy was grateful.

Feeling good about our good deed, we settled into the business of getting the car ready for a win.

I won my qualifying race, which meant I would be starting second on the outside of row one. (On regular race nights, cars with the lower points started up front. On special event nights, qualifying set the lineup.) Tonight's feature race was a thirty lap special event, so it was longer than the normal twenty laps. With pride in my step I walked over to look at the chalkboard that had the lineup for the feature event. The chipped-up old chalkboard had been erased so many times it was light gray instead of black, and the rag they erased it with didn't totally take off the previous numbers so the brighter numbers were the ones that drivers were interested in. This chalkboard was mounted on the wall of the food stand in the center of the pit area. I had to keep swatting away the bugs attracted by the bare 60 watt light bulb mounted just above the board. The bulb actually looked pretty neat as it had a small cone-shaped pile of dust built up on top of it from the racing that had taken place over the past weeks.

A couple of guys were ahead of me so I got on my tiptoes and stretched upward to see over them. I knew where I was starting, but I wanted to see who was around me. A soon as I got a look at that old chalkboard, my face turned to a look of horror. Pure *horror*. I felt my face muscles involuntarily distort. I came down off my tiptoes so hard that when my heels hit the ground, the jolt went all the way to the back of my neck, snapping my head sharply forward. All the enthusiasm I had for the upcoming race had just drained out of me like water swirling down the toilet. At that instant, I had a strong premonition that my night was ruined. I walked back to the car in a daze.

"You won't believe it," I told the guys. "Goddamn it. You won't fuckin' believe it. We're doomed!"

"What the hell are you talkin' about, you idiot. You're on the outside pole," Joe said.

"I just looked at the lineup and we are outside row 1," I said.

"What the hell's wrong with that?"

"Guess who the hell is inside?" I said (meaning on the pole).

There was a guy—I can't remember his name—that drove a Javelin (American Motors) Late Model. The only problem was—he had one arm. Know your competitor. I knew this one. He was unpredictable. Inside, outside, no one knew where he would be next. He had a blue plastic knob on the steering wheel to drive. Sometimes, he drove straight as an arrow, but if he got in a bind it was hard for him to react with one hand. I realized he couldn't help it and I gave him a ton of credit for racing as he did. If I'd been in his shoes, I'd have done anything I could do to race also. Drivers couldn't help but like him—he was a great guy, and he or his dad would do anything to help anyone. His father, who was with him every night he raced, was also a great guy. *But tonight, why does he have to start next to me tonight?*

I had a bad premonition. All I knew was my strategy was blown all to hell.

At first, I thought about it and I figured that if I let him go and get out in front, he would go too fast into Turn 1 and I could duck under him and get by him there. Then he would be on the outside. But if I did let him go, chances are the guy behind him would follow him closely and end up on my inside. Then I'd be stuck outside, behind him. The only chance I had was to pass him on the outside before we got to Turn 2 and beat him down the Back Straight. I discussed it with Joe, who agreed with me. I had to beat him through Turns 1 and 2. I felt a little better but I was not as confident as when we had arrived at the track. When it was time, I climbed into my Chevelle.

As we went down the Back Straight on the pace lap, I glanced over to my left to the light brown Javelin. It felt like it was stalking me!

I am in a Stephen King movie, I thought.

Out of Turn 4 the starter was holding the green flag high in the air. It was time to concentrate. I had been thinking on the pace lap, "I can win this race. I won the heat, and now I'm going to win my first race at the Wheels." As the flagman began to wave the green flag, frantically, in a figure eight, the entire twenty-eight-car field accelerated at the same time. Along with the mighty roar of eleven thousand horsepower from twenty-eight engines, the spinning wheels were kicking up huge, billowing clouds of dust. That mass of controlled mayhem headed for Turn 1. Through Turn 1 the Javelin and I were side by side. I was running a little higher line than my usual, making sure to give the Javelin plenty of room. Between Turns 1 and 2, through my peripheral vision I could see his right front fender rapidly moving backward. I was almost clear. *Thank God.* Just then, I glanced up at the Back Straight flag stand, which was just off Turn 2. There was Charlie Trickler, a friend of mine from Waterloo, New York, waving at me. For a split second I thought, "I didn't just see that, did I?" Then it was quickly back to racing! I took a quick glance to my left to look for the fender. It was gone but I could still hear his engine. Thank God. "Throttle to the floor. Try to gain some ground before we get to Turn 3."

My foot was to the floor coming out of Turn 2. I was way up on the outside keeping my high line. Just as I was headed down the back straight thinking "I made it! I'm clear!" I heard, and at the same time felt, a thud on the left rear fender. The Javelin had hit me and instantly my car began a slow, looping, counterclockwise spin at 80 mph down the Back Straight. I turned the wheel hard right to counter the spin but there was no catching this one. I was gone. The car spun around 180 degrees and for a second, out of my windshield, I could see the entire field—including that damn brown Javelin—chasing me down the straight at 80 mph. I may have been going backwards but I was still leading. The front of my car slowly rotated to the left and then careered backward across the track from the outside of the track to the inside. I was still moving at about 70 mph backward. Sliding on a dirt track a car doesn't slow down much. I was hanging on, just along for the ride. I smile at the way the track

"Crash at Rolling Wheels": Standing behind car by windshield with beard, Don Romeo. Leaning down looking at rear wheel, Joe Matwiejow. Little guy to the side of him is Eddy Vickio. (Photo by Gater News)

announcers of today say after a car spins out, "He did a great job keeping it off the wall." Let me tell you something. That driver—90 percent of the time—was simply along for the ride.

I read somewhere that when you're racing and something happens, adrenaline pumps into your system and speeds up your senses so much so that everything actually seems to slow down. Well, for me, this turned out to be true! It was like the spin was happening in slow motion. I knew there was a guardrail along the inside of the track and thought I would miss it. I was wrong.

There was a loud *bang* and my car plowed into the steel guardrail at about 70 mph. My head snapped back into the headrest, which had no padding. The G-force was incredible as the car crashed to a halt. I must've sat there for a few seconds, possibly knocked out, because the next thing I remember was Joe hollering in the window at me. "Are you all right? You hear me?"

"*Wow.* That was a hell of a hit," I mumbled. Joe was reaching in, trying to help me unbuckle the belts. I slowly got out of the car with the help of Joe, my cousin Eddy Vickio, and the ambulance guys. I was a little shaky. My knees were not doing their job. I was holding onto the roof of the car with my left hand while looking at the back of my car which was sticking through the guardrail. A huge crowd had gathered. In a few seconds, I was able to stand without help. With Joe and Eddy still trying to hold me, I slowly took off my helmet. I looked again toward the back of the car where the crowd was gathered.

"How bad is the car?" I asked anyone who would listen. No answer. Along with the ambulance on the track surface I noticed another ambulance on the inside of the guardrail in the pits. I was getting my senses back and it was hard to understand anything anyone was saying as they are all talking at once. Someone said, "Get out of the way so we can hook it up."

Finally my senses returned enough for me to take in everything. My car was halfway through the guardrail. A ten-foot section of rail had bent in a U-shape and was sticking into the pit area. Several wood posts were broken off. I had hit hard. The rear of my car was wrecked pretty badly. The worst part was that the rear axle housing was bent, broken, and leaking. I could smell it—Wolf's Head gear oil does not smell good when it's where it doesn't belong! The rear tire was flat and the rim was bent, too.

I looked right behind my wrecked car. "Holy shit," I hollered to no one. "I almost hit my own truck." My hauler was parked along the Back Straight rail not five feet from where I'd hit. The truck that was hauling the yellow Sprint Car—the one I moved over to make room for—had a huge dent in the door where a piece of flying guardrail had hit it. The ambulance wasn't for me, it was for the guy's wife who'd been lying down in the front seat. Lucky the guardrail did not penetrate the door! She was not injured, just shaken up by the jolt and noise. Back then, the ambulance guys asked, "Are you OK?" If you nodded yes, they left. I nodded my head and they were gone!

Later I found out that Joe and my cousin Eddy, standing by the guardrail to watch the race, had had to run for their lives when I headed right for them. Joe said the sound was incredible. When the guardrail blew apart, the old paint on the rail had been blasted sending paint snowflakes into the sky. The pits had white paint flakes all over them.

On the way home my luck didn't get any better. I was driving, Joe was in the center and Eddy rode on the passenger side of the race car hauler. We were all pretty depressed. The adrenaline was wearing off, and my neck right between my shoulder blades was really starting to hurt. I probably had a concussion too, but in those days no one got checked for concussion. (With my brain, I wouldn't have known the difference anyway!) But my neck and shoulders sure did hurt as I steered the truck down the road.

We were on Route 414 just south of Seneca Falls when Joe leaned forward and picked up a faded old red M-80 fire cracker (one of the kind called quarter sticks) that had been gathering dust on the dash for a year.

"What the hell you doing?"

"What's it look like?" Joe said, looking at Eddy sleeping on his right. "I'm lighting this and tossing it out the window. We might as well wake some people up."

I turned back to driving and out of the corner of my eye I saw the sparks and could smell the fuse as soon as it lit. An M-80 is nothing to fool with. They're powerful. Really powerful. I glanced over as Joe flipped his arm right in front of Eddy's face toward the window and watched the trail of the sparks, twirling over and over as it flew toward the passenger window. Well, in his effort to wake some people up, Joe should have checked one thing first. *Was the damned window open??*

It wasn't. That M-80 bounced off the window and back toward us. It landed on the floor of the truck right under our feet. Instead of jumping on it, like in the war movies when a grenade comes into a foxhole and the hero soldier takes one for his comrades, Joe was trying to stand on the seat while leaning over in front of me trying to stick his head out my open window. I was lifting both of my feet up off the pedals and trying to keep the truck in the road while Joe's shoulder was stuck in my mouth. I couldn't see past Joe's body as he tried to squeeze through my window. Eddy woke up with all the commotion and jumped just as the fuse spurted its last spark. *Ka-boooommm.* There was a bright orange flash and suddenly it was daylight inside the truck. It was the loudest explosion that I have ever heard. The smell of gunpowder and sulfur was terrible. All I could think of was to get the damned truck stopped. I thought we were on fire! The cab was filled with sulfur-smelling smoke. Eddy was trying to peel himself off the ceiling of the cab as I pushed Joe back to the center of the seat and pulled off the road.

As soon as the truck stopped we all bailed out.

"You stupid bastard. Didn't you check the stupid window? What the hell is the matter with you?" I hollered.

At first I was mad. We were standing in the pitch black night along the side on Route 414 just outside of Seneca Falls watching the smoke from the M-80 drift slowly out of the cab and rise into the air. Then I started to laugh. I don't know if all that had happened that night built up to the emotional outburst or what, but I was laughing. Maybe it was crying but it sounded like laughing. We were standing by the cab of the truck, smoke still coming out of the open doors, and laughing like crazy. Joe did succeed in getting our minds off the wreck.

 # I Learn a Hard Lesson

After the smoke from Joe's M-80 cleared (coming home from the Rolling Wheels debacle) we piled back in the truck and headed home. I got to thinking—tomorrow was Saturday. "Let's start work on the car at 7 a.m.," I said. "There's a big race at Five Mile Point tomorrow night, and I want to go." I was probably talking louder than normal but I couldn't hear myself!

"We don't even know what's wrong yet," Joe said. "The damned rear end is really bent and the frame probably got it too. That's not mentioning the body. There's a hell of a lot of work," he said. Then he added "I'll be there." That's Joe!

"I'll tell you what," I said. "I want to go to Five Mile Point Speedway but it's an hour and a half trip. How's this sound? If we are not done with the car by 4:30 p.m., we quit and drink beer instead. Deal?"

"Deal, but I'll have a Pepsi," Joe said. He didn't drink.

When we got home, I parked the truck as quietly as I could so I wouldn't wake up my parents.

It was too late to unload the car, anyway. I backed the car hauler up to the front of the garage and shut it off. My back and shoulders were really hurting and when I turned my neck there was a sharp pain at the base of my skull. My ears were ringing so much I couldn't stand it. It sounded like a high-pitched bell. I kept looking around to see if an ice cream truck was coming. All I wanted to do was to go home, get in my bed, and sleep.

The next morning, I managed to arrive at the garage at 7 a.m. Just as I turned into the driveway, I looked up and saw Joe coming down the road in his old Chevy pickup. My dad was already out there inspecting the car. "See you didn't win last night," he said.

"Nope," I said.

As Joe walked up to the car I hollered to him because I still couldn't hear myself talking. "How're your ears, you dumb ass?"

Putting his right hand up to his ear he laughed and said, "Ringin' like hell. Now let's get this pile of junk unloaded."

We walked around the car, which was still on the truck, checking to see how extensive the damage was. The body was a mess but that could be hammered out and straightened. The fuel cell was dented, but the inner bladder was sound. One tire rim was bent beyond repair and the tire was cut, but I had spares.

The main thing was the rear end. We had to pull it out and replace it, so we decided we would jack the back of the car up right on the hauler and put jack stands on the ramps of the truck to hold the car. The day was beautiful, and it was easier to work outside anyway. After all, it took a wrecker to get the car on the hauler and I would need one to get it off as long as the wheels weren't turning. Kirk Williams—one of my crew—showed up to help out. I got the rear-end jig out so we could modify another Oldsmobile rear axle housing to make into a floater rear end.

Bill Meehan, my friend the machinist, had kept me supplied with spare parts such as the spindle adapters that I would need for the new rear end housing. It was very nice to be able to just walk over to my workbench and pick out the new adapters from the shelf underneath. I even had a spare Olds rear end housing. As I was cutting the new housing to the right width with an acetylene torch, I thought about the day I had picked it up from Morrow's Junkyard.

Morrow's Junkyard was out in the boonies a few miles past the Watkins Glen racetrack on County Route 16—just outside the little village of Townsend (population of about two hundred) near Pappy's bar (now called Monterey Jacks). At Morrow's, there was nothing but junk as far as you could see. Many of the old vehicles had been there so long they were almost entirely covered with brush, vines, and rust. Large trees grew out of the open hoods of a few of the cars. The one clear area—a dusty spot in front of a faded green and white, old house trailer—was surrounded by transmissions, brake drums, engines, and rims and tires.

Back when I picked up the spare housing, I'd found Larry, the owner, under the front end of a red '57 Buick LeSabre. The LeSabre's front end had been four feet off the ground suspended by a hook and chain to the homemade wrecker boom of a WWII-era Army pickup truck. No jack stands or other supports were under the car. All that had been holding it up was the chain wrapped around the car's front bumper.

Jerry, a heavyset guy about forty years old with long, scraggly hair, crawled out from under the car dressed in the grungiest pair of jeans I had ever seen. He kicked up some dust as he got up. "What the hell do you want today?" he said, not brushing himself off.

When I told him I was looking for an Olds rear end, he turned and pointed toward the woods. "Go down that path over there. Stay left and about ten cars in, by that big oak tree, is a blue '67 Bonneville." That car used the same rear end as the Olds. Jerry came down and lifted the housing out for me, and I was on my way. (I wish I had pictures of the junkyard. It definitely was movie material. Jerry's gone now and the yard is cleaned up, well almost.)

My friends and I worked hard repairing the damage to my race car. Kirk and my cousin Eddy (who lived next door) spent the morning straightening the frame and body. Joe worked the bent rear end out and disassembled it on the ground next to the car. That was a hell of a job as he had to remove the hubs, brake drums, and all the brake parts and spindles. Then the axles came out, and then the differential (the gears). Kirk was banging away with a three-pound hammer straightening out the sheet metal on the body. I was sweating as I welded the new spindle adapters and the spring mounts to the new housing. The hot day didn't help. It was at least 90 degrees! Too hot to wear a long-sleeved shirt, so I had all these little red burn spots on my arms from the weld spatter. We worked right through lunch while my dad supported the operation. (He mostly observed but when I needed an extra hand to hold something, he was right there). We only stopped when my mom brought out sandwiches.

I figured we did three days' work in ten hours. By 4:30 p.m. we still didn't have the new rear axle bolted back in the car. "That's it, boys!" I said. "It's four-thirty. That was the deal. Remember? I told you guys last night that at four-thirty, no matter what, we were done. Well, it's four-thirty and guess what? We're done. Time for a beer." I sounded disgusted as I had really wanted to race that night. We'd made one hell of an effort but we just ran out of time. I walked to the refrigerator in the back of the shop and pulled out a couple of cold Genny Cream Ales and a Pepsi for Joe. I walked outside and handed Kirk one. He pulled the tab off and tossed it into the old rear-end housing lying by the side of the car hauler. I did the same and took a big swallow. Oh my God, did that taste good! "AAAHHhhhhhh," I hollered out loud, "That tastes so damned good."

Joe, who was still under the car bolting the rear end in place, crawled out and sat up on the side of the ramp on the back of the truck. He leaned back against the car, slouching down to get in the shade. His hands and arms were covered with oil.

"Your Pepsi is right behind you." I said to Joe.

"What the fuck is the matter with you?" he retorted. The angry outburst startled Kirk and me. Joe never raised his voice. "I thought you were a fuckin' racer. Racers don't quit. Don't drink another sip. Dump that damned beer and get the hell back to work. You wanted to race tonight? Well, you're gonna race tonight." Joe climbed back under the car and we heard the sound of bolts spinning so fast he could have been using an air wrench.

Kirk and I didn't dare say a word. We looked at each other wide-eyed, then shrugged and dumped our half-full beers on the dirt driveway. We went back to work without as much as a whisper.

An hour later, I said, "Five-thirty! Five-thirty, guys! That's it, Joe. Kirk, that's it! We got a ninety-minute drive and we will not make the qualifying race. It's five-thirty! *We . . . are . . . done.* Do you hear me, Joe? We're done, goddamn it. Is anybody listening?"

Apparently not. Joe and Kirk didn't answer—and they didn't stop working. I went back to work and plugged away. No one wanted another ass chewing from Joe. Thirty minutes later I called out again. "All right. Six o'clock is the end. You got it, Joe? You hear me?" As I think back on it now, maybe Joe didn't hear me. He was still deaf from the night before when he almost blew us up inside the truck!

We finished work on the car, and by 6:30 p.m. Joe, Eddy and I were pulling out of my driveway and heading to Five Mile Point Speedway. The track, located just south of Binghamton, New York, was about ninety minutes from my garage. Poor Kirk couldn't make the trip. After the tremendous work he had done all day long, his

Kirk Williams and I unloading my 1969 Chevlelle for a test run at Watkins Glen International. When the track went bankrupt in the early eighties it was my private "test facility"!

wife had other plans for his Saturday night.

Don Romeo, my engine builder, joined us as well. He was hobbling around on crutches. A month earlier, at Rolling Wheels Raceway, there was a huge wreck coming out of Turn 4. Everyone was out of their cars and standing around watching the wreckers hook up all the cars. I noticed an ambulance leaving the track. It had the red lights on but it was not in too much of a hurry. I found out later than Don had jumped over the rail after the wreck and snapped his Achilles tendon.

Heading towards Five Mile Point Speedway, I drove like crazy. It was stupid, but we pulled up to the pit gate an hour and ten minutes later! It felt like I had already been in a race, and I wasn't even at the track yet. The pit sign-in shed was closed. The window was covered with a piece of gray plywood. Luckily the pit gate was open, so I drove into the pit area and parked on the end of the line of cars already there. I could hear the roar of the cars on the track and see the dust swirling up and over the safety fence and into the bright lights. This was not good; I don't like dusty tracks. As Joe unloaded the car, I finally found an official. I told him my story, and without any expression he said, "Sorry, buddy. The qualifying races are over and you missed the lineup. See ya next week."

He was turning away when I started to beg my ass off. Another official got involved, and finally they came up with a deal. After asking a few of the local drivers if it would be OK, they said that I could start the consolation race *dead last* if I wanted to try to get in the feature race.

As I've said, the consolation race was the last chance for everyone who didn't qualify in the heat races, which made it the most brutal of any of the races. When you mention the consi to racers, they always get goose bumps. If there was one race a driver wanted to avoid, it was the consi! Generally, in a consi, you have the less skillful drivers that didn't qualify and were now crazy to get to the front. It was never good to be in a consi, but choosing to start dead last, even in relatively small sixteen-car field was insane.

Knowing my chances of qualifying from the last spot approached zero, the officials figured they had a safe solution for letting me race. I would have to finish third or better as only the first three cars qualify to make it into the feature race. This would be next to impossible but it took so much to get here to just turn and go home, I could not turn it down.

"Sure. I'll do that," I said.

The official looked at me with a smirk, like he was thinking, "You dumb shit. You're in for an ass bustin'."

I thought, *At least I'll get to race in one event.* It was going to be tough—I'd only raced at this track once before. It would be a good test for the car to make sure we got everything back together right since I also wanted to race at Weedsport the next night (Sunday).

Well, all I kept thinking was, *Third, I've got to get to third.* The problem was that I only had eight laps to do it. I figured the chance of getting third from last place was about a hundred to one. You wouldn't want these odds at Vegas.

As I drove out of Turn 2 on the pace lap, I was flooring the car, spinning the tires and working the steering wheel back and forth to see if all the work we did was right. No vibrations; that was a good sign. Anyone watching probably thought I was showing off. Not the case. After a wreck like the one the night before and without any warm-up laps, it was a little intimidating to go into a corner with no testing. On the pace lap, I came out of Turn 2 and the cars on the pole were already going into Turn 4. Right then reality struck. I felt kind of sad because I realized there was *no way* I could make it to third.

As the green flag waved, the race became a blur. Five Mile Point is a very tight 1/3-mile oval. It was so short that at the start of a race, the leaders could catch the cars in the back of field on the first lap. With sixteen cars on a tight, fast track, you didn't have time to breathe. It was like being trapped inside a friggin' tornado. Cars were all over the place. If that wasn't bad enough, the dust was tremendous. Have you ever seen a movie where a dust storm was blowing in the desert? Well I was in one. Maybe it was better that I couldn't see. I might have pulled out if I could have seen where Pit Road was.

Going through a corner I passed a car on the outside. His right front tire rubbed into my door, not a foot from my shoulder. I could hear his engine screaming in my ear and smelled burning rubber. At the same time, my right front tire rubbed into someone's door on the other side. This was a full contact race! There wasn't a second when I was not banging into someone or someone wasn't banging into me. Sometimes I got banged on all four sides at the same time. My head bounced off the head rest as the guy behind me rammed the rear bumper. I didn't spin out, but that was just because I had two cars on either side of me holding my car straight.

When the tornado finally stopped and all the dust cleared, I did not get third. I did the impossible—I *won* the race. I won the dreaded consi from last place. I don't know how. I wish I could have seen a replay. It had to have been a hell of a race! I hoped the feature race would not be as bad.

My car, despite the wreck the night before, handled perfectly. We must have done a good job on the repairs. And we'd guessed right on the stagger (the difference between the circumference of the left and right rear tires), which was doing pretty well, since this was the shortest track we'd raced on. As I said before, in oval racing, you want the outside rear tire to have a greater circumference than the inside tire, so the outside wheel is traveling further than the inside wheel and forcing the car to turn left. I think we ran about seven inches of stagger that night.

Don Romeo and Joe hollered and waved with joy as I pulled into the pits from the consi. Kathy, still my wife at that time, was also at the race. She had driven down with a friend, and they were sitting in the grandstand. I had wanted to win the night before (at Rolling Wheels) so bad and now I had just won the consi from dead last at Five Mile Point. I was sure the feature race was going to be a lot different. That race would not have the cars that didn't qualify like in the consi. The feature race would have the best racers.

As I went out to line up for the feature event, Joe banged his fist on the hood. "Give it your best, damn it," he said. Don, on his crutches, stood there, hunched over a little. He lifted his hand off the crutch handle and gave a halfhearted wave.

I started the feature in eighteenth place. That night was only the second time I had ever raced at Five Mile Point's bull ring. (No bulls involved. A bull ring is a type of track—a short dirt oval with grandstands all around it.)

As the green flag fell and the race started, I saw the usual accordion effect: the lead cars immediately sped away while cars in back were still going at the pace lap speed. On a long track, this was not much of a problem. On this track, the leaders came right up behind me on the first lap! An early caution, caused by someone spinning out, saved me from being lapped. That was when I figured I'd better get my ass movin' as soon as the green flag dropped again. There was no foolin' around!

The first half of the race was full of wrecks and spins. Nothing serious. Mostly spins. This was good as it kept the leaders from lapping me. Again, the cars stirred up a tornado of dust. It was so dusty that I could barely see the car ahead of me. His bumper was all I could see. My game plan was to stay right on the bottom of the track (that is, the inside) and not back off at all. This was a different kind of racing from what I was used to! Push the guy ahead of me. Keep pushing. There was a lot of bumping and banging, just like in the consi. I was bumping the car ahead of me. The guy behind me was bumping me. Suddenly there was a car right next to my door. His engine was screaming right in my left ear! He must have had his left side tires on the inside dirt berm to get to the inside of me. I slammed into the car on the outside of me. Luckily, there was no real damage to my car. The engine noise with the cars racing so close was insane! The engines just screamed. My ears hurt at times when the engine got to a certain rpm. When you were close, like we were, the engines harmonized. It was a weird sound! From the grandstands the engine noise was different. The noise was loud when the cars went by, then it quieted down. In the car, the noise did not go away. It was with you from the start of the race to the finish.

The heat from my engine coming through the fire wall almost overpowered me. The racing fuel and hot oil smells, mixed with dust, filled my nose. I could smell Wolf's Head gear oil coming from the rear of my car—not a good smell.

The second half of the race went green flag all the way. The dust was so heavy that I could feel the grit grinding between my teeth. It was getting really hard to see. Sweat was starting to drip down the center of my forehead and down the sides of my nose under the shield. It itched like hell, but in the middle of a race you couldn't open your face shield. (It would take too long, and in any case the stones and dust would surely blind you.) I tasted the salty sweat on my dry lips. The only things any race car driver could do were concentrate and forget about the abuse. Drive as hard and fast as you could possibly go. If you can't take it, you lose. I had been passing cars almost every lap. Sometimes two cars at once! Very few of them without rubbing, banging, bumping, or getting bumped! I was possessed by a speed demon.

With only a few laps to go, I headed into Turn 3 and saw the car ahead of me slide a little to the outside going into the turn, leaving room for exactly half of my car to fit under him. Well, I (or the speed demon possessing me) put my whole car in that space. When an opportunity presented itself, there was only a split second to react. That's what I had been doing all night. I didn't know what lap it was but it had to be nearly over. *Please be over soon, please,* I thought to myself. I was mentally and physically drained and my eyes were full of sweat and dust! The car that I wiggled under in Turn 3 rubbed and bounced off me down the Front Straight. I could smell that rubber smell again. White tire smoke from his left front tire, or my tire, rolled up and over my hood. *I hope my tire stays up,* I thought. I finally pulled ahead of him through Turn 1. Most drivers would not have pulled that risky slam-bang, but I had to gain every position that I could on a short track like Five Points. If I wrecked going for a win, it didn't bother me as much as wrecking while just following somebody around the track in tenth place. I had been in traffic the whole race but had also been lapping cars at an amazing pace. I didn't have a second to relax. I passed two more cars down the Back Straight. "Must be lap cars." I thought. They were too slow to be leading.

As I came out of Turn 4, through the dust, I could barely see the starter on the starter stand high above the track overhanging the front straight. He waved the white flag and with his other hand pointed at me. The white flag meant there was only one more lap and pointing at me meant I was leading the race. *That can't be,* I thought. After one more lap I looked at the starter again. Sure enough, there was the checkered flag waving through the dust cloud.

That slam-bang move in Turn 3 got me the *win*. It was an incredible race. I was so proud. Not only of myself but of my crew, Joe, and Don. I was completely drained. I was spitting out dust while tears helped clean my eyes. That was a race to remember.

Me, Kathy, Don Romeo, and Joe Matwiejow at Five Mile Point Speedway after my feature win.

Not just the race but the work it took from being wrecked the night before and winning the next night.

I parked on the Front Straight for pictures. Kathy came down from the stands and Joe and Don came out from the pits. There were more boos than cheers. I was considered an outsider. I didn't normally race there and fans didn't like outsiders winning—but when I win you can boo me all day long. I loved it. When you get booed you know you have been noticed. Hell, Earnhardt and Gordon got booed.

The cash window was in a small gray woodshed behind the grandstand. I picked up my pay for winning the feature event. *Two hundred bucks wasn't lavish, but it meant a whole lot more then than it does now.* As I collected my winnings, I noticed an old man sitting outside the shed near the end of the grandstand. The light, hanging from the side of the shed, shone down on him as he sat in an old green-and-white aluminum folding chair. He was about seventy years old and wouldn't have weighed ninety pounds soaking wet. He wore a filthy red racing hat and an old red nylon racing jacket. His grayish hair, a little long and uncombed, stuck out from under the hat and curled up by his ears. A five-day beard covered his skinny, puckered face. The cigarette between his two yellow fingers gave off a steady column of smoke.

As I walked by him, the old man said in a loud but frail voice, "That you drivin' that seventeen car, boy? Yoose a stranger here, huh? Only seen ya here once before."

I turned toward him. "Yeah," I said. "That was me."

"Helluva good run, boy," he said. "Gotta tell ya sup'um though. If ya come back next week, watch yer ass. These guys don't like outsiders takin' their money home. Just a word of warnin', sonny. Don't come back and think ya's gonna win another one." Just then, his eyes suddenly widened to huge, white globes and a serious look came on his face. It was like he was putting a period on the sentence with his eyes. He put the cigarette back in his mouth and drew on it so hard the end turned bright red, lighting his face in an eerie reddish tint. I took a double take. Suddenly, with that eerie, red glow, he looked just like the devil. A chill ran down my spine as I imagined little horns rising up out of his head.

"Thanks, man," I said, turning quickly to walk away. I thought about what he said for a second, then I shook it off and headed to the pits to celebrate with Kathy and the crew. I didn't think about the old man again until the following week, when his words came back to me.

On the way home, Don and Joe were quiet. I think we were so happy that we were all lost in our own thoughts of how the last two days went and how unbelievably it ended. I thought of the night before and my car sticking halfway through a guardrail and how I was ready to give up when 4:30 p.m. came.

That Saturday in front of the garage working on the car, Joe had taught me something. You never give up. It resulted in winning two races and both of them from near last place. From that day on, I was a changed man. I never gave up on anything again. As I was driving home, I had a huge smile on my face.

❧

The next Saturday night, instead of going to Canandaigua, my regular track, I went back to Five Mile Point. Yeah. I got greedy. *I won there last week,* I reasoned to myself. *I can do it again.* I was not thinking about that old-timer and his words to me after the last race. "If ya come back next week, watch yer ass."

I started the feature race in the middle of the field this time. I was doing fairly well. By the halfway mark, I was in third place. I was running right on the bottom, steadily moving my way up through the field. I felt really comfortable. I was not being overly aggressive because I only had half as many cars to pass as I did last week. That night, the track was not so dusty. I was using my head and with less dust there was less contact.

With six more laps to go, I only had to get by two more cars. Coming through Turns 3 and 4 my car, without warning, took a sudden, hard 90-degree turn to the right. I happened so fast that I hardly had time to lift my foot off the throttle, let alone hit the brake. I hit the concrete wall nearly head-on without slowing down. The last thing I remember was the hood crumpling up. My car had tried in vain to punch a hole through the foot-thick concrete wall. The wall won. After the hit, it was quiet. I just sat there. I knew I had been in a race, but for some reason, I just calmly sat in my car. I remembered hearing, "Get the ambulance out here. Get it now." I thought another car must have been involved. *Hope that other guy isn't hurt too bad,* I thought to myself.

As I regained my senses, Don hollered in the window, "Hey! You OK?" That's when I realized they were calling the ambulance for me. I had been out cold. The strange thing was I could hear everyone talking. I didn't get in the ambulance, although I probably should have. I guess my brain wasn't damaged too badly.

Seems someone was on the outside of me and between Turns 3 and 4 came down against my right rear fender. This turned me 90 degrees right and straight into the concrete wall. I never did see that old guy that night, but I'll bet that he had a smirk on that puckered old face. He sure knew what he was talking about. Plain and simple, they took me out. Just as the "devil" told me they would do the week before.

I should have listened.

 A Love of Painting

When I was not at work at Shepard Niles, racing, or working on my car, I was painting something. I put lettering on all types of cars at the track. Formula 1, Indy cars, prototypes, sports cars. If it raced at The Glen, I lettered it. Every October, Watkins Glen hosted the United States Grand Prix, but many different classes of cars raced at the Glen all year. SCCA sports cars were the ones I worked on most. The Indy cars and the prototypes did not give me much work. One thing about lettering race cars at the Glen: it's always in front of hundreds of people. This cured my shyness.

Lettering and pinstriping my brother's van with the name of his band, Sopwith Camel.

From that point on, through the 1970s to 1980, whenever the Formula 1 cars came to town, I was in great demand. Formula 1 teams traveled all over the world together. When one of them found a good place to eat, they all ate there. After Graham Hill's crew found me, I was the sign painter they all used. During the following year I was actually getting better at lettering and I wound up doing some sort of lettering on most of the Formula 1 race cars that raced at Watkins Glen.

Back then, most of the racing teams had one sponsor—if any. Most of the cars had a simple white circle with a black number in it. Over time, they started to get more creative. Some had a colored number with an accent outline. Sometimes I would paint numbers and the driver's name on new body panels after a car was wrecked. I got so I could paint numbers on the cars really fast. For example, I would paint the number in black first and then carefully paint the white circle around it while the black paint was still wet. This saved a day as I didn't have to wait for the white to dry to put the number on.

I was so new to sign painting that I was never sure what to charge. One time a team manager, a short, heavyset guy in a gray suit, opened his black leather briefcase and said, "What do I owe you, son?"

I thought to myself that $10 or $15 would be fine. But I was too tired to pick one, so without thinking, I said, "Just give me what you think it's worth." I wanted to get home, so I just left it up to him. He bent over his briefcase as he pulled a bright chrome pen from the inside vest pocket of his suit. Leaning over the briefcase he signed something. He tore the paper from a pad and handed it to me. I looked at it. I had never seen one before. "What is it?" I asked.

"It's a traveler's check," he said. "Thank you. You did good." He had given me a $50 traveler's check. What a great idea that turned out to be.

I started to leave the payment up to the people who hired me and I would often get five times what I would have charged. The Team managers always carried traveler's checks, usually 50s or 100s and they would normally say, "Got change for a fifty?"

"Nope," I would say, "I don't have any money on me." They would rip off a traveler's check and hand it to me. *Holy Cow!* Now I saw what the sign writers in Europe were charging. Life was good.

Sometimes, after I was paid, the team would take me to supper with them at Seneca Lodge. At times, the whole table didn't speak a word of English, so I just smiled and nodded a lot. They were probably saying, "Look at that dumb ass down there thinking he's a sign writer. He oughta see the guys in Europe paint." I didn't care. The Black Angus steak sure tasted good.

Sometimes I would go to the track at night, after the garage was closed, to do my work. This was great. No crowds or crew members. No one was in the garage except me, a guard, and a big, gnarly German shepherd attack dog. I was scared of that damned dog, though. I didn't trust it. When I arrived, I would scratch its nose—but after I walked away, I would look back and it would be glaring at me. It would put goose bumps up the back of my neck.

The fun part of working nights was, after I was done working on a car, I would sit in it. I have sat in some of the most famous cars in the world. Ferrari, Lotus,

Typical F1 car showing the white circle with the black number. (Photo from Bill Green collection)

McLaren, you name it and I've been in it. Getting paid was even better.

In the late 1970s, I worked on the cars driven by Graham Hill, Jody Scheckter, Mario Andretti, James Hunt, Jackie Stewart, and just about every other Grand Prix driver of that time. I have a list, and it is long. Although I worked on their cars, I only met one Formula 1 driver during that time—South African Jody Scheckter.

Getting ready for the 1976 United States Grand Prix in Watkins Glen, Jody had crashed his car in practice, so new body panels had to be put on. After the repairs, the car only needed Jody's name lettered on it. His name on the old car was simply JODY, at a slant, on the sides of the driver cowling. I lettered that on the new car as close as I could to the old one, which was lying on the floor by the wall. I was just starting to clean my brush when Jody himself came by. I was kind of proud of the job I did and was expecting a "Good job!" from him, when in fact, he started hollering. He was pointing his finger and frantically waving it back and forth.

"No, No, No, not right . . . not right," he said in a very loud voice. "Not slanted enough. Take it off," he said, waving his hand in front of himself. "Get it off there!" He then turned and stormed off.

Jody had caused such a big commotion that people were drawn from around the garage area to the car. The crewmen were looking at each other and back at me. I didn't know what to do. I held my arms out and shrugged my shoulders. They were as shocked as I was. This was embarrassing, to say the least.

I took a rag and some thinner and wiped the still-wet paint off. Just as I got the paint off, Jody came back with his helmet which had JODY painted on the sides. I thought he was going to show me what the angle of the slant he wanted on the sides of the car. To my surprise, and everyone else's, he put the helmet on and got into the car. He slid down into the cockpit, put the steering wheel on and sat as if he were driving the car. We all looked at each other in amazement. I could hear a muffled voice from inside his helmet while he pointed to his name on the side of his helmet. "Slant, like this. Just like this."

This drew a hell of a crowd. Jody sat there in the cockpit with his helmet on looking straight ahead while I lettered his name on his car. When I was done, he got out and took the helmet off. He looked at the helmet, then the car, and back to the helmet. There was total silence. Not one of the crew said a word as we all stood motionless and silent. He smiled. Then, holding the helmet down to his side by the chin strap, he quickly turned and walked away without a saying a word. I looked around and the entire crew and I started laughing at the same time.

In 1976, Formula 1 added the Japanese Grand Prix (at the Fuji Speedway) to the end of the racing season. Up until that time, Watkins Glen had been the last race on the schedule. Starting in 1976, the crews stayed at the track for a week after the early October race at the Glen getting the cars ready to ship to Japan. I would go up during that week and letter some of the cars that needed changes. Teddy Yip, an Indonesian shipping tycoon, owned two Formula 1 cars. He told me he wanted them lettered in Japanese for the race in Japan. He drew the layout on a sheet of paper and I carefully lettered the cars. He was happy with the result. Sometime later that year, I was in the Ten Limited Tavern having a cold Genesee Cream Ale and a few of us were talking about lettering that Formula 1 car in Japanese.

Someone said, "Hey Vickio. Since your lettering is now going all around the world, you gotta be world famous." That's how I got the nickname "World Famous" which was later shortened to "Famous" by several painter friends.

Looking back, I wish I had taken more pictures of my racetrack work.

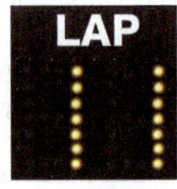 Applying Life's Lessons

For years after I built my low-riding Chevelle Late Model in 1976, I had one of five cars that could win at any track in the Northeast, and everyone there knew it as soon as we showed up. It was great. I even signed some autographs once in a while. I *never* drove a race car onto a racetrack, whether it was a qualifying race or a feature event, without one thing on mind. *Winning*. If I knew some reason that I couldn't win, I wouldn't go out and just drive around. I had developed a WWT mentality: *Win or Wreck Trying*. This got me a lot of wins, but my enthusiasm occasionally cost me.

Early in my racing career, I was preparing to run hot laps—practice laps—one

In the pits at Weedsport with a new car.

night at Weedsport Speedway. Don Romeo, my engine builder and part-time crewman, was also a photographer for Gater Racing News, a racing paper covering dirt and asphalt tracks in the Northeast. Don was inside Turns 1 and 2 shooting photos and noticed that the track was very wet—the track crew had watered it to keep the dust down. He turned to the photographer next to him and pointed (like Babe Ruth did when he called a famous home run) to a spot way over across the track on the Turn 4 concrete wall. Don said one word: "Vickio." Don knew how I raced. It was just warm-ups, but I had to be the fastest. I couldn't just go out there and cruise around. I was still new at the time and my brain quit working every time I put my helmet on. *Maybe my helmet was too tight.* On the first lap of the warm-ups I got a little high going into Turn 4 and. . . . *Bang.* I slammed the concrete Turn 4 wall about three feet from where Don said I would. (Don told me all this later as he chewed my ass about using my head.) That stunt cost me a race and quite a few bucks to fix the car.

I did back off in the hot laps from that point on, but I never set foot on a track without knowing I could win the race. That was until a rainy Fourth of July weekend in 1978. It was Sunday afternoon and I was sitting in my apartment watching TV. I looked outside. The sky was getting lighter and the rain had almost stopped. I did not want the rain to stop.

The week before I was racing at Weedsport when the ring and pinion in the rear end broke. I had still been able to run at Rolling Wheels on Friday and at Canandaigua Saturday night, because I could use the same rear-end gear ratio at both tracks. The Sunday race was at Weedsport which was shorter and tighter. To be competitive there, I'd have to change the gear ratio—but the replacement for the broken part had not arrived yet. I was out of luck. I wouldn't feel so bad if the Weedsport races were canceled. If I couldn't race, I didn't want anyone to race.

I was bored just sitting home when it looked like the races would go on. I said to Kathy, "Let's go to Weedsport tonight just to watch the races. I can't sit home and watch the stupid TV. The rain has just about stopped."

"You're not thinking of taking the car, are you?" she said.

"Hell no," I said. "With those gears, I could never win. Why take it?" As we were walking to the car, I said, "Let's go up to the shop first. I have to get something."

As we pulled in, there was the hauler with my dirty race car still on the hauler from the night before. I hadn't even washed the mud off of it. The roof and top of the hood were clean from the rain, but the sides of the car were wet and muddy. The car looked like a wet, tired dog. I could barely read the number.

The race that night at Weedsport was a special event, a July fourth deal, and qualifying would determine the starting positions. While at the shop, I said to Kathy, "It's rained all day. If I can draw one of the first two qualifying races, the track will be wet and with those low gears on a wet track I might just qualify. If I do, I can start the race and run two laps and pull out. Last place is paying $75 bucks tonight."

Kathy said, "*No.* Damn it. Leave the damned thing here. You already told the guys to stay home. No one will be there with you and I'm not changing a tire. Leave the damn thing here. Don't be stupid. I'm saying it the last time. *Leave it here.*"

When she said, "Don't be stupid," I knew she was right. At that point I should have turned around and driven my 442 Olds to the races. But I didn't.

We drove to the races in the car hauler with the car on the back. It wasn't a good ride. I don't think Kathy and I said one word to each other the whole hour drive. I probably should have listened to her. This was not the right thing to do. Not only were we not talking, but I was breaking my own rule. As I drove in the pit gate a guy held a faded old Maxwell House Coffee can toward my window. I turned to Kathy. "I'll tell you what. If I don't draw a number that gets me into the first or second heat, I won't even unload the thing. The track has to be wet for me to have a chance." She gave me the glare. "I promise. I want it muddy," I said to her.

She didn't even look over at me—just sat there, glaring straight ahead. The guy at the gate said, "Pick your number for the heat." I reached in and drew a small piece of white paper out the can. I unfolded it and saw the number 10. I spoke the number in an excited voice—it would get me into the first heat. I handed it back to him. He rolled it around and flipped it over as it was upside down and said, "Ten." I nodded, thinking, *That's what I just said.* We drove into the pits and parked.

"You aren't really going to try to run the car, are you?" Kathy said, with the same glare she'd had when we left home. "I'm going in the stands," she said, not waiting for an answer. "Go talk to all of your buddies, and then come to the stands. I'll save you a seat." She stormed off before I could say OK.

A lot of cars were at the track that night. Big races draw lots of cars. Many of the cars I had never seen before. The place was packed. There were a few cars from Five Mile Point. *Wonder if the guy that put me in the wall is here tonight? I could return the favor if I knew who he was.* I started to pull the ramps from under the truck. They screeched putting my teeth on edge. They were heavier than hell and dirty. *Crap,* I thought, *now I know why I have a crew. This is work.* Just then it stopped raining. Fitting right into my plan. I got into the car and coasted it down the ramps. It jolted to a stop just behind the truck as I hit the brakes. The car was clean after the drive in the rain. I left the ramps down. I was not picking those damned things up again.

The gears I had in the car were 4:56s. I needed a 5:12 ratio to run here. I probably could have run using third gear, but I'd pulled the second and third gears out of the transmission to reduce friction, keep the heat down and increase horsepower to the rear wheels. My concern was that when the track dried out, it would be like trying to drive off in a standard shift car from a dead stop in fourth gear. My car would lug down so much, I would not be able to keep up. But in the early qualifying races, with the rain and the track being muddy, lugging the engine would be a benefit, keeping the wheel spin down and actually getting more traction. This would probably work for the qualifying race only. After that, when the track would dried out, and I'd be done.

My plan was: (1) Qualify. (2) Start the race. (3) Run two laps. (4) Pull in and collect $75 for last place. For the first time in my life I was at a track knowing I *could not* win. I was disobeying my own WWT strategy. I knew in the back of my mind, I should not be doing this! I could hear Kathy's words echoing in my head: *"Don't be stupid."* I was getting a feeling of pending disaster. Another premonition?

Drawing the number 10 put me in the first heat, but almost last in a field of twelve cars. They were taking the top four cars. I needed fourth. I can imagine that when Kathy saw my car come out onto the track, she almost fainted. I couldn't see where she was sitting, but as I drove down the Front Straight on the pace lap, just after the flag stand, I suddenly felt a ray of heat on the right side of my face. It was the *glare*.

I started the first heat and, taking into consideration the track conditions, I drove with my brain, for a change. I won my heat race! The other cars, not changing gears, were spinning and sliding around like they were on ice. I just drove, or should I say *putted*, by them at the bottom of the track like I was on a rail. With the win, I would start the thirty-lap feature on the pole. (Since this was a special event, qualifying set the lineup.)

I was *sick*. *I was on the pole and would have had a good chance to win.* I would have to pull off at the start of the race as I'd be a definite hazard out there. *Damn it. This sucked*, I kept thinking. *I should have listened to Kathy. I shouldn't have brought the car and I wouldn't be feeling like this. Damn.* Nothing left to do but stick to my plan.

Back in the pits, I knelt down in front of the car to clean the radiator. I don't know why as I would be pulling out in two laps anyway. I guess it was habit. I just wanted to race so damned bad. I kept thinking, *I'm on the pole. It isn't fair.* Just then I felt a sharp slap on my shoulder that almost knocked my head into the hood.

"What the fuck you doin' workin' by yourself? Where the hell is your crew?" I turned around and there was Jim Jarvis. Jim was a hell of a runner. Not only that, he was crazy. I don't mean crazy like a guy having too much fun . . . I mean *crazy* crazy. He always had a wide-eyed look on his face and a red bandana wrapped around his head that added to the crazy look. I think a few of the drivers were scared of him. I gotten to like Jim a lot and we had become good friends.

"*Hey*, Jarvie," I said. "Believe it or not, I'm here alone. Where are you starting?"

"Third. Right behind you."

I told him my story.

"You idiot," he said.

That was twice I'd heard a similar thing today. "I've got a plan," I told him. "Going into Turn 1, I will drive up high and force the guy on the outside of me up the track. You be ready and go under me. That way I won't slow you down."

"Cool," he said. "I still can't believe you came here alone." He turned and walked back to his car.

I was still kneeling in front of my car and staring at it thinking what could have been. *I'm breaking my own rules. I never went onto a track without being able to win and now I'm telling the guy behind me I'm moving over for him.* This was a bad omen. I really felt like shit. *This just isn't the way I race. Is it worth $75 bucks to humiliate myself?*

Just then I heard a clatter and voices coming my way. It sounded like something was being dragging across the stones on Pit Road. The noise was getting closer to my car. I looked up over the hood and there was Jim Jarvis, Jerry Schweitz (who became a gasman for Sterling Marlin), Charlie Trickler, and the rest of Jim's crew coming toward my car. Jerry was dragging a jack behind him. Jerry was *big*–about six-foot-eight and 220 pounds. The other guy was carrying a center section for an Olds rear end and Charlie had some tools. "What the hell ya doin?" I asked.

"Get the hell out of the way," Jim said. "We got work to do and there isn't much time."

"You don't have time," I said. "The consi is just going out. We will be next." They didn't listen. I stood back as they went to work. They jacked the car up and at the same time, two guys were pulling the axles and the drive shaft. It was incredible. They got Jim's spare set of gears (Jim had a spare everything) and put the right gear ratio in the rear end just as the consi race ended. "Man, thanks," I said. "I don't know what to say."

Jim said, "Just don't wreck me," and they all walked back to their car.

I stood there all alone by the side of my car, thinking about what had just taken place. I got goose bumps. I couldn't believe it. I looked across Pit Lane to Jarvis's car and watched them doing last-minute work on it. After helping with my car, they were now intent on beating me. If he could, Jim would beat me fair and square. I opened the truck door and stood behind it and took my pants off. Then I put my fireproof Nomex socks and long underwear on. The fire suit was next and my sneakers. All alone, standing by the side of my car, I heard the speaker blare, "Late Model Feature. Late Model Feature to the line." *Wow.* I got in the car.

I drove out onto the track for our thirty-lap feature and went drove down the Front Straight for the lineup lap. I could feel the heat from the stands again. This time the glare felt even hotter. Man, did I feel good. Kathy had to think I was nuts for coming out in the feature and starting on the pole. She probably figured I would start last and then pull in. Down the Back Straight I had my WWT feeling back. I was smiling. *All this worrying and now I have a chance to* win. Kathy had no idea of what just took place in the pits.

About half an hour later and after thirty laps of dusty, unbelievably hard racing, I was standing in front of a full grandstand with a checkered flag in my hand doing

A win at Weedsport Speedway. (Photo by Gater News)

an interview. I led that race from start to finish. I had a couple of good challenges but that night there was not one car that was up to the task. I was going to win and it would have taken a superhuman effort to beat me that night. Jim finished where he started, third. I publicly thanked Jim and his crew as I told the story to the crowd.

Over and over, on the way home, I couldn't stop saying, "Oh my God. Can you believe it? I can't believe it." Kathy sat on the passenger side smiling. There, between us on the seat, was a big, shiny trophy and a roll of cash in my pocket.

I couldn't wait till the next morning so called the boys when we got home and told them the story. They all came over to the garage, where I had the trophy sitting on the roof of the car. At first, they called me all sorts of names. Then they realized, even though they were not there, they still were a part of the win.

That was one of my most memorable wins. Back then, racing was fun. You helped each other even if it meant getting beat. Today, money has taken over and racing isn't the same. Some guys would put their own daughter in the wall to win. *Well, maybe I would, too, if she was in the way. (Remember the Go-Carts, Beth?)*

A win later that year at Rolling Wheels—with Mark and Kathy, my son and wife.

Shangri-La Speedway

My First Asphalt Race

I was at one of the dirt tracks on a warm, calm summer Friday night. I think it was Rolling Wheels Speedway in Auburn, New York. I was working on the car getting ready for the feature event, when my friend Dale Marion walked up and said, "Hey. How's it goin'?"

"Good," I said. "The car is really runnin' and I might even win tonight." (*I didn't.*)

Dale Marion owned a NASCAR Asphalt Modified. These things are nasty, fire-breathin' monsters. They can average 110 mph on a half-mile oval, hit 120 on the straight, and run 90 mph in the corners. Dale's car featured a tubular chassis (He used a Troyer chassis), a Ford Pinto body, a quick change rear end, four-wheel disc brakes, and huge twenty-one inch Goodyear slicks. Dale's car was powered by a 433 cubic inch Chevy engine that developed 650 HP. That is an honest 650 HP in a 2100-pound car. This added up to one of the fastest short track series going.

"How'd you like to drive my car tomorrow night?" Dale asked. He might as well have hit me with a two-by-four.

I stood up. "You're kiddin' me, right?"

"No," he said. "Chuck is driving a Dirt Modified race someplace tomorrow night and I thought you might be interested. I need a driver." Chuck Ciprich had driven for him a few times.

"I've never driven on asphalt before," I said. "That's a whole different ball game." Part of me said, *Are you sure you want to do this?* The other part said, *Holy shit. Driving an Asphalt Modified. Go for it.* "I guess I can try it."

"Good. Be there [at Shangri-la Speedway in Owego, New York, now called Tioga Speedway] around five o'clock and we'll get you fitted to the car." (Chuck was a little taller, so the seat and pedals and steering wheel would all need adjusting.)

I showed up at Shangri-La Speedway so early that almost no one was there yet. The parking field had only three cars in it. I headed for the open gate to the track at the end of the Front Straight. This was the first time I was going racing without my dirt car. It felt strange. Just before the gate, on the left, was the sign-in shack, a 6'×10' gray wooden shed.

Two women were sitting on high wooden bar stools inside the shed as I walked up. The one on the right looked like she was in her late fifties. She had bright blonde hair and glossy red lipstick. I guessed that her ton of makeup was an attempt to patch up and hide the wrinkles. The other woman was a little older. Her hair was jet black, like she'd painted it with a can of Krylon gloss black spray paint. Her hair had a bluish tint to it when she turned just right. She was very thin and puffed on a cigarette like it was her last one and she was going to enjoy it.

"Hello," I said. "I need a Pit Pass."

"Driver or crew?" asked the woman with the Krylon hair.

I said, in a fairly proud voice, "Driver."

"Can I see your license, please?"

I reached into my left side pocket, as I never carry a wallet, and pulled out a wad of papers. I had a ten, twenty, some ones and mixed in were some quarters, two of which fell to the ground. Among the dimes and pennies was my bone-handled pocketknife; I'd wondered where that thing had been. I laid the pile of stuff on the countertop as I bent over and picked up the quarters. "Sorry. I don't carry a wallet," I said as I stood up.

The women just glared at me. They weren't impressed. The smoker puffed a huge cloud from her cigarette. I fumbled through the pile and found my driver's license. I smiled and handed it to her. "There it is. Sorry about that," I said.

She looked at it and said, "What are you? George Carlin? You're a comedian, aren't you? That's not it. You need a NASCAR license."

"What? I don't have one. This is my first time here," I said. "I'm only driving tonight for someone else who couldn't make it."

"Sorry, honey. You can't drive without it."

I couldn't believe it. *Give up a night of dirt racing, drive all this way, and I need a NASCAR license? Why didn't Dale tell me?* I felt sick. I picked up the huge pile of papers and things and stuffed them back into my pocket. "How do I get one?" I asked. "Is there an application? How long will it take?"

Krylon-woman's lipstick-stained cigarette bounced up and down as she spoke. "Twenty bucks."

"You mean I can just buy one?"

"Twenty bucks." she repeated.

I reached back in my pocket and pulled all the stuff out again and laid it on the counter. Searching, I found my only twenty and slid it across the wood counter top.

"Now gimme back yer driver's license," she said.

"There it is," I said. It was all wrinkled up and stuck to a yellow receipt.

She copied some stuff from my driver's license, probably the speeding tickets, and wrote it on the NASCAR license. She slid them both across the plywood countertop. I picked up my brand new NASCAR Modified driver's license and looked at it. *Wow.* I walked down the dirt road to the open gate near Turn 1, carrying my duffle bag with my fire suit, gloves, and helmet in it. As I went past the concrete wall at the end of the Front Straight, I walked out onto the track surface. I noticed it was banked a little. I was in the middle of the track when I stopped and looked left toward the Front Straight. Then turned and faced right toward Turn 1. *Wow. This is cool. Asphalt. No* mud. In a little while I would be going right over this spot at 100 mph. Looking up the Front Straight, I saw the flag stand hanging over the track. "Man. It doesn't look very high. That's gotta be scary standing in that." I thought. The grandstands were not very big and at the top was a small, glassed-in announcer's booth. *It looks smaller than the Wheels,* I thought. I looked down and noticed something strange—grass was growing out of the cracks in the asphalt. *Wow.* Then I figured it out. This was way out of the racing line and toward the wall. *No cars would be up here unless they were crashing,* I thought.

Part of me couldn't wait to drive on the track. The other part wanted to run back to my own car and get the hell out of there. There weren't many race cars here yet, but I could feel the excitement building. I looked down toward the far end of the pits, toward Turn 4, and saw the red and white number 21. My heart jumped at the sight. *My car.* I walked over to Dale and shook his hand.

"Get in the thing and we can set the seat and pedals to suit you," he said. "This takes a while, but it's worth it—you have to be comfortable."

After the car adjustments were completed, I went to the dressing room and put my fire suit on. As I walked back to the car, I noticed the curious glances from other drivers and crews. I had long hair and a jet-black beard, and I was a newcomer.

Dale was warming the engine up. The sound of that bored-out 427 sitting there idling was awesome. It gave me goose bumps. Man, this thing just thumped away with heavy, dull thuds that moved my clothes. It was hard to talk with that engine

First night at Shangri-La Speedway. The look on my face was priceless! What did I get into?

running. Dale suddenly cranked the throttle and revved the engine to about 3,500 rpm as he set the timing. *In a few minutes I'll be sitting six inches from that engine and it will be under full power.* Every once in a while it let off a strong whiff of the aviation gas and CAM 2. It smelled good. It smelled *fast.*

I got my helmet out of the blue canvas bag. The front of my full-face orange Simpson helmet was caked with dry brown mud from the night before. Dale looked over and said, "Get that shit off. We can't have any dirt around here. It's bad luck." I smiled and with my fingernails scraped the mud off before setting it down on the roof of the Modified.

The pits were filling up with cars. I looked around and saw guys that I'd watched race years ago. Off to my right was George Kent, one of the top Modified drivers in the Northeast. He'd won a lot of championships.

I knew George as I used to letter his race cars. Seeing him reminded me of a night years before, when I was in his garage lettering one of his new Modifieds. I had just painted the number 26, in bright red, on the driver's door. I knelt down on the concrete floor and started to letter the opposite side when I felt the car move. I looked up through the window and there was George, leaning in the driver's side and doing something with the steering wheel. I said, "Hey. The numbers are wet." He looked up at me with a "deer in the headlights" look and stood up with a perfect top half of a red *2* on his white T-shirt. We all had a good laugh.

Off to the right I could also see Brett Bodine, and over on the backside of the pits was Jimmy Spencer. I was very nervous. I figured it was a good time to hit the restroom.

When I got back, Dale still had the car warming up. I walked up to it wondering if I could handle a Modified. I couldn't wait to step on that throttle to find out. I noticed Dale pointing in a frantic manner and trying to shout over the sound of the engine. "Get in," he yelled over the noise. "Practice is going to start in a couple minutes."

I slipped through the window. It was a tight fit. I had to put my right leg through the driver's window first, then bend over with my chin down near my right kneecap (like doing some sort of aerobics). From there I slid my upper body through the window and plopped onto the seat. My left leg followed me in. (The steering wheel was outside the car at this point, making it possible to get in. A driver didn't just sit in a Modified race car—he wore it. That's how confined it felt in there. And those cars are *low.* My rear end was less than six inches off the ground. I buckled the five-point harness (the two lap belts, two shoulder straps, and a belt that ran from the center lap belt buckle to the floor, right between my legs). The idea was to stay in the harness and not slip down and out in a violent sudden stop.

Dale reached in and snapped the steering wheel in place. I grabbed it and pulled it hard toward me a couple of times to make sure it really engaged. I looked over the steering wheel to an awesome sight. The hood, made of fiberglass, was so low and narrow I could see the two huge front tires. The Holley Carburetor and air cleaner stuck right out of the hood. It felt like driving a large go-kart. In front of me was a flat red dashboard with a water temperature gauge and an oil pressure gauge. To the left of the water gauge was a black plastic toggle switch to turn all the electrical on. Right next to that was a chrome push button starter and next to that was the tachometer, which I would ignore. (The crew uses the tach to set up the car's gear ratio; it didn't matter on the track.) On the right side of the gauges was the two-inch-wide, red oil pressure warning light (about the size of a tail light off of a '58 Chevy Impala). The driver can't look at the gauges all the time while driving, but the warning light was an unmissable signal telling the driver to shut down immediately and maybe save the $25,000 engine.

Like dirt cars, Modifieds do not have a windshield. Dale's car had a piece of clear Plexiglas about the size of a sheet of copy paper mounted right in front of the steering wheel.

The last step to dressing was putting the Simpson fireproof driving gloves on. I slipped the left glove on first. Always the left glove first. I don't know why—I'm not superstitious at all. It's just that the left glove always goes on first. Just as I got the other glove on, I saw a car start to go down Pit Lane toward the track. Dale stood up and twirled his finger in the air and pointed to the Pit Exit, telling me to get the hell moving.

I pushed the clutch in and shoved the Hurst shifter into first gear. I couldn't hear it, but through the shifter and glove, I felt the synchro in the transmission meshing. Letting the clutch out while giving it a little throttle, I slowly rolled away. *OK*. Now I was really nervous. For the first time, I felt I might be way out of my league. I had no idea what to expect. From the stands, Modified races looked so fast they almost scared me. I couldn't believe how they could go around a corner so fast and drive so close to each other with no fenders on their wheels. I was going out onto a half-mile asphalt track and in a few minutes, I would find out.

Chuck Ciprich and me wheel to wheel. (Photo by Don Romeo)

Pit Lane comes out onto the track just before Turn 1. I drove around the very inside of Turns 1 and 2 following a white car. I drove slowly down the Back Straight on the inside of the track. I didn't want to be in the way of the other cars as checking the steering and the brakes and just getting a feel for the car. Modifieds have power steering which was a little hard to get used to. Dale's car had a power rack and pinion unit and it was very tight. It didn't have the play that my dirt car's steering had. I putted around the track for about five laps when I saw the starter wave the green flag to start the hot laps. A few cars flew past on my right as I started to speed up. I shifted up through the gears and down the Back Straight I shifted into fourth. I was following a blue and white car, just trying to keep up. The power was unbelievable. I learned I had to be very smooth with the gas pedal. You sure as hell couldn't drive a Modified like a dirt car.

Soon I was moving pretty fast. I went into Turn 3 fast. Too fast. A huge shot of adrenaline pumped into my system. I thought the car would never stick and I was going to hit the wall. To my surprise, the car didn't even slide. *Wow.* I went through the next corner faster. Then the next one a little faster. The G-forces were incredible. I found myself grunting from the pressure on my body when I was in the turns. Dirt cars slide, so there isn't much G-force in a dirt car. In Turn 1, I found myself getting dizzy. I was not used to the tremendous lateral G-forces that those cars were capable of in the corners. *Man, I have to pull in,* I thought. I pulled to the inside down the Back Straight and slowed up. As I pulled into the pits, I was really dizzy. I stopped by my pit and Dale ran to the car and leaned his head in the window.

"What's the matter?" he hollered.

I said, "I'm dizzy."

"Get the hell back out there. It will go away. Get going."

Back out I went. I'll be damned. It went away and I never felt it again. Just as he said it would.

These cars had so much power, I had to learn to be smooth on the throttle; a sudden movement, smashing the throttle down, I could easily spin myself out. As my confidence grew, I realized *this was fun!* I was running fairly well for the first time out and ran the whole hot lap session. My dirt experience helped a lot. *If you look around, some of the best asphalt drivers came from dirt racing. Jeff Gordon, Tony Stewart, Mario Andretti, and A.J. Foyt are a few.* I pulled into our pit and parked the car, happy with my run. Dale was excited too. One thing I really appreciated racing here: *no dust!*

We were scheduled to run in the first heat. I really wanted to qualify in the heat race, but I figured that might be a little too much to expect. This was high-level racing.

I started the heat toward the back, and coming out of Turn 4 on the second lap, the right rear tire blew. Luckily I was on the outside when the car did a quick snap spin and no one was behind me. I had spun right at the entrance of the Pits and by more pure luck, I didn't hit anything. When you watch a race on TV, you sometimes hear the announcer say, "Wow, what a job he did keeping it off the wall!" Well let me tell ya, avoiding the wall was usually *pure luck*.

A wrecker came out and picked up the back of my car. Dale, in front of George

Kent's pit, motioned the wrecker towards him. George's crew had an air wrench and put one of George's tires on the right rear of my car. They dropped me from the wrecker and I shot down Pit Lane and back onto the track. The caution was still out and I didn't lose a lap. When the race restarted, I realized the importance of new tires on asphalt. With George's new tire on, it felt like I had another engine in the car. Dale didn't have the best tires. With the new tire from George's car on the right rear, I qualified! That one tire made it feel like I was driving a different car. It was unbelievable.

We had to give George back his tire after the heat. I didn't want to. Handing it to George's crew, I didn't want to let go. I almost started a tug of war with me pulling one way and George's crewman pulling the other way. It must have looked comical. When I finally let go of the prized tire, I asked Dale, "Why don't we have a new tire for the feature?"

He looked at me with sad-dog eyes and said, "A hundred fifty bucks."

"Don't look at me," I said. "I don't have any money. I just spent my last twenty to be a NASCAR driver."

We slapped on one of Dale's old spares, and I started the feature in eighteenth place. On the pace lap I was shaking—something I'd never done before. I was starting my first race on the inside row. I didn't mind running inside. It felt safer for my first race.

The green flag waved. I held my own for the first five laps. I felt about ten good taps on my rear bumper. *Hey. I'm going as fast as I dare.* The speed was mind-boggling. So was the sound! About the halfway point, I was still about sixteenth. I wasn't going anywhere. Everyone was single file, hugging the inside line. Then I did something that was not really seen much in asphalt Modified racing. I went to the outside, I didn't know at the time that it was not the recommended way to pass. After all, I passed that way on dirt tracks all the time. Traction on the outside was not that great and at times I felt myself sliding like I was on a dirt track. I had to run very close to the guy on the inside of me as there was not much room for error on the outside. Also

Racing the late, great Richie Evans. (Photo by Don Romeo)

you have to watch your tires as they are out in the open and to touch tires would most likely cause a wreck. That concrete wall came at you fast.

When the race was over, I finished ninth. A top ten finish my first time out! When I pulled into the pit, Dale and his crew were jumping up and down like cheerleaders. When I finally got out, Dale started hugging me—and you know, I felt pretty damn good. I thought they were jumping around because I didn't total the car. Come to find out, it was their best finish ever, and they wanted me to come back the following week and the rest of the season.

On the way home I couldn't get the race out of my head. I kept thinking, *What if I had new tires on. How far could I have gone?* It didn't matter. I was very happy with a ninth-place finish. It was a whole new way of racing. You had to be smooth. From this night on, I would be running two nights on dirt and one night on asphalt. It couldn't get any better than this. This was fun. I couldn't wait until the next Saturday.

 # From Hobby To Career

In 1980, Watkins Glen lost the Grand Prix. There were minor SCCA races, but for the most part there was a lot less business. The track was dormant for almost three years. Despite the lack of race cars to letter, my painting business continued to grow. It had turned into a great part-time business, but my day job was still working as a structural draftsman at Shepard Niles. I finally had to make a choice to stay at the drafting job or start my own business.

When I was lettering wreckers for Keith Messinger, he introduced me to two of his friends, Ken Coates and Mike Wells. Ken and Mike owned a custom interior business in Ithaca and they kept telling me to open a sign painting shop there. In 1982, an old building became available next to Ken and Mike's shop. Their landlord owned both buildings, and they talked him into repairing the building so I could rent it.

My personal life had been going through changes during this time as well. Kathy and I had divorced a while back. I met Harriett Cole when I was not in the best of shape. Harriett really turned me around and saved my life. We were married in 1982. With Harriett's support, I made my decision. I left my job at Shepard Niles, and opened Vickio Signs in Ithaca, about twenty miles from home. Leaving a full-time job and going out on my own was not something most people would find sensible. *But then again, I never said I was sensible.* Harriett went to work for me in my Ithaca sign shop, which really made this venture into the unknown possible. A year later, Harriett and I were blessed with the birth of our daughter, Beth.

Running my own shop—and becoming a husband and father for the second time—took all of my time and energy. I stopped building and racing my own dirt track cars.

I started my business painting small signs by hand and worked my way up to larger things. In the early 1980s, it didn't take much equipment to run a sign business. All I had to have was paint, some brushes, some wood, a saw, and a roof over my head. Also I needed the one thing that tied everything together—skill. I had to be able to paint. I had developed some great painting skills while working on race cars like how to handle a brush and how to mix paint. As I branched out into painting signs, I found that almost every job was unique. This made me a pretty darn good

At Vickio Signs in Ithaca, NY with Knute Schmidt, from Germany, who taught me the art of wood carving. In return, I taught him how to hand letter.

sign painter.

Back then, computerized cutting machines were just coming onto the scene, forcing me to break into the vinyl era. I saw one of these newfangled machines at Cornell University, and I knew I had to have one. I made the big jump and became one of the first sign shops in the area to offer vinyl. This was my start in the computerized sign business. At that time, I didn't realize that the computer would eventually take away my brushes. Computer-generated lettering was the future, even if it took a while to catch on.

The racetrack in Watkins Glen got some good news in early 1983. Corning Enterprises—a newly chartered subsidiary of what was then known as Corning Glass Works—purchased the track and formed a partnership with International Speedway Corporation (ISC). Together they brought Watkins Glen International back to life and worked to restore the track to its former glory. ISC also owned Daytona International Speedway, Talladega Superspeedway, Richmond International Speedway, Phoenix International Speedway, Michigan International Speedway, Martinsville Speedway, Kansas Speedway, Homestead-Miami Speedway, Darlington Speedway, and Chicagoland Speedway.

During the ten years my shop was in Ithaca, I gained an unbelievable amount of knowledge in the sign-painting business. I kept involved with the racetrack as well.

The track contracted me to do numerous signs and when race teams needed work, the track would give them my number.

☙

Strange things happen when you work around racetracks. I was in my shop in Ithaca when I got this frantic call from the track. The 1988 IROC race was about to start and was going to be shown on live TV. Another sign company had installed two new Camel Cigarette signs at the track on a tower, about twenty feet up, by the Glen Club near the Esses (near the top of the hill in Turn 3). It was a TV camera location, meaning the signs would show up on live TV shots as the camera panned by.

The Food and Drug people were at the track inspecting (because of the live TV) and discovered these new Camel signs had the wrong warning label on them. The inspectors were not going to let the race be broadcast with the wrong warning label on the cigarette signs. The track wanted to know if I could correct the signs.

I had a guy working with me at the time, John Russell, and I could send him for the fix all right. Unfortunately, Ithaca was thirty minutes away from the track. "We can't get there that fast," I told them.

"We are going to send a helicopter." They weren't kidding around—but that didn't work. There was no place near my office for a helicopter to land, so the track had the State Police provide an escort, and John drove his own car. He said it was just like in the movies. He and his police escort practically flew to the track. He said it was a blast. On the broadcast of the IROC race, you can see John in the bucket truck putting the vinyl stickers on the sign as the cars took pace laps. (I'm glad John was there as I'm petrified of heights.) The cars had to take two extra pace laps, on live TV, before John got the stickers changed and the FDA approved the signs for live television. This shows how important it is to get the details right.

Shangri-La Speedway

Dark Side of Racing

I really enjoyed driving on asphalt. I was finally accepted by the other NASCAR Modified drivers as not being a hazard, and I was just part of the weekly competitors at the speedway coming in steadily in the top twelfth to fifteenth position.

One Saturday on the way to Shangri-La Speedway, I was riding in the race car hauler with Joe Matwiejow and Dale when—right out of the blue—I got an overwhelming premonition that I was not coming home from the track that night. I instantly turned sweaty and cold. I started to take deep breaths as I felt faint and sick to my stomach. I came within a hair of telling Dale to turn around because maybe I shouldn't race that night. Instead, I kept the feeling to myself.

I went on with the task of racing. Once the green flag flew the thought of the premonition faded. It was a normal, hot Saturday in Owego. Racing took over and I was in another world.

I figured we could be a top-ten car if we could only afford new tires each night. Tires were the secret on asphalt. The top teams put at least two new tires on for the feature race. Dale bought used tires that the other top drivers pulled off their cars. I doubt Mario Andretti could have won on old tires. It bothered me a lot, but at least I was driving an Asphalt Modified and getting experience. Even with new tires I figured we did not have a winning car, but maybe a top-five ride.

In racing, when things happened, they happened fast. In the feature event, I was running in my usual twelfth position. We were about nine laps into the twenty-lap race. A gold car was ahead of me by about four car lengths. Just to my left was Brett Bodine. Jimmy Spencer was behind me. We raced down the Back Straight at 120 mph. Just ahead, the gold car came out of Turn 2 a little high and drifted a little too far. His two right side tires went off the edge of the track and into the dirt. Nobody lifted. I watched through the dust and small spray of stones as the gold driver continued straight down the track with two wheels on the pavement and two in the dirt. The rest of the field gained two car lengths on him in a second. I thought I could get by on his left as it looked like he was going to hold his line. Just then, he tried to come back on the track—and started to spin. Throwing dust and stones, his car kicked sideways turning left and started to come across the track right in front of us.

Leaving the track as Jimmy Spencer goes past. (Photo by Gater News)

I bore down on him at 120 mph. As he started across the track, I realized I was going hit him in the driver's door. Making a split-second decision, I pulled left hitting Brett Bodine and sending him into the infield. I thought I was going to miss the gold car when I heard a loud bang and the steering wheel jerked in my hands.

My right front wheel hit his front bumper. I almost made it by but six inches was enough to ruin my night. My left front wheel, spindle, brake caliper and rotor flew off the car. The shock of the wheel coming off broke the rack and pinion steering—and with the brake line to the right front wheel torn off, I had no brakes as I headed toward the retaining wall at the end of the Back Straight at 110 mph. I honestly thought, *This is it.* As I got close to the bank I mysteriously relaxed. Maybe your brain relaxes you when you know it's the end.

I hit the bank with such force that the car didn't stop as I thought it would. The retaining wall was made of dirt. There was no guardrail or concrete wall. As I hit, the bank acted like a ramp, launching my car up at an incredible angle. The car flew twenty feet into the air (as high as the light poles) and started a slow roll to the left. I was still conscious and couldn't believe I was still alive. As the car continued to rise and turn over, the thing I noticed most was that it was getting dark and it was dead quiet. When a race driver wrecks and hears no sound, nothing good was going to come of it.

On the other side of the dirt bank, the track dropped off about forty feet. The twenty feet I went up, plus the forty feet of drop, put me sixty feet up in the air. I remember it took a long time to land. Witnesses said the car inverted and when it went out of sight over the bank it was going down nose first.

The car hit the ground with tremendous force. It was like a bomb went off. My lungs felt like they completely deflated. The smell of hot oil instantly filled my nose. I sure as hell didn't know what was going on. I thought I was dead as the car started a series of violent end-over-end flips that threw a cloud of dirt, grass, and dust high enough into the air it could be seen from the grandstand.

When the car finally stopped, my senses started to come back. To my amazement, I was still alive. I started to move one thing at a time. *Right leg OK, left leg worked. Right elbow hurt, but not too bad. Christ. I'm alive.* It was very dark and I was hanging upside down. My right elbow started hurting a little more, and I could still smell gas and engine oil. I wanted to get out. I tried to unhook the window net but I was so disoriented I couldn't do it, even though all it required was putting my fingers in it and simply pulling forward. No one from the track had reached me yet. I put my left hand over my head to try to hold myself up a little while I unbuckled the belts. I dropped on my head and lay in a clump on the roof of the car. Remember that five-point harness? Remember that belt that went between my legs? It kept me in the car, but holy shit, it hurt!

I was on the roof of the car on my hands and knees. *I'll crawl out the passenger side window*, I thought. To my amazement, my right front tire, rim, and brake caliper were stuffed tight into the window blocking my exit. They were still smoking. I crawled out the back window and got about ten feet from the car when the effect of the crash hit me. I lay in the cool grass in total silence waiting for someone to come

Crash aftermath. Note the right front tire sticking out from the side window. (Photo by Gater News)

to my aid. *Where the hell are the rescue guys?* I was thinking. What I didn't realize was how far away from the track I was. I looked around and could see the glow of the lights of the racetrack way back up the hill.

A NASCAR official finally showed up. He ran all the way out to where I was lying in the grass. As he approached, I was kneeling on the ground. He came over and held me steady until help came. From the reaction when he saw me, he was surprised I was alive. I got in the ambulance and we went back to the pits. In the pits they wouldn't let me out of the ambulance or let anyone in. There was quite a crowd outside. Kathy came over from the grandstand. Joe was also standing outside. Finally they let me out. Adrenaline was still coursing through my system. The car was brought to the pits on a flatbed, and a huge crowd gathered around it. It took two wreckers to load it onto Dale's truck. The main right frame rail was bent and shoved noticeably back. The aluminum engine mounting plates were bent and the whole roll cage had been bent back. The hood and nose piece were gone. The body was dented all over, especially the roof. It was in bad shape. It was a good thing it was a Troyer chassis. They bent but didn't break.

Joe and Kathy (who'd come to the races that night in her own car) were really shook up. They said the grandstands went silent for about fifteen minutes until word came back that I was OK. Then a loud roar went up. Joe said that when I cleared the bank and was going out of sight upside down, he started running toward Turn 3. Suddenly, he said, he stopped dead. He didn't want to see what he thought they would find. He slowly walked back to the pit thinking I wasn't going to make it. For a while he was devastated. Kathy said she felt the same way. I guess everyone had been happy to see me walk out of the ambulance.

On the way home that night, I had to stop at the hospital in Elmira, New York. My right elbow started to really hurt and X-rays showed a fracture. I had also fractured my left collarbone (from the shoulder harness) and a couple of ribs (from the seat support that wrapped around the rib cage to hold me upright). I was hurting.

As I headed home from the hospital, all I could think about was the premonition I had on the way to the racetrack that afternoon. I proved the premonition wrong. It didn't kill me. I only got the hell beaten out of me. It was close, but I went alive home that night.

☙

After about four weeks, Dale's car was ready to be picked up from the Troyer shops in Rochester. I rode up with Dale to pick it up, my arm still in a cast. Maynard Troyer, the car builder, said it was the worst-bent-up car he ever had to fix. We got it back to my shop and unloaded it. I couldn't wait to get in it again.

"There's a hundred-lapper coming up next week," Dale said. "When does the cast come off?"

"Not for a while yet," I said.

The next day I called Dale and in an excited voice. "The cast is off," I told him. "I'm ready."

"I thought it was going to be a while?"

"I took it off myself. It doesn't feel too bad. I'll wrap it up for the race." My ribs hurt worse than the elbow did and my collarbone was a little sore. Kathy was *not* happy about my decision to take the cast off and she let me know it. She said, "You will be sorry someday when you get older!" *Yup—she was right!*

My elbow was in an ace bandage but felt fine. My collarbone was tender but healed. My ribs were sore. I'd been to Lane's Yamaha and talked with Cal Lane, a Motocross racer and dirt stock car driver, about my concern that my ribs might hurt too much to drive. He recommended I get a kidney belt (Motocross motorcycle riders use them) for the ribs. A kidney belt is a foot-wide elastic belt that has three steel straps in the back to give support. The front is held tightly together with a large Velcro strip. This would hold my rib cage tight. I was ready and anxious to be back behind the wheel.

Back in the car at Shangri-La Speedway, I drove slow laps before the warm-ups. We have all heard stories of how hard it is for a driver to come back to the scene of a bad wreck. People ask, "Will it affect his driving? Will he lose his courage?" As I drove through Turn 3 and passed the exact spot where I thought I was going to die, I did get a new feeling. Not one of losing courage, but just the opposite. The thought that came into my head was *Hell, that wreck didn't hurt that bad. I think I can go faster!* I couldn't wait for the green flag to fall.

The race went well. I didn't wreck. I finished about eighteenth. My right arm got tired but the kidney belt did its job. The following week at my sign shop in Ithaca, I was carrying my trash can out when I tripped over the curb. I didn't see the curb as I carried garbage pail with both hands out in front of me. Not wanting to put my right arm out to stop my fall, I put my left arm out. I heard it crack as I landed. *Yeah, I broke my damned left elbow.* I called my buddy Ken Coates, and he took me to the hospital.

Just like my right elbow cast, I took that left elbow cast off early to go racing. Both elbows still bother me to this day. Sometimes they want to dislocate if I try to reach out and lift something at an awkward angle. As I get older, I find that my decision to take those casts off early has started to interfere with my golf game! Still, if I had to do it all over, I would make the same decision. I would take the casts off early to go racing.

As much as I enjoyed racing Late Models on dirt and Modifieds on asphalt, money came in to play. I finally quit driving to concentrate on my sign business. Although I thought my racing days were over, I eventually had other opportunities to do more driving in totally different kinds of cars. It seems I couldn't get away from speed.

 # The Superspeedway

The shop in Ithaca was doing well, but in 1992 a graphics design job opened up at Watkins Glen International. After much thought—and because my landlord didn't want to sell the building I had been renting for ten years—I reluctantly closed my business and went to work for the track. I think my love for racing also had a little influence on my decision. My new title was graphics design manager.

My boss was Matt Matusicky, general manager at Watkins Glen International. Matt, or Mattman, as I called him, had worked his way up at the Glen from his first job of painting guardrails all the way to general manager. Mattman was about six feet tall and sported a goatee. He could make small talk with a temporary worker who was carrying around a weed eater, and then turn right around and talk business with Bill France, founder and former president of NASCAR. Mattman had a gift for talking!

Early in the new job, Matt came into my office. "Dick Hahne just called from Daytona and wants you in Talladega to do some signs before their race."

Talladega Superspeedway is located in Alabama.

"Are you kidding me?" I said to Matt. "I ain't goin' to Talladega. *No way.*"

Dick Hahne was the operations manager at Daytona Speedway (and later vice president of operations there). Seems their sign painter (Daytona had their own sign guy who also took care of Talladega Superspeedway) was trying to get more money and was holding out just before the Talladega race. That put ISC in a tough spot. Dick had remembered me from his trips up to Watkins Glen in the 1980s. We first met in 1986 during the first NASCAR race at Watkins Glen. Dick had asked me a lot of questions at the time about the track signs. One day I took him down to the Mechanics Club, a small private club in nearby Montour Falls, for hot dogs at lunchtime. *Dick loved those hot dogs.*

When Dick requested help, my boss agreed to send me on a trip to Talladega. So I guessed I was going. I had forgotten I was not working for myself anymore. It didn't matter what I wanted anymore!

Watkins Glen International thought it would be good advertising for the track if I drove the track's pace car down. The Watkins Glen race was a few months after Talladega's race. A week later, reluctantly and all by myself, I found myself behind the wheel of the brand new bright red 1992 Thunderbird Super Coupe on my way to Alabama.

Aerial view of Talladega Superspeedway (built on a WWII airfield). (Photo by Aerial Photo Lab, Inc.)

Talladega Superspeedway, which opened in September 1969, sat off I-20 not near anything. It was about fifteen miles from the city of Talladega and a bit farther from Anniston and Oxford. I rolled into Oxford, Alabama, about twenty-five miles from the track, on a bright and sunny Sunday afternoon two weeks before the Die-Hard 500.

I drove around for a while trying to locate the motel in Oxford, where the racetrack had me staying. It was off on a side street, and I had a bad feeling as soon as I checked in.

The motel was very old, and the man behind the desk did not have a good attitude. Maybe it was my northern accent or the fact that I had interrupted the football game he had on the TV, but he was really happy to tell me I couldn't get the beer I wanted because the county was dry on Sundays. I checked in and walked back out to find my room. It was at the back of the motel and on the ground floor. People were partying noisily outside and it looked like a welfare halfway house. Kids were running all over. The people two rooms down had a barbecue right on the sidewalk and—to add to the decor—two white plastic chairs were floating in the pool. It was evident some of the people lived here. I went to unlock the door to my room and found it was not locked. I stood in the doorway and looked around. The room was terrible.

When I built up enough courage to actually go in, I found the phone on the small table between the beds, called Matt, and told him the story. "Tomorrow, I'm getting out of here and into a different motel," I said, "or I'm driving back home. I don't care how you do it, but get me the hell out of here!"

An hour later Matt called me back and said the speedway would put me in another motel the next day. I slept that night with one eye open and a chair propped against the door handle. Outside my hotel room, it sounded like Mardi Gras. Of course, if I hadn't been so tired from the drive, I probably would have gone out and joined them. I'll bet they had beer! If I'd known that for sure, I know I would have joined them.

☙

I set my alarm for 5:30 a.m. as I wanted to be the first one at the track. A McDonald's was just down the road, so as soon as I pulled out of the motel I went through the drive-through and ordered a cinnamon breakfast bun and a black coffee. I drove out on I-20 and headed to the track. I was excited. When I arrived at the track, the gate was closed and padlocked. I figured I was thirty minutes early, so I waited. Seven o'clock. Seven-thirty. Eight o'clock. Eight-thirty. Still no one. What the hell was going on? Didn't anybody work here?

Finally, someone in a white truck with a black Talladega decal on the door pulled up. The guy, weighing about 250 and wearing a white T-shirt, white pants, and a large straw cowboy hat, slowly and with much effort rolled out of the driver's side of the truck. He crossed in front of my car and slowly approached the gate and unlocked it. He walked just as slowly back to his truck, got in, and drove in. He glanced over to me and nodded as if to say, "Follow me." I followed him through the gate and smiled—I'd finally arrived at Talladega. (I discovered later that the place was just across the line in the Central time zone. That was one of the reasons I had to wait so long—when my alarm went off, it was only 4:30 at the track.)

Once inside, I kept following the truck since I didn't know where I was going. Talladega had been built on top of an abandoned WWII military airstrip in the 1960s. Bill France (of NASCAR) had been having troubles with the city of Daytona, Florida, over issues pertaining to that racetrack and had threatened to move elsewhere. The issues in Daytona were resolved, but Bill opened Talladega in 1969 anyway under the name Alabama International Motor Speedway. It quickly surpassed all expectations because of its size, speed, and competition.

In 1992, the speedway was nothing like it is today. Then the track only had about 30,000 seats. (Now there are 190,000.) A small chain link fence circled the track property. It was a bare-bones operation.

I followed my guide until we pulled up to the Maintenance Shop. Three maintenance men drank coffee standing outside near the gray metal building. *How the hell did they get in here?* I was thinking. *Must be a back gate somewhere.* I got out of the car and walked over to where they were standing.

Two of the men were black and the other was white. They all wore matching dark-green coveralls. It was already hot, and it was beyond me how they could wear those coveralls.

"Mornin'," I said. "I know I'm early. I'd like to wash my car. Is there a hose that I could use?"

I wanted the pace car to look sharp—it was lettered with the Watkins Glen logo and the Official Pace Car decals—but it had over a thousand miles of dirt and dead bugs on the front and on the windshield. Without saying a word, one of the men walked over and got a hose that was hanging from an old rusted chrome tire rim bolted to the wall. "Have at it, man," he said, handing me the hose.

I had started to spray the car with a blast of water, when the white guy approached me. He walked slowly over, stopped, and just stood there. He was short and thin, maybe five-foot-three and 120 pounds, and his face had a deep tan that disappeared into a thick, graying eight-inch beard stained brownish from chewing tobacco juice. He had a hat on that was so sweat-stained and dirty I couldn't read what was embroidered on the front. I think the hat was red, but I wasn't even sure of that. God, he reminded me of the grungy cowboy Festus (a character on the old TV show *Gunsmoke*).

After thirty seconds of standing there, he pointed at my car with his right hand and said, "I see you're from Watkins Glen." The pace car obviously gave it away. Holding out his hand to shake mine he said, "They call me Outlaw."

"Hello, Outlaw," I said shaking his hand. "Up north, they call me Tony."

He turned his head to the side and spat a huge load of dark brown tobacco juice on the pavement. I must have jumped a little making him look at me strangely. I couldn't help it. I thought the dark brown oyster was going to splatter on my new white sneakers. He almost got his own boot. Looking down, he stuck out his left foot and, with his well-worn brown western boot, twisted the toe of his boot on the freshly spit tobacco like he was squashing a bug. He looked back up at me. "My wife," he said, "she's from Dundee." Dundee, where I used to race, was only twelve miles from Watkins Glen.

"You gotta be kidding me," I said. "Dundee, New York?" He nodded his head up and down. "How the hell did you end up here?" I asked.

He thought for about five seconds, as if he couldn't remember. "That's a good question." He turned his head to the side and spat again. This time he put it about four feet to the left of us. He spoke while keeping his bottom lip up as to hold the tobacco juice in, "I used to drive tractor trailer up in New York. I was haulin' juice fer Seneca Grape Juice outta Dundee down here to Alabama. Sometimes, when I was in Dundee, I would stop for coffee in that little diner on the corner. My wife, before I married her, was a waitress there. I was haulin' a load of juice down here and I talked her into going for a ride with me. Well, one day we were down here deliverin' juice and I got a DWI with my truck. We've been here ever since." He turned and spat again. "That was seven years ago." It was as if he was putting a period on every sentence with spit. (He brought his wife to the track the next day to meet me. They were nice people. A few days later she stopped by the track and asked me if I would deliver a package to her mother in Dundee, which I did when I returned home.)

After washing the car I walked about fifty feet to the Operations office. There I met Larry Johnson, the operations manager. I really liked Larry; we hit it off right off the bat!

He took me over to a metal building (near his office, which was outside the track) and showed me my office during my stay. The only window was high on the wall. I had to stand on tiptoe to see out. They'd shipped a computer, a vinyl lettering machine, and materials up from Daytona. "There it is," Larry said as he turned around and left.

It took me three hours to hook everything up and when I hit the switch—nothing. Finally, after I'd pushed and fiddled with everything I could think of, the computer monitor came to life and brightened up the dimly lit office. The graphic design and lettering software was a program I had never seen before. It was nothing like the program I had at home. To add to the frustration, I was fairly new to computers. I had no information, no manuals, nothing! What a mess.

They had given me some sign orders, nothing big, but they wanted them that day. I tried to figure out how to use the strange program, but after a lot of wasted material they had a local sign person come over and try to teach me the basics of using the computer program. Finally, I picked up enough to run the computer and crank out the signs.

Around 4 p.m. that first day, I looked out the window and saw a tall guy wheeling out an old barbecue grill. He fired it up and proceeded to cook chicken. I can't remember his name, but he owned North Carolina Speedway. Man, could he cook chicken. Some of the workers would stop by and grab a piece of chicken and continue on their way. He just loved cooking chicken. He didn't charge anything. I guess he just enjoyed doing it. I went outside, and we talked racing while I ate chicken.

Today when you see Talladega Superspeedway for the first time, it's hard to comprehend. As you turn off of I-20, the main gate road is overwhelming. It is thirty lanes wide (to accommodate the huge numbers of cars that arrive on race day), and someone has come up with the perfect name for it: they call it the Thirty Lane. As you drive up this wide entrance, you come face-to-face with a huge grass-covered bank, the outside of Turns 3 and 4. Looking straight ahead, you see a tunnel made from half a large culvert pipe that runs right through the base of this mountain.

As you get closer, a narrow one-lane road leads into the dark tunnel. A row of fluorescent lights line the ceiling without casting much light, and the road inside drops off at sharp angle. It was a little intimidating at first. A concrete walkway hugged the right side, but there was no room for a second car. But down you go. The road flattens out in a puddle at the bottom of the tunnel and then climbed up the other side at the same sharp angle. At the bottom, I could hear something like a jet engine: water splashing off the tires and echoing off the tunnel walls. Of course, while I was in there I had to blow the horn.

The first time I drove out the other side and into the sunlit infield, I looked back over my left shoulder—then instantly slammed on the brakes and stopped the car dead. From that point, the view of the track between Turns 3 and 4 hit me so hard I couldn't speak. I can't describe the view of the track at this angle, but I've gotta try. Seeing the steep 34-degree banking up close was breathtaking. It almost looked like an asphalt wall. I had never seen this angle on TV. No matter how many times I see it, I still stop and stare.

On my second night in Alabama, I was asleep in a motel in Anniston when a strange siren woke me at about 2:30 a.m. It wasn't the normal fire siren I was used to back home. Then I heard a loudspeaker blast out a message, "Take cover immediately. Tornado warning! Take cover." I jumped up and looked out the window of my motel room. The lightning was nonstop and rain was blowing sideways past my window. Instructions on the back of the motel room door told a guest what to do in case of a tornado. Basically you went into the bathroom and sat on the rim of the tub and waited. I guess if everyone was in their bathrooms, it would be easier for the first responders to find the bodies. They would all be in the same place. In the bathroom! I was scared. I sat on the edge of the bathtub in my underwear for about twenty minutes. Finally there was another announcement, "All Clear." I dragged myself back to bed. Welcome to the South.

༺༻

After a couple of days working at Talladega, I met Billy Swinford. Billy owned a large construction company and did work for the track. He was a big, cheerful, funny guy that anyone would feel comfortable around. What a personality! The way Billy acted, you would think he owned Talladega Superspeedway. Everyone knew him. He was a fixture at the track along with his rusty old blue Ford Ranger pickup. It was full of dents and had barely room for two people inside the cab. The rest of the space was taken up by two-way radios. He had track radios, company radios, and God knows what else. He always wore at least three radios at once. One would ring and he would jump, slapping himself with both hands on the hips, pockets, and belt, searching around for the right radio and answer it with, "Hey, my man!" I think it was Billy that gave me the obsession to have a radio on at all times while working at a track. (Billy turned out to be a great friend. Although he is no longer with us, I consider myself lucky to have met him.)

Billy called me one afternoon on the radio. They had given me a track radio, explaining that the place was so big it was necessary to be able to contact someone on the radio—it would take too long to drive around to find him. I was out on the track painting "TALLADEGA" on the Back Straight retaining wall. Back then they only had the name painted twice on the retaining wall. One painting was on the Front Straight wall and the other on the Back Straight wall. The retaining wall was about forty-three inches tall. It didn't look large on TV, but the word *Talladega* can be as long as 120 feet. At the time, all I had to do was repaint what was already there. Good thing, as I didn't have a clue how the hell to lay out something that big yet.

"Hey, my main man!" Billy said over the radio. "Ya done yet?"

"Yeah," I said, "I'm just about done for the day."

"Meet me at the office," he said.

About twenty minutes later, I finished painting and went over to the Maintenance Office. There was Billy, sitting in an aluminum folding chair. I remember it had yellow and white woven nylon straps because two of them were broken and were hanging down just touching the dirt. Billy was talking to Larry Johnson. Billy looked up at me and—smiling as he always did—said, "Hey. There's my main man. I'm taking you to get some supper."

"Good." I said.

"Get in the truck," he said. As I got in, I heard him say, "The cooler is in the back." There was always a beer cooler in the back of Billy's truck, and it was always full. We left the track with beer in hand and drove about three miles down the narrow two-lane road. Billy suddenly stuck his beer between his legs, grabbed the steering wheel with both hands and whipped it violently around without slowing down much. The truck turned left down an old dirt road. I held my arm straight out trying to balance my beer so I wouldn't spill any as my right shoulder banged against the door.

We drove a half mile through the woods, at a much slower pace, and finally came to a clearing next to a fairly good-sized river. We pulled into the clearing and got out of the truck. We threw our now empty beer cans in the back of the truck and Billy opened the old Coleman cooler and grabbed two more. He tossed me one over the bed of the truck, which I missed. It landed on the ground and rolled under the truck. I knelt down and noticed the ground was completely covered with a thick layer of pine needles. I reached under the truck feeling around for the can. Billy hollered, "Hey. It's over here." He tossed it in the back of the truck and threw another beer toward me. I caught that one.

I popped the tab and looked around. It was peaceful down here. This place was beautiful. Three or four cars were parked near us in the clearing. As I took a sip of beer, I looked over by the river and saw two very old black men fishing on the riverbank. The sun was getting low, shining through the tall pines by the river and reflecting off the slowly moving water. Over to the right, in the shade under some pine trees, sat an old warped wooden picnic table. The paint was long gone and the boards were twisted and cracked, but a two-foot-square piece of plywood covered some of the cracks. Two more black men were singing, sort of like something you hear of men singing on a chain gang, while dipping the fresh fillets in this white stuff that was in an old, white plastic five-gallon spackle bucket. One of them would then lay the battered fillets on the grill. The grill was a fifty-five-gallon drum that had been cut in half. People were lined up waiting. As a fillet was done, the man put it on a paper plate and handed it to the next person. They handed the man some cash and then drove off. For a buck, I got a big fresh fillet of catfish. I can still picture Billy and myself sitting on that old Ford tailgate next to that river, with the sun shining through the pines, watching the water slowly flow along. We drank beer and ate catfish until dark. That was heaven. *Man, am I glad I came down here to Alabama*, I thought. *This is so nice and peaceful.*

The next day Larry told me that he was going to give me a helper, a guy named Raymond. (I don't recall anyone telling me his last name. It was just Raymond.) He was about twenty-four years old, tall and wiry, all muscle, with sharp features and dark brown eyes. He had a strong Southern accent, bad teeth, and a brush cut. His jeans had holes in the knees and the back pocket was so frayed I could see the corner of his brown leather wallet sticking out from the bottom. He held his jeans up with an old leather belt about ten inches too long. The loop was wrapped around the belt and still hung down six inches from the belt buckle. His once-white T-shirt was dirty, and he had a pack of Camels rolled up in the left sleeve. The tattoo on his left arm was really bad. It looked like he did it himself. I think it said "Rita," but I didn't want to stare at it trying to figure out if I was right. Raymond had little education, but it turned out he was always willing to do anything as long as I explained to him exactly what I wanted.

Being told to help the sign guy from the north put him above the other workers. I could tell he was proud to be chosen. He followed me around like a dog. If I turned around or stopped quickly, he would bump into me. I knew that if I told him, "Raymond, I need your right arm," he would saw it off with a hand saw without even asking why I needed it. I really liked Raymond. He was a good guy and we got along great.

It was the Monday before race weekend and I had completed all the small sign work they'd given me. I figured I was done a week early. I couldn't understand why they sent me down here for this length of time and why they had given me a helper—but the next day I got the answer.

 # The Bombshell

The bright blue Alabama sky was perfectly clear as I drove to the track the next day. Sun shining, birds chirping—an absolute Disneyland morning. I turned up the Thirty-Lane and headed left onto the huge strip of yellowish-brown concrete that would take me to the Operations Building and my office. When the track was being built, the two-foot-thick concrete runways of the old Anniston Air Force Base were too hard to remove, so the racetrack was built right on top of them. As I drove down one of the old runways, I could picture myself in the cockpit of a B-17 just reaching takeoff speed. Thump, thump, thump. The tires of my red Thunderbird Super Coupe pace car pounded out a beat as I drove over the cracks in the concrete.

I slowed just in time to turn left and pull up to the front of the building. I got out and went into the Operations Office. There was Larry Johnson, the operations manager, and his ever-present cigarette. He was surrounded by a cloud of smoke so strong I had to take short breaths until I got used to it. I walked over to the counter to check out the coffee. I'd been getting coffee at McDonald's on the way, but skipped it today.

"Can I get a cup of coffee, Larry?" I asked.

"Git yerself a cup," he said without taking the cigarette out from between his lips. "Cupser over there."

With a cup of coffee in hand, I chatted with Larry for a few minutes. I was hungry and needed a doughnut or something. Since it was still early, I went back to my car and drove out the gate. Just down the road was a gas station with a large deli. I parked and went inside.

Wow. They have a lot of stuff in here, I thought. Along the front window were four booths. The tables had tan tops with chrome trim. The bench seats were covered in blue vinyl with two thick white stripes going up and over the backrests. They were right out of the 1950s. Vinyl wasn't the best material to sit on, considering how hot it got down in Alabama. There were about three aisles of shelving with candy, Band-Aids, and the normal deli stuff. (I found out later that a few days before the race, the owners pulled out the booths and the three rows of shelving and replaced them, floor to ceiling, with cases of beer.)

The back of the deli was lined with coolers full of all sorts of drinks, frozen pizza, and ice cream. On the right was a long counter and behind it was an open kitchen where two women were cooking lunch for the day. To the right of the counter was a large display case with glass shelving for the pans that held the different items for lunch. Everything down here was fried. I noticed some stringy green stuff in one of pans—I wasn't sure what it was and didn't care to find out. Still, the place smelled good. It was only 8 a.m., but the smell made me hungry for lunch!

I got a muffin and walked up to the counter. "Is that it, Honey?" The cashier had one hell of a Southern accent. Getting called "Honey" made me feel special until I heard her call the girl behind me in line "Honey" too. She called everyone "Honey." I grabbed my muffin and change and went back to my office.

On my desk was a list of stuff someone wanted that day. It was a few small signs—only about an hour's worth of work. Since it was such a beautiful morning, I went outside and sat on the tailgate of a truck parked in front of my shop and drank another cup of coffee. The demand for signs hadn't been huge, and I wondered why Dick had wanted me down here. Why not just hire a local sign company? Right now all the signs were well in hand. I hadn't seen anyone from the main office yet even though it was fairly close to my sign shop.

It was still morning when I finished the list, so I went back outside to enjoy the weather. What a beautiful day. The sun shone brightly and a light breeze blew in from the west. With not much left to do, I felt a little homesick. I was also feeling hungry and considering a trip back to the deli. I was so hungry I could almost consider trying some of that green stuff I saw in the glass case. Almost.

I walked over to Larry's office and sat down in an old green and white canvas folding aluminum chair he had out front. Soon, around the corner of the building came Larry with his cigarette smoke preceding him by five feet.

"Tony!" he hollered when he saw me.

Immediately I got a bad feeling. I didn't know why. Maybe it was the tone of his voice, one I'd never heard before, or the fact that he actually took the cigarette out of his mouth long enough to say my name. I couldn't put my finger on it, but I could sense something really bad was about to happen. I started to feel really uneasy. Until now, things had gone very smoothly. Too smoothly.

"Yeah, Larry," I said. "Whatcha need?"

In his left hand, Larry was carrying a piece of thin white plastic about thirty inches long and a foot wide. Taped to the plastic was a piece of paper with the Talladega logo on it. Taped to the logo was a piece of transparent tracing paper held in place with old masking tape. On the tracing paper, someone had marked the letters with dimensions and locating points. The whole thing looked well used.

What the hell is that, I wondered? *Must be they wanted me to replace that worn out little sign with a new one. Shouldn't take ten minutes,* I thought. Boy, was I wrong!

Larry swung the piece around and handed it to me. "There ya go," he said. He turned and kept right on walking to the door of his office without missing a step. "I almost forgot to give it to you," he said without turning around. "It's the drawing for the grass." He opened the door and stepped inside.

"Grass?" I hollered. *What grass? What the hell is he talking about?*

I keep this Talladega layout drawing in my shop as a reminder that anything is possible!

I jumped up from the chair, holding the piece of plastic out in front of me like I was a hot piece of metal. Larry turned and looked back through the doorway. "Dick said you were coming down here to do the grass. This is the drawing the other guy used, so I guess you can use it too."

I was standing there dumbstruck as Larry disappeared inside. I must have looked hilarious. I stood there stunned, head tipped down a little and my mouth wide open, staring at this piece of plastic with a drawing on it. *Did he say painting* grass?

The color drained from my face and a feeling of panic flowed over me. I had absolutely no idea of what Larry was talking about! Dick never mentioned grass! Just because I painted some signs at Watkins Glen did not mean I knew everything. I felt like a guy going skydiving, but just as he jumped out the door, he realized he didn't put the chute on. I was starting to feel a bit faint. I snapped out of it when I heard Larry holler from inside his trailer, "Didja get a coffee?"

I just shook my head as I thought to myself, *Fuck the coffee—we've got trouble here!* Grass? What were they expecting me to do? Paint grass? What the hell was he talking about? I followed Larry into his office. He stood in front of his desk in his own personal smoke cloud.

"What are you talking about?" I said. "Grass? What grass? You paint grass down here? I have never heard of anything like this. I've never done anything like this. I don't know what Dick told you but I can't do this. Christ, I didn't even know you could paint on grass!"

Larry walked around his desk and sat down in his chair. He leaned backed clasping both hands behind his head. "All I know is what Dick told me," he said between puffs on his cigarette. "That's the grass painting layout, and you were sent down here to paint the grass. We will have the paint gun and paint out there for ya when you're ready. It has to be done before Friday. I wouldn't dilly-dally around. You might want to start it tomorrow." With another big puff on his cigarette, Larry slowly disappeared into the cloud of white smoke.

For a second I felt totally calm. *I know what's wrong! I'm in a nightmare,* I thought to myself. *I'm dreaming. I have to wake up.* I realized I was not dreaming, and just when I thought I was doomed, Larry poked his head through the cloud and offered a ray of light.

"Oh, I forgot," he said. "Dick is sending up a painter from Daytona to help ya. He should have been here by now." *Thank you! Thank you God!* I thought. Relief! I was saved! Oh Man. I was really scared for a minute. I actually felt a smile form on my face.

I went back outside and plopped down in the chair still looking at the drawing, which meant nothing to me. Twenty minutes later, still staring at the drawing, I heard a vehicle approaching. I looked over to the driveway and there was a white Chevy pickup pulling in with Daytona Speedway on its doors. I jumped straight up out of the chair. I had just dodged a bullet. My white knight was here to save me. *Thank God. He'll know what to do, and we can get this done. I might even learn something in the process.*

I ran up to the truck before it even stopped. Larry was coming out of the office, and as I got to the door of the truck, it opened. A small white-haired man got out of the pickup. He looked like he was in his early sixties, maybe five-foot-six, and thin. So thin, he looked very frail. His pure white hair matched his white painter's coveralls and white T-shirt. His face was a little drawn, and he had reddish cheeks and a red nose.

The first thing I said to him was, "Hi. Man, am I glad to see you." I shook hands with him so hard it made his head shake. "My name is Tony. You don't know how scared I was a few minutes ago. They wanted me to paint this thing on the grass," I said, holding out the small sign. "Christ. Can you imagine that? Painting on grass?

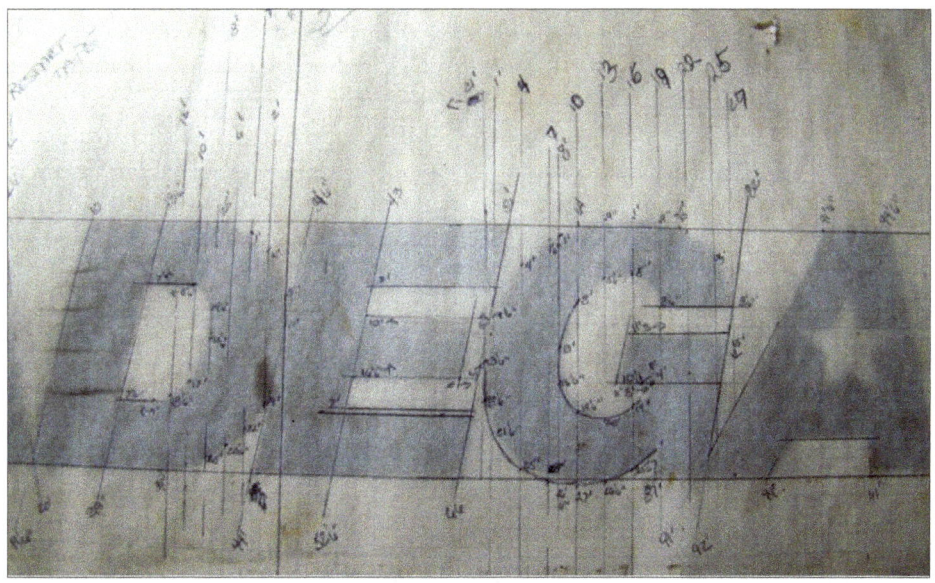

Close-up of the layout for the grass painting.

Now you can show me how to paint the Talladega logo on the grass. I have never seen anything like this done before. Hell, I didn't know they even painted on grass. This is all new to me. Sure the hell glad you are here." I handed him the plastic drawing with my left hand. I was so happy to see him. Someone was here who knew how to paint this goddamned logo in the grass.

"Glad to meet you, too, Tony! My name is Mike," he said. "But what the hell ya talkin' about? What the hell makes you think I know how? I don't know how the hell to do it either. One thing for sure is I don't want to know. If I did, them damned fools down there [in Daytona] would have me going all over the friggin' place paintin' that crap."

I was stunned. My panic attack returned. In a quivering voice I said, "Larry told me you were a painter. That you were sent up here to help paint the grass."

"He's right. I am a painter," he said. "I paint the retaining walls, the buildings, and anything else they want painted white at Daytona Speedway. I don't letter any damned grass. Matter of fact, I don't letter nothin'."

I stood there with my arms hanging down to my sides, wondering if this was how having a stroke felt. I couldn't lift my arms. My mouth was open and my jaw moved up and down—like I was a fish gasping on a riverbank. *I'm dead,* I thought. This was my first venture out into the real world of racetrack painting and the realization hit me that I didn't know crap! What made things worse was that everyone would soon know that too!

"Oh no," I said out loud just as he threw the layout back to me like it was Frisbee. It bounced off my chest and fell to the ground—my arms still wouldn't move. Good thing he didn't throw it at my head. I wanted go home. I felt completely lost. I had this feeling once before, but not to this level, back when I lettered the wing on Graham Hill's F1 car. I'd gotten through that nightmare, but this one felt worse. It was like a big black cloud moved in front of the bright Alabama sun. I had no clue what to do.

Larry broke in. "Let's go out to the Tri-Oval," he said, "I will show you guys where the logo goes." I picked up the drawing, and we all walked to Larry's truck. The Tri-Oval was the Front Straight that had a slight left turn in it compared to a traditional straight front stretch. I was still in shock as Larry, Mike, and I climbed into Larry's truck. I sat in the middle. Driving down the old concrete runway toward the tunnel, the truck bounced us up and down in perfect harmony as we hit each crack. If I wasn't so sick I would have been laughing.

My mind was a blur. The smoke from Larry's cigarette passed right in front of my face and swirled around my head twice before continuing out the passenger side window. I don't even remember going through the tunnel. We reached Pit Lane and Larry pulled to a stop.

I got out of the truck and breathed in some fresh air. I followed Larry as he walked out onto the grass about twenty feet, turned around, and looked toward Pit Lane. "This is about where the logo will go," Larry said.

Oh God, I said to myself. *Why the hell did I come here? I could be home working out of my own shop and having a cold one.* Mike started to say something in a real low voice that I couldn't hear.

"What?" I asked him.

"I think I remember him [the other sign man] using some long measuring tapes," he said, "One up there and one down here." He pointed with a crooked, arthritic index finger. He was pointing toward Pit Lane but the end of the finger was pointing to the right at a 30-degree angle toward Turn 1. This is when I realized that Mike had been around, maybe just watching, as someone had done a grass painting.

Mike's information was a piece to the puzzle. Someone else had done this. I should be able to do it too. I just didn't have much time to figure things out. We needed to start painting in the morning. I looked at the grass, then at the piece of plastic with the logo on it, and then back to the grass. Numbers, grass. Numbers, grass. Nothing was coming to me. As I stared at the numbers and the overwhelming size of the grassy Tri-Oval, the look on my face must have been pathetic. I wanted to disappear. I honestly thought of leaving my job at Watkins Glen, telling Larry I was quitting, and going home. It honestly was that bad. This painting was beyond anything I had ever dreamed of. I realized that if I quit, Dick (from Daytona Speedway) would never call me back and the Watkins Glen International would never give me any more work. I had to do this, but I didn't know how. What the hell was I going to do? I was in a real mess. I had no choice but to figure this out and get it done.

Preparing to Paint

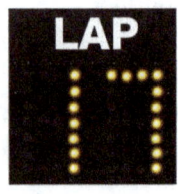

At 6:30 a.m., trying to get an early start on the day, I drove from my hotel towards the track. I looked up at the sky as I drove, trying to distract myself from the lingering stress of that damn grass painting. Not a whisper of a cloud. No wind. It was another beautiful day in Alabama.

Last night, I had taken the drawing of the grass painting to my motel room to study. After supper, I lay on the bed with two pillows stacked up behind me and my legs drawn up forming a table for the layout. I studied the drawing while listening to the TV. Decoding the drawing was like trying to decipher hieroglyphics in an Egyptian tomb. It was just a mass of numbers and lines. *Someone did this before*, I kept thinking. I had to figure it out.

I stopped at the deli (after finding this deli, I no longer wanted anything from McDonald's) to get a small cup of hot black coffee. I only drink one small cup of coffee first thing in the morning and then not a drop more until the next morning. I poured a cup at one of the self-serve coffeepots at the back of the deli—making sure not to pick the Decaf one! As I walked to the counter I moved my cup back and forth between my hands trying not to get burned by the heat of the coffee through the paper cup. There were three people in line ahead of me at the cashier, so I glanced at the glass cabinet to the left of the cash register displaying doughnuts, cakes, and pies to take my mind off of the hot cup.

Silently sitting there inside the glass case, resting on the second clear glass shelf from the bottom and protected from the public by thin pane of glass, was a huge, perfectly cut slice of fresh, homemade apple pie! It was about three inches high. The apple slices and filling were thick and slowly running down the sides of the well-cut slice onto the flowered paper plate. The crust was flaky, baked to a perfect golden brown. The rolled-up outer edge of the crust that rings the outside of the pie was extra thick. God, it was beautiful. It was a piece of culinary art.

I stood in front of the glass, staring at it for about a minute. I must have looked like a kid with his nose crushed to the window looking at a puppy in a pet store. I looked up and everyone that was ahead of me was now gone and the woman behind the counter was looking my way. I pointed to the pie and gave a quick nod toward it with my head. She smiled and came over to the back of the glass case. "Alice made it fresh this mornin'," she said. "Actually not fifteen minutes ago. That is the only piece left. It usually doesn't last long."

With loving, motherly hands—the same way she would pick up a newborn child out of a crib—she gently picked up that fine piece of heaven that was sitting on a white paper plate with the blue flower print and carefully carried it over to the counter. She gently set it down as if it were made of delicate crystal. She put a pure white napkin on top of the pie and with both hands holding the paper plate and with a motherly smile, she slowly handed it to me over the counter. I didn't remember setting my coffee down as I reached out for the pie. My eyes were like saucers and I could actually feel the drool running down the corner of my mouth. I had to look pretty foolish with the grin I had on my face.

I paid the lady and walked to the door with my prize in my left hand and my small black coffee in my right hand. I slowly turned around, backed into the double aluminum door, pushing it open with my butt.

Outside I noticed couple of guys in their mid-twenties, one heavy and one thin, standing by a beat-up maroon and black 1972 Ford pickup. The truck had rusted chrome rims and worn-out tires with almost no tread. On the back was a ladder rack made from some old wooden two-by-fours bolted together with round-head stove bolts. The rack had been there for a while—rust streaks from the bolts ran all the way down the unpainted two-by-fours. The rack held a couple of well-used aluminum ladders covered in several colors of paint.

The heavier of the two guys wore paint-covered denim coveralls and a tank top while his friend—about a hundred pounds lighter—sported a pony-tail, a T-shirt with the sleeves torn off, and arms covered with tattoos. Both were smoking cigarettes

On the Front Straight at Talladega with the Watkins Glen pace car.

as they checked out my Watkins Glen pace car. They wanted to know what every gas station attendant and race fan wanted to know when I pulled up with that car.

"How fast ya had 'er?"

"Not very fast." I told them. We talked for a few more minutes, but I got a little nervous as the heavy guy kept staring at my pie.

I ducked into the car and gently laid the pie in the center of the passenger seat. I put the napkin on the seat right by my slice of heaven and drove away. The smell of that apple pie was driving me nuts. I couldn't wait to eat it. I kept looking over to the passenger seat where it was riding. *Damn*, I thought to myself, *I forgot to get a fork. Oh well, I'll have to eat it the old-fashioned way, by hand.* I would have tried to take a bite while I was driving, but it was just too big a piece to hold with one hand.

I turned off the two-lane road onto Thirty Lane, and then down through the dark, wet tunnel. The water splashed against the sides of the tunnel as I drove through, then I was up the other side and into the sunlight. Yeah, I couldn't help it. I had to blow the horn while I was in there.

I proceeded down an access road, turned right, and drove through a gate to the garage area. I wanted to get to Pit Lane so I could park—and, before anyone showed up, eat that beautiful piece of pie. I wasn't going to share. At the north end of the garage area, I stopped and unlocked the gate. Then I proceeded through another gate. Talladega had gates all over the place. And there was a rule: if you unlock a gate, make sure you lock it once you're through. I drove past the empty garages and headed down a short entryway that led to Pit Lane. I took a left turn and I drove down Pit Lane to the center and stopped.

I looked to my right and there was the Tri-Oval grass, where the logo was to be painted. Then, as I looked out the windshield I saw the high banking of Turn 1 at the end of Pit Lane. Suddenly I was not thinking about the grass! I had the urge for speed. I looked over to the passenger seat and that perfect piece of apple pie. I swear that the position of the huge apple slices made it look like it was smiling at me. I then looked straight ahead. With my hands 10 and 2 on the steering wheel, I thought, *What the hell, nobody's here yet*! This was a dream of every race fan. Driving a hot lap at Talladega.

I slammed the '92 Ford Thunderbird Super Coupe pace car into first gear and floored it. The rear tires let out a loud squeal as the smell of burning rubber seeped into the car. Under full acceleration, I flew down Pit Lane. I was feelin' good! I slammed into second gear and the tires let out another squeal. At the exit of Pit Lane, I slammed into third gear speeding around the access lane at the bottom of the banking in Turns 1 and 2 and onto the racing surface on the Back Straight. On the flat I shifted to fourth. I brought the motor up to the redline and shifted to fifth. It was foot to the floor with speeds of 90, 95, 100, 110 down the Back Straight. Not lifting off the gas, I went into Turn 3.

The banking was unbelievable. The track was so long and the banking so steep, I couldn't feel the speed. I put the car right up next to the wall. What a feeling on the 34-degree banking! Even at 120 mph, I could feel the car wanting to turn down the banking. Off Turn 4, pedal to the metal, the motor was slowly winding up to

The banking was unbelievable.

the redline in fifth gear. The Super Coupe was flying down the Tri-Oval as its engine wound to the redline! The motor screamed as if to say, "*Yesss*. Give me more!! I'm runnin' man, I'm runnin'." I hit 132 mph. That was as fast as the Thunderbird would go. Going through the turns, the banking and the G-force slowed me down to 128 mph or so. With my ten years of racing experience driving Late Models and Modifieds, I felt right at home. I couldn't help myself; I started a second 2.66-mile lap. I slowed down in Turn 3 and slowly came down off the banking before I blew the engine or a tire. That would have been hard to explain.

Pulling onto Pit Lane at 90 mph I took a deep breath. I pushed the clutch in and kicked the shifter into neutral. I coasted down Pit Lane and rolled to a stop right in the two black rubber tire marks I'd left there two laps ago. I let out my breath slowly and I thought, *WOW. Who the hell needs drugs when you can do that? What a ride!* I reached down for the key and shut the car off and I got out and stood alone on Pit Lane in the beautiful Alabama morning sun. My heart was pounding. With my arms crossed and resting on the top of the open door I looked toward Turn 1. It was dead quiet. My eyes were wide open and I had a grin from ear to ear. I looked over to my right, over the roof of the car. There was the grass. My hands dropped down to my sides as my grin turned into a grimace. My eyes closed to just two small slits. *The grass*. That damned grass had become the enemy.

I don't know how long I stared at the grass before I snapped out of the daze and realized that I could finally eat that huge piece of fresh-baked apple pie. I bent down inside the car and started to reach over the driver's seat to grab my coffee cup out of the holder. I picked up my coffee and glanced to the passenger seat to look at my prized piece of pie. *My pie!!* "AAGGGHHHH. Oh God!" I screamed out loud. It was gone. My fresh, homemade three-inch-thick pie with the crispy, golden brown crust with the thick rolled-up edge was no longer on the seat. I jumped out and tore around the back of the car. I jerked open the passenger door practically ripping the door off its hinges. I leaned into the car as the door hit the hinge stops and bounced back into my ass so hard it blasted me into the passenger seat and crushed my shins in the door opening. I ignored the pain as my eyes darted all over the place trying to catch a glimpse of my pie.

"Aagghhhh. There it is!" I jumped back in horror. My face and jaw muscles distorted in spasms of pain and grief. I staggered further back.

There, on the floor of the Thunderbird, squashed between the passenger door and the seat, was my pie. Instead of the original three-inch thick slice, it was now a mere half-inch thick. The freshly cut apples were squashed out from the sides and the filling was stuck to the carpet. It was covered in sand and grass from the carpet. I pulled a Juicy Fruit gum wrapper that must have been under the seat from the pie filling. I slowly picked up the remains of the pie with both hands as some of the slippery fresh apple slices slid through my fingers and fell onto Pit Lane. I carried it away from the car, realizing it was dead. "Oh God, it's still warm," I muttered. A tear might have run down my left cheek. I honestly thought, for a second, of brushing it off and eating it anyway. While holding my dead pie in my hands, I looked up at the sky and let out a loud, echoing "NOOOOooooooooooo!"

I walked over to a blue fifty-five-gallon garbage can on Pit Lane and gently put the pie to rest. I must have stood there for three minutes staring at that blue garbage can. Then I licked all the filling off my fingers.

Oh well, the laps were worth it, I thought. I walked back to the car and got my coffee cup. As I took a sip of my coffee, I straightened up as the sweetest of sounds reached my ears. Goose bumps covered my arms and the back of my neck. It was sweet music to any racer, and it was coming from directly behind me. The Thunderbird's engine, headers, and exhaust pipes snapped and crackled as they cooled down from the heat of our high-speed run. I loved that sound. "You just rode the horse hard and put it away wet," I said as I looked at the car, and I smiled. It made me feel good and I sensed the car was happy too.

The sun was rising higher over the retaining wall in Turn 3. The shadows were moving away quickly. I looked out at the Tri-Oval grass. After all the doubt I had yesterday, this morning I finally had some confidence. Somehow I was going to do this. I took a sip of coffee. Then, as I continued to look at that grass, my confidence started slipping.

I heard a vehicle approaching and turned to look. My helpers had arrived. Mike, the I-don't-paint-grass guy, from Daytona, my helper Raymond, and extra maintenance man all pulled up in a couple of white Chevy pickup trucks. They jumped out, and Raymond ran to the middle of the six-acre Tri-Oval grass looking around like he was thinking, "How the hell did I get here?"

Today, on the grass, surrounded by my army, we were about to attack the problem. "Well, let's git movin'," I said. "We got a lot of work to do." At the same time, I thought to myself, *God, somebody help me!* I didn't want to show how I really felt—which was like running away, waving my arms and screaming obscenities as I went.

Last night, after constantly staring at the drawing, an idea had started to form. I might have figured out how to read the grass layout drawing. If Mike hadn't remembered the part about the two tapes, one across the top of the letters and one across the bottom, I might never have figured it out.

Acting like I knew what I was doing, I had the guys find a center line of the grass from end to end of Pit Lane. This was the easy part. Knowing the length of the logo would be 165 feet, we put a peg in the ground at one end of the logo's location and another one at the other end. We connected the pegs with a string. This string ran parallel with Pit Lane and would define the top of the word TALLADEGA. Next, we laid a 200-foot tape right by the string. The tape would read from left to right. The letters would be thirty feet tall so we measured down from the top string and put pegs in the ground with a string line between them. From there we laid a second 200-foot tape, defining the bottom of the letters, parallel with the top line. This 4,950-square-foot logo would be the largest sign I had ever seen. I realized I needed more help so I got on my radio and requested two more men from the shop.

Mike had suddenly remembered another part. Flags. I drove to the Maintenance Shop and in the storage shed was a pail full of heavy gauge wires, each about eight inches long and with a little red flag tied on one end. They also had white paint on them (the logo was white) so they must have been used for marking the points of a previous logo. That's what I figured, anyway.

With our two tapes on the ground, one above the letters and one below, running parallel to each other, I placed one man on the top tape and one on the bottom. They started at the zero measurement on the two horizontal tapes on the left side of the layout. I read the first point off the drawing, fourteen feet. The two men moved together fourteen feet to the right. They were holding a thirty-foot tape between them. I read out another measurement—twenty-four feet, six inches—and the third man, who was walking up and down the thirty-foot vertical tape, moved up to his mark and put a flag in the ground on that spot. The letter T took eight points to mark out. We proceeded, letter by letter, down the logo. Once we got the hang of it, things went pretty well.

Five hours and fifteen minutes later, after hollering numbers all day long, we were done. The last of the flags was in the ground. I couldn't really believe what we had done. When I stepped back and looked at this layout, all I saw was green grass and a mass of red flags. Was it right? Standing on the ground I couldn't visualize the logo—it was too big. I had to trust the layout.

I sat down on the grass, completely drained, not by labor but by the mental stress. Just as I slumped to the grass, one of the guys yelled at the top of his lungs, "Don't sit on the grass, you idiot!" I wondered what the hell his problem was. One of the tape-holders walked over and in a deep, calm Southern drawl said, "We got fire ants down here, boy."

I jumped up, slapping my butt with my hands, trying to wipe off any fire ants that might have gotten on me. "Thanks, man," I said.

Billy Swinford was at the track that day working on different projects. He had stopped by to see how I was doing. I told him the layout was done but I could not tell if it was right. He said, "Let's go up in the grandstands and look at it. We got in his truck and drove around to the Front Straight grandstands, then went up the center of the grandstands to try to see the flags. They were barely visible at that distance. I could make out a T and GA. It looked OK. I felt a little better. Billy wanted to drink beer, but I was done for the night. I was mentally drained. I walked to my car muttering, "Tomorrow, *we paint.*"

Off to the motel I went, but I couldn't get to sleep. I kept thinking, *What if we did the layout wrong?* One mistake would screw up the logo from that point on. The only way to see it all was to paint it. Then I thought, *What happens if I made a mistake?* I couldn't erase it once we painted. *What should I do?* Then to make matters worse, another thought came into my head. *This painting is going to be seen by millions of people on live TV!* I curled up on the bed in the fetal position and finally drifted off to sleep.

 # Painting the Grass

I left the motel and headed to the track early. I was nervous. I had come down to Alabama alone, and if I screwed this up I would probably be out of the track painting business for good. I'd only been employed at Watkins Glen for a few months, and I had never thought of painting anything like this before. If I painted a thirty-foot letter on the grass and it was wrong, I couldn't just wipe it off. I had to be right the first time. I had to trust the layout. The layout was the key. I also had to get the thoughts of disaster out of my head.

I pulled into the deli, got my coffee and another piece of apple pie, and drove to the track. No hot laps this time. I sat on Pit Lane sipping coffee and enjoying every bite of that delicious pie. My thoughts were turning to the job at hand—painting the grass—when I heard the sound of two old pickup trucks approaching. I could see the first truck carried two airless paint sprayers. The second truck hauled a trailer with about fifty five-gallon pails of paint. My painting helpers were piled on the trucks like bales of hay. The trucks stopped near me and began unloading the paint and sprayers.

I suddenly realized I didn't know how to operate an airless sprayer. I had never even touched one before.

I looked at the paint stacked on the trailer and saw another problem. There was a big guy wearing a cowboy hat and sunglasses. With a toothpick between his lips, he picked up five-gallon pails of paint like they were empty and set them down on Pit Lane. "Hey," I said. "That paint is enamel. We can't put 250 gallons of enamel on the ground. That's not legal." In New York, the Department of Environmental Conservation considered enamel paint a hazardous material. "We'll be in trouble with the DEC."

The big guy looked at me without expression. "You're in Alabama, boy," he said. "There ain't no rules down here."

I walked out onto the grass with the courage and stride of a Roman gladiator walking into the Coliseum to do battle. Today, this stretch of Talladega Speedway would be my Coliseum. I looked across the track and up into the stands. The seats were empty. In a few days thousands of people would see the grass painting on race day. Chances were they never think about how it got there.

Unlike a gladiator, I wouldn't be armed with a sword or a spear. I would have a spray gun. My enemy was not a lion or fellow gladiator, it was grass. I looked down at my field of battle, the Alabama green grass at my feet, and my courage began to disappear. I felt like I was about to be eaten, not by the lion but by the grass.

Relax, I thought. Just then I looked to my right and saw Mike and Raymond kneeling on the grass opening a five-gallon pail of white enamel paint. They were fighting with the tabs on the plastic lid, using an old screwdriver trying to pry the tabs open. It reminded me of two cats playing with a ball of yarn. I wanted to say, "Be careful. Don't spill that," but I didn't think they were listening. I just shook my head and turned away.

Just then I heard loud yelling. "You stupid ass! See what you did?"

"I didn't do it. You did it, you dumb jerk."

"You are going to get it now."

"He ain't gonna be happy."

I didn't want to turn around—because, without looking, I knew what had happened. The contents of the pail, five gallons of pure white enamel paint, was now in a thick, five-foot-wide puddle on the green Alabama grass. My eyes bugged out and I couldn't speak as I looked at the large paint spill. The loss of five gallons of paint was nothing compared to the problem of the five-foot white spot on the grass. As I watched, the spot slowly grew larger.

This was a disaster. This was a major screw-up. And my God, *we hadn't even started painting yet.*

I could feel the veins that run around the outside of my brain stretching and putting pressure on the inside of my skull. I ran over and hollering for someone to get some shovels. We tried to scoop up the paint with shovels and then dump it back in the pail. What a horrific mess. We managed to get the bulk of the mess shoveled up, but it was impossible to clean it all. "Just let it dry," I finally told them. "We will clean it later." Somehow. I couldn't let this distract me now. We had to get painting.

Mike suddenly stood straight up. "I remember," he said with a strange, gleeful look on his face. He scared me for a second. I thought he was hearing "happy music." He was smiling and looking surprised about having another thought. "I remember more," he said. "They had string and some two-by-fours. Yeah. I remember they tied a string between the flags and laid two-by-fours on the ground along the string for a straight edge to spray along the outside of the letters. Yeah. That's how they did it." He turned toward me with this silly smirk on his face.

That's not a bad idea, I thought. *Why didn't I think of that?* This would give us a nice, straight edge on the letters. I could use the solid edge to outline. Once the outline was sprayed, it would be easier to come along and fill in the letter. As I was thinking and looking at the red flags on the ground, I saw a problem. I had to figure out where the hell a letter was in that maze of red flags before I could paint.

After a couple of minutes of staring, squinting, and making my eyes blur, the outline of the T magically appeared. "I can see the T," I yelled.

I looked at the guys and they were staring back at me. I had to remember that they thought I knew what I was doing. Oh well, we were rolling now. We used string to connect the wire pins to get an idea of where the letters were. It would be easy to lay the two-by-fours along the string and paint. When I finally saw the T, I also saw something that indicated things might be going my way. The big white spot in the grass where Raymond and Mike had spilled paint was just inside the lower part of the T. We would be painting right over the spilled paint. We had just dodged a bullet. Oh man, this was good.

The airless paint sprayer was gas powered. It didn't just look well used—it looked well abused. Dried white paint was smeared all over the engine. The hose was covered with dry white paint. The rusty exhaust pipe still had threads on the end where there once had been a muffler. The rope cord was so frayed it didn't look like it had many pulls left. It wouldn't retract all the way.

Raymond gave seven hard pulls on the rope starter with his right hand while bending down and fooling with the choke lever with his left. I noticed the air cleaner was missing and I could see the silver choke valve opening and shutting as Raymond flipped the flat metal choke lever up and down. Finally, the five-horsepower Briggs & Stratton engine sputtered to life. It shook like crazy, causing the whole machine to shake around on the cracked old rubber tires. Dark smoke poured from the exhaust and engulfed Raymond where he stood. His pants rippling in time with the exhaust. He quickly reached down through the dark cloud and flipped the choke lever to the off position. The black smoke turned white. At the Vatican, when a new pope was selected, the smoke coming out of the chimney turned from black to white. Here, the white smoke signaled the start of our new adventure.

The engine continued to run a little rough and the whole machine looked quite pitiful. I had a feeling it hadn't been started since the last time the grass was done a year ago. That old Briggs sputtered so badly that at one point it shot a couple of perfectly round, white smoke rings out of the exhaust. The smoke rings floated peacefully, about a foot off the ground, out across the grass. They rolled around and around, turning inside themselves, before they reached the asphalt of the racetrack about fifty yards away and disappeared into a whisper of light gray smoke. Watching the smoke rings gave me a peaceful feeling, although I couldn't help thinking, *I wish I was going with them.*

After about three minutes of Raymond fooling with the choke and carburetor, the engine smoothed out a little, although it never did run perfectly. With no muffler, the steady drone of the airless sprayer's engine replaced the semi-quiet of the nice, peaceful Alabama day. I imagined it was the same sound a WWII B-24 Liberator would make taking off from one of the old runways. I wished I had ear plugs. I grabbed the airless sprayer's gun handle. As I moved the hose around, pieces of thick, dry paint cracked and fell off. Through the cracks in the paint, I could see the hose used to be blue. The nozzle looked like a golf ball, it had so much paint built up on it. *I can't be fussy,* I thought. All I cared about was that paint came out the end.

"This is it," I mumbled to myself nervously. Raymond set a full five-gallon pail of white enamel paint next to the airless sprayer and put the suction hose in the paint pail. He turned the prime lever on the pump to ON. The engine started laboring. Puffs of dark smoke came from the exhaust while large bubbles appeared in the bucket having come up slowly through the thick paint. It looked as if the sprayer might work.

I had two guys kneeling on the grass outside the letter T, one at each end of an eight-foot wooden two-by-four. Raymond hollered above the drone of engine, "I think it's ready, man." He bent over and flipped the switch on the pump to PAINT. I could feel the steady thumps of the pressure pump through the handle of the spray gun as I stepped inside the outline of the T. The spray gun's pistol grip had a large trigger that took all four fingers to pull. I grasped it and took a deep breath, then pointed the nozzle to the ground, holding it about six inches from the grass. The thirty inches from trigger to nozzle helped my back as I didn't have to bend over too far. Pulling the trigger, I sprayed a test pattern well inside the T. The second I pulled the trigger, the engine changed its tone. The spray gun kicked back like I had just fired a .357 Magnum. Grass and chunks of dirt flew in the air.

"My first spray," I said out loud. *Wow. Pressure's gotta be too high.* I experimented with the pressure and continued spraying paint.

The engine noise was so loud that Raymond and I couldn't talk to each other—and he was only twenty feet away. Every time I hollered to him to adjust something, he had to walk over to where I was to hear me. I ended up devising some creative hand signals. Pointing my left index finger up and twirling it around gave Raymond the signal to increase the pressure to the nozzle. Pointing my left thumb down and moving my hand up and down gave him the signal to decrease the pressure. When I sent a signal, Raymond would do the strangest thing. Each time, he would move his head to mimic my hand signals. I couldn't look at him because I would start to laugh. When I twirled my finger while pointing up to increase pressure, his head would tip up a little and he would rotate it in a circular motion. His eyes would twirl in their sockets while his head rotated so that his eyes kept looking directly at me. When I signaled less pressure, he would bob his head up and down like I was moving my thumb up and down. He would do all these motions while turning the knob on the sprayer.

It took five minutes of frantic hand signals (Raymond must have been dizzy by then) until we got the pressure to what I thought was just right. If it was too high, it would blow the grass right out of the ground. Too low and paint would just dribble out the golf-ball-size nozzle.

With Raymond feeding five-gallon pails of paint to the hungry monster, we started to get serious about painting. There were two guys kneeling on the ground with our two-by-four straightedge and a man standing about five feet behind me holding the hose so it didn't drag through the wet paint. I took a deep breath and pulled the trigger. I got into a zone, almost like racing. On the pace lap, a driver is nervous as hell, but when the green flag drops, it all goes away. That's what this felt like. As soon as I pulled the trigger, I mellowed out and concentrated on the task at hand.

I didn't know it at the time, but this was the start of a new era. My sign business was about to take a new turn. It all started that first trip far from home on the grass Tri-Oval in the middle of Talladega Superspeedway in the beautiful state of Alabama. If someone told me the night I met Bob Shaw (the pinstriper who gave me his brush in that dingy Esso gas station in Watkins Glen) that I'd be in Alabama in the center of Talladega Superspeedway painting grass, I would have called him crazy. But here I was, painting grass.

My heart was beating faster as I squeezed the trigger and sprayed a pattern along the two-by-four. I sprayed a little more, and then the guys kneeling on the grass picked up the two-by-four and moved it along the string up the side of the letter another eight feet. I sprayed more paint along the board, and they moved it again. The paint was thick. We didn't use any thinner as we wanted it to cover the grass in one pass. I found myself thinking, *This is fun.* Of course I had forgotten about all the stress it took to get to this point and the consequences if the layout was wrong. We painted on. No one spoke to anyone as we couldn't hear anything above the sound of the unmuffled paint sprayer anyway. Just as we were developing a rhythm, we had to take a time-out. The guys had to move the eight-foot-long two-by-four four times as the letters were thirty feet tall. We needed to get more two-by-fours. This first board had gotten so covered with the thick white paint that it was starting to mark up the grass near the letters as it was moved along.

Getting more boards took time. I felt like I was watching an old Keystone Cops movie. Instead of one guy getting into the pickup truck and driving to the Maintenance Shop to get more boards, everyone was trying to get into the cab at once. Those that couldn't fit in the cab jumped into the back of the truck—while it was moving! This showed me one thing for sure. I wasn't alone in not wanting to be out here! I walked over to the sprayer to shut it off. Looking down at it, I thought, *With that frayed starter rope dangling there, will it start again?* I turned the throttle down and let it run on idle. It took twenty minutes before I saw the old white Chevy appear on the horizon. Dust flew as it approached. I could see three guys standing in the back leaning on the roof of the cab and waving. The Keystone Cops were back.

With new boards, we moved on. At first, I tried not to get paint on the hands of the two guys that knelt on the grass and held the boards. They didn't have to hold the board while I painted as it wasn't going to blow away, but I guess it made them feel important. I quickly realized it was useless trying to avoid their hands. I finally got to the point that when I sprayed up the side of the two-by-four and got to their hands, I didn't stop. I painted right over them. At first they jumped and looked at each other. I'm sure they were thinking "What the hell." After the first time, they didn't seem to mind and told me to keep going. Rubber gloves? Too late. Once I had a letter outlined, another man on the other spray gun came along behind me and filled the letter in. The guys fought to take turns on the other gun, shoving each other and hollering. *"Hey,"* I hollered back. "I don't care who paints, just take turns. Spray outside of my line, I will kill you. *Understand? Kill!"*

They made me nervous, so when I sprayed along the two-by-four, I would paint inside the line about two feet. This gave them a big cushion. I ended up going over each letter anyway, as they wound up leaving light and dark spots in paint.

To anyone watching, it had to be a sight. Two guys were kneeling on the ground holding a two-by-four while I sprayed along the board and right across their hands. Then three guys were fighting over the other spray gun and two more were holding the hoses up off of the wet paint while we painted. And there was Raymond, with a

Filling in the white on the Talladega logo.

Camel cigarette hanging from his lips and a cloud of smoke in front of his face as he stood by the sprayer waiting for my signals.

It wasn't long before everyone was splashed with white paint, including me. I finally got to the letter D and thought, *After this I only have a few more letters to go.* I looked at my flags and all of a sudden felt a slight panic attack. The letter D is round. Our two-by-fours were straight. All production stopped. We all stood around looking at each other and the guys holding the two-by-fours wondered what was up. I looked at the flags defining the D. They were about ten feet apart. I had gained some confidence spraying and was getting bolder. *I'm going to try to freehand this. I have to. How else could it be done?*

I stepped inside the D and took a few practice strokes toward the inside of the letter. The nozzle was spraying in an eight-inch-wide pattern. I turned the wand sideways and swung it in a straight line along the grass and I got a one-inch wide line. The first test spray was terrible. Trying to walk forward and spray caused the nozzle to wobble. After a little more testing I stumbled onto a solution. I found it was easier to walk backwards and draw the nozzle toward me. I took a deep breath and away I went. All eyes were on me. The guys oohed and aahed as I outlined a giant letter D. I was dancing like Fred Astaire with a spray gun.

Walking backward and swinging the gun, my footwork was awesome. Like the old saying, I was poetry in motion. To this day I will argue with anyone that I invented the Moonwalk, not Michael Jackson. Moonwalkin' with a spray gun. I finished the D and found that freehand painting was much easier and faster. I realized that I could spray a decent line without the board. With just three more letters to go, I had finally started to get the hang of it. On the final letter, A, I painted along the string instead of using the boards. I'm sure those two guys who had been holding the two-by-four were happy. One thing that was hard for me to get used about painting grass—I didn't have to be perfect. After all, this painting would be viewed from a camera high above in the Goodyear Blimp. No one would see small wobbles in the line.

Six hours with the paint sprayer engine blaring in my ears had been painful. With the last letter A completed, I signaled Raymond by slashing my index finger across my throat. Raymond, whipping his head to one side, followed my finger motion and shut the sprayer off. All of a sudden all I could hear was *silence!* Beautiful silence.

I was still hunched over from the spraying, so I tried to stand up straight. *Oh, my back.* It took a while to get fully upright. The spray gun hung loose in my hand. I looked over at Raymond. His head tilted and with cigarette smoke rolling in his face, he had a sheepish grin on his face. I smiled back. I walked over and high-fived him! It was done. The grass was done. I raised my head slightly and sniffed. I put my forearm to my nose a smelled it. Holy cow! I realized I smelled like a Briggs & Stratton engine. The smoke from that old engine running all day had covered me with its fumes. I didn't care. The grass was done.

Just then, Billy Swinford came on the radio, which still hung from my belt. "Hey, my main man," he said. "Up here." I looked around. I heard his voice call out again. "Up here. In the grandstand." I looked way across the track and there he was up on top of the grandstand waving his arms over his head. He looked like an ant. "Come up here and look," he said on the radio. "It looks great."

I dropped the spray gun down near the spray unit and I ran over to the pace car. As I started to open the door, I looked down and I stopped. My sneakers! Oh my God, they were covered with wet, white enamel paint. Mixed in the paint were green grass clippings. The mixture was about a half-inch thick and slowly sliding down the

Grass painting from the grandstand on race day.

sides of my shoes. It looked like my shoes were a fresh salad covered with too much ranch dressing.

"Let's take my truck," Mike said. "I'll drive ya over."

Talladega was so big that it took a while to go from the infield to the back of the grandstand. Mike pulled up, and I jumped out before the truck stopped. I couldn't wait to look. I ran to the grandstand, leaving white footprints on the pavement. I ran up the metal stairs (being careful not to slip), all the way to the top where Billy stood. He was smiling. (He always smiled, even if things were bad.) I looked past Billy and stopped dead in my tracks. My mouth dropped and my eyes opened wide. There it was. A huge white TALLADEGA. I was speechless.

I got goose bumps on my arms and up my back. If I'd been up there alone, I might have cried. I had done it, but I could barely believe it. I didn't realize at the time what doors this one job would open for me in the future. Oh man, I felt good. I had been sent down here not knowing why and had been asked to do something that I had never heard of before—lettering grass—and I had pulled it off.

Smack! I jumped as Billy slapped me hard on the back. "Beers are in the truck, my main man," he said. As we turned to walk away, I had to look back one more time to make sure it was still there and this was not a dream. I looked over in the grass again and could see the guys picking things up.

That night, in my hotel room, I lay on the bed smiling and thinking of the past week. *I can't believe I painted that logo. I honestly can't believe it.* I slept well that night.

With my work done, I looked forward to watching the weekend races. The race on Saturday went smoothly. None of the racers slid through our logo. On Sunday, May 2, Ernie Irvan took the checkered flag winning the NASCAR DieHard 500. It was a great race. The best part for me? I didn't care if someone had slid through our grass painting on Sunday and damaged it. It didn't matter anymore.

When the race was over, I couldn't wait to get home. First, I dropped by the staff party after the race. All the workers had gathered at the Maintenance Shop for food, beer, and talk. Mike Helton, the president of Talladega Superspeedway, was there. He called me over in front of everyone, put his arm around me, and thanked me for coming down and getting them out of a bind. He also praised me for the fine job on the logo. (Mike Helton is now president of NASCAR. I see him a couple times a year at different tracks, and say hello. I consider him a friend.)

At the party, Mike asked, "When are you going home?"

"I'm headed out right now," I said. "I like it down here but two weeks is a long time to be away from home."

"I think you better stay another night," he said. It was late afternoon and I had a long drive ahead of me.

"Oh, no. I am leaving in five minutes." I said. "I'm ready to go home now." But that was the weekend Rodney King got beaten in Los Angeles. Riots were going on all over the place and Mike didn't want me driving that marked pace car at night. He was right, I stayed.

At daybreak, while everyone was still asleep, that Thunderbird Super Coupe pace car was smokin' the tires heading up Route 59 toward Gadsden, Alabama. From there it was up to Chattanooga, Tennessee. I was admiring the beauty of the Great Smokey Mountains when I realized I was almost out of gas. I pulled into the first gas station I saw. Driving the pace car attracts talk whenever I stop someplace. The attendant came over to fill up the gas tank. The first words out of his mouth were "How fast ya had 'er?" I smiled and told him about the laps at Talladega. He was impressed.

"Maybe I'll see you next year," I told the guy as I paid him. I got in the car, buckled up and got ready for some serious driving. It was pedal to the metal as I pointed the front bumper of the Thunderbird north.

༄

The following year, while working on the "High Banks" one sunny afternoon at Talladega Superspeedway, painting PEPSI logos on the retaining wall, we (Larry Orr and Steve Hughey) noticed another crew painting Winston logos on the wall about a hundred yards from us. I finished my part of the painting and walked down to where the other sign company was painting. This walk (not easy walking on 34-degree banking) turned into a 30-year relationship with one of the best "Racetrack" painters I have ever met! Not only that, but the kindest, most sincere person you could imagine. Keith Grubbs is his name. I introduced myself and the conversation continued when Keith said, "Man, we have been on the road for weeks and I wish this week was over so we could go home. If there is a hit on the logos, we have to be here to repaint them before the Sunday race". It was Wednesday. I said, "Well, Larry Orr and I are here until Sunday. You leave me the paint, brushes and rollers and we will do the repainting as we will be here anyway, and you guys can head home". Keith said, "Are you serious? How much will you charge so I can call my boss (JKS Incorporated in Winston Salem, NC). "No charge", I said. "Head home"!

Well, since then, whenever we ended up working at the same racetrack, we always ended up helping each other out. The side benefit was Keith taught me so much about large format painting. His partner, Paul Bennett, was like Keith. They were an awesome pair!

As a perfect example of this, Larry Orr and I were finishing up painting logos on Pit Wall at Watkins Glen as it was too dark to paint. Heading up Pit Lane to go home, we noticed lights on the crossover bridge in turn 11. There was a manlift with two guys in it. We drove up and it was Keith and Paul. I hollered up to them, "What the hell are you doing? It's dark!"

The vinyl wrap material (Sprint) had just came and it had to be up before tomorrow's practice. They were just starting at one end. The bridge is 92 feet long. The vinyl sheets are 4' x 10'.

I went over to maintenance and found another manlift. Larry Orr and I started applying the sheets on the other end of the bridge. I don't know what time it was when we met in the middle, but the last pieces came together perfectly!

I am so fortunate to have met Keth. Our families are friends, and this is one of the benefits of painting at racetracks.

 Back to My New Job

Returning from Talladega, I couldn't wait to see my wife, my son, my daughter, and my dog. Harriett said my dog, Brandy, had been moping around for a week while I was gone. I also looked forward to getting back to my new job at Watkins Glen International. I drove straight through on Monday, about eighteen hours, and I was in my office at the track on Wednesday. I shared stories of my adventures at Talladega with my new boss, Matt Matusicky, and my coworkers Michelle LaDue, Tim Coleman, and Steve Ely.

My job as graphics design manager at the Glen included working with clients on their sign needs, making a detailed map of the track property, and some other stuff.

My daughter Beth and her teddy bear, named Teddy, posing in front of a newly painted Watkins Glen Victory Circle sign.

I was also starting to paint larger signs. All I had done up to that point was 4'×8' signs. I didn't consider the grass at Talladega a sign—it was more like a painting. Standard billboards that I painted at the track were 12'×36' and made of aluminum. Why 12'×36'? I didn't know, but that was the standard size billboard used at the track since the 1970s, when Formula 1 ran there. Someone built these billboards, using an eight foot high and four foot wide sheet of aluminum with a 4'×4' sheet at the bottom. They made a wood frame out of wood two-by-twos and screwed the aluminum panels to the wood. This made one '4×12' panel, and it took nine panels to make one billboard.

A corporate logo had to be perfect. You cannot alter it in any way. You work to the specs they send you, matching the font for the letters and the colors exactly. Often the company will send digital files of the logo. To make things tougher, most graphics companies use the Pantone Matching System (PMS), which was developed for the printing industry—and some colors are impossible to match with paint. (Paint uses different pigments from the ones in ink; you can get close, but it's not easy.) The part I did not like as a painter was the complete lack of creativity on my end. I had to paint what they sent me.

When I first did a Budweiser billboard at Watkins Glen, before it could be installed, Budweiser sent a woman up from St. Louis just to check the colors I was using. She told me, "We have people doing signs for us all over the country and we don't know the quality of their work. Budweiser wants all signs held to our high standard. You wouldn't believe how bad some of the work we run into can be." That afternoon she was on a plane headed back to St. Louis. Now that I know the people at Busch Media, they trust my work—they don't send anyone out to check on my work anymore.

Painting signs that big required a building with lots of space. At the Glen we used the Service Garage, a 70'×300' building with a fourteen-foot ceiling. It was the garage for all the different series of cars that raced at the Glen, including NASCAR. The building was one huge open space. At the south end, I had the maintenance guys build a wooden rack on the end wall that would hold a 12'×36' billboard. I put individual 4'×12' panels on this rack, one by one, until the whole 12'×36' billboard was attached to the rack.

To paint the surface, I used an overhead projector and projected the pattern onto the billboard. I had learned this projector tip from a furniture shop owner in Ithaca who did fantastic wood carvings of animals. He used a projector for his carving layouts. *I need one of those,* I thought at the time.

Turned out the furniture shop owner had an extra one that he sold me for $125. With this transparency projector, I put the image I wanted on a piece of clear plastic film. The light under the glass passed up through the film and into the lens where mirrors projected the image out to the sign. The image was very detailed and with the superpowerful thousand-watt bulb, I could project an image onto a 12'×36' billboard in one shot and then paint it.

When I finished lettering a billboard, the panels would be taken down one by one. When they had fully dried, Maurice Rudy, the track sign installer, would take

Larry Orr and Steve Hughey helping me hand-paint a 12'×36' billboard.

them and put them up in their locations around the racetrack. Rudy had worked at the Glen forever. He started doing fence work (and believe me, there is a lot of fence) before adding sign installer to his duties. He'd had put up countless signs, and all that practice made him the absolute best at installation. No matter the size of the sign, the panels always lined up when Maurice was done with them.

For these large billboards, I usually worked at night—with good reason. First, it was much less crowded at night. No one was there to bother me with stupid questions or comments—no "I knew a guy that would shake like hell until his brush touched a sign" or "I knew a guy that painted that stuff freehand with no layout." That was all crap and I was tired of the same old tales. When I had to work around race cars that were in the garage for the weekend, I was always concerned about dropping a quart of paint on somebody's new BMW. Second, while working at night, it was easier to see the projected layout on the billboard. I had the lights on in the section of garage I was working in while setting up, then I would turn them off when I projected the image. In the dark, the projected layout was sharper.

One night, around 9 p.m., I was in the huge empty garage, alone—except for my dog, Brandy, who was curled up on the floor in his usual sleeping position. The only time he would wake up was when I hollered, "Brandy! Let's go! Get in the truck!" I was halfway up a ten-foot step ladder working on a 12'×36' billboard. All the lights were off except for the projector. Since it was warm, I had a couple of the garage-type overhead doors open. From the ladder, I traced the projected image onto the panels and sang along with a Bob Seger song playing on my radio. (I loved that old radio. It was held together with masking tape and covered with every color of paint I had ever used. It worked great even though it was missing a couple of knobs and had an antenna made from a brass-tone coat hanger.)

As I sang, I stretched to the left from my position on the ladder. As I reached to trace a line, my arm froze. Right on the billboard, not two feet from my left shoulder, was a huge animal. I screamed. It was more like an "AHHHaaaaaagghhhh!" because I was so petrified my vocal cords were frozen. A mass of goose bumps formed on my ass and traveled up the center of my back. Part of them went up the back of my neck into my hair. Yes. My hair had goose bumps. Adrenaline raced through my body as I jumped backward off the ladder from the fourth step. With my arms flailing and my feet churning in the air, I landed flat-footed on the floor and was instantly backpedaling from the board to get away from the monster.

I was twenty feet from the ladder when I stopped and looked back up at the billboard. The creature was gone. Where the hell was it? If it didn't run out the door, it had to be in the building with me. I whipped around, looking down the building past the projector. The 300-foot building faded into total darkness. *This was not good.* "What the hell was that?" I yelled.

I looked over toward the projector. A tiny little moth was flying around in a circle in the light of the projector. As I watched, it landed on my clear plastic sign layout. I turned and looked up at the billboard. There was the monster. A yard-long, highly detailed moth, right on the billboard. "Oh my God," I said out loud as I started laughing. The light from the projector had attracted the moth through the open doors and into the building. I had almost had a friggin' heart attack. I could have broken my leg when I jumped off the ladder. Through all this, Brandy had only opened one eye to see what the fuss was about. The rest of the night, I was on edge. I kept looking around inside the 300-foot-long building, where my lights faded to jet black in the far corners. I saw a tiny, eerie red glow at the far end of the building and imagined it was a monster down there in the dark. It could have been the EXIT light above the door, but I wasn't walking down there to find out. Even after all these years, I still jump when a bug lands on the projector and think of the night when I survived a monster attack.

Those 12'×36' billboards were big, but other signs were getting even bigger and getting put in unusual places. My boss, Mattman, gave me a new task one day. "The Camel GT Center sign needs to be changed," he said. The GT Center was a single-story building serving as the track operations office and the Maintenance Shop. *It wasn't tall but I was so afraid of heights that it was tall to me!* The GT Center was actually two buildings, attached together, and the sign was on the roof. The sign measured about 6 feet high and 120 feet long, with a gold background with blue lettering. Now they wanted a blue background with gold lettering.

Now I have a bad flaw. As I said earlier, I am petrified of heights. I am not scared of heights, I'm *petrified* of heights. I get so terrified of heights that I can't even look up at high things.

The sign at the top of the GT Center was on an angled iron frame about four feet

The 6'×120' sign on the roof of the GT Center at Watkins Glen International (with John Russell on one ladder and me on the other).

above the roof. Ten cables attached the top of the sign to the roof at intervals as the wind never stopped blowing up there. And we couldn't use scaffolds with the cables in the way and the thin metal roof material under the sign. My helper John Russell and I would have to work off of ladders.

Before I could paint the Camel sign, I would need to use pounce patterns to apply the layout. Pouncing—a simple technique for transforming an image from one surface to another—was invented by Michelangelo centuries ago. A pounce pattern starts with a piece of paper sized to match the size of the sign you want to paint. You draw the layout of the sign onto the paper and then roll a pounce tool—a small star-shaped wheel attached to a handle—along the lines to make small holes. Then you put the paper pattern with the holes on top of the blank sign and pound a cloth bundle of very fine charcoal dust—a pounce bag—against the paper pattern. The dust passes through the holes and transfers the pattern as a charcoal outline you can follow when you paint the sign.

To repaint the Camel GT sign, I had to make large pounce patterns that I could tape to the existing sign. It takes a lot of paper and it needed to be done in sections so we could handle them easier. We could have done the layout right on the sign, but this sign was double-sided so we could save time by reusing the patterns on the other side. I created the patterns in my sign shop at my house with a computer and printed them out on my large printer, which could handle thirty-inch-wide paper. Instead of a pounce wheel, I used an electro pounce machine, a more modern way to create the pounce holes. The electro pounce machine was grounded to a table and had a pounce cord attached to an insulated electric pencil. The electric pencil was the size of a Sharpie pen and had an inch-long metal stylus point sticking out of it. This electric pencil burned a line of small holes through the paper pattern as I moved it along.

When I first got that machine, I was showing my friend Don Romeo how it worked. "You never, ever, touch that tip," I told him as I leaned on the table with my elbow (a big mistake as it turned out). "It has almost three thousand volts." As I told him this, I pointed to the tip with my index finger. I knew not to touch it, so I was keeping my finger about two inches away from the tip. This wasn't as safe a distance as I thought—without warning . . . *crack*! A bluish-white arc flew off the shiny metal tip and twisted and turned in midair before snaking its way to the tip of my finger. I watched as a puff of white smoke exploded off of the end of my finger tip and three thousand volts (luckily not many amps) went into my finger and out my grounded elbow to the metal top of the table. My hand remained clamped shut on the insulated handle, but the rest of me jumped, twisting and turning in midair just like the little lightning bolt that got me. My antics pulled the new machine right off the table and I watched in horror as it crashed to the concrete floor. "Oh my God!" I screamed in electronically induced pain. "AAAaaaahhhhh." I was standing there over my electro pounce machine, which was upside down on the concrete floor. I was looking in disbelief at my smoking finger as Don turned and walked toward the door. He was laughing so hard he couldn't even say good-bye. I could hear him laughing as he got in his car and drove away. My finger was numb for the rest of the day and the elbow that was grounded to the metal table hurt like hell. This is why some people still use the nonelectric pounce wheel! To my surprise, the pounce machine was not hurt at all. I figured they must have designed it so that it would withstand sudden jerks off the table caused by idiots like me!

Once I put the holes in my Camel GT pounce pattern, I had to get all the patterns up to the roof. Climbing up and down the sixteen-foot extension ladder was the hard part. Being scared of heights and carrying rolled-up paper patterns under my arm was not fun. Once on the roof, the rooftop so big I could pretend that I wasn't up in the air. I usually worked with John, but one day I was painting alone on top of the GT Center. I was in my own little world, when all of a sudden I heard a metal-on-metal sliding sound. I looked toward the sound, at the west end of the roof, and just stared in horror at what was *not* there. My ladder. The wind blew my ladder sideways, and it disappeared from sight and clattered to the ground. I couldn't get down. Adrenaline shot through me like a jolt of lightning. Once again, this showed the importance of having a two-way radio on me at all times. It was my radio to the rescue. I always have a two-way radio with me when I am at racetracks. I am never without one. Someone from the Maintenance Shop came to my rescue and put my ladder back up. Of course I got harassed for my panicky radio message.

About a year into my employment and in addition to my sign painting duties, I got picked, along with Matt, to work on a secret five-year development plan for the track. The development plan was the idea of Claude Sullivan, the CEO of Corning Enterprise, and John Saunders, the track president. They wanted to keep it under wraps until it could be presented to NASCAR. Corning Enterprises owned the track during the years I worked there and Claude (a wonderful person) was personally involved in the operation of the Glen.

I was fairly good with computer graphics programs by that point, but the detailed layouts and the maps for the development plan would require a more sophisticated program than I was using. I wanted to learn AutoCAD, the best computer-aided design program available at the time. AutoCAD licenses cost about $3,000 back then. Claude would stop by the track from time to time and see how things were going on the plan. He saw my efforts and asked me if I was interested in going to evening classes at Corning Community College for AutoCAD. "Sure," I said. He told me to call his secretary and she would set it up.

Claude liked people who wanted to better themselves, and he used his position to help when he could.

When it came time for my first night class, I arrived early and picked a seat in the middle of the room. I waited as I was the first person there. I looked around at the blackboard, the chairs and the room. It all brought back memories of high school. Even the smell reminded me of my school days. By the time the rest of the class and the instructor showed up, I realized I was older than all the other students. I was also older than the teacher! There were only eight people in the class and they were all sitting up front. "Why don't you come up and join us?" the teacher said. I looked around. Yeah, he was talking to me. I moved forward.

Being out of school for so long was a disadvantage, and the class was hard for me. The other students were great, though, and would help me with any problems I had. I think they felt sorry for me because I was so old—forty-six. As the weeks went by I got better, and I'll be damned—I passed the course.

Through Corning Glass, Claude supplied the track with the latest AutoCAD program. I used AutoCAD only for the mapping of the track. I used CorelDraw for my own graphics work.

 # Midgets Speed

Most of my time at Watkins Glen International involved my painting career, but I did have a few opportunities to exercise my need for speed. I am addicted to speed, after all, and I'm resigned to the fact; I don't even try to fight it!

During my first winter working at the track, I took a trip to Buffalo, New York, where I saw some Midget car racing—indoors, at the Niagara Falls Convention Center. These cars were called 3/4 Midgets. They had a tubular frame and were built on a smaller scale than a Sprint Car or Super Modified. They had disc brakes, a quick-

My son Mark and I discussing an upcoming race at Watkins Glen International where I would be driving the back up car of Can Am Midget Champion, Keith Dempster.

change rear end, and a modified motorcycle engine that developed 185 HP. That might not sound like much, but the entire car weighed only six hundred pounds. This power-to-weight ratio turned the cars into missiles.

When I went to work Monday morning after the races, I couldn't get those cars off my mind. I started talking to John Saunders, the president of the track, about these Midgets, telling him I thought they would make a good show running on the Inner Loop at the Glen. Finally, to shut me up, John (now president of ISC, which owns NASCAR) gave me the go-ahead to organize a Can-Am Midget race.

To help organize the race, I reached out to my friend Ken Coates, owner of Inlet Glass and Mirror in Ithaca. Ken put me in touch with Harry Macy, who headed the Can-Am Midget series based in Buffalo, and I soon found out that once you met Harry, you would never forget him. He was quite a character, and I really liked him. As I got to know the drivers in the series, I found out everyone loved Harry! After much discussion, Harry and I put together a Can-Am Midget Series race at Watkins Glen International.

While organizing the event, I got to know most of the officials, drivers, and crew members that belonged to the Can-Am Midget Racing Series. These guys were awesome to work with. Being around these drivers made me feel rejuvenated. I hadn't raced in a few years, but when I got involved in this project, I came alive! My addiction to speed raised its ugly head! It was like setting a shot of Jack Daniels in front of a reformed alcoholic. *I had to figure out a way to race!*

And the impulse didn't go away—I kept trying to figure out how I could race in the event. I knew that if I did get to race I wanted to be in a good car, so I was happy to get a line on one. At one point, I went back to Niagara Falls to observe another Can-Am race, and there I met Keith Dempster, the Can-Am Midget Champion from Toronto. He had a backup car—probably better than most of the other cars in the field and likely to be almost as good as his primary car—and I worked out a deal to rent it for the Inaugural Can-Am Midget race at Watkins Glen. That meant I could run it if I could come up with sponsorship money.

I hit the bricks in search of sponsorship. My cousin, Fast Eddy Menio (who owns Menio Contracting), Bob Carson (the owner of Maria's Tavern in downtown Watkins Glen), and Johnny Ellison (of Central Asphalt, a paving company in Watkins Glen) came to my aid and put up the money—I think it was about $500—to run the car for one event.

This Midget race, the first of its type at Watkins Glen, was scheduled for the night of Saturday, July 17, 1993, during the Glen's U.S. Nationals weekend. We decided to use the Inner Loop at the end of the Back Straight and the run-off portion of the track to make a 1/5-mile oval. Racing at the world famous Watkins Glen International was huge for the Can-Am Midget Series and had caused quite a stir in the Midget racing community. Before the race, track officials, Bill and Harry Macy, and a couple of other Midget drivers brought their cars to Watkins Glen to run a test at the track. They wanted to see how well the cars would adapt to the planned 1/5-mile oval. I got to take a turn driving Bill Macy's car during the practice session. (It was nice of Bill and Harry to let me take their car out.) I just wanted to see how it felt—Oh my

Crew chief giving me instructions. (Photo by Jack Eckert)

God was it fun! I couldn't wait for race day.

During the Camel GT weekend some weeks earlier, temporary grandstands had been set up at the Inner Loop. This worked perfectly for our event. We brought in some portable lighting for the night racing. About forty cars showed up for the race. We had qualifying heats and a consolation race, just as we did when I ran on the dirt tracks.

In my qualifying race I had to finish fourth or better to lock a position in the feature race. I also had to start last in a ten-car field as I was a rookie. Everyone there was a member of the Can-Am Midget Series; they raced each other every week, while I was a newcomer. I had yellow ribbons tied to my roll cage to flag my rookie status and also to warn the other drivers to that fact. With two laps to go in my qualifying heat, I was fifth. Two cars ahead of me had been battling side by side for the past three laps. Going into Turn 4, they separated just a little and I shot between them.

Just then they came back together. One of the cars hit my front wheel and he spun. I went into the foam barrier. (Watkins Glen was just starting to use the foam blocks as a safety barrier in front of the rail.) My right front wheel caught the foam and it broke the steering linkage and bent the wheel back. J.J. O'Malley, the press director, later presented me with a trophy for the First Car to the Foam award.

Keith Dempster's crew fixed my car in time to run the consolation race. I got into the feature through the "consi," and in the feature, I finished in fourteenth place (out of twenty cars). The race was well received, and I managed to set up a second Midget race later that year. My sponsors came back, and I raced Keith's backup car once again. This time I managed to qualify without incident. In the feature, I was running seventh in the fifty-lap race with fourteen laps to go. I was moving forward when one of the two ignition coils failed. Although this ruined a great finish, racing the Midgets was still a blast.

About a year after the Midget race, another opportunity to satisfy my need for

Racing at the Glen in the yellow 5 car. (Photo by Jack Eckert)

speed came when George Duke, owner of Zippo Manufacturing, rented the whole Glen for Zippo Day. This was a day of high-speed fun! George invited some of his employees to come up and take rides in one of the two Grand Am Ford Mustangs that Zippo sponsored. The Grand-Am Series was a great racing series. The cars were basically stock with only minor modifications allowed. Even in their stock form, they were incredibly fast. George also had a couple of his personal cars at the track that he would give rides in. George had taken driving schools and had raced in some Grand-Am races.

Thanks to my friend George, I got a chance to drive a Grand Am Mustang that Zippo sponsored. George told John Kohler (co-owner of the Grand-Am Zippo team with Gary Smith) that I was experienced enough to take the car out. John, however, was not convinced. They don't let just anyone drive these cars. John had Gary take me around the track in the Mustang at almost full speed. The cars have two seats, each complete with the five-point harness. Then Gary and I switched places. He checked out my driving for a few laps to see if I could handle the car. After turning a few laps at a good speed, Gary gave me the OK, and I got to drive on the track by myself. Those cars were really fast and way too much fun. I could lap the 3.4 mile track in two minutes and nineteen seconds. I drove in what I call my comfort zone—where I felt I would not get in trouble and wreck the car, but still going fast enough to get my adrenaline pumping.

⁂

Zippo Day led to another racing opportunity later that year when John and Gary invited me to go to Mosport International Raceway (in Ontario, Canada), which they were renting for a test session. There would be a Grand-Am race there two weeks later, and John wanted to make sure the cars were ready. Mosport, about an hour east of Toronto, was famous for holding the Canadian Grand Prix from 1967 until 1977.

I drove up the night before in the Watkins Glen pace car with friends Scott and Greg Freeman, owners of Freeman Communications. They went up with me to hang out and enjoy the day. The next morning, we arrived at the track at sunrise—just as John and Gary pulled up to the gate with their tractor-trailer car hauler. John got out of the truck and unlocked the gate. No one from the track was there, which seemed very odd to me. At Watkins Glen, when you rent the track, the security, fire truck, wrecker, ambulance, and corner flaggers were all included. Here, we were on our own. As they were unloading the car, a Ferrari pulled up and a young man stepped

I am in the pits at Mosport Speedway in Canada.

out. He was the driver that was teaming up with John and Gary to drive the race in two weeks.

It took until 10 a.m. to get the three cars ready. Shocks and springs had to be changed, brake pads put in, and the cars fueled up. Two of the cars were the ones they were planning to race in two weeks. The third was a backup car, and that was the one I was driving. We got to go out around 10:30. I had never been to Mosport even to watch a race and here I was driving on the track! That first slow lap was awesome. We drove around and around, and by noon I had worked my way up to what I thought was a decent speed—until John or Gary would blow by me on the Back Straight.

At speed in a high-speed, downhill left turn at Mosport speedway in Canada.

At lunchtime I noticed a gray-haired man sitting on pit wall. He had arrived in the bright, red Ferrari with the young driver. I noticed the older man had no right arm. He just sat there on pit wall staring at the track. I walked over to where he was sitting and sat down next to him. "Man, that sure is a nice Ferrari you got here in this morning. Someday I am going to own a Ferrari," I said.

"Yeah, it's a beauty," he said as he looked over his shoulder toward the car. "I have had it a long time. Wish I could drive it. I would love to get it back on the track." It was a six-speed standard shift and with no right arm there was no way he could drive it.

I sat on the wall next to him eating a slice of pepperoni pizza. Then I got an idea. "Hey," I said. "You wanna take it out? No one is out there." Everyone was at lunch.

He nodded his head to his right side as if to say, *Didn't you notice?* "My son drives me around in it now," he said.

"I'll tell you what," I said. "You drive and I'll shift for ya. Take it slow on the clutch. I'm not used to shifting left-handed."

He looked at me. "You aren't serious, are you?"

"Hell yeah I'm serious," I said. "I've never ridden in a Ferrari."

He got up without saying a word and walked over to his son. I could see them talking and his son handed the man the keys. Away we went. The first lap was awkward but the next two laps went fantastic. We did three very fast laps and pulled in. The old man got out of his Ferrari with a smile that wrapped completely around his head. He shook my hand. That made his day—and I got to ride in a Ferrari.

The young Ferrari driver was a pro who was going to drive one of the Zippo-sponsored cars at Mosport in two weeks. During lunch, I asked him to take me out in the Watkins Glen pace car and run a few laps to show me how to negotiate a corner that I was having trouble with. He explained that this corner could not be taken as I was trying to do it because it was double apex corner, and you had to carry speed through it so as to gain speed on the back straight. After he showed me this, it made a huge a difference in retaining my speed going onto the Back Straight. That afternoon, driving the Grand-Am car, I felt like I had a hundred more horsepower. That day I put more than six hundred miles on the Zippo backup car.

I also went through three sets of brake rotors and pads. I was not used to being treated like a king. Whenever I felt the brakes fading, I would pull onto Pit Lane and the pit crew would come out, jack the car up and proceed to change the brakes and tires!

These Grand-Am cars had an onboard computer that recorded data all the time. When we arrived at Mosport, the crew chief took a Mustang out and made about three slow laps. This allowed the onboard computer to draw a map of the track. The map was then uploaded into the computer in each of the race cars. After a run, the data from the race car was then downloaded to the computer in the hauler. The track layout was displayed on screen. It also showed what gear a driver was in at locations on the course, how hard a driver was braking (they had G meters in the car), along with the engine rpm, shock travel, lap times, and top speed. In all, it monitored twenty-one different actions. (Back when I was racing my dirt track car the only monitoring that was done was listening to the sounds from the car, smelling it, or looking at a couple of gauges!) At the end of the day at Mosport, we were all sitting on pit wall having a beer when John announced who had the fastest lap and the top speed down the Back Straight. I got a surprise. Of the four cars there, checking the computer read-outs, John announced that I had the fastest straightaway speed of the day—151.7 mph.

∽

I was always looking for chances to feed my need for speed. I had a great opportunity to race in August 1996, but it unfortunately led to a tremendous letdown. Plans had been made to run a NASCAR Modified race along with the Winston Cup race at Watkins Glen. The Modified Series had never run on a road course, so this race was a new venture not only for the drivers, who are used to going in circles on the short oval tracks, but for the pit crews as well. The suspension setup on those cars would be totally different from what they were used to. A few weeks before the race, the track had me give some of the driver's orientation laps in the pace car to try to show them the basics of racing on a road course, something most of them had never done before. At that point, I had thousands of miles of driving on the Watkins Glen track, mostly giving pace car rides. I knew the track like the back of my hand.

While working with those guys, I suddenly realized that if I had a decent car I'd have a very good chance to win this race. I had to find a car! During the orientation day, I met a Modified driver from Connecticut named Dan Avery, who told me that he had a backup car. A good one. It was exactly the same as the one he drove in the series he raced in. With the race approaching, I hunted him down and asked if he would be interested in renting his backup car for the race. We made a deal that the car could be mine for the race if I could raise the $5,000 sponsorship money. I placed a call to George at Zippo Lighters and I had my sponsor. I was so excited.

A week before the race, the new Zippo decals had arrived at Dan's shop and were placed on the car. Then, one night, Dan called with disastrous news! He had wrecked his primary car at Thompson, in Connecticut, and needed to drive his backup—my ride—at Watkins Glen as he was racing for NASCAR points. I was devastated. I think that would have been my only chance to win a race and stand on the podium at Watkins Glen. (To this day, thinking of it makes me a bit sick.) What might have been?

Working at Watkins Glen International was a great time in my life. The memories of the racing and all the people I worked with and the people I met will be with me forever. But the entire time I worked at the Glen, I also kept up my own sign painting company—working mostly nights and weekends. After five years at the Glen, however, I was nearly burned out working full time there, then going home and working on my customers' signs. While my wife and I were on a rare short vacation to Alexandria Bay on the St. Lawrence River, I lay on a motel bed and realized I had a difficult decision to make. After much thought, weighing the pros and cons, I decided to leave my job at Watkins Glen International and go back to my sign business. I simply could not do both. I was working too many hours.

It was a hard choice as I loved both. When I got back to work that Monday, I went into Mattman's office and I told him my decision. He looked like he was going to cry. I gave two weeks' notice and ended up staying six weeks. They needed me to prepare for the 1997 Bud at the Glen NASCAR race in August and I couldn't leave them hanging. Although it was hard to leave, I parted the best of friends with everyone at the track and at NASCAR. My coworkers even had a party for me, gifts and all. The card they all signed hangs in my shop today. I continued to do sign work for the Glen out of my shop even after I left my track job.

Risking a Grassy Death

I focused on my own sign business until it was time for NASCAR's Bud at the Glen in August 1997. Matt Matusicky (Mattman)—my old general manager—gave me a call from the track. They wanted a grass painting done on the inside of the "Ninety," the 90-degree first turn. The Ninety had a grassy stretch between the asphalt of the track and the guardrail that lined the pit exit. Road courses rarely have much room for grass paintings, and the Glen was no exception. So this one would be small, a forty-foot NASCAR logo. It would also be the first grass painting ever done at Watkins Glen International.

Of course, I agreed to do it. I went to the track and did the layout. Since it was a small logo, I was working alone on this one. *I love it,* I thought to myself as I started spraying the water-based latex we used up here. *Not near as hot as Alabama.* After a while, I stopped painting and shut down the sprayer to take a break. I paused to look around. A cool summer breeze was blowing as it usually did on the hilltop where the racetrack was located. It was so beautiful up at the track, a little over a thousand feet above sea level. Looking to the east, I could see the hills on the far side of the valley disappearing into the distance. Looking north, I could see the south end of Seneca Lake. (Watkins Glen is located on the southern tip of this forty-mile lake, in the heart of the Finger Lakes Region.)

Break over, I got back to work. I started spraying some white paint on the grass. I just wanted to get a first coat of white down today. It was about 3:30 p.m. and the track was nearly deserted. Not a soul there but Maurice Rudy (the track sign installer and maintenance guy), Mattman, and me. Rudy was out on the track checking the guardrail. He was in his four-wheel-drive Ford track truck (oxygen and acetylene tanks in the back, tools and a Speedy Dry Spreader hanging off the tailgate). I was just about finished with the first coat and ready to call it a day when Rudy drove by on the track surface heading toward the Ninety. He blew the horn and waved to me through the passenger window. I looked up and waved back. Rudy had a huge smile on his face as he drove by. The same smile that he always had. While watching Rudy go around the corner, I looked down the track toward Turn 2 and I saw Mattman driving the reverse direction around the track in his official vehicle, a new white Ford

Taurus. He was taking a shortcut on his way out to check on my progress. He had turned left out of Baker (the track access road between Turns 1 and 2) to avoid having to go all the way around the course (although in the right direction) when I was only a hundred yards away. Rudy, still looking back and waving at me, turned at the last instant to see Matt heading (the wrong way) directly at him. Matt was heading west with the later afternoon sun directly in his eyes. Suddenly, he saw Rudy. I stood there not believing what I was seeing!

The scene is frozen in my mind. The Watkins Glen track is 3.4 miles long and has over 1,800 acres. There are three people at the track: me, Rudy, and Matt. There are two vehicles on the whole track surface. *And they hit head-on.* I stood there, spray gun in hand, mouth open, and yelled, "Holy shit!"

Matt had seen Rudy seconds before impact and stomped down on the brakes. He had even tried to slam the Taurus into reverse to back up. Rudy had seen Matt at that same instant and had tried to turn. That big four-wheel drive Ford ran right over the hood of the Taurus and ended up just short of the windshield. Then the truck came off the driver's side hood and bounced on the asphalt.

I ran over to the wreck, where Rudy and Matt were blaming each other, and saw there were no injuries. So I walked a distance away before I started to laugh. I laughed by myself since neither Matt nor Rudy would see the humor. The next day was spent telling the story to John Saunders, the track president. (To this day, I get a smile on my face when I think of the "Big One" at Watkins Glen.)

The next day, I was back at the track to finish the logo. I worked on the painting all day, and I was cleaning white paint out of the gun so I could spray the last color when my friends Greg and Scott Freeman stopped by. Greg and Scott, who owned Freeman Communications in Elmira, New York, were working at the track that day hooking up phone lines. I was talking with them and cleaning the nozzle on the spray gun at the same time when I noticed a piece of grass and a chunk of dried paint that was stuck to the nozzle. Not thinking, I reached up and picked it with my finger. Bad move. Very bad move. You don't think about it, but in one instant, one mistake and you can die. The trigger of the sprayer was built into the handle of the gun. I was holding the handle with my right hand and the thirty-inch extension with the nozzle on the end was pointing straight up. I reached up to the nozzle with my left index finger and pushed on it to scrape the piece of grass off. At the same time, my right hand tightened on the handle to hold it steady—firing the spray gun. Before I could move, a small burst of paint shot into my finger at 1,800 psi.

"God Damn it! Shit!" I hollered as I dropped the gun on the ground and grabbed my hand. The tip of my finger was swollen and hard as a rock from the paint now inside my finger.

"What the hell did you do now?" Greg said. I told him and he didn't hesitate. "Get in the car," he said. "You gotta go to the hospital."

I didn't want to go, but when I felt my rock-hard finger, I didn't argue. It was also starting to *hurt.*

Looking back, I can't believe how lucky I was to have Scott and Greg stop by at the time they did. I really didn't know how life-threatening it was. The local hospital was only about two miles from the track. We got to the emergency room where a nurse took me into a curtained room and told me to sit on the examination table. Before long, the doctor came in and looked at my finger. As I told him what happened, the doctor looked more scared than I was. Now I was uneasy. *This is not good*, I thought to myself. The doctor examined my finger, squeezed and poked at it, and then turned and walked briskly out without saying a word. He went across the hall to a small office where he immediately sat at a small desk and picked up a phone. I was sitting on the emergency room table, feet swinging back and forth, muttering, "Hurry up and fix my finger so I can go. Christ. All you gotta do is poke a hole in it and let the paint out. I've got to finish a painting." I watched the doctor talk into the phone, glancing up at me a couple of times—which made me nervous. He came back with a concerned look. "Do you have a car?" he asked.

I thought, *how the hell do you think I got here? By helicopter?* "Greg has one," I said. "He's in the waiting room."

We went out to the waiting room and the doctor asked Greg, "Do you know how to get to St. Joseph's Hospital in Elmira?"

"I live in Elmira," Greg said. "I know where it is." (Elmira is about twenty-two miles south of Watkins Glen.) The next sentence from the doctor scared the crap out of me. "Great," he said. "Get him there as quickly as you can. I can't do anything here and there is no time to get an ambulance. Go to the Emergency Entrance. They will be waiting for you. *Get moving.*"

We hurried out to the car, where Greg jumped in the driver's seat. Scott got in the back leaving me the passenger seat. I got in and looked over at Greg. I had never seen him with a more serious look on his face. We didn't say a word as we sped out of the parking lot.

The twenty-two-mile trip to Elmira was over two-lane roads, but we were lucky the traffic was light. Greg didn't waste any time and in twenty minutes we were approaching the hospital. Not bad.

As we rode along, I couldn't understand why the doctor at Schuyler didn't want to mess with my finger. "Why couldn't he just fix it? Why do we have to go through this mess? It's not that bad." I said to Greg. "All you have to do is cut it and let the pressure out." That was my diagnosis of the situation.

"Hey," Greg said, "You don't want to take any chances."

As we approached St. Joseph's Hospital, Scott said from the back seat, "We made it and you're still breathin'." He added a halfhearted laugh.

"You ass," I said. Greg turned the last corner quickly. "Christ," I said, "slow down or we will all need a hospital." When we pulled into the Emergency Entrance, I was surprised to see a gurney on large rubber wheels complete with IV bottles hanging from the chrome pole attached to the side of it. Standing beside it were two men and a woman, all wearing nurse's badges.

"What the hell is that? Is that for me?"

We got out of the car and the woman asked, "Are you Anthony?"

My mouth opened but before I could say anything, Greg answered for me. "That's him," he said, while pointing at me like I was the criminal in a police lineup.

In a split second, I was on my back on the gurney with an IV jammed in my arm, and I was being rolled into the emergency room. The hospital staff asked all kinds of questions as we rolled down the hall. I felt like I was in a movie. The lights in the ceiling zipped past and everyone was talking as they pushed me down the hall. The nurses were almost running. We paused for a second as they spun the gurney 90 degrees to the right, and *bang*—I was shoved through a set of silver metal doors like I was a side of beef coming out of a slaughter house. They didn't even open the damned doors. The gurney did it.

They told me to slide off the gurney and onto another table. The big white operating light was right above me. Now I was scared. I was sitting up when a male nurse put his hand on my chest and pushed me back onto the bed. My head sunk into the pillow. Someone took my left arm and taped it, with what I thought was duct tape, to a stainless steel tray-like attachment on the side of the bed.

"Do you feel OK? The doctor is on the way," the nurse said. "She should be here soon."

"I felt good before I got here," I said. "Now I'm not so sure. You said the doctor is a she?"

"Yes, she is the best microsurgeon around," the nurse said as the door burst open. I looked down between my multicolored paint-covered sneakers and there was a beautiful woman. Her red hair was down to her shoulder blades, and she was wearing a red and white sundress. She was about forty years old, wearing round, granny type sunglasses. *No, this can't be. This isn't the doctor. Did I die and go to heaven?*

She was talking to the nurses when she turned toward me. "Are you ready?" she said.

"I guess so," was all I could say. "Whatever you're going to do, I don't think I'll even need Novocain." That brought a smirk on her face.

"You're right," she said. I smiled. "We don't have time for the Novocain to work," she continued. "I'm going to give you a nerve block, minus the Novocain. And believe me, sir. It *is* going to hurt like hell."

"Oh, that's nice," I said, trying to pull my arm from the restraints.

I lay there with my left arm taped tightly to a metal tray off to the side of the bed. I looked over trying to see what the doctor was doing. She picked up a needle from another shiny stainless steel tray full of all kinds of tools. It was not one of the small needles that you get your normal shots with. This was the Mother of All Needles. The tube was chrome and about an inch in diameter. At the top were attached two rings for her fingers. The plunger had a chrome ring for her thumb. I wondered if she was actually a veterinarian as this thing should only be used on large animals such as horses. Surely it was not designed to be used on humans.

The doctor held up a bottle with some clear liquid in it and turned it upside down with the rubber stopper facing down. The needle was about two inches long. It slid into the rubber end of the bottle and she drew the clear liquid into the chrome tube.

"Knock me out," I said.

"No time," she replied. She spun around, holding the needle straight up then squirting a stream of the liquid into the air. "I'm really sorry," she said. "This is really going to hurt. I have to give you a nerve block without the Novocain."

"Go ahead, I can take it," I said. As the words came out I wondered where the hell that comment came from. My left arm was secured to a stainless table. My left hand was facing up and my fingers were held down with tape.

"I have to give you three shots in your finger," she said.

"That's not so bad."

"No, you don't understand," she said. "I have to put the needle into the large knuckle and get it down in the socket. I'm going to have to move it around in between the knuckle, and I have to do it in three places."

I didn't even have time to say, "*What*?" before the needle went into my hand. Holy shit! The pain was unreal. I tried to inhale so I could scream, but I couldn't. It hurt so bad I couldn't breathe. The nurse wiped the sweat from my head and constantly asked, "Are you OK?"

I couldn't answer. I felt like an hour went by, but it was only about half a minute before the doctor stopped. "There," she said. I finally let out a breath. "Holy shit," came out as well. I didn't like the doctor anymore.

The doctor turned to one of the nurses who handed over a rather large, strange-looking piece of headgear resembling a set of military night vision goggles. The doctor looked at me. "In a minute," she said, "when the block kicks in, I can start working. This is a magnifying device I have on. I'm going to cut your finger down to the first knuckle and clean out each of the veins."

I could feel her working on my finger. I didn't hurt but I could feel a dull, pushing sensation. "How far will you have to cut?" I asked.

She didn't answer for a minute. She sat on a stool next to the bed, bent over working. "As far as we have to," she said. "If the paint is in a large vein, we may have to go up your arm until we find the end of the contamination. This is why we had to hurry. This is classified as an 'injected wound injury.' *The* most dangerous. Time is the factor. It also depends on what was injected and where in your body you did it. If the material gets into the bloodstream and gets to your heart, it's all over."

She stopped talking and it was all quiet. They must have given me a shot at some point because I suddenly felt a calm sensation come over me. Aaah. I lay there counting the tiles on the ceiling. (My wife can tell you I have an obsession for counting things.)

The doctor's voice finally broke the silence. "You are a lucky man," she said. "I got it all. The paint was thick and the veins that were contaminated in your finger were small. The nurse will stitch you up and after you lie here for an hour you can go." I thanked her. They stitched me up and I lay there for about twenty minutes before I got up and talked my way out of that torture chamber. I was put in a wheelchair and wheeled out to the waiting room, where I found my friends Scott and Greg. They had waited not knowing what was going on.

"Hey. You OK?" they said when they saw me. "You were in there a couple of hours."

"Yeah," I said, "let's get the hell outta here."

They got up, slapped me on the back, and we walked out into the sun. "Hell, it doesn't hurt at all," I said, holding my heavily bandaged hand up in front of me. *What's all the fuss?* I thought to myself. The needle was the worst, but my hand didn't hurt at all. (Of course I didn't realize the nerve block hadn't worn off yet.)

On the way home, we talked about how everything worked out to my benefit. I shot myself doing something stupid—cleaning the nozzle with my finger—but I only hit small veins in my finger *and* Scott and Greg happened to be there to give me a ride *and* one of the best microsurgeons in the area was available to operate. Ahhhh, I didn't want to think about what might have been. Almost getting killed by a paint gun! God, what a day.

That night, I sat in my easy chair looking at my injured hand. My whole hand was wrapped in white bandages halfway to my elbow while my index finger pointed straight out with the help of a white plastic splint.

"Boy. This is really starting to hurt," I said to my wife, Harriett. My hand was *throbbing*. I lay back in the chair trying to find a comfortable position. I tried resting my elbow on the armrest with my hand pointing straight up in the air. That made it feel better. I decided I'd sleep in the chair that night and closed my eyes to relax. I was glad to have survived my day of painting the grass.

At that instant, *boom*, a thought jumped into my brain and slammed into the inside of my skull. The damned grass painting wasn't done yet! "I've got to finish it tomorrow." I hollered out loud. My wife heard me mumbling obscenities and came out of the bedroom.

"What's wrong? What are you hollering about? Does it hurt?"

"I just remembered. The damned painting isn't done!"

"Look at you," she said. "Don't worry about it. You can't go to work like that. Look at how you are whining like a little kid about the pain now. You'll have to find somebody to finish it. They can't expect you to go to work."

"Damn."

As Harriett walked back to the bedroom, I thought to myself, *I'll feel better tomorrow. I'll figure something out.* I couldn't sleep thinking about this new problem. I reached for the telephone and called Mattman at home. He wanted to know how I was feeling and what happened. I told him the story and asked if anyone took care of the gun.

"We cleaned it the best we could. It's all set," Mattman said.

"I have an idea," I said. "I will come up tomorrow and finish the painting, but I will need help. I only have one hand. I need someone to be my slave."

"Everyone is busy," Mattman said, "so I guess I will have to help you."

I should have been encouraged, but have you ever had—and ignored—a premonition that things weren't going to go as planned? As soon as my good friend Mattman promised to help, I had the feeling of impending disaster.

 # Not Again!

When I woke up the next morning, I was still sitting upright in my easy chair. I was stiff and sore all over. I tried to raise my head, but the pain in my neck made me groan out loud. I looked down at my bandaged left hand, thinking to myself that at least my hand didn't hurt too badly anymore. I couldn't feel my heart beating in my finger like it was last night. But that was just because every joint in my body hurt more than my hand from sleeping in the chair. I finally gathered enough strength to stand up and stretch. My neck was the worst casualty of the night in the chair. On the bright side, I was already dressed when I woke up.

"This doesn't feel so bad," I told my wife while holding my bandaged hand out looking at it. "I think I'm going to call Matt and tell him I'm coming up to finish the grass right after lunch." Harriett didn't answer. She didn't have to. I could read her mind. "Hey," I said, defending myself from her thoughts. "I don't have a choice. I can't leave the painting half finished. I have to go." I called Matt. He told me he would have the maintenance guys bring the spray equipment out to the painting after lunch.

My finger started to throb like hell as I pulled into Gate 2 at about 1:30 p.m. I should have listened to my wife. How many times have I said that! I was greeted by Katie Messinger, who headed up the gate personnel. (She was the best gate person in the world!) "I didn't expect to see you back so soon," she said. She asked about my finger since the story of yesterday's excitement had made the rounds at the track.

"It feels OK," I said with a smile, "but my main concern is that I have to work with Mattman today." We both laughed, and I drove in. Matt and I are so much alike it is scary. Both of us are, you might say, a little crazy. We have the same sort of sense of humor and love sitting back and just watching people and then commenting on them. Matt has had a lung operation and so have I (the same side). One day in the office, Matt was showing someone a strange-looking stretch mark on the skin on the life line on his right hand. Everyone looking at said how strange it was and that they have never seen such a thing before. I walked over and looked at it. I said, "That's not such a big deal." I opened my right hand and I had the exact same mark. Matt, along with the others, couldn't believe it. I knew that working with Mattman was going to be an experience.

I drove down to the Ninety, where I found my spray outfit, the paint, and my almost-finished grass painting. I parked my truck about a hundred feet away to make sure it stayed out of the range of any overspray. I walked over while sipping my Pepsi and inspected the painting. It was just as I had left it. I got on my radio and called Mattman to let him know I was out there. About ten minutes later, I heard a car approaching. I looked up toward the start/finish line to see an older gray car coming down the track. *Who the hell is on the track?* I was ready to get on the radio and call Security but then I saw it was Mattman. He pulled off the track and onto the grass right next to the logo and shut the car off.

"*Hey,*" I said, "move that thing over there so I don't get any paint on it." I pointed toward my truck.

He looked over at my truck and then looked back at his car. "I'm not walking that far!" he said. He got out of the car and shut the door.

"What are you driving?"

"It's Betsy's car." Betsy was his wife. "Remember?" he said, nodding toward the part of the track where the head-on collision occurred. "Seven thousand bucks' in damage and I'm still trying to explain it to John." (John was the president of the track.) "How's your finger doing?" he said, looking at my hand. "Man, from what Scott and Greg said, you were damned lucky."

"It's OK. It hurts a lot, but I'm still here. It was a good thing Scott and Greg were here."

"Yeah, you were lucky. OK, let's get this done," he said. "I've got important stuff to do."

I started giving Matt instructions on what I needed him to do. I soon realized that this was going to be much harder than I thought. Things that I would do by instinct, I now had to explain to someone with no knowledge of what we were doing. It wasn't Matt's fault. I was happy he was helping, but it was frustrating when simple tasks that I would do without even thinking about now took thought and time. When I fired up the sprayer, I quickly learned how hard it was to work with one hand. Normally while painting, I would simply grab the hose with my left hand and whip it around to get into position so the hose was behind me when I started spraying. Now I had to have Matt move the hose. This took a lot of time. I had to wait a second when he moved the hose because pulling on the hose could pull my gun sideways. I kept worrying I'd accidently paint a three-foot streak out from one of the letters.

It was 6 p.m. before we finally finished the painting. Now it was time to clean the gun.

"Hey," I said to Matt, who was standing there looking like he wanted to be anywhere else.

"What?"

"Get over here and help me get this gun cleaned so we can have a cold one," I said. Matt had a cooler with some nice cold Budweiser waiting for us. That got him moving. I also realized that today I was the boss of my boss! That felt good. *I could get used to this.* "Get that pail of water over here and I'll clean this thing." I had an old white five-gallon pail of nasty-colored water that I'd used to clean the previous colors from the gun. Matt struggled carrying the plastic pail over. As he set it down, he spilled some of the water on his shoe.

"Shit," he said. *Lucky he didn't spill it all,* I thought to myself.

I had to talk Matt through the process of how to set the sprayer to clean the lines. "Turn that blue knob on the nozzle to the left," I said, explaining how to set the sprayer up so it would pull in water and clear out the paint. When we were ready, I shoved the nozzle into the bucket of dirty water—and then I double-checked to see if my fingers were all safe before I pulled the trigger. I laughed as I said to Matt, "Never put your finger in front of that goddamn nozzle."

I took a deep breath and pulled the trigger—only to hear a loud *bang* and see a huge white flash. I dropped the gun into the bucket of water and grabbed my face. "What the hell?" I screamed. "Shut it off. *Shut it off!*"

The hose for some reason had blown off the handle of the gun, spraying paint everywhere. I could taste the paint in my mouth. I wiped my eye with my paint-covered hand so I could see, at the same time spitting white paint onto the ground, I looked around for Matt.

"Matt, get me some water. Hurry! I've got to get this paint out of my mouth." Still bent over, spitting, I looked up at Matt. He stood by with a look of horror on his face. "Hurry," I hollered louder. *He was right near me when I pulled the trigger, so why doesn't he have any paint on him?*

He turned and ran toward the car. I looked up again and did a double take. Matt really was near me when I pulled the trigger. As he ran to the car, I saw the back of his windbreaker and the ass of his pants were covered with white paint. "Oh my God," I screamed—half laughing but still bent over with both hands on my knees, spitting paint.

"There's no clean water," Matt said when he returned. "Here's a can of Bud."

I grabbed it and Mattman pulled the tab. With a sticky, paint-covered hand, I took a big gulp of Budweiser to wash my mouth out. As soon as that beer hit the latex paint, it turned into foam and boiled up in my mouth and shot out of my nose.

"Holy shit," I heard Matt say. I was gagging, coughing and spitting up a mixture of white latex paint and Budweiser beer while trying very hard not to swallow. Matt got on the radio and called for the track fire crew, who were onsite setting up their camp for the upcoming race. "Emergency, emergency! I have an emergency in the Ninety. I need water . . . fast."

The track fire trucks responded with sirens blaring, thinking there was some sort of fire.

When they arrived, they saw me standing in the grass with a white face. My front side was covered in white and I was holding my bandaged hand in the air trying to protect it from the paint. They got the hose out and filled a pail. They offered me some rags and I started to clean up. When I could finally talk again, I told Matt to turn around. Everyone broke out in laughter. He looked over his shoulder. "Holy Christ," he said. "How did I get this on me?"

One thing for sure, instead of holding the fort and helping me in time of need,

Mattman standing in front of the painting in the Ninety.

Matt was running away from me at the time of the explosion. Man, did we have a good laugh.

After I cleaned up and we finally got the spray gun cleaned, we all sat on the back of the fire truck and drank some nice cold Budweiser.

"What the hell happened to your hand?" asked Meatball, one of the rescue guys.

"You won't believe it." I told them the story starting with Matt and Rudy's head-on collision, explaining how I shot my finger full of paint and ended up in surgery, and finishing with how Mattman and I got covered in paint. We sat on the back of that fire truck on the Front Straight of Watkins Glen International telling stories and laughing at each other.

My first Budweiser tasted so good. "I'll have another," I said. My good friend Mattman reached over and handed me a fresh one. The sun was starting to dip behind the mountains off to the west. Despite my sore hand, I enjoyed that day, drinking and laughing with friends. (I'm also glad I have those memories of Meatball, who passed away not that long ago.)

 Back to School

The Skip Barber Competition Driving School is one of the most famous racing schools in the world, and I wanted to try it from the moment I first heard of it. They run open-wheeled rear engine cars that reach 130 mph in their sessions at Watkins Glen International. The school was 80 percent track time and 20 percent classes, and it drew some big names: Michael Andretti and Jeff Gordon, just to name a couple. But it was expensive. It cost about $3,000. Worse, if you damaged or totaled a car, you had to pay for it.

One Sunday in September, 1997, I pulled into the pit area behind the pit wall around 4:30 p.m. A three-day school session was winding up, and I knew my friends Mike Schuler, president of Zippo Manufacturing, and George Duke, owner of Zippo, had been enrolled. They'd be coming off the track, and I wanted to see them before they headed back to their headquarters in Bradford, Pennsylvania. I walked over to them. They still had their fire suits on and were walking toward pit wall. All I could ever do was dream of attending this racing school. My love for speed was, and still is, an addiction. Sadly, the cost of the school was out of my reach. As I got closer, I saw Mike and George sitting on pit wall and cracking open a Coors Light. I said, "How was it, guys?"

They could not contain their excitement. All I heard was, "Unreal, fabulous, I learned more than I can tell you!" And then George said, "Tony, with your racing background, you have to get out there. You gotta do it."

I looked at George and said, "Are you nuts? I would love it, George, but it's too expensive. I don't have that kind of money. Besides, I'm here for the beer. Which car is the cooler in?" George and Mike always have a full cooler.

Mike pointed over his shoulder. "In back of the Suburban. Grab two more for us."

I was sitting on pit wall having another cold Coors Light while George and Mike changed out of their fire suits. I waited about twenty minutes. *Where the hell are they?* Finally, on my second beer, I looked toward the Press Tower and saw them approaching. We sat on pit wall, and I listened to them rattle off tales from the three-day school. After about a half hour, it was time for them to head back to Bradford. George suddenly turned to me and said, "What are you doing tomorrow?"

"I'm working. What do you think I'm doing? I have to work."

George walked off to the right, motioning with his can of Coors to come with him. We stood together by pit wall. "Be up here at 7 a.m. tomorrow," he said. "I signed you up for the school. I know how bad you want to do it."

I was stunned. "No, George," I said. "You can't do that. I can't pay you back. I can't do it, man." I reluctantly added, "Thanks anyway, George."

I'll never forget what happened next. George put his hand on my shoulder and said, "Tony. Blaze [his cousin] and I were born very fortunate people. I know how you feel about racing, and I know you are dying to get out there."

"George, I can't. It's too much money," I said again.

"There is a way to repay me," he replied. "You have my home phone number. Wednesday night, when you are done, call me and tell me how much fun you had." With that, he wrote something on a piece of paper. I looked at it. It's a line of numbers.

"What's this?"

"It's my credit card number. If you get in trouble, give them this." Meaning *if you wrecked a car.*

I shook George's hand, and as he pulled away in his white Porsche convertible, I honestly had to hold back tears. I could not believe what had just happened.

That night I had a hard time falling asleep. I was turning laps in my head imagining what it would be like haulin' ass down that back straight at 130 mph in an open-wheeled rear-engine race car. I was soon going to find out.

Thank you George. I'll never forget it.

༺༻

I woke up at 5 a.m. too excited to sleep any more. Imagine something you've thought about for years but you knew you could never afford. Then suddenly, out of the blue, you get the chance. All I could think of was what the next three days would bring. Harriett just smiled at me. She knew I was acting like a kid, but she didn't saying anything.

After I took a shower, I put on a pair of red underwear. I haven't mentioned it before, but whenever I raced, I always wore red underwear. I figured it took balls to get into a race car and race to win. Red underwear—red being an aggressive color—would help. Some nights at the racetrack it worked. Some nights it didn't. On second thought, I guess it worked all the time. Even when I crashed, you could say I did so aggressively. Well, today I had them on and I was ready for the unknown.

I arrived at the track early and went straight to Pit Lane. Twenty-four cars were lined up in rows of two along the side of pit wall. It was dead quiet, with only one man there, a mechanic from the Skip Barber School who was kneeling by the front of one of the cars. I walked over to him and said, "Mornin', how's it going?"

Without looking up, he said, "Christ. You're here early. There won't be anyone here for an hour."

"Yeah, I know," I said. "I live just down the road. It doesn't take me long to get here. I didn't want to be late." I was kind of early. Suddenly I thought, *Don't be talking to this guy. It might distract him and he will forget to tighten a nut on the steering and it may be on the car I'll be driving.* I turned and walked away.

I was so excited that I'd left my coffee in the truck. I walked over to the backside of the pits where my truck was parked and got my semi-warm coffee. I walked back to the pit wall where the cars were, sat up on top of pit wall, and took a sip (or more like a gulp) of the coffee before it got totally cold. It was so early the concession stand wasn't open yet so I couldn't get another one. It was nice and cool and there wasn't a sound. There is something about being at a racetrack when it is empty. I looked around toward Turn 1 (the Ninety) where the track dropped down and goes out of sight. In the dead calm morning, I could see the ghosts of Sports Cars, Can-Am, Indy, and Formula 1 cars speeding down the Front Straight and into that corner. Over the past thirty years, the best drivers in the world had been on this track at one time or another. Today, with no haze, I looked north and could see Seneca Lake off in the distance between two rolling hills. I looked back to the track and pictured driving down the Front Straight at 120 mph, picking the brake marker 200, stepping hard on the brakes and at the same time double clutching (heel and toe) and shifting down to third gear to 70 mph then turning in from the far left side of the track, hitting the perfect apex point on the inside of the corner, accelerating through the corner, drifting out, just running up on the outside curb and down the straight. I snapped out of it. . . . *I can't wait.* I turned to my left and there, not three feet from me, sat the open-wheeled rear engine race cars for the school. I immediately got goose bumps.

"Christ, I can't believe this is happening." Then I thought of all the laps I'd run on this track. At that time, Bill Green, the track historian, told me it would have been around 3,000 laps or almost 10,000 miles. He claims that I had more laps at Watkins Glen than anybody else. I couldn't wait to get out there. I know every bump and curve in that track.

"Come on, you guys, where are you?" I said out loud.

Finally two red Dodge Neons and two red Dodge vans with white Skip Barber decals on the doors pulled up to the front of the NASCAR garage, where the office and classrooms are. I walked over to the man that was setting up a table. He was arranging the stacks of paperwork in separate piles. He looked up at me. "Man, you're here early."

"Yeah, I live just down the road. Guess I can't wait to get started," I said.

He gave a slight laugh and said, "You must be George's man."

"I guess I am."

He smiled and quietly said, "That's George." Apparently George has done this for many others who couldn't afford it. *Yup, that's George,* I thought. My thoughts were interrupted by the man saying, "You might as well get started and fill out these papers."

On one form was a space for a credit card number. I dug in my pocket for the piece of paper with George's credit card number. A shot of adrenaline went through me as it wasn't in my pocket. I took everything out of my left front pocket and laid it on the table. I carry everything, money, cards, and change in my left pocket. It wasn't there. I frantically stuck my hand in my right pocket where I never carry anything except my car keys. There it was. I remembered—I'd put it there so I would know where it was when I needed it. I thought as I wrote down the number on the form, *If I have to use this, it will mean I had a really bad day.*

Everyone showed up at once. It was hectic. We were separated into groups based on our racing experience. I was in the Competition group. There were only about five of us. One young kid, about twenty, had come from Sweden. He even had a handler with him to take care of all of his affairs. He was hard to understand. I can't remember his name, but he had to take the school in order to get his license to race in the United States.

It was class time. There were about twenty-five in the school. Class lasted about four hours on that first day. After lunch we went to the cars. *Ahhh Yesss!!* The cars have four-cylinder Dodge engines. Unlike Indy Cars, they don't have wings—you're supposed to drive the car, not let the car drive you. They are capable of 160 mph, but at Watkins Glen, 138 mph is the max you can get on the Back Straight before you hit the Inner Loop (a series of right, left, left, and right turns designed to slow the cars down after J.D. McDuffie was killed in a NASCAR race here). NASCAR calls it the inner loop. I call it what it is—a *chicane*.

After we got suited up, we were each assigned the car we'd be driving for the three days. (That way, if one was damaged, they know who did it.) My car was blue and had the number 72. I was standing by it looking at this really neat race car thinking . . . 72. Let's see, 7 plus 2 is 9; 7 minus 2 is 5. No, that's not going anywhere. Let's see, 7 plus 2 is 9, 7 minus 2 is 5, 5 plus 9 is 14 which makes 5. I'm standing there staring at the number realizing it doesn't mean shit.

Two crewmen came over and it was time to get fitted to the car. The steering wheel was off so I could easily slide in. The wheel and pedals were all adjustable, and at the beginning the front bodywork was off so they can adjust everything to fit you. In a race car you have to be comfortable. Once the cars were set up for everyone, we went over instructions on what to do on the track. There were spotters (Skip Barber instructors) all over the track at critical points to observe every driver. You make one lap at a set rpm (your first day the speeds are not very fast) and then you stop at the start/finish line. There, an instructor would get on his radio and if there were any issues with any of the spotters, he would hold the radio to your helmet and the instructor would tell you the problem. You then went another lap and stopped at the same spot for more instruction. There was very intense scrutiny. On the third day you are turned loose. This is what I was waiting for.

I will give you a lap of the Watkins Glen Circuit as seen from the seat of a Skip Barber car:

Crossing the start/finish line, you speed down the front straight at about 115 to 120 mph. It's slightly downhill into a 90-degree right turn (it is called the "90"). You double clutch (no synchros in the transmission), heel and toe (that means you brake with your right heel while you rev the engine with the ball of your right foot) to get to the proper rpm so you can downshift. At the same time you are doing the braking

Buckling in for a session on the track. (Photo by Jack Eckert)

maneuver you are pushing the clutch with your left foot. At the same time all of this is going on you are shifting with your right hand and steering with your left. As you can see, one hell of a lot is going on when you are braking and downshifting. You want to keep the revs up on a downshift so you don't slide the rear tires when you gear down. This is critical. Not enough revs when gearing down could lock up the rear tires and you will spin out before you know what happened.

You go into the Ninety at 80 mph. Halfway through, in third gear, you accelerate to full throttle. As you pass Seagraves Road (a road that crosses the track) you shift to fourth. It is full throttle around Turn 2 as you fly up through the Esses flat out. The Esses are a series of uphill corners. It is a blind corner at the top and the guardrails are very close to the track. This is a very dangerous section of track. No room for errors here. One mistake and you are in the guardrail.

Near the top of the hill you shift to fifth gear. After a long, sweeping right-hander, you are headed down the Back Straight. The engine is about six inches from your back and the sound of it at full revs is awesome. The vibration even disrupts your vision a little. You hit 138 mph at the end of the straight and at the 200-foot brake marker you step very hard on the brakes. (Brake markers are usually 2'×4' signs alongside the track leading up to a corner. The first one you come to is 600. They go down from there—500, 400, 300, 200, 100. They tell you how far, in feet, it is to the corner. When cars are in front of you, it's hard to see the corner, so the markers give you a braking point.)

Two downshifts to third and you shoot through the chicane, tires squealing. Halfway through the loop (a series of right, left, left, right corners) you accelerate, and when you exit the chicane you are in what I call old Turn 5. It is a sweeping, high-speed downhill corner. Geoff Bodine and Tommy Kendall have had spectacular crashes in this stretch, and J.D. McDuffie, a NASCAR driver, was killed there.

Shift to fourth as you go downhill into the Boot (we were running the Long Course and the one-mile extension is called the Boot because from the air that's what it looks like). Hard on the brakes and downshift to third as you enter the laces of the Boot. This is a nasty, downhill, slightly off-camber left-hander. I rate it as the second toughest corner on the track. You shift to fourth for a second and right back to third for the toe of the Boot. Some even go to second gear here. Around the toe is a very tight 180-degree uphill corner. Coming out of the corner you are back to full throttle and you shift to fourth. Back to third at Turn 8, the heel of the boot. This is a 90-degree right-hander. Accelerate to fourth up a slight hill and back to third for Turn 9. This is the hardest corner. It is a sweeping left-hander that comes out onto the NASCAR track. The apex is hidden from view as you approach this corner. Hitting the apex here is a must. Miss it and you won't miss the guardrail, which is just a few feet from the track.

Now it's down a shoot (a short straightaway between the two turns) to Turn 10, a fast left-hander. Third gear through Turn 10 and coming out, shift to fourth and down another short straight to Turn 11 (the last turn). Hold fourth through Turn 11. That's a little risky because if you get in trouble, fourth won't give you the power to pull yourself out of a slide. But fourth gear is faster through Turn 11. Full throttle out of Turn 11 and down the Front Straight and across the finish line.

The whole 3.4 miles takes about two minutes. As you can see, you have about fifteen gear changes per lap. You are busy all the way around—but I loved it. If not for the kid from Sweden, I would have had the fastest lap. He was *fast*. I kept him in

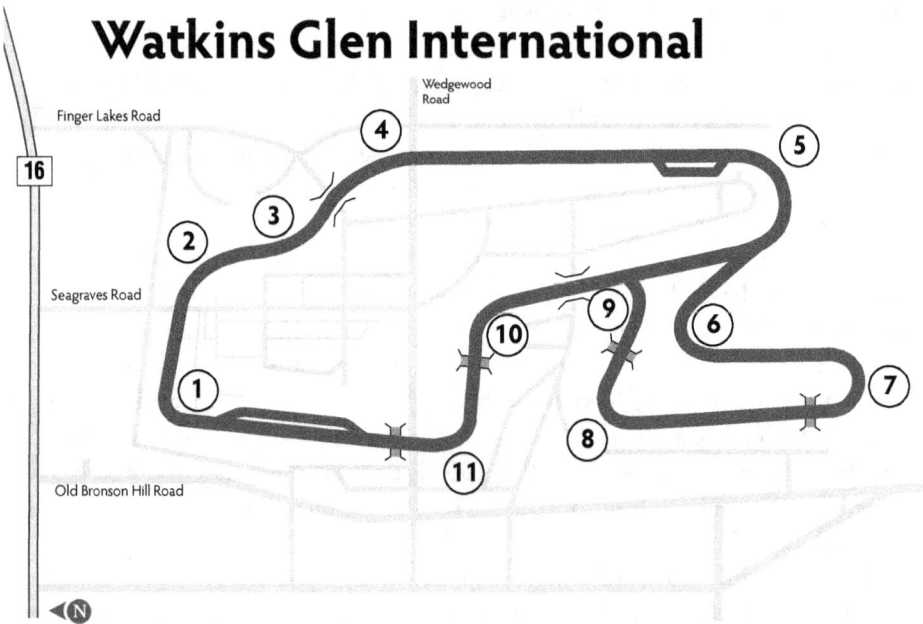

Map of Watkins Glen International showing the corners.

sight for four laps, then he was gone.

Wednesday night, after the school was over, I called George Duke. I couldn't contain my excitement. George is a true friend. I'd learned more about how to go fast in the past three days than I did in my twelve years of racing. It was awesome. I wish I'd had the opportunity to do this school before I went into racing. I might have taken up road racing instead of the oval track racing that I did.

On the track, coming out of the Boot (Turn 9), I passed a 12'×36' Zippo billboard that I'd painted. I had my friend the photographer, Jack Eckert, take a picture of me, at speed, in front of the billboard. I framed it and sent it to George as a thank-you.

If you're thinking of getting into racing, take this school. It will give you a head start that you will not believe.

Coming through Turn 9. Thank you, George! (Photo by Jack Eckert)

 # Back With Friends

Talladega turned into a regular gig, painting the grass twice a year for almost five years. Then one day I walked over to the wall phone mounted near my 1923 Mills slot machine. (That's my own one-armed bandit, a nickel slot machine that was a gift from my wife, Harriett.) I grabbed the dirty, banged-up Radio Shack phone off the wall and said, "Vickio Signs." A woman's voice came on the line. "Hello. I'm Mary from Britten Banners. I am looking for Tony Vickio. Is he in?"

I said, "It's me." *Nobody else here except my dog Brandy,* I was thinking. You would be surprised by the number of people who think I have a huge shop with lots of employees, when in fact I work alone.

She said, "I'm calling from Britten Banners in Michigan. We have won the bid to do the grass painting at Talladega Superspeedway." I thought, *I know, rub it in.* Then she said, "We have never done this type of work before." *Oh boy,* I was thinking. *Sure, they' have never done one before. Now they probably underbid it to get the job, plus she wants me to tell her over the phone how to do it. I should just hang up.* She continued, "We called the racetrack [Talladega] and they gave me your number. We were wondering if you would be interested in going to Talladega to run the job for us?" I perked right up. "We will pay your expenses and your rate and we will supply the men, materials, templates, everything. You just oversee the job and make sure it is done right."

"Could you repeat that," I said. I was going to say yes right away, but one word sent up a red flag. Templates. When the word *templates* came up, it meant I was not running the job from the start. I didn't have control over the whole project. I almost said no right then. "Let me think about it. Could you call me back tomorrow?" I asked her.

Later that same day, Paul Britten, the Britten Banners president, called me to talk over the details. I told him about the size of these paintings and that templates were not the best way to do them. He insisted on his guys making cardboard templates for all the logos except the DieHard 500. He said he figured it out and his men could make cardboard patterns in his huge warehouse and when they got there, they could just lay them out and put them together like a puzzle and spray them. Like I said, grass painting was getting more popular. Things had changed since my first simple

Talladega logo. For this job, there would be one large 70'×320' DieHard 500 logo and six smaller 70'×70' paintings for Winn Dixie 500, TORO, NASCAR, Winston, and a telephone company that I can't remember. The six smaller paintings would all be done with cardboard templates. The DieHard 500 was too big for their patterns. That was why they needed me.

As we talked, I was hesitant. Something wasn't right. I wasn't in the kind of control I wanted. They were controlling me with templates. I pondered it. I thought, *It is their job, not mine, and I couldn't talk him out of templates.* Still, I couldn't resist going to Talladega.

Why not? I said, "OK, I'll do it." I didn't really want to go alone, so I asked Paul if I could take a helper.

"That would be fine," he said.

I thought about who could get a week off and go with me to this fabulous speedway and have an unbelievable time to boot. That October night I was sitting in Maria's Tavern having a nice cold bottle of Budweiser—my favorite—talking to the bartender (who later became the owner), Bobby Carson. Bob was the guy that cured me of drinking and driving.

❧

You see, the first night I met Bobby, back in 1992, we hit it off real well. I sat there shooting the bull well after everyone with a brain had left. At closing time, I went out and got into my Chevy street rod. (I miss that car. It was a 1951 Chevy Sedan Delivery that I chopped off the front of the frame and welded on the front of a 1970 Camaro frame. Now it had power steering and power disc brakes. Then I put a Camaro rear end under it. The body still looked like stock, but it had a beautiful custom green paint job. Denny Snow of Snow's Custom Auto in Montour Falls did the paint work. It even had the old sun visor on it. My friends Mike Wells and Ken Coates, who owned Welco Custom Interiors in Ithaca, did the interior in a saddle color. It was beautiful. Another friend, Rich Seely who built race car engines, did the motor: a 350 Chevy, with high-performance heads, cam, Elderbrock intake, and a Holley four-barrel. That car would run.)

Anyway, I left the bar at about 1:30 a.m. and not a thousand feet from my house I was doing 85 mph. I had a Bob Seger tape playing full blast. As I rounded a corner, a deer crossed the road in front of my Aunt Lega's house. The deer was already more than halfway across the road, but in my condition, I overreacted. I lost control and my right rear tire dropped off the newly paved road and turned the car sideways. Just then, the right rear tire hit the culvert pipe of my neighbor's driveway. My car barrel-rolled three times and hit a large pine tree roof first. From my racing experiences, I have never driven or ridden in any car, especially a street car, without wearing a seatbelt. A '51 Chevy didn't have seat belts, but when I built the car I put them in. If I hadn't, my story would have ended right here. I was less than eight hundred feet from my home by the time I stopped—I'd barrel-rolled two hundred feet up the ditch before I hit the pine tree.

In the pitch dark I walked home. I couldn't find my keys, so I banged on the front door. Harriett almost fainted when she came to open the door for me. Even though the seat belt had held the bottom part of me in the car, the top part of me was flopping outside the door like a rag doll as the car rolled over and over three or four times. My T-shirt was ripped down my whole left side. I had a fractured jawbone (from a fire extinguisher that hit me when it broke loose while the car was rolling), my left collarbone was broken, and I had large brush burns on my left shoulder. Because I put a seat belt in, I survived. That's how I met Bob Carson. After this encounter, I was cured of drinking and driving! I was almost killed, and I lost a beautiful car, and I was in pain for weeks! It's a hard thing to do, but if you have been drinking, give your keys to a friend. Just make sure he isn't as drunk as you are!

෴

The night after the call from Britten Banners, I was drinking a Budweiser at Maria's Tavern. I was telling Bobby of my latest pending adventure at Talladega. I said, "Why don't you go with me, man? You've never been to a race—and this is one of the best. And it's free." He talked it over with his wife. She said he could use a vacation.

Of course, this would be no vacation. I was talking to Mattman about the upcoming trip and his eyes lit up. *Oh-oh. This may not be good*, I thought. "Hey! I have a plan," he said. "Why don't you drive the pace car down? It'd be good advertisement for us down there at Talladega since our race is a little while after theirs."

He didn't have to say it twice. The car was a brand new Red Ford Mustang convertible. It was all lettered up (I'd done the lettering). On the trunk was a yellow caution light bar. We packed the car with clothes for a week and once again, I was headed south. This time with my good friend Bob Carson.

We pulled into the motel in Anniston, Alabama, at three o'clock on a Sunday afternoon. The weather was beautiful. After throwing the suitcases into the room, we went back to the car and got the cooler full of Budweiser (I had planned ahead when I remembered this was a "dry" county on Sundays). I carried the cooler to our room and placed it outside, under the large window. We found two of those molded white plastic chairs and set them along the brick wall on each side of the cooler. There. We were now sitting out front of the room in those white plastic chairs enjoying the bright Alabama sun. We must have looked like two motel bums, slouched down in our chairs, legs stretched out straight with our sneakers sticking out to the sidewalk and tipped at forty-five-degree angles. Each of our left arms were hanging down over the plastic arm of the chair, knuckles dragging on the ground, and each of our right hands was wrapped around a bottle of cold Bud. I had the bottle sitting on my stomach, as it was too heavy to hold. As the sun shone on us, I said in a low, contented voice, "Man. This is the life."

Bobby just said, "Mmm."

Little did we know this was the calm before the storm. I laid my empty bottle of Bud gently down beside the cooler, opened the lid, fished around in the half-melted ice, and found my prize. I twisted the top off another cold one and tossed the bottle cap back into the cooler. We were waiting for the crew from Michigan, who were supposed to be here by now. About fifteen minutes later, the bird chirps were interrupted by the sound of a vehicle. My first thought was, *Please don't let this be them. I am way too comfortable to be disturbed right now.*

Bobby and I both turned our heads to the right at the same time. Around the corner of the motel came an old brown Ford pickup truck. It had a tin cap on the back with a black roof. The flip-up side windows were half open. The truck was pretty ordinary except that the front wheels were almost off the ground while the rear bumper had only about an inch of clearance. The rear door of the cap was open and the tailgate was down. They couldn't shut it because sticking three feet out of the back of the box was a solid stack of brown cardboard, packed in tight from the floor of the box to the roof of the cap. That had to be the templates. That truck was almost doing a wheelie just trying to move. I couldn't believe it.

"They drove all the way from Michigan like that? That musta been damn near fifteen hours in that beater. Holy shit." I said to Bobby.

The truck turned in next to the pace car and jerked to a stop. Bobby and I struggled to get up from our chairs. Two guys and a girl climbed out of the cab, and we all introduced ourselves. First there was Ben. He was there, but you could tell he didn't want to be. He was about twenty-four years old, average build, short blond hair and a hunched-over sleepy look. His handshake was weak. To me, that's not a good sign. Missy was next. She was about twenty-one, perky, and all excited to be on the mission. Missy Hromada was attractive, and she was ready to go to work; this was a new adventure for her, and—adding to her excitement—she loved racing. Then there was Charlie. As soon as his foot hit the pavement, I liked him. Charlie was really comical. I mean, he was so funny he could be a standup comic. He had fuzzy reddish hair and he was hyper. We hit it off immediately. He was a blast.

"Anyone want a beer?" I asked. Charlie was the only one that wanted one. We looked around and found Charlie another white plastic chair. Now there were three of us slouched in front of the large window in front of our room. I dug through the ice and pulled a Bud out of the cooler and handed it to Charlie.

"It's all we have," I said.

"It's cold and it's a beer. I'll drink it." Charlie said. Ben and Missy were tired from the trip and decided to go to their rooms.

Breaking the silence, I said, "How was the trip? Looks like it could have been a chore driving that truck down here."

Charlie said, "Man, you can't image it. My eyes are stuck wide open from the terror of driving that goddamned thing down from Michigan."

We laughed and then I said, "Hey, Charlie. When is the rest of your crew going to show up? Weren't they right behind you?" Charlie didn't answer right away. Between slugs from the bottle of Bud, he leaned his head over and looked at me with two tired, bloodshot eyes. His hair was all fuzzed out like an Afro, and his eyes were glazed from driving. He had a little beer running down his chin through his two-day growth of beard and dripping onto his T-shirt. A really wise-ass smirk came on his face.

With a twisted smile he said, "Help? You're lookin' at it, man." My eyes got big.

I hollered out loud, "Are you crazy?" Leaning hard back into the chair and looking straight ahead, Charlie said in a low, slow voice, "This is it, man. I'm not lying to you. To be honest, you're lucky ya got us." Charlie had a real sorry look on his face, like it was his fault. He took another sip of Bud, slouched back in his chair and quietly said again, "Yup. This is it, man. You're lookin' at it."

We had only three days to do the six logos. You cannot start them too early because the grass will grow too much and the logos will look fuzzy by Sunday. Timing was critical. So was the weather. We'd been lucky so far. I looked at him and with my best mean look, hiding my panic, I said, "You better get on the damned phone right now and get more help down here by Wednesday. This isn't enough help. I'm telling you right now, we ain't gonna make it. You don't know how much work this is. I mean, call right now."

"I'll call Paul [the owner of Britten Banners], but there is no one else up there. We've been working nonstop on these friggin' patterns for a friggin' month," he said. I looked over at Bobby—who had returned to join us for a beer—he just shrugged his shoulders and with that "Don't look at me" smirk and took another slug of beer.

Here I go again. Can't anything go smoothly? I'm down here in Alabama, surrounded by people that the only grass they have worked on was when they mowed their lawn and we have six logos to paint. I sat, or should I say slouched, back into my white plastic chair and with a look of total disgust I glanced over to the brown Ford pickup sitting in the parking lot. The rear of the truck was facing us. The tailgate was down, the cap door was open, and in between was tightly packed layer on layer of cardboard patterns. From floor to ceiling. I just stared at the sight. I didn't even know what those patterns were. *Will they work? Oh God. This is not good.* I could feel the rest of my black hair turning gray as I sat there.

The beautiful Alabama hills were in the background and the sun was just starting to dip behind them. The birds were chirping and flying from tree to tree looking for a place to bed down. I started to put my hand in the cooler when I snapped my head and took a second look at the truck. I took a double take. With the sun in my eyes I squinted to see better. I could swear, with all that cardboard in the back, just sitting there, the front wheels of that Ford had come off the ground. I didn't even say, "Oh, God." I just reached down with my right hand, opened the cooler and dug through the ice, and grabbed the first thing I felt. It was another cold Budweiser. I screwed the top off and tossed it back into the cooler. Just before I put the Bud to my lips, I did say out loud—and in a voice that Bobby and Charlie could hear: "Oh, God."

 Getting Started

Our motel was between the speedway and the town of Talladega. It was the one closest to the track (at twelve miles), while the next nearest were in Oxford or Anniston, almost twice as far away. It was old and small and painted a strange dull blue with black shutters, but it did have a dining room and a bar. Kathy the bartender got to know us well, as we were in there every night after coming from the track. We had nowhere else to go. By the time we made it to the bar each night, the buffet in the dining room was over, but Kathy kept two big Styrofoam containers of food for Bobby and me behind the bar. When we came in, she would set the huge platters of food in front of us. "They we going to throw it away anyway," she would say. There never was a charge. The food was great. I think she simply felt sorry for us.

At the track, everyone talked to us. We were the foreigners with the accent. There was a guy who drove a large blue Ford tractor with a huge mower behind it. They called it a Bat Wing mower. In the center was an eight-foot-wide mower section that housed three blades. On each side was another eight-foot section with hydraulic rams that could lift these sections up at a 90-degree angle when not in use. It looked like the fold-up wings on the fighter planes they had on WWII aircraft carriers. The guy rode that tractor all day, mowing. The track is on about 1,400 acres and it is mostly all grass. They have about three large mowers that run every day. It takes about four days to mow the entire facility. By then the grass where they started mowing has grown back and they would start over. It was a nonstop operation.

The tractor driver was about six-foot-eight and probably weighed an eighth of a ton or more. If you cut your hand off at the wrist and put a huge fingernail on the stub of your arm, you'd be looking at something the size of his thumb. If you shook hands with him, you couldn't use your hand for an hour. But for all his size, he was a nice guy—and it turned out his wife was Kathy the bartender at our motel.

For a sign gig, I usually arrived at a track two weeks before the race. Basically, except for the mowers and a few maintenance men, my crew and I were alone at that point. This time, we were here only one week before the race, and there was a big difference in the amount of activity going on. Monday morning, Bobby and I went out to the Tri-Oval to see how it looked prior to painting the logos. Driving around this huge facility was fun. When no one is around, you can drive eighty on those big old runways that the track is built on. No one bothers you. We flew out to the Tri-Oval, pulled the car out onto the track and stopped in front of the grass near the center of the Tri-Oval. We got out of the car and looked at the grass. It looked like crap. The Southeast was in the middle of a drought and the grass was an ugly dark brown with a few small patches of green mixed in. I got on the radio and called Mike McWilliams, the new general manager. (Larry Johnson had retired.) Mike was about forty-five years old, five-foot-eight, and heavyset. He had a neatly trimmed white beard and short salt-and-pepper hair. He was a slow talker but had the respect of everyone. When he wanted something done, he only said it once.

Whenever I talked to Mike on the phone, I always asked, "Mike, how are you doing?" I always know the answer I am going to hear: "I'm workin' like a dawg." It was his favorite saying.

I called Mike on the radio to ask if he could have the grass mowed on Tuesday. It was quite high. "Where are you?" he asked.

"Out on the grass."

"I'll send a groundskeeper out to see you."

I looked at Bobby. "*Groundskeeper?*"

Sure enough in about five minutes, the groundskeeper arrived driving a green John Deere Gator. [A Gator is a small all-terrain utility vehicle used by track maintenance crews] He had short hair and sharp features and he was all muscle. He did not look friendly.

He walked out to us and said, "What's the problem?"

"No problem. I just was wondering when you could cut the grass for me? We are going to paint the logos." I didn't want to cut it this early, but I was afraid of the time it was going to take to do the painting, especially with the crew I had and only four days to work. "I would like it cut down to one inch," I told him.

He didn't like that because the grass was already looking bad from the drought. He finally said, "OK. But right after we mow it, I want to spray for fire ants and then we will paint it green."

I gave him a puzzled look and said, "You're going to paint six acres of grass green?"

He said, "Yup. Can't have it look like this on TV." When the fans come to a racetrack, most of them never think about what went on before they arrived. Behind-the-scenes work was so interesting.

About an hour later we were back at the Tri-Oval. In the distance, a large John Deere riding mower was coming across the west section with the groundskeeper sitting upright in the seat and riding it. He had his feet on two pedals and his hands on two upright levers to steer the thing. The engine was in the rear with the mower deck right under the driver. He revved the engine up and he was off. We went back to the shop, as it would take a few hours for the mowing, and found Charlie, Missy, and Peter trying to sort out the patterns. As I watched them fool with all that cardboard, I wished I had gotten the artwork for these logos before arriving so I could have done a grid drawing.

A grid drawing was the normal way to do large paintings although not as accurate. For a grid drawing, quarter-inch graph paper was used. As an example, imagine a capital A is drawn six inches tall on the graft paper. On the grass, string is used to create horizontal and vertical lines—not at quarter-inch as on the paper, but twelve inches apart. The letter A on the paper is twenty-four of those quarter-inch spaces, four for each of its six inches. On the grass, twenty-four one-foot squares are counted giving a twenty-four foot letter A.

I went over to where they were getting the patterns ready and walked up to Charlie. "Charlie," I said. "Did you get hold of your office? Is any help coming down? We need help."

"Paul is coming down," he said. "He will be here until we are done." One more man wasn't really enough, but thankfully I had brought Bobby with me. Otherwise, I would be in serious trouble. Bobby became my right-hand man, literally.

Back out on the Tri-Oval grass, the mowing was done and the spraying of fire ants was under way. Three guys with small tanks strapped to their backs, similar to the ones firemen use on brush fires, were walking all over the Tri-Oval grass looking for fire ant hills. They pumping poison on every anthill they found. More waiting. I was getting nervous. "Come on." I whispered to myself. I walked up to the groundskeeper and asked, "How much longer?"

He didn't answer, just walked away. Another hour went by.

I heard a tractor coming. Looking over toward the pit gate, I saw another John Deere with a big plastic tank mounted on the back. A young girl was driving it. Walking alongside the tractor were an older woman and a man (her parents, I later found out), each holding a coil of hose with a spray gun attached to the end, a lot like the

Painting the Tri-Oval grass green before we apply the logos.

ones we were going to use to paint the grass. As it got closer, we could see a greenish mixture that was sloshing around in the plastic tank. The girl at the wheel twisted around in the driver's seat and pulled a lever. The engine revved up and the adults started spraying the burned grass a healthy green. I couldn't believe what I was watching. No paint masks, nothing. Painting the Tri-Oval at Talladega Superspeedway green. *Wow.* When they were finally finished, they were green too. When you watch a NASCAR race on TV, look at the Tri-Oval grass. It will be a nice dark green. Then look as the cars go around the track at the other grass. You might see a big difference.

I kept having these mood swings about this job. I'd feel good about things for one minute, and then I would swing to severe depression. I thought to myself, *I opened my big mouth and I said I would do it. . . . Now I have to do it. Stop thinking of all this crap and get this job started.*

It is hard to describe the pressure of this type of work unless you have experienced it. When you take on a job like this, no one wanted to hear an excuse. There are none. Not even the weather. You may have to work all night. When the race is televised live on Sunday afternoon, the grass better have lettering on it. Period. The sponsors pay the freight.

Charlie and the gang started unloading and sorting the patterns on the freshly painted grass at 7:30 a.m. Piles and piles of cardboard were stacked on the grass. "Do you have a drawing of the placement of the logos on the grass?" I asked Charlie.

"We have it," he said.

I felt better. *Something was going right.* Next came the slow job of measuring the six acres of grass to place the six logos. You do a lot of walking. I looked up as the sound of a car driving up Pit Lane broke the silence. It pulled to a stop on Pit Lane and a man got out. He was in his late thirties and dressed in Haggar slacks. He wore a golf shirt and sunglasses.

"It's Paul," Charlie hollered.

"Great," I muttered. "One more man."

We shook hands as he thanked me for being there. He looked all around like he was ready to work. I hesitantly asked Charlie, "Did you order the paint?"

He gave me a "Why didn't I think of that?" look. My heart sank. Then he said, "Sure. Isn't it here yet?"

Oh, wow, I thought. *Things are looking better.* I got on my radio and called the Maintenance Office. "Has anyone seen any paint for the grass yet?" I asked.

Someone came back on the radio and said, "Yup, we unloaded the tractor trailer yesterday and put it on two of our trailers. Do you want it out there?"

No is what I felt like saying. "Bring the trailers out here and park them on Pit Lane," I said. Paul said he ordered what the drawing called for, plus some extra, just in case. Damn good thing he did.

Sitting in the first race car that I built. My brother Chip is behind me. Too bad that car didn't survive its inaugural run at Watkins Glen (LAP 1).

I moved my drag racing from country roads to King's Dragway because it was safer and I could win trophies (LAP 2). Safer until I met someone coming the other way while drag racing my friend's Corvette, Acid Indigestion (above).

LAP 10

I found a new passion in 1972 after watching a painter pin-stripe a friend's Corvette. My first painting paycheck came from the crew of a famous Formula 1 driver (LAP 7).

My first painting kit which I still use today.

LAP 4

I built my first Late Model dirt racer out of a 1965 Chevelle (LAP 4). It took a lot of work, but it was worth it to feel that pure adrenaline rush during my first race at Rolling Wheels Raceway (LAP 5). I would later win my first race driving that car.

I used a 1969 Chevelle to build my second car (LAP 8), but later changed the number and color to improve my luck. My third and last Late Modified was based on a 1970 Camaro.

My son Mark and my 1965 Chevelle.

1965 Chevelle

1969 Chevelle

1969 Chevelle (repainted)

LAP 8

1970 Camaro

After years of dirt track racing, I got my first chance to race on asphalt (LAP 12) thanks to Dale Marion and his NASCAR Modified (above). Even though I would live through a serious crash (LAP 14), it was painting, not racing, that was almost the death of me (LAP 21)

Images from a racing life (*clockwise from below*): Our lovely Granddaughter Rachel (*left*) with Betty & Mark; Jeff Gordon getting to meet my mother (r) and my Aunt Henrietta (l); My daughter Beth at Watkins Glen victory circle; With my father at Weedsport; Weedsport win with my son Mark and first wife Kathy; Hanging with race car driver Sarah Fisher; My wife Harriett getting a Terry Labonte autograph at Talladega;

LAP 18

I have a healthy respect for heights (meaning I am afraid of them). This can be an occupational hazard for a professional sign painter who sometmies has to deal with really high signs (LAP 18, LAP 53).

LAP 53

LAP 20

LAP 20

I loved to go fast! I have a need for speed and will take every opportunity to get in a race car. This included a Can-Am 3/4 Midget at Watkins Glen (LAP 20), a Grand-Am car at Mosport International Speedway in Canada (LAP 20), and, thanks to my friend George Duke from Zippo for sponsoring me, the Skip Barber Competition Driving School race car (LAP 23).

Talladega Super Speedway (LAP 18)

Talladega Super Speedway (LAP 26)

Talladega Super Speedway (LAP 27)

Talladega Super Speedway (LAP 50)

I had no idea what I was doing when Talladega Super Speedway first asked me to paint on the grass (LAP 16). With some perseverance and determination, I figured out the trick (LAP 17) and got pretty good at it over the years. It helped to have a crazy fun group of painters working with me (LAP 26).

Nazareth Speedway (LAP 56)

Painting the walls at Talladega Super Speedway is not difficult. The difficult part was climbing five stories up the 34-degree high banks to get there (LAP 35)! After all that hard work, we could only sit back and hope the early races didn't have too many wrecks that would require us to repaint the logos (LAP 40). Thankfully, we only got attacked by drunken bombers once (LAP 41).

I thought I had a great solution for working on the steep banks at Talladega — but it didn't end well! (LAP 42)

Painting huge signs on asphalt requires two coats of white paint for the background. This has a wonderful benefit. We were ten times cooler working on the white surface than standing or kneeling on the black asphalt (LAP 44).

When I bought my 1965 Fuel Injected Corvette Sting Ray (LAP 3) from Jim's used cars, I never would have guessed I would still be driving it over 40 years later (LAP 57)!

Here We Go... Painting

Charlie and the Michigan gang now had the cardboard templates scattered all over the grass. They resembled a giant jigsaw puzzle. I couldn't imagine the man-hours they must have put into these templates. I chuckled to myself, thinking, *Hope the wind doesn't decide to blow.* The Winn Dixie logo was in the center toward the track surface. It was fairly large. Looking at the drawing, it showed a white background with red and blue letters. Charlie had already started laying out the templates for Winn Dixie when I walked over and told him, "Hey, Charlie. Pick those templates up. I think it would be best to paint the white rectangle background first. It will make the red and blue stand out better if they are painted on a white background. OK?"

"You're the boss, man," he said, grinning.

"Let's get a gun set up and get a couple of pails of white paint and we can spray the rectangle background today," I said. The Winn Dixie painting measured about 70'×75'. We used string for the guidelines for the background, and then I gathered everyone around to give them lessons on the sprayer. Paul jumped right in, clean clothes and all. Before I could explain something, he was already trying to do it. He was down here and he was ready to work. I was nervous about any of these guys spraying as they'd never done it. If you make a mistake on grass, you couldn't erase it! And besides, I was hoping he wouldn't spray his finger.

For some strange reason, Charlie was immediately at war with the sprayer unit. If he touched it, he got paint on himself. The airless sprayer was brand new, but was either alive or possessed. While watching Charlie, I thought of Raymond. I missed Raymond, the guy that helped me when I first came down here. He had moved on. He would have earned his keep just hauling the paint buckets out to the sprayer on this job, as we had two hundred five-gallon pails. The projected amount of paint required for this job was eight hundred gallons. We had a thousand gallons sitting on the trailers on Pit Lane.

After an hour or so and thirty-five gallons of white paint, the rectangle was done. By the time we lay out and painted that rectangle it was too late to start a new painting. We packed up and headed to the motel. I wanted to be at the track by sunrise as the next day was going to be a long one; I wanted to paint all five small logos. Bobby and I headed for the bar at the motel. Kathy, our bartender, had our supper behind the bar. Time to relax.

The bartender's huge husband was at his usual seat at the end of the bar right by the fake wood panel wall where the light was dim. He was sitting on the bar stool in a smoke cloud, smoking nonstop as always. Off to his right was a square clear glass ashtray full of freshly smoked butts, some of them still smoking. A mug of draught beer sat between him and the computerized poker game he was playing. The glare from the screen gave a bluish tint to the smoke that was slowly twirling in the air in front of his face. He sat there, taking a sip of beer and a puff on the cigarette hanging from his lips. He would play that poker machine all night. I turned back to my beer and slowly took another sip. We ate like pigs out of our Styrofoam containers right there at the bar. After a few more beers we headed for the room. It was going to be a long day tomorrow.

⁕

The alarm went off at 5:30 a.m. I reached out to hit the button. My eyes suddenly opened wide and I remembered where I was. "Damn," I hollered out loud.

Bobby said in a low, sleepy voice, "What?"

"It's time to get up."

"Yeah," he said.

"Let's get moving. It's going to be a long, hard day today," I said.

"Christ, it's still dark."

"I know. It'll be light by the time we get there," I said.

As we were driving in, I wondered if the Michigan crew was up. I'd told Charlie what time to be at the track the night before. I should have called him. *Now we will have to wait until they show up*, I thought. I should have called just to make sure. Today was an important day.

We drove right by the back entrance to the track on purpose and headed for the deli. I turned left into the parking area and stopped. Inside, I got my coffee and apple pie and walked up to the counter. "Hi, Honey," the cashier said. *She's still here*, I thought. The other girls were already starting to cook lunch. You could smell it. *Mmmmm, smells good.* I looked at the stuff they were cooking. I realized I didn't know what it was, but it smelled good. I said "Hi" to the cooks, who were now staring at me as I walked out the door.

By the time we pulled into the track, the Michigan crew was right behind us. I couldn't believe it. *Good*, I thought. *This is good.* We pulled up to the thousand gallons of paint on Pit Lane and stopped. Where do we start?

We gathered in a group meeting at the paint trailer. Everyone had coffee in hand and they were waiting for me to give the orders. I saw it on everyone's face. They were excited and anxious to get started as they had never done this before. I decided it was best to split into groups of two. I wanted Bobby with me to get the spray guns set up. Charlie, Missy, Paul, and Ben would start laying out the Winn Dixie patterns on the white rectangle we sprayed yesterday. Some of those logos took more than thirty pieces. It was just like a huge jigsaw puzzle. Working on six acres of grass, it took time just to walk from one logo to another. As they put the Winn Dixie patterns down, I thought of the hours, or days, it must have taken to cut these cardboard patterns. I could see where it would make it fairly easy to paint the logos, but the time it must have taken to produce them didn't seem like the way to go. Doing a grid would have taken much less time and effort. Anyway, as we were stuck with this method, we would work hard to get it done.

We had two new spray units that didn't blow smoke rings and were fairly quiet—Mike McWilliams gets things done at Talladega. Bobby fired up one of the guns and put a new five-gallon pail of red paint on the sprayer, and in five minutes we were spraying. This time we were shooting turf paint (a water-based latex). It goes on better, with better coverage, and it doesn't hurt the grass. Spraying paint, once the patterns were down, was brainless and fast. I would spray the edges and the guy on the other gun would fill in. Today Charlie was on the other gun.

After Raymond spilled the paint on the grass the first time I painted a logo, I learned to set up a paint zone. So this trip I'd covered a big area with a blue tarp, and that was where the sprayer and the opened pails of paint had to sit. It's a good thing I did this as Charlie's war with the sprayer was heating up. Honestly. It was right out of Stephen King's book *Christine,* where the car had a life of its own and was out to kill people. This spray unit was alive. I swear, at times I actually caught Charlie and the sprayer staring each other down.

The first shot in the war between Charlie and the spray gun had been fired when Charlie put that first pail of white paint in the sprayer. He was getting ready to prime the gun, that is, to bleed the air out of the hose. (There's a special setting for that, and you point the spray nozzle into the empty pail and hold the trigger down until it's done.) Somehow, the nozzle got turned from Prime to Spray and the pressure was set to High. The instant the air stopped coming out of the hose, the paint hit the bottom of the empty five-gallon pail at about 200 mph and 1,500 pounds pressure. Naturally, the pure white latex paint bounced right back at Charlie. Instantly, the front side of Charlie turned white. Paint covered Charlie. Good thing it was latex. He glared at me with this "What the hell did I do?" look. I looked over to him and I swear I saw him lick his lips to taste the paint that covered his face.

You can think what you want, but I know the nozzle was on Prime, because I put it there. This machine was alive. For the next two days, I actually found myself nodding to the sprayer as I walked by as if to say, "Hi, how are you today." I also tried not to make any eye contact with it. Humbly, I would think, *You are a nice sprayer, please don't hurt me.* I don't know what he did or said to it, but it was clear to me that the sprayer was out to get Charlie. After the first few hours of spraying, it seemed clear that Charlie was doomed. The sprayer hose came loose once, right by where Charlie was holding it, spraying him again. He was covered with a different color of paint every night.

We settled into a routine. Paint all day, go to the bar, drink a Bud, eat out of Styrofoam containers, and hit the sack. Wake up by the alarm at 5:30 a.m. and then hit the deli, "Hi, Honey," apple pie and grass. On Wednesday, we were back at the

Charlie made this painting of us at Talladega. It shows how smooth the job went! From left to right: Ben, Missy, me, Paul, Bobby and Charlie.

track again. Once again the weather cooperated perfectly. It was a beautiful, sunny morning. The grid layout for the DieHard 500 went pretty smoothly. The flags were all in and we had the string between the flags. I was feeling good. With the big logo laid out, I decided to finish up all the other logos. That would leave Thursday to paint the DieHard 500 logo. Thursday was the last day we could really work, because NASCAR practice and the qualifying runs would take up most of Friday. We were not using boards for the lines; it was all freehand. We finished painting the small logos. I was smiling as it was going really well. I tried to keep it out of my head, but one thought kept haunting me. *It is going* too *good.*

We took a break at noon and headed to the deli. It was hot, and I needed some Gatorade. You could tell it was getting near race weekend. The tables were gone, as was the aisle shelving. Cases of beer were stacked from floor to ceiling. Thousands of them, filling the entire space where the tables and aisles used to be—cases of beer stacked seven feet high with their own aisles between them. They were unloading the cases from a tractor trailer as we walked in. The closer to race weekend, the more things changed. The people were so busy in the deli, the counter gal didn't even call me "Honey". I walked away with my Gatorade. My head was sadly tipped down. Get a few new guys around and all of a sudden no more "Honey?" Oh well.

Back on the grass: I needed something from the shop. I can't remember what it was, but I do remember Bobby saying, "I'll go get it." Either he'd seen enough grass or he just wanted another chance to drive the Mustang. I think it was the Mustang.

Away he went, tires smoking. The crew from Michigan watched in awe. I didn't want to look. We were so used to no one being here we usually ran on the old airport runways around 70 or 80 mph. Well, a few days before the race, they open the jail. Yeah, they have a permanent jailhouse right at the track. For the weekend, this fat guy parks his motor home right across the road from the jail and sets out a sign. It reads "Bail Bonds Here." No kidding. State police and sheriff's deputies come in and take over security at the track. The track grounds run under state law from about four days before the race.

Bobby got the part I needed and was on his way back, doing about 70 mph down one of the old concrete runways. The Mustang had a strobe caution bar light mounted on the trunk with yellow lights. The top was down and Bobby was haulin' ass back to the grass. As he was driving across the old runway the lights flashing in the mirror caught his attention. *Where the hell is the switch for the damned caution lights? Must've hit the caution light switch with my knee*, he thought to himself. He didn't slow down a bit. He just kept going while leaning over a little fumbling for the switch to shut the caution lights off. He was flying down the runway. Suddenly there was the sound of a siren. He sat upright and thought, *I don't have a siren.* His eyes widened when he looked in the mirror. The Alabama State Police were in hot pursuit of Bobby Carson.

Being color blind, Bobby didn't know his own yellow light from the State Police blue light. He slowed down and pulled to a stop on the old runway. The trooper who followed him was not happy. He stepped out of the car, adjusted his hat and sunglasses and slowly walked up to Bobby. There was Bobby, hands 10 and 2 on the wheel, sitting there with a slight hunch, top down and waiting for the ass chewin'. The trooper—right out central typecasting—was about six-foot-two, 230 pounds, and towering over Bobby who slouched even lower in the seat. "What the hell you doin' boy? You can't drive like that around here. Who the hell do you think you are? When you come down here you gotta obey the rules."

All Bobby sat in the official Watkins Glen pace car with a huge Alabama State Trooper towering over him and chewing him out. All he could think of was, *What were the Watkins Glen managers going to say?*

"Yes sir, no sir," was all Bobby could say to the trooper. To his surprise, the trooper let him go with a warning. Must have been because of the pace car, I would guess.

When Bobby got back, his eyes were wide and he was all jittery. The weird part was how slow he was driving as he drove up. "What the hell is the matter with you?" I said. "You look pale. You sick?"

He said, "You ain't gonna believe what the hell just happened." We all gathered around and with his arms waving and sticking his stomach out to mimic the trooper, he told the story. We all had a good laugh. It was too late to start the DieHard 500 logo, so we called it a day. At least, all the smaller logos were painted. One more to go.

Back to our routine: bar, Styrofoam, bed, Thursday morning alarm, deli, "Honey" lady, and back to the grass. On Thursday, it was time to paint the DieHard 500 logo. Then we would be done! We all gathered on Pit Lane. I couldn't hold back the excitement as today we would finish up–nothing left to do but watch the practice and qualifying runs and hope nobody spun into the grass. All that worrying and everything looked like it was going to turn out OK. We loaded the guns with paint and I started outlining the forty-foot letters. I was getting really good at spraying lines. We moved right along. Of course, instead of white, Charlie was now black and red. The battle went on. Bobby and I were spraying right along when the groundskeeper came onto the grass with his John Deere Gator. He pulled up to me and got off of the Gator and slowly walked over to me. "What do you need?" I said.

He said, "Mike just got a call from the NBC cameraman on top of the tower." He nodded over his right shoulder and across the track to the thirteen-story tower above the main grandstand. "He said that you better go look at the zeroes in the 500. Something doesn't look right."

I said, "I haven't painted the zeroes yet." I whipped around and looked to the right toward the far end of the logo. Down toward the start/finish, about three hundred feet away, I saw one of the Michigan Gang trying to paint a zero on his own. Up until now, things were going good. Now we have a major crisis. The feeling I had earlier had come true. Everything was going *too good*.

Major Problem

"*Stop! Stop!*" I yelled as I took off at a dead run, leaving the groundskeeper standing there talking to himself. I ran down the bottom side of the DieHard 500 logo with Bobby right on my heels. When I got to the zero section, I frantically looked at the black paint on the ground. Paul, Charlie, and Ben were standing there, looking at me. They said in unison, "What?"

"The cameraman says there's something wrong with the zero in the 500."

"It looks OK to me," said Ben.

From where I was standing it looked like the arc between four of the marker flags was too sharp, but I couldn't really tell by looking at it at from ground level. Looking at a thirty-foot letter next to your feet, you can't get the right perspective. It was hard to see a mistake. When doing these large signs you have to totally rely on your layout. The cameraman saw something bad enough to make him call it in, and that was enough for me. He had a good view as he was thirteen stories high, up on the roof of the control tower. I'd have to go up and look for myself. *Oh man, I don't want to do this. I don't want to, but I have to see what's wrong and the only way was to go up.*

"Nobody move until I say so," I hollered out. As I was walking away I glanced over my right shoulder—and to my surprise, no one had moved. I smiled a little as I noticed I actually sounded like the boss. Bobby and I got in the Mustang—*I was a lot more careful and experienced and had learned not to paint my shoes!*—and drove down Pit Lane the opposite direction the race cars go. We passed through the mass of gates and the tunnel then turned left and drove around the outside of Turn 4. Soon we were driving down the back of the main grandstand. We spotted the elevator right behind the control tower, and parked the Mustang right by it. Bobby and I got out of the Mustang and walked toward the elevator. When you looked at the back of the grandstand and craned your neck to see the top of the tower, it gave you a whole new perspective of how big this place really was. It was *huge*.

Yes, there was an elevator that went up to the control tower. At least, they called it an elevator. I immediately said to Bobby, frantically shaking my head back and forth, "I'm walking up. I'm not gettin' in that goddamned coffin. *No way.*"

This was not the typical inside-a-building elevator. It was what a construction company would use on the outside of something they were building. It had four angle-iron columns in a six-foot square hooked to the outside of the back of the grandstand, and inside the square was a cage made of heavy angle iron with walls lined with aluminum diamond plate. The ceiling was made of a heavy wire mesh; the floor was metal grating—and *yes*, I could see through it. Part of it looked like it was purchased from a bankruptcy auction and the other half looked homemade. The thing had been painted red, but it was so sun-faded that it was a sort of light pink.

Since I was petrified of heights, riding it would be a real challenge. But thirteen stories was thirteen stories, way over a thousand stair steps. The seriousness of the situation called for extreme measures, and no matter what I said, going up that elevator was one of them. I reluctantly got in this thing they called an elevator with Bobby. *Don't look down*, I told myself.

A maintenance guy standing outside pulled the sliding door shut. Clang. It sounded like a jail cell shutting. He turned around and reached toward a gray box that was attached to a wooden light pole. He stuck his thumb out and pushed the green button. Nothing. *Oh no*. He wiggled the junction box and there was a sudden jerk. With a hideous clanging and the screeching of dry metal rubbing on dry metal, we broke the surly bonds of earth and in a spit second lunged upward. The elevator clanged, banged, jerked from side to side, and continued to make the metal-on-metal grinding sounds that were as pleasant as fingernails scraping on a chalkboard.

Halfway up I could actually picture the cable—one strand at a time—fraying and snapping! We were going to get almost to the top and drop like a stone, I could feel it. I looked up and about forty feet above us I could imagine the cable wrapping around the large pulley at the top of the tower. I had another horrid thought: we'd get to the top without stopping, just wrapping right around the pulley and coming back down upside down. I put my head down and with my fingers sticking through the wire mesh door, I shut my eyes tight. Finally we stopped. It was quiet. Bobby lifted the latch and slid the metal mesh gate open and I stepped (more like jumped) out of the thing onto the platform of the control tower. I wanted to get out before the elevator plummeted from beneath our feet. It was going to plummet. I could feel it.

I quickly looked around but I didn't even see the track, only the mountains in the distance. Now I was really scared. We walked over to the outside of the race control booths where a metal ladder clung to the wall. It went up to the roof. We were now thirteen stories in the air and I was not doing so hot. We still had to go up on the roof. I slowly climbed the ladder, hand over hand. Yes, my knuckles were white. I got to the roof and cautiously stepped off the ladder. *Oh well. At least there's a small railing around the edge,* I thought.

"Oh God!! This is high," I said to no one.

I looked over to the camera platform and the cameraman was walking around the edge of the roof like he was two feet off the ground instead of thirteen stories. "You the painter?" he asked.

I just nodded. I couldn't talk yet.

"I thought I'd better call someone before you got too far along," he said.

I finally got enough courage to say, "Thanks."

Another thing I noticed at this height was that my voice sounded squeaky. *Maybe just my imagination, but at these heights, the air is a lot thinner*, I thought.

"Come on out here, you can see it better. I'm no painter—but if I can see it anyone can."

I thought to myself, *Are you nuts? I'm not movin'.*

"You gotta come out here to see it," he said again, waving us closer. I cautiously walked over to the cameraman. The little railing around the roof didn't do a damned thing for me. I realized my arms were stretched out from my sides and I was walking like I was on a tightrope. Slowly, still hunched down a little, I reached out with my left hand and grabbed onto the camera mounting leg and looked down. Oh my God! I could feel myself being sucked over the side of the tower by some unseen force that was whispering to me, "Fall. Faaaalllllll"!

"Are you OK?" the cameraman asked.

I snapped straight up, shut my eyes for a second, and took another breath. My sweaty hand was locked on the camera stand leg and I could feel more sweat forming on my forehead. *If I'm going, the camera is going with me. I don't like this.* I looked again.

"Holy shit," I said out loud. "I see it." I forced myself to focus on the zero in the 500. Yup. He was right. It was deformed, just like I'd thought on the ground.

"We're screwed. Let's go down," I said out loud. I looked at Bobby and said it again. "We're screwed. Let's go down." I got that cold feeling of panic when all of a sudden you are confronted with a serious situation and you don't know what to do to fix it. *This is where you earn your money. Calm down and think.* I told myself. There has to be a way out of this. There has to be. I just haven't thought of it yet.

I got back from the edge and I sat on the roof and immediately jumped back up. No, not because I had an idea of how to fix it—that roof was *hot*. I walked to the wooden camera platform and sat on the side of it. I had to think. After about a minute of deep thought, an idea popped into my head.

I turned to Bobby and said, "I think we can fix it. I have an idea." I stood up and patted Bobby on the back, saying, "You will have to do the painting."

"What the hell you talkin' about? I can't paint that."

"We will have to repaint the left edge of the second zero and maybe part of the edge of the other zero," I told him.

He looked at me. "Are you nuts?"

"It's the only way. Here's the plan. I will stay up here. When you get back down, go to the Maintenance Shop and get a radio. Go to the spray gun and I will use the radio to guide you from up here where I can see everything. You will be my hand," I said.

He shrugged with an "I don't know about this" look on his face. "OK," he said. "I'll try it."

He turned and headed for the elevator. My sweaty hand was still locked on the camera leg as I took some deep breaths to get my heart rate down. I looked at the cameraman and shook my head. He had no mercy on me. He figured I was a wimp.

I had to wait on the roof for about a half hour until I saw, way down below,

The repainted logo is the one on top. Can you see the difference in the zeroes on the 500? It was the one on the right.

Bobby driving the Mustang down Pit Lane. He pulled up to the grass. He looked like an ant. Bobby walked to the zero and looked up at me, waving the two-way radio in his left hand above his head. I thought, *Oh God. You don't use hand signals with the goddamned thing. You talk on it.* I clicked the button on my radio and in a strong voice I said, "Talk on the damn thing, you idiot. Don't wave it around."

He jumped and looked at the radio. Fumbling with the talk button, he said, "I'm here."

"Yes, I know," I said. "I'm looking at you."

Bobby looked up and waved.

Oh God. This is going to be bad, I thought to myself. I thought about just jumping over the edge.

I started to give commands over the radio. At first it was little awkward, but we got into it as we went along. I even forgot how high in the air I was. It went like this: Bobby had the spray gun in his right hand and with his left hand he was holding the radio up to his ear. I told him, "Face Pit Lane. Take five steps to the right . . . stop. Now start walking straight ahead, slowly . . . slow. Walk, walk, walk . . . Straight . . . OK, spray. Keep walking and spraying . . . Right, right, straight, right, right. . . . Stop."

This took hours. The Michigan crew stood and watched. The cameraman watched us for a while too, and then he got bored and left. When we were done, I was happy with the results. It was acceptable. The average person (one of the mere mortals as I call them) would never notice the slight errors that were still there. I told Bobby, "Good job, man. We're done." I got back in the elevator for the ride down. I was so burned out I didn't even care if the cable broke. I would get down a little quicker. I didn't even hear the clanging and banging. All I knew was we were almost done with this job.

I walked out on the grass, looked at Bobby, and with a slap on the back said, "Good job, man." Bobby was truly my right-hand man.

By the end of the day, the entire job was done and I was happy with the results. We left the extra paint on the trailer, hoping we wouldn't need it for the weekend. *Hit the walls all you want, just don't slide through the grass!* While we were cleaning up out on the grass the Michigan gang surprised me by saying they were headed back to the motel to pack up and head back north.

"You're going right now? It's only Thursday," I said to Charlie. They didn't even want to stay to watch the race. Paul had a business to run and being away from that was not easy.

But off to the side, Missy was crying. She wanted to stay so bad to see the race. Part of the deal was they would be able to stay and watch the race. She had never seen a NASCAR race and was a true Dale Earnhardt fan. To be at Talladega, Earnhardt's favorite track, was a dream come true. It truly is a race every NASCAR fan should see in person at least once. The general manager's son, Andy McWilliams, found out how badly Missy wanted to see the race and—just to show you how nice the people that run the track are—they let her stay at the motel and even bought her an airline ticket home Monday after the race. That made her extremely happy.

Bobby and I were staying until Sunday. No way would I miss a race here. We planned on leaving right after the race was over. Actually we had to stay until Sunday whether we wanted to or not. If someone slid through a logo during Saturday's race, it had to be repaired before Sunday. It had to look perfect for the TV cameras.

Back at the motel we said our good-byes, shook hands, and wished the Michigan crew a good trip home. Their old Ford pickup now sat level. I could still see traces of paint on Charlie, but I guess you could say he won his duel with the sprayer. He was still alive. One of the good things that came from this trip was meeting Paul Britten, the owner of Britten Banners. Paul is one heck of a guy and we've remained friends from that day on.

The Bar Brawl

Friday was just as much fun—and as little work—as we'd hoped. Lots of fast cars, all staying out of the grass. That night we headed for the motel bar and our Styrofoam feast. We had a whole new attitude as everything was done and it turned out OK. When you're done with one of these jobs, you feel lighter and a little prouder. Especially when you had a serious problem and you figured it out and fixed it. All the pressure was finally gone! What a feeling. We ate and we drank a few more Budweiser.

Race weekend had arrived and so had the crowds. We were at our usual seats, thanks to Kathy for saving them for us, and were just relaxing. I glanced over to my left and there, four seats down and right next to the wall, was Kathy's husband, Jerry, engulfed in his smoke cloud and playing the electronic poker machine. He glanced back and nodded as if to say, "How ya doin'?" I nodded back and tipped up my bottle of Bud.

It was very crowded at the motel and the atmosphere had changed. Race week atmosphere was hard to imagine unless you've been there. Everyone was hyped up for the same reason.

The tables behind us were full of people eating dinner and most of the crowd was casually dressed. Two couples right behind sitting at a round table stood out from the rest of the bar. All four were in their sixties and were dressed up: the men wore suits and the women wore dresses and lots of jewelry. Just by the way they talked, ate, and looked, you could tell they were wealthy and they flaunted it.

Bobby and I decided to have one more cold one to celebrate before we turned in. From behind us, we heard loud voices, not the normal bar talk. Not wanting to get involved in anything but curious, I turned and looked over my right shoulder. A waitress was at the table of the wealthy couples and was talking to them in an unusually loud voice. Within minutes, right out of the blue, all hell broke loose.

"You stole a hundred-dollar bill and I want it back!" rang out above the normal bar babble. Bobby and I looked at each other and turned on our bar stools to see what was happening. One of the overdressed men at the wealthy couple's table was yelling at the waitress.

"Sir, I would never steal money. I didn't take a hundred-dollar bill. You must be mistaken," she shouted back.

Kathy, the bartender, came over and leaned over the bar right behind Bobby and me. We turned in unison and looked at her. She said to the man at the table, "She's my daughter and she doesn't steal."

Just then, Jerry, the bartender's huge husband, turned around from the poker machine. His cigarette still hung from his lips. He tilted his head to the left so he could see through the smoke and just glared at the man. Bobby and I turned toward him. It was a good thing we had swivel seats. "Mister, you don't know what you're talkin' 'bout. My daughter doesn't steal from anybody." He pointed his finger at the man that was making the fuss.

The fat old man at the table stood up and glared at Jerry. Bad move. He pointed back at Jerry. Another really bad move. "Why don't you sit down, boy, and go back to playing your stupid poker mach—"

Yup . . . He didn't even get the word *machine* out of his mouth before a fist about the size of my head made contact with his face. Like I said, Jerry, the mower driver, was about six-foot-eight and *big*. He came off that stool so fast, he was a blur. The speed of him moving across the floor combined with the speed of his fist lifted that guy right off his feet. He flew backward into the fake wood panel wall with a loud crashing thud. He was now on the floor, sticking partially into the hole in the wall he made with his head. Jerry was kneeling on top of him pounding away like a Chicago Pneumatic Model CPCP 1210 jack-hammer.

Kathy was screaming at the top of her lungs, right into our ears, "*Stop. Stop.* Somebody stop him. My husband is recovering from a heart attack. Somebody stop him." I knew them both and she fed us well, so I jumped up and ran to the two guys fighting on the floor. This could have been a very stupid move.

The women at the table were screaming at the top of their lungs, as were others in the bar. You could hear tables and chairs sliding on the wooden floor as the people seated near the action were trying to get away from it. Just as I ran to Jerry, the other guy at the table stood up and started to come after me. Bobby, covering my back, jumped up and restrained him. I grabbed Jerry's right arm as he was pummeling the man's face. He turned, eyes glaring and glazed and drew back and aimed that huge fist at my head. "Jerry. Jerry. It's me," I yelled out of pure fright and to get his attention, bracing for the blow. He stared at me for a couple of seconds—it felt like a whole minute—and slowly relaxed his grip on the guy. Then he stood up and walked back to the poker machine, glancing back at the guy on the floor.

Holy shit. What the hell did I just do? That was really dumb. Really dumb. Good thing he recognized me. One hit from that fist and I wouldn't have seen the race.

Bobby let go of the other guy, who ran to his friend still lying on the floor. The two wives were screaming as they ran over to help. The guy's face looked like a spaghetti dinner. They picked the guy by his arms and carefully guided him out of the dining room. There was blood all over his suit jacket and tie. The people in the room stepped back as they walked toward the door. The whole place was dead silent. The other guy picked up their coats and followed his group. On the way out, he came over near the bar and said, "She didn't steal a hundred. He was just being an asshole.

I'm sorry."

Bobby and I looked at each other, turned and walked back to our stools. As I was sitting at the bar, I looked up over the top of my Budweiser into the mirror behind the bar. I had to verify I still had a head. Everything got back to normal. Bobby and I were heroes. We didn't have to buy a drink the rest of the night. We closed the place.

TALLADEGA

Saturday Excitement

The alarm still went off at 5:30 a.m. *Oh God.* One good thing, it was Saturday and all we had to do today was enjoy the Busch race. No work. All the work and stress was forgotten and now it was time to enjoy ourselves. It made getting up a lot easier.

We didn't even stop at the deli. On race day I want to get to the track early. If you arrive a little late, you could be stuck in traffic for hours. At the track Billy Swinford came up to me and said, "See you boys had a little trouble last night?" Turns out Jerry was Billy's cousin. When word got around we were the talk of the day.

"Where are we watching the race from?" Bobby asked. When we worked at the track, we had credentials that are "all access." We could even go on the racing surface. This spoils you. With one of those passes, if you wanted to go up with the spotters or cameramen, you just go. What a bonus. We even had NASCAR garage passes.

"Let's watch it from the Turn 2 rescue truck area," I said. The Turn 2 rescue boys were stationed inside the turn, just behind the concrete retaining wall. They were very close to the track, so close you have to look up at the cars on the banking as they go by. What a view.

The NASCAR Busch Series race that Saturday had its share of accidents but the cars stayed away from the grass. Billy's voice came over the radio, "Hey sign man, two more laps to go and you're home free."

I hollered to Bobby, "We are home free. Man, does that feel good. We will be relaxing and drinking Bud tonight."

Then Billy came back on the radio "The last lap. You made it!" he hollered over the radio. All the safety crew was giving us the thumbs-up.

"The race leader is across the finish line and the checkered flag is waving," one of the rescue guys hollered over to us.

I looked at Bobby. We high-fived each other. Now we could celebrate a great job finished and a great time down here. Nobody spun into the grass and that meant no repairs.

"No. . . . Wait," Billy was hollering on the radio.

"Oh man. Two backmarkers sliding through the grass." A backmarker is someone who is not in contention.

We couldn't see the grass from Turn 2, but I know Billy. He was joking. He jokes all the time. I was thinking, *You nut, that won't work with me* and laughing. "Nice try, Billy. HaHaHa. It won't work, pal. We may be northerners but we ain't stupid. HaHaHa. . . . " I said over the radio.

Then my cousin Ernie (he was the safety coordinator for Daytona Speedway) hollered over to me, "He's not kiddin' ya. It just came over the track emergency frequency. Two cars in the Tri-Oval grass."

I looked at him and I could tell he was not fooling. The joke was on us. Come to find out, two backmarkers got together coming down for the checker and these two idiots slid through two logos. Our plans changed in a few seconds. Tonight we had to work.

As soon as the cars were off the track we jumped in our John Deere Gator and went buzzing around to see the mess. The grandstands were not even empty when we pulled up to the Tri-Oval on the Front Straight. I was on the radio to maintenance to get the trailer with the paint (and paint guns) out to Pit Lane. I heard a mower coming. I looked up and it was the groundskeeper. As he drove onto the grass, I ran over to him waving my arms for him to stop. I walked up to the mower and hollered over the engine noise, "What are you doing?" He got off the mower and said, "I'm mowing the grass (and this meant the logos) for tomorrow's race. My eyes popped out. "*What?* You aren't mowing these logos," I said.

You see, normal practice was, when the grass grows to a certain point the logos start to look fuzzy. At that point the whole Tri-Oval got mowed. Mowing over the logos meant they had to be repainted, but they remained visible so repainting them was easy–no layout required. A quick color coat needed to be sprayed over what was already there.

I'd been afraid of this happening from the time we started the logos a day early because I wanted to leave a cushion in case the patterns didn't work out. "There is a problem," I told him, "Number one, all my help went back to Michigan. Number two; there isn't enough paint to repaint all of the logos." We only had about forty gallons of extra paint. The grass has hardly grown an inch since we painted it. Thank God for the drought. The groundskeeper paid no attention to me and got back on the mower and started to mow. I walked up to the side of the mower and put my left hand on the armrest. I hollered, "You are not mowing those goddamned logos." He continued to drive away and I ran around the front of the mower. He stopped with a jerk. He jumped off the mower and now we had a heated discussion on who was boss.

Finally, he pulled his radio off of his belt and called Mike (the general manager). He said, "We have a problem. Can you get out to the grass logos?" Mike arrived in a few minutes and could see there was a problem. Mike walked up to us. Neither of us looked happy. The groundskeeper said, "He's keeping me from doing my job."

I told Mike my story. I wanted the groundskeeper to mow around the logos if he had to mow something. Mowing around the logos was something they have never done before. After listening to both of us, Mike turned to me and said, "Tony, will they look OK on TV tomorrow?"

I know one thing. When Mike asks a question, you better have a damned answer and you better have it fast. If it had rained that week I would have been in trouble. But as luck would have it, the weather cooperated. "Mike," I said, "it will look OK."

He turned to the groundskeeper and said, "Tony says it will look OK. Mow around the logos." Mike turned and left. The groundskeeper glared at me and then got back on the John Deere mower and did a burn-out.

Mike called me on the radio and said, "I'll get some construction lights out here for ya. Looks like you'll be workin' late."

"Thanks, Mike," I said.

I'm proud of how much Mike trusted me. It made me feel good! Bobby and I walked out to survey the damage. When a car going 180 mph slides through the grass, it didn't stop in a hundred feet. It was more like a thousand! By pure luck the cars slid together and hit only two logos. We usually only had to repair tire marks, but this time one car had had its wheel ripped off, and the suspension dug into the ground. The car had skipped along digging a trench every ten feet or so and eight inches deep. There were about ten trenches. I figured I had no choice but to try to paint the trenches, but one of the maintenance men who were setting up our lights said, "We used sand before to fill gouges in the grass. It worked well after we tamped it down. I'll get a dump truck and some guys and we'll take care of it for you." They got me a dump truck full of sand and three maintenance men to help me, armed with wheelbarrows and a gas-powered tamper. A couple of them filled the gouges with sand and the third followed behind them with the tamper. Like I said before, when someone needed help on race weekend, the help was always there. They don't even wait for you to ask—they just show up. Sure makes you feel good.

We worked hard for three and a half hours, until about 9 p.m. With all the help, it didn't take as long as I first thought it would. I kept looking at the logos and wishing I could have repainted them. Mike trusted my judgment call on leaving them and that made me feel good, but the right way would have been a repaint. It was going to be close on the grass length on Sunday but we really didn't have much choice. Thank God it wasn't going to rain.

We drove over to the Maintenance Shop where everyone was gathered. The night before the race was always exciting. The Sunday race reminded me of a tornado. You can see it coming in the distance; it gets closer and closer but you can't stop it. Whether you were completely ready or not, on Sunday, the race was going to happen. Everyone had last-minute projects, except us. "Anyone need help with anything?" I asked.

Someone hollered from the shop, I think it was Sarge, "No, we want it done right." David 'Sarge' Sargent worked in maintenance. He was tall and one hell of a guy. Everyone laughed.

We were having a beer when Mike walked up to us with a quart glass canning jar. "You guys earned it, take a sip."

"What is it?" I asked.

"It's good old Talladega Ice Water," Mike said. The guys standing around all laughed. I took the jar from Mike. It was a Ball quart regular Mason jar. The top was off and it was filled half full with a perfectly clear liquid. With a classic two-handed grip I put the jar up to my lips and I took a sip. The instant the first drop of that stuff hit my throat, my windpipe contracted completely shut. It was like a movie. I was gagging and making a horrible gasping sound trying to get a little air into my lungs from my collapsed windpipe. I was frantically looking around for a knife to give myself a tracheotomy so I could breathe. My eyes bugged out of their sockets as I bent over gagging and coughing. I stuck my right hand, with the jug in it, straight out to my side. Bobby took the jug. I sounded like some sort of malfunctioning air pump. After I caught my breath I thought, *Oh God. This has got to look embarrassing.* I could hear the laughter all around me but I couldn't see anyone as my eyes were watering so badly everything was a blur.

After I put on a pathetic show with everyone laughing, what does Bobby do? That stupid nut, after watching me gasp for air in front of the whole staff for five minutes, took a slug. Yup. Same thing. Gasping, wheezing. A pathetic show of plain stupidity. A hell of a hilarious sight. I was a little embarrassed as I now knew how I looked. But now I was laughing. How can one be so stupid? Well, I'll tell you how. . . . Take another sip. And another. Then pass it back to Bobby.

"This is smooth," we both said. I don't know what the hell *smooth* meant. It actually tasted like kerosene. Not only like kerosene, but like kerosene already on fire. Strange, but it had no effect at all . . . we thought. We headed for the motel and our supper. Lucky we did.

We were on our stools eating supper and having a Bud. That moonshine had finally reached my bloodstream. I was just putting my first bottle of Bud to my lips when the whole back bar, mirror included, slithered off to the right. It was like getting hit broadside by a freight train. I slammed my bottle down and grabbed the bar so I wouldn't fall off the stool. I looked at Bobby and said, "Did you see that?"

He said, "What?" Then, I don't know if he saw it or not, but he said, in a slow, low voice, "Let's get to the room . . . *now.*"

I don't remember getting off the bar stool.

 # Talladega Race Day

  I was awakened by a sound. I could barely hear it, but something woke me up. Not opening my eyes, I strained to listen more closely. *Maybe it was nothing. It was nothing. It's gone. Go back to sleep. No. Wait. There it is again. It's so far away I can't quite make out what it was. What the hell was it?* I strained to hear it again, but as soon as I heard it, the sound disappeared. Suddenly I realized it was the damned phone ringing with our wake-up call! I don't remember ordering a wake-up call as I had been setting the alarm all week. I guess in the condition I was in the night before, I couldn't set the alarm and must have called the desk to order a wake-up call. I could hear it, but I couldn't move.

  A moonshine hangover was the worst thing you could imagine. My tongue was stuck to the roof of my mouth. I opened my mouth and stuck two fingers in and grabbed the tip of my tongue. I had to peel it off the roof of my mouth with my fingers, just like peeling a strip of Velcro. Finally, I had to use my left hand to pick my head up by my hair so I could reach over and grab the phone. I went to speak and my mouth was so dry, all that came out was an "AAaaagttttttthhhhh." *Oh my God!! The worst may be happening. I might live. Oh God, my head.*

  I tried to get Bobby up. For a second, I thought he was dead. I am not alone with this moonshine thing. Bobby was as bad as me, maybe worse. Sitting up, eyes still shut, he said, "I'm stayin' right the hell here and watchin' the friggin' race on TV."

  "No way," I said. "We are going to the track." I don't know how we made it to the track but we did. It was 6 a.m. and I could only breathe out. If I inhaled, my head would have exploded and blown off of my shoulders. This was a rough start to a hell of a race day at Talladega.

  We were at the sign shop slowly going about our task of packing things up. We planned on heading home right after the race. Thank goodness for the coffee! Coffee was brewed fresh in the Maintenance Office, which has a room with a couch, a few chairs, and a countertop where the coffee maker sat. On race mornings, it became the war room. Mike and the maintenance guys gathered there to talk over the game plan for the day. On race day they had boxes of cookies and all types of pastries, thanks to the hospitality vendors at the track, who keep the staff supplied with all kinds of good pastries. We hung out in there, telling anyone who would listen how bad we felt.

After talking to Mike and a few others, it became clear we'd been suckered in with the moonshine. As I look back, I don't remember any of them drinking the evil brew. *Those bastards! They got us—it was our own fault.* If my head hadn't hurt so bad I would have started planning a way to get them back, but I just said the hell with it for now. *I'll get 'em some other day.*

We walked outside into the bright sun, the warmth easing our faces. It was a beautiful day. Coffee in hand, we walked over to Mike, who was leaning on the side of the box of a new red GMC pickup. One foot was up on the rear bumper and his elbows were on the top of the box. He was holding a cup of coffee with both hands. We leaned on the truck, just like him, with a foot on the rear bumper. (Not to be cool—to keep from falling over.) There was activity all over the place. Race day. Everyone was hustling to get last-minute stuff done. We were lucky. Our work had to be done by Saturday night. There was no pressure now. We looked over to our left and there was Bill France, then president of NASCAR, standing next to us at the Maintenance Office. Over to our right was a group of maintenance guys filling a pickup with waste cans. It was awesome. Every level of people mix together on race day.

We had been at the track for two hours and it was only 8 a.m. I said to Bobby, "Let's go over to the main grandstand and see how the logos look." He didn't say a word, just gave me an "Are you kidding me" look. I went alone.

I drove our John Deere Gator over to the gate to the main grandstand and parked. People were starting to come in. It looked like a dam had cracked. The crowd was flowing instead of walking—there were so many people. It was easier to walk than try to drive the rest of the way. I got to the grandstand and walked up a few rows and looked out at the Tri-Oval. I was a little nervous. Thank God, the logos looked good. Not as good as they would if we could have repainted them, but good enough. What a relief. *I didn't lie to Mike.* I walked back down and in five minutes the crowd coming in had doubled. It was like swimming upstream trying to walk back to the Gator. Back at the shop I told Mike that the logos looked good. He said, "I already saw them. You surprised? You told me they would be OK." Yeah, I guess I did. It was time for more coffee. I went into the room thinking, *I felt better after that walk up to the grandstands.*

Bobby was not doing well at all. He was sitting in the passenger side of the car with the door wide open. His head was tipped back and he was not moving. I felt bad for him. If I'd had my pistol with me, I think he would have pleaded with me to shoot him. He was that bad. It is really boring being there so early, but like I said, it's basically be there early or wait in traffic for hours. I was leaning against a post that held up the canopy of the Maintenance Shop, contentedly watching people run around like ants getting last-minute chores done. I sipped my coffee again. It had gotten cold. I tossed the remainder out onto the asphalt and turned to go back inside to get another one when I spotted Dick Hahne walking toward me. Dick was the vice president at Daytona Speedway who had been responsible for my first trip down to Talladega.

I thought he was headed to the Maintenance Office, but when he spotted me, he turned and walked toward me. I waved and said, "Mornin', Dick."

"Another beautiful day in Talladega," he said. "How did your painting go?"

"Went good," I said. "Glad we're done. I'm ready to go home."

"Where are you watching the race today?"

"I don't really know," I said. I didn't want to tell him Bobby wanted to stay in the room and watch it. "I guess we are going over in Turn 2 with the rescue guys."

He reached into the right-hand pocket of his brown tweed jacket and pulled out two large, classy-looking tickets. He held them out toward me and said, "My guests can't make it so I have two credentials to the Presidents Seats. Do you want them?"

Holy cow, I thought. I didn't want to look overly excited. "Yeah. I guess I could use them." I looked at them and they even looked expensive. I couldn't believe it. I took them and thanked Dick for the tickets. I turned to show Bobby. His eyes were now open, but I don't think he was in there. I told him of our good fortune and he still just looked at me. God, he looked like crap.

As the morning dragged on, Bobby started to come around a little. I was full of coffee and the race was about an hour and a half away. I said to Bobby, "Let's go find these seats and sit there. At least we will be in our seats and not fighting the crowd at the last minute. Plus, the walk will do you good. You can sleep up there."

He struggled to his feet. We drove the John Deere Gator to the side of the grandstand and parked it by the security guard. He just looked at us as we left on foot. It was a long walk under the main grandstand to our seats. The crowd coming in was unbelievable. At that time, the track had 150,000 seats, and they were all sold. We

The crowd coming into the grandstands on race day.

walked and walked and walked.

This place was huge. Walking under the main grandstand was like walking in a huge tunnel. Signs hanging down from the steel I-beams show the grandstand sections. The stairs on the left appeared at regular intervals. The right side was lined with souvenir booths, food stands, and restrooms. They all had lines to them already.

We kept walking. The crowd was elbow to elbow. I looked over to Bobby and I swear he was sleeping. He was standing stiff and straight with the tightly packed crowd carrying him along like a log floating upright down a river. "Bobby. Hey, Bobby," I hollered. He looked left, right, and up and down. I hollered, "Over here. We are up there." Pointing over my head. He managed to pierce the crowd and walk toward me. We were at the bottom of the metal stairs that went up to the President's Seats. As we got to the stairs, I felt like we'd just swum to the shore of a river; the crowd, like a river, was still slowly going by.

The security guard for the President's Seats section stood at the bottom of the galvanized steel stairs, with her hands clasped behind her back. She looked ex-military by the way she was standing. She had a rugged build and was dressed in the typical security uniform: black shoes, black pants, and a white blouse with blue stripes up the sleeves. The patch on her left sleeve said "Talladega Superspeedway Security" and on her right shoulder was the American flag. Her hair was black and pulled tight in a bun on the back of her head. As I walked up to her, she was looking off to her right, smiling in the spirit of race day at Talladega. As we approached and she looked our way, her expression changed to a tight-jawed frown. As soon as I saw that look, it was crystal clear what she was thinking: "What the hell do you two want?"

I stood in front of her, unshaven and with uncombed hair. Bobby was slouching right behind me looking like his chin was stuck to my back and I was towing him around. I looked back at him to make sure he was there and, *Oh My God,* he was drooling. His eyes were half-shut and he had a day's growth of beard. He actually looked worse than he had when we left the Maintenance Office.

I handed her the tickets. With a frown and not saying a word, she reached out with her left hand and took the tickets. Instead of tearing off the stubs, she looked at the tickets, then looked back at us. She looked back at the tickets and again looked at us. She didn't say it, but I could read her mind. "How the hell did you two get those credentials?" I think she wanted to get some help because she knew these had to be stolen. The two guys in front of her who wanted to get in the Presidents Seats looked like two winos that just came from a street corner in Talladega. She reluctantly tore the stubs and handed the tickets back to me. As we walked past her to the stairs, her whole body turned and I could feel her eyes glaring at us. She said, in a manly voice that sound like an order, "Enjoy the race."

"Thanks," I said, and walked up the stairs.

At the top of the metal stairs, we turned left and walked out to a platform just under the tower seats and just above the lower grandstand. There, we found a single row of seats. The great thing about these seats? No one was in front you and no one was behind you. There were no obstructions to viewing the race. It was great. The view was fabulous, and we had lots of leg room and lots of space. We looked over to the left at some people down the row. They were all looking at us. I gave a quick short wave. They didn't wave back. They continued to stare. I know what they were thinking: "How the hell did those bums get in there?" You have to be somebody to be in these seats as they are not for sale; they're reserved for VIPs. I felt like hollering down to them, "Hey, I got friends in high places," but we just sat there soaking in the sun and letting them wonder.

Finally, the race started. The pace laps were done and the pace car pulled into Pit Lane. The cars came down the Front Stretch right in front of us. A hundred and fifty thousand people were on their feet waving and screaming. Everybody, that is, except one. Bobby. I looked to my left and did a double take. There he was, slouched back on the bench, feet straight out in front of him, his head tilted back and to the left. His eyes were shut and his mouth was wide open. Oh God. There was even a little drool showing on his chin. He was out cold. I'll be damned if he didn't look a little like Homer Simpson.

I hollered over to him, "*Hey.* Here they come, man. Here they come. This is what we've been waiting for."

He snapped straight up and with half-opened eyes saw the green flag waving. I could tell by the look on his face that what he was seeing wasn't quite registering. Damned if his mouth wasn't still open. What a sight! I slid over to the right a little bit to make more space. Maybe people wouldn't know we were together. Bobby might have seen every other lap, but he didn't enjoy the day. Neither did I after an early wreck took out half the field, including Earnhardt. We were glad when the checkered flag finally fell.

At the Maintenance Office we gathered for an after-the-race party. We didn't drink anything. We said good-bye to everyone as we planned to drive home that

Sitting in the Presidents Seats.

night. They all tried to change our minds. "Leave in the mornin'. You guys look like shit."

"Nah, we are headed back," I said. But our plan to head straight home didn't pan out. We were so tired that we made it to the first motel we saw, which was about thirty miles from the track. We were asleep by 7 p.m. That was a smart move.

The next morning we woke up around 7 a.m. As we walked out of the motel and into the warm morning air, the humidity hit us like a ton of bricks. We both said at the same time, "Holy shit." Bobby was looking much better (he had at least stopped drooling). Looking up at the sky, I thought we might run into some rain. *Good,* I thought. We'd hit perfect weather the last week, allowing us to get our work done, so I actually didn't mind if it rained. We jumped into the Mustang and I took the first tour of duty driving. I turned the key and the engine came to life as I thought, *This poor engine doesn't realize it isn't going to shut off for more than a minute or so for the next nineteen hours.*

We stopped at the first gas station we came to. I filled it up, got some snacks, and headed north. I couldn't wait to get home to Harriett and back to my usual customers. Bobby and I made it home with no further adventures. It was over a month before either of us touched a drop of alcohol. That Alabama moonshine was that brutal.

This trip would be my last big grass painting job at Talladega—but far from my last big job there.

The Road to Daytona

    Winter in upstate New York can be bleak. It's dark when you get up and it's dark by 5 p.m., but it goes have some good points. When the temperature hovers around 32 degrees and the snow starts to fall, I like to walk to the center of my driveway and tip my head back, squinting straight up with my eyes almost shut at the huge snowflakes coming straight down. It does look stupid—people honk when they drive by—but I just stare up as the big flakes float down in slow motion, drifting back and forth like bits of paper falling out of the sky. After a few minutes, you begin to feel like you are moving up into the air. How high you go is determined by how long you can stand there, eyes half open, with snowflakes falling on your face. Open your mouth and the big wet flakes land on your tongue and add to the sensation. I don't look down (remember, I'm scared of heights), just straight up. When I want to land, I shut my eyes, lift my arms straight out from my sides, lower my chin, and wait a few seconds. When I look around, I'm back in my driveway, miraculously right in the exact same spot where I took off. Then I go inside, wipe the snow off my face, and return to work thinking, *Man, I musta been a hundred feet in the air before I came back down.*

    Even that gets old after a while, though. One day I'd spent the afternoon lettering a new Ford Victoria for the Schuyler County Sheriff department and looking at the gathering gloom. *Man, is it cold,* I thought as I walked from my shop to the house, anxious to see what Harriett had made for supper. I got to the sidewalk in front of the house and I knew what it was. I could smell it. My favorite. It was venison. Man, can she cook venison. She can cook anything, for that matter, but this was the best. I walked in, shaking my whole body like a dog does when he gets out of the water except I wasn't wet just cold.

    "Man, does that smell good," I said as I set trays in the living room. We watch TV while we eat. Usually we watch and play *Jeopardy*. (I don't even know why I play against Harriett. She gets me 90 percent of the time, but I'm a glutton for punishment. They never have my categories—painting, racing, or WWII aircraft.)

    After supper, I was sitting in my easy chair watching the news when the phone rang. Harriett was in the kitchen, so I hollered out to her, "Get that, will ya? It's probably for you anyway."

She walked in with her hand over the mouthpiece and said, "It's for you." She had that look of "Why didn't you answer it in the first place?"

She was doing dishes when the phone rang. Now she handed me the phone and it smelled like dishwater. I didn't really want to talk on the wet phone. Also, I didn't want to be bothered as I was stuffed, relaxed, and slouched in my chair with a blanket over me. I was finally warm.

"Who the hell is it?" I snapped as I grabbed the phone with two fingers. She shrugged her shoulders, gave me that look, and walked back to the kitchen. "Aw shit," I mumbled. *Probably it's one of my buddies wanting to go snowmobiling. I'm not moving out of this chair for anything.*

"Yeah," I said in a sort of disgusted way.

"Tony, how are you doing up there? Dick Hahne here."

"Dick," I said, shifting myself upright in the chair as if it would help me hear better. "What are you up to? It's pretty cold up here. I was just watching TV."

"I called because I need some help. Remember what you told me? Well, I'm calling you on it."

My mind raced back. *What the hell did I tell him?* Dick continued, "I hired two guys to run the sign shop." Now I remembered. Many times Dick offered me a job at Daytona Speedway, where he was the operations manager. He wanted me to move down there and run their sign shop. After thinking of all the pros and cons, I turned him down. It came down to the simple fact that *I cannot live in Florida.* I like to visit, but to actually live there . . . *no way.* When I told Dick my final answer was no, I didn't leave it at that. I never learn. I had to open my big mouth. Like Jackie Gleason would say—*"My biiiigggg moouutthhhh."*

About a year ago I'd said, "Dick, you don't know how honored I am that you considered me to run the shop at Daytona, but. . . "

"I already knew the answer," Dick said at the time. "But I wanted to make sure. You'll never leave the North."

Instead of just letting it go at that, I had to keep my mouth running. "Dick, you know that whatever happens, I'm only a phone call away." Yup. He remembered and this was that phone call.

Dick said, "Do you remember, way back when, you said you were only a phone call away?"

"Oh, yeah."

"Well, I need you down here for a month to train the two guys that I hired to run the shop. I want you here for all of Speed Week and the 500, just in case."

I said in a loud voice that got Harriett's attention, "A *month?* Let me talk to Harriett and I will call you tomorrow."

Dick said, "Call me. I need you."

I hung up the phone and Harriett asked, "Who was that?"

"It was Dick Hahne from Daytona. He wants me to go to Daytona for a friggin' month. I don't wanna go down there for a month."

Harriett said, "I remember when you told him the phone call thing. It's your own fault. You have to go."

"I know. I'll call him tomorrow."

I called Dick and told him I would come down. Now he was happy. Come to find out, the two guys were not even sign men. One was an artist and the other was a graphics guy doing ads at a local newspaper. Neither had ever done a sign. I thought to myself, "Oh God."

✧

My airplane ticket came from Daytona Speedway by FedEx, and in a week I would be heading south. The month that I'd be down, from the middle of January to the middle of February, included Daytona's Speed Week and the Daytona 500. I had never been to Speed Week (a race fan's orgy that consists of NASCAR Sprint Cup practice, a seventy-five-lap Sprint Unlimited race, a Sprint Cup Pole Qualifying race, the NASCAR Camping World Truck Series, practice, qualifying, and race, and the Nationwide series race).

When the day came to leave, Harriett drove me to Elmira/Corning Regional Airport. It was bad enough being away for two weeks at Talladega, but a month? *Well, I can call every day and I figured if you look at it this way, a month isn't that long. It's only four weeks.* I gave Harriett a big hug for both her and my daughter Beth and headed out of the terminal to the plane. As I walked across the asphalt, I had to put my right hand up to the side of my face to block the 20-degree, 15 mph wind that was blowing straight out of the west down the runway. The back of my hand was getting sandblasted with ice crystals. I looked up at the plane and it was a black US AIR Gulfstream. Nice plane. I figured this would be a good trip.

I looked out the window to see if I could spot Harriett. I couldn't see her, but I waved anyway hoping she could see me. The plane fired up. I'd have to connect in Boston—a bit out of the way—before flying south to Orlando. We had been in the air only a short time when the pilot came on the intercom and said that we would be landing in Rochester. I thought, *Why Rochester?* I looked out the window. The right wing was still on and the engine wasn't on fire, so why were we landing in Rochester? I never did find out. They put us on a commuter plane in Rochester. The pilot was a young guy, as was the copilot. As he turned onto the main runway, he didn't even stop to power up. Full throttle. *Holy Shit. Man, does this plane have power.* We did a steep climb under full power. It was awesome. I loved it. In Boston, we got on a 737 that took me nonstop to Orlando without fuss.

I walked out of the airport in Orlando. It was *warm!* What a difference. I had to stop for a minute to pull out my sunglasses and squint up at the sky. Nothing up there but sun. *A month of this might not be bad after all.* I found my rental car, a new Monte Carlo, adjusted my Serengetis (the only sunglasses I wear), and headed out of the terminal and up Alligator Alley toward Daytona. I had the radio blasting away and the air conditioning on full bore.

Then I got thinking. I turned off the air conditioning and rolled the windows down. I wanted to feel that warm breeze blowing my hair around. Even with my Serengeti sunglasses on I had to squint a little. The sun was really bright but I didn't mind—considering just five hours ago I was walking to a plane with my head down, getting pelted with ice crystals. I soon noticed I was the only car with the windows down.

The drive to Daytona was only about an hour. Before long, I could see big green overhead road signs in the distance. I reached the first of the Daytona Beach exits. I kept going. As I approached the next exit, I turned onto the off ramp without slowing down. I hugged the inside of the right turn, making the tires on the Monte Carlo squeal. Ahhhh. Squealing tires brought back my Skip Barber Competition School instructor's voice: "A happy tire is a squealing tire." With a big smile on my face, I drove down I-95 for a short way and found Speedway Blvd. *Almost there*, I thought. As I drove down the four-lane road to Daytona Speedway, I thought back to the first time I was here with Harriett in 1984. *Man, has this place changed.*

෴

Harriett and I had come down to Florida for a short vacation shortly after I met her. It was so long ago that I-95 was a two-lane road. We wanted to see the World of Outlaws Sprint Car series race at the Gibson Speedway near Tampa. It rained for two days non-stop rain. To save money, we had camped in a tent and got soaked. Harriett had never seen a Sprint Car before but now it's the only type of racing she likes watch. She loves Sprint Car racing. After the races we headed to Orlando. We planned to find a campsite and visit my cousin David 'Butch' Orcutt for two days before driving down to Daytona Speedway. In Daytona, we were going to catch the Twin 125 qualifying races. (We only had enough money to buy tickets to see the Twin 125s.)

On the way to Butch's house, we got lost in Orlando. Before the days of cell phones, we had to find a payphone to call Butch for directions. "There's one." Harriett said in an excited voice as we drove down a strangely deserted street in the middle of Orlando. It was around noon and we were in a section of town where we hadn't seen a car with wheels on it in the past five minutes. I pulled over and got out of the car. "This is strange." I thought. There was not a person or a drivable car on the street and it was the middle of the day. When I got near the phone booth I noticed it had no glass. I just figured it was built that way because it was so warm down here. When I got inside I saw that at one time it did have glass but now it was all in little pieces on the floor of the booth. The frames that held the glass were all bent out of shape as if someone had beaten them with a bar. The dial on the phone caught my eye. *That's right, it had a dial. That's how long ago this happened.*

The dial had been melted into a blackish, brown pear shape. It hung off the center of the phone. All the finger holes were in a grotesque oval shape with a long, stringy glob at the bottom. It looked like the face of an alien from outer space. The moneybox was bent, as someone had tried to pry it open. I put a dime in the slot and was pleasantly surprised to hear a dial tone. Holding the receiver with two fingers and away from my mouth (you never know where it's been), I had to dial the number by guessing where the right holes were. I could hear the line ringing.

"Jallo," came a booming voice through the earpiece.

"Hey Butch. Tony here. We're lost. How do we get to your house?"

"Where the hell are ya? Can't help ya if I don't where the hell ya are," he said, laughing.

"We are in Orlando, but I don't know where. Hang on—I'll look."

Over by the corner was a street sign on the pole. One sign was ripped off and the other was bent so that I had a hard time reading what it said. I ran back to the phone and gave Butch the street name.

For a second there was silence. Then Butch screamed into the phone, *"Jesus Christ. Get the hell outta there. Call me from another phone. Get the hell movin'."*

Before I could say a word, he slammed the phone down. I looked around. Now I was nervous. I was naive back then and thought everywhere was like small town Watkins Glen. I ran to the car (Harriett's Toyota Celica as I didn't have a car that would make it to Florida at the time), dropped it in gear, and floored it.

"What's the matter?" Harriett said.

"We gotta get the hell outta here," I said. We flew down the street with my eyes reflecting the fear and panic in my cousin's voice.

Up the street, about three blocks away, I saw traffic flowing to the right. "Traffic. Oh man, traffic," I hollered. Harriett sat there silently, looking nervous. I couldn't believe I was so glad to see traffic. I blended into the flow, tucking between several cars like someone was chasing me and I was trying to hide. Thinking back, that was pretty scary. When we did arrive at my cousin's, I found out we were in what he called "No-Man's-Land." He couldn't believe I had gotten out of the car in that part of town and still made it out alive.

After visiting with my cousin, we headed to a campground that was only a few miles away. We got lost again. We didn't arrive at the campsite until 1 a.m. That night it was *cold*. Temperatures reached a forty-one-year record low that night of 28 degrees. *I still have the newspaper to prove it!* We survived in our tent and the next day we drove to Daytona. We only had to pay $5 to watch the Twin 125 qualifiers. That's right, five bucks and we could sit anywhere we wanted. I was in awe watching the races. I'd never seen a track anything like Daytona except on television. Harriett didn't want any part of it as the sound was ripping her head apart. I was in heaven. After the checkered flag fell, we started the long drive back to New York.

☙

I found a smile on my face, remembering that trip, as I drove toward Daytona. *That was a long time ago*, I thought to myself, *I wish Harriett was here with me on this trip*. I suddenly got a huge, homesick feeling—but it disappeared when I saw out my window the grandstand at Daytona Speedway. *Wow*. I got goose bumps up and down my arms and legs. What a sight—and to think, this little sign painter from Watkins Glen was going to be part of that. I got a proud feeling and my eyes actually watered a little as I tried to find Gate 7. "They need some signs out here," I muttered. *Dick told me to come in Gate 7 and tell the guard I was there to see him.*

There it was. A small yellow sign with black letters—GATE 7. I pulled onto a tar-and-stone access road that ran through the parking area to the back of the main grandstand. The road continued right under the grandstand, where I pulled up to the glass-enclosed guard booth. The guard was a large man in a white short-sleeved shirt and black pants. On his head he wore a dark blue Daytona Security hat turned slightly to the left. His shirt had a Daytona Security patch on the left shoulder and an American flag on the right. He was sitting on a chair in the booth. It took a lot of effort for him to get up and slowly walk from the small aluminum glassed-in booth to my car. "Can I hep ya, Sir?"

"I'm Tony Vickio and I'm here to see Dick Hahne," I said.

He walked back to his little glass enclosure and grabbed a clipboard. He flipped through the pages on his clipboard looking for my name. As he reached my car he said, "Yup. Here ya are."

I signed in and handed his clipboard back to him. He pointed toward the track. "Go straight forward and proceed through the opening in the wall," he said, like he was reading from a script. "Immediately, turn right and proceed down the track. Make sure you stay to the left side of the racing surface. Then proceed left and go down Pit Lane. *Do not* go around the track. Take the first opening in the pit wall on your left. Follow the road and you will see the Operations Office on the right."

"Great. Thanks," I said.

Wow. I'm actually going to drive on Daytona Speedway. I proceeded under the huge grandstand. It was dark under there and it was huge. I drove through the opening in the retaining wall just off Turn 4 and into the bright sunlight. Now I was driving right on the Front Straight of Daytona International Speedway. *Wow.* What a feeling. It reminded me of Talladega. *Boy, would I like to take a lap. Maybe later.* I slowed down and stopped to look at the view. This place was *huge*. I drove down Pit Lane and through the opening toward a white cinder-block building. A little sign above a door read "Operations." Must be the place.

I walked into the office and the secretary was sitting at a desk typing away on her computer. I said, "Hi, I'm Tony Vickio. I'm here to see Dick Hahne." She jumped up and held out her hand to shake mine.

"Oh. Tony. We've been expecting you. My name is Bonnie. We've heard so much about you." *Oh no, what had she heard about me?* "How was your trip?"

"It was great. I can't believe how warm it is."

She laughed, not knowing how friggin' cold I was when I had started out this morning. "It's not that warm. Actually it's a little chilly. I had to put a sweater on. Dick is in his office—go right in."

I opened the door and there was Dick. He stood up, shook my hand and thanked me for coming down. After a lot of small talk, he said, "Come with me and I'll show you around. You have to get to know your way around and we might as well start now." Walking out the back door, we got in the cleanest golf cart I had ever seen and away we went. After a two-hour tour of the place we pulled up behind Pit Lane at a row of about twenty medium-sized motor homes. "Here is where you will be staying. You'll be right at the track so you won't have to drive at all." I thought to myself, *I don't know about this.* "Does it have TV?" I asked.

The first night was damp and cold. I did not like it. The TV only had local channels. The next morning the shower was cold. *I'm not doing this for a month.* As soon as I got dressed, I went to if Dick was in yet. Bonnie showed me in to his office. Before I could say anything, Dick said, "How'd it go last night?"

"Dick, I have a question."

"Shoot," he said with a big smile on his face.

"If you were coming to work at Watkins Glen for a month, would you like to stay in a motor home parked behind Pit Lane?"

He stared at me for a second, then toward the motor homes, then back to me—and without answering he pushed the button on the intercom and said, "Bonnie, get Tony a room." He looked up and said, "There."

"Thanks, Dick," I said and walked back outside. I smiled. Life was good.

As I was walked back to the sign shop, I was nervously thinking about meeting the two men Dick hired and beginning something that I'd never done before. *I had to teach total newbies how to run a sign shop.*

 # Teaching Class

The more I thought about it, the more nervous I got about my latest job. Teaching? I could paint thirty thousand square feet of grass—no problem! But teaching? *Man, I don't know.* I didn't even know where to start. I figured it was sure as hell too late now. *I'm here. Stop thinking about it.* I walked to the sign shop—a one-car garage, 30'×30', with an overhead door. I walked in and looked around. It was laid out pretty well with a work table, a large easel, and some open floor space, but it was really cluttered, and that bugged me. I hated clutter.

In a 10'×30' room off to the right side of the shop, I found a Gerber thirty-inch plotter, a fifteen-inch plotter, and a computer, printer, and scanner. I fired up the computer and found it had the same program I'd used in Talladega. I hated that program—it was really cumbersome compared to what I use at home. *Oh well.* "Get used to it," I said out loud. I looked around and saw a ton of unopened vinyl rolls. When the guys showed up, the first thing we were going to do was reorganize. We were going to get rid of this clutter. This shop would be tidy.

It was still early morning when I opened the overhead door. The sun was shining in a light blue sky. There wasn't a cloud in sight—just a few seagulls. I looked up at the sky with my arms stretched out to my sides like a human cross, shut my eyes and stood there enjoying the sun. I got some strange looks from the maintenance crew gathered at their shop sixty feet across the asphalt lot. Six men, holding white Styrofoam coffee cups, stared at me. I could hear one of them say, "Who's that new guy." I wore a T-shirt and was enjoying the 65-degree weather. They all had sweatshirts on. *They shoulda been where I was two days ago and they wouldn't be looking at me so crazy,* I thought. I walked over and introduced myself. We all got talking and I learned that a few of them had been up to Watkins Glen to work at the track for the NASCAR race. One of them was from Australia. They brought me in the Maintenance Shop and showed me the coffeepot, which they kept full. Then one of the guys said, "Hey, Vickio, here comes your class."

I looked to my left and two guys were walking toward the shop. "Are these my students?" I asked. Sure enough.

I caught up to the two guys before they reached the sign shop. They turned toward me and one of them asked, "Are you Tony?"

"It's me. You guys must be the new sign guys. How are you guys doin'?"

They introduced themselves and we talked a few minutes, then went into the shop. One man was sort of tall and slender, about forty-five years old. His name was Jack Lane. The other guy was pretty rugged and about thirty-five years old. His name was Glenn Morris. Jack was an artist—oil paintings, pencil and charcoal drawings, and things of that nature. Glenn had worked in a graphics department of a newspaper, laying out ads. I told them this was going to be completely different from what they were used to—and we only had one month to get them going. I also asked them to bear with me as I had never done any teaching like this before.

I thought the first place to start was to organize the shop to suit ourselves. "You have to have a good work environment to do good work," I told them. I thought about what I just said and suddenly realized that when I got back home, I had some major cleaning to do myself. I just might teach myself something here.

Since the day was sunny, I said, "Why don't we take everything—and I mean everything that isn't bolted down, tables and cabinets and all—out in the parking lot and we can clean the entire shop. Then we will put everything back in that we need and scrap the rest. Whatever else we need, I will see if Dick will let us get it."

We worked all day. It was actually fun. People walked by and stared at the huge pile of stuff that had accumulated in the parking lot in front of the shop. It was hard to believe all that stuff came out of the sign shop. Boxes with empty boxes in them, old rolls of forty-eight-inch-wide paper that would never be used, some old signmaking equipment that did not work, thirty gallons of dried-up paint cans—the list seemed endless. There was a dumpster nearby, and a lot of junk went straight in it.

At the end of the day, the shop looked great. "There. Now we can work. See you guys in the morning," I said. I could tell they were excited about their new jobs and would be there early. "Tomorrow, I *teach*."

I went into Dick's office and sat down in a nice maroon overstuffed leather chair. *Plop*. I almost sank out of sight. "Well what do you think?" he asked. "Will they work out?"

"It's only the first day. We'll see in a week. They have a good attitude. We spent the day cleaning and arranging things. I've noticed a few things that we don't have. One of them is a panel saw. It is almost a must in a small shop. I was wondering if we could get one. I have one at my shop and I can't see working without one." A panel saw is a large metal frame that mounted along a wall. It has a saw mounted on a vertical arm that ran up and down. One man could put a 4'×8' piece of plywood in it and cut it perfectly, crosswise or lengthwise, in one smooth operation.

I was going to explain, but Dick waved a hand. "You're here to set up the shop and teach these guys. All you have to do if you need anything is order it. Bonnie will show how to use your purchase order."

"Oh, that sounds good. Thanks, Dick," I said, and walked out thinking, *Wow, this is neat*. I went in to see Bonnie and she showed me what to do. I had my own account and PO forms. I was in charge of the sign operation and basically the boss. The first thing I did was order the panel saw. Spending $2,000 was so easy.

In the computer room were boxes and boxes of unopened rolls (thirty inches wide by fifty yards long) of the kind of vinyl used in computer-cut graphics. Expensive stuff. The person here before me also had this open account and really used it. I never saw so much new, unused material in my life. Vinyl does have a shelf life—and that stash would have taken so long to use that the adhesive would be unadhesived! We started to stack it up and I wrote down the description and item numbers of the unopened boxes, wondering if I could send this stuff back. It all came from a sign material distributor in Orlando. I called them and the first guy I talked to was apparently a salesman. He wouldn't take anything back, so I asked for the boss. I got a guy on the phone and said, "Hi, my name is Tony Vickio. I'm down here from Watkins Glen, New York, working at the sign shop at Daytona Speedway. I have a huge inventory of unopened vinyl rolls that the person here before me ordered from your company and it has never been used. I would like to send them back." He says, "What do you want to return?" I said, "I have all the invoices and it adds up to $14,865." I waited a few seconds and said. "Are you there?"

After a long pause, he came back with, "*No way.* Those must have been there for a while and we will not take back that amount of material."

I thought for a minute and said, "I'm new here and if you don't take it back I will find another distributor to service the speedway. I'm sure anyone else in the business would love to have the Daytona Speedway account." I waited. . . . Another long pause.

Glenn Morris standing in the "cleaned out" sign shop. The graphics computer and plotter are in the room to the right.

Finally he sort of muttered, "OK, we'll take it. I can only give you credit and you will have to get the stuff here. We can't pick it up."

I sat up in the chair, smiling and thinking. . . . I have *power*. The word *Daytona* is power. Sitting perfectly upright in the chair, I thought, *Power, power!* A little drool might have run down my chin.

I said to the guy on the phone, "I will get it there." *My third day and I just saved the track $14,800.*

Dick could not believe it. Then I told him I had to get it there and he looked at me with a puzzled expression. "Tony, just take it to the Shipping Department and tell them where it's going. They will take care of it. You don't have to ask me everything. You do what you need to do while you're here. That's why I hired you."

I walked out thinking, *I really don't know the power I have down here yet. I will find out.*

We finally started to do some signs. Glenn was a good computer guy already, and things were going very well; he and Jack were both picking up on how to use the (lousy) graphics program (the same one I used at Talladega) for the kinds of work needed. We were not doing any painting, just some design work and vinyl graphics. We would soon get plenty of on-the-job training as Speed Week was approaching and the sign jobs were starting to roll in from different departments at the speedway. The day went by so fast. After some basic training and a few small sign jobs, it was time for Jack and Glenn to go home. After everyone was gone, I stood outside the shop alone. Once I started teaching, I really was shocked to find out how much I knew. The information just kept coming out. At times I wondered, *How the hell did I know that? No wonder I'm down here. I've never thought about the amount of knowledge I've accumulated, but holy shit, I do know a lot of stuff.* I smiled and went back inside. All our work would be signs we could produce right in the shop. Daytona had no billboards and another company was doing the grass, so Jack and Glenn would not do any hand painting. This was fine. The small signs gave them the basic knowledge of layout and procedure.

At 11:30 the next morning I noticed this big black guy going into an unpainted cinder block shed near the shop. It was only about 12'×12' and had a big opening in the front, so I could watch as he started to cook something on an old barbecue grill. Smoke rolled out of the opening, swirling up and around the building. I went over and he said, "Dick has me cook burgers and things every day for the guys. Just put a buck in the jar and eat. All the stuff is over here," he added, pointing to a table with mustard and so on at the other end of the opening. It smelled great so I thought I would try it. I ate there almost every day from then on. All the maintenance guys and even Dick ate there.

Glenn and Jack really caught on fast. We were sailing right along when I got a phone call from the president of the speedway. He needed to talk to me about some gate information signs that would be placed on Speedway Blvd. the morning of the race. I told one of the maintenance managers about the call and he responded with, "Oh boy. He is a fanatic. He will want it to look like a book on those signs. One other thing. You *will not* change his mind."

"Believe me," I said. "I'll change his mind." I knew I had to—the more information you try to put on a sign, the less anybody will get from it.

"No you won't," he said. "You'll see."

I thought, *Oh boy. Oh well, we will see when he gets here.*

In an hour, a little guy about sixty years old walked in, wearing a dark blue suit. "Is Tony Vickio here?" he said.

"I'm Tony," I said, walking toward him.

He shook my hand. "Tony, glad to have you down here. Dick tells me you are the best. How are things going?"

"Thank you," I said. "You know you can't believe Dick all the time. But it's going great. You will have two good guys running the place in no time." I looked at Glenn and Jack.

"Hey," he said next. "I have some signs I need made. Got a minute?"

A minute turned into an hour. *Oh my God.* The manager was right. He did want a book on each sign. When he was finished, I said, "Let me make a layout on the computer and tomorrow I will show you what they will look like."

He said OK and left.

I couldn't do them like he wanted. His layout was not going to work. These signs were to be read from a moving car on Speedway Blvd. You would have to stop the car, get out and walk up to the sign to read any of them. In an effort to change his mind, I made two layouts—one with his wording and the other the way I thought they should read. My layout gave the same information as his, but only needed four words and an arrow.

The next day I got a call from the anxious track president. He wanted to come over to the shop and look at what I had. He was dressed in another blue suit, this one pinstriped, as he strolled into the shop. I had the two sign layouts sitting side by side on the computer screen. He looked at his, turned and looked at mine. Back to his, mine, his, mine. The silence was aggravating. After a good three minutes he straightened up and looked up to the ceiling. His head did a quick jerk to the left and he said, "I like mine."

Oh no. I didn't sell it. It didn't sell. I can't believe it. I had no Plan B. Right out of the blue an idea came into my head. I told him, in desperation, "I don't know, sir. There's a lot of copy on yours and remember you are reading this from a car. Here is what I'll do. I'll actually make two signs. One with your layout and one with mine. Tomorrow morning I'll have the maintenance crew put them up on Speedway Blvd. and we will go out in your car and drive by each one. You can read them just as a fan driving in would. The one you like best is the one we will make. How's that?"

He paused, standing there in a thinking pose with one arm supporting the other and his thumb and forefinger holding his chin. "Call me tomorrow when you want me here," he said, "and we will go out and take a look."

Yes. I won a round! At least he was now thinking. I looked at Glenn and Jack and said, "Making headway!" This is good. That afternoon we made two signs—good practice for the boys. The next morning I had maintenance put the two signs out on the highway far enough apart so they couldn't be seen at the same time. I called the president and he showed up at the shop in his gold Cadillac.

I put my Serengetis on and slid into the passenger seat, saying, "Let's ride."

He looked at me with a weird expression and said, "Yes." We drove up the road, turned around and headed back down Speedway Blvd. toward the speedway. "Where are the signs?" he said.

"I'm not telling you," I said. "That's part of the effectiveness of a sign. It has to grab your attention, then you have to be able to read it."

We drove up to his sign and he said in an excited voice, "I see it—I see it." He slowed down to about 15 mph on that four-lane road as we approached his sign. I slouched down in the seat hoping our speed didn't cause a wreck. His hands had a death grip on the steering wheel as he leaned forward trying to read the sign. We were down to 10 mph. He didn't seem to hear the other cars blowing their horns and giving us the bird as they drove by. I expected us to get slammed in the rear at any second. *Oh God.*

A short distance after we passed the first sign, he said, "There's the other one. I see it. I see it." We slowly drove past. A woman pushing a shopping cart down the sidewalk passed us. After we drove by my sign, not a word was said all the way back to the shop. I pretty much gave up and figured on making the dozen or so signs the way he wanted. I should have just made them his way and we would have had them half done by now. But, if I'm in charge, I wanted everything done right. I got out of the car and shut the door, thinking, "Oh boy. What do I do now? I lost."

As I walked around the front of the car, his window rolled down and he stuck his head out and said, "Tony. Your sign looked great. Make them all that way."

I stopped dead. I didn't even answer. The window silently went up and I watched him drive off. I gave him the thumbs-up. No one could believe that I changed his mind. I just smiled.

Race day was fast approaching and Jack and Glenn were cranking out signs. The newly opened Daytona USA was in need of a lot of small signs. Perfect. Good practice. The phone rang. It was Lisa France Kennedy, sister of Bill France, president of NASCAR. She needed a sign for the front of a podium being used at a dinner function in two days. "It has to look elegant," she said. I did a beautiful sign of computer-cut vinyl (cut in reverse) on the backside of a piece of clear Plexiglas to give it class. I thought it looked great. The next day I got called in to see Dick. He said, "Lisa sent me a note and said she wants a different sign for the podium." He handed me the note she sent him which read, "Dick. I would like a different sign for the podium. This sign looks too much like a sign."

I looked at Dick, who had a smile on his face, and said, "Oh my God." Then I made a plain old thing and she liked it.

Jack and Glenn were learning fast. After about three weeks, with Speed Week approaching, we were caught up on sign requests. Time to enjoy the scenery.

 # Speed Week

On Thursday, about a week before the 1998 Speed Week, I drove to work listening to the radio. The announcer was talking about a night launch of Space Shuttle Endeavour at Cape Canaveral at 9:48 that evening. *Wow.* I couldn't believe it. Aviation, second to racing, was my passion. *Damn. I'm this close! I have to drive down and watch it.* I couldn't stop thinking about the launch.

The guard at Gate 7 waved his left arm and pointed the clipboard to the track like I didn't know where to go after three weeks. With his right hand he held a half-eaten glazed doughnut in his mouth. I heard him say, "MMMurrnin," while shaking his head up and down. I waved and hollered out the window without slowing down, "Mornin'."

I stood in front of the shop and drank a cup of coffee. Glenn and Jack came walking across the lot. I was so excited about the news of the launch that I couldn't wait to tell somebody and maybe get them to go with me. "Hey," I hollered as I ran to meet them, spilling coffee down my hand. "Hey, guys. Guess what I heard on the radio. There's a shuttle launch tonight at 9:48. A night shuttle launch. Holy shit. You guys wanna go? Come on. Let's all go. It'll be great."

They gave each other a weird look. Jack said, "Yeah, he's a tourist." They both laughed and Jack said, "Naw. You can see it right from here. Why drive all the way down there?"

"Why? Because, I wanna be close enough so it blows my clothes off. That's why. I'm goin'. You sure you don't wanna go?" I said.

Jack said, "My wife works at the Cape. I'll call her and she can fax a map up here that will get you as close as a civilian can get."

My eyes bugged out and I said, "Are shittin' me? Great. Call her. Call her right now!"

He laughed and said, "God. She isn't even at work yet. I'll call her at nine."

I kept checking the fax every five minutes until, suddenly, it rang. I ran over to the shelf and waited for the paper to start coming out. A groaning sound began inside the machine. Was this it? Was this the map? As the paper slowly rolled out of the slot on the top of the machine I could read "Kennedy Space Center." I hollered, "*Hey. It's here.* The map is here." To me, it was like finding a pirate treasure map. I ripped the paper from the fax. This was *gold.* Looking around, I realized that no one else was paying any attention to it at all. I went over to the far corner of the shop, turned the map over and stared at it. *Gold, pure gold! A Secret Map.* I studied it for a while and then folded it up carefully and put it in my pocket. I tried all day to get someone to go with me, but all I got was, "You can see it from here."

Map in hand, I gave Glenn and Jack some menial tasks to finish and left Daytona Speedway at 3 p.m. heading south toward Cape Canaveral. The drive was only about an hour and a half, but I wanted to get there early. Jack warned me that I wouldn't believe the traffic down there on a launch day. I reached Titusville and it was like race day at Daytona—wall-to-wall motor homes and cars. I kept driving. Vendor tents were all over the place selling things as masses of people walked along the roads. I parked the car at a motel lot and walked across the road toward the bay. I checked my secret map. I was at the right location. I looked around and thought, *How the hell did twenty thousand people get the same map I have?*

It was a hundred feet from the edge of the road to the water. Straight across the water, about six miles away, I could see the Space Shuttle with my naked eye even though it was six miles away. Not many people were by the water yet as it was early. I got talking to a man who had a rather large video camera on a tripod. "Just wait," he said. "You won't be able to move." He had videotaped every launch. He also had a scanner and it was tuned in to launch control. I stayed by him. He knew what was going on.

After a while, with my new friend promising to save my spot, I walked over to a nearby diner to get something to eat. The diner was packed. A shuttle launch was an event. After having a Launch Pad Burger and a Rocket Booster Pepsi, I walked back to the spot by the bay. The crowd was filling in fast, but I found my way back to the guy with the camera. We enjoyed a few beers from his Coleman cooler. We were about a foot from the water and that made me nervous. Gators live down here.

As the sun set, the crowd was now shoulder to shoulder. In the darkness, the pure white shuttle and the large orange fuel tank glowed white on its illuminated launch pad. It gave me a weird feeling of excitement, danger, the unknown, bravery, challenge, envy (I'd do anything to go up in the shuttle), and pride in my country all at once.

Through the scanner we could hear the countdown, which went on for an hour. Finally, it got down to T minus ten seconds, nine, eight, seven, six, five, four, three, two, one. . . . Ignition. . . . Liftoff.

When it got to *ignition,* I could not move. From the pitch black night sky, everything turned a bright, yellowish orange—bright enough to read by—and we were six miles away. The shuttle sat there for a second, while the huge white smoke cloud (which looked solid enough to walk on) billowed up and slowly rolled around, completely engulfing the shuttle. An orange glow appeared in the center of the white smoke. Slowly, the glow started to rise. The nose of the fuel tank pushed through the cloud and up it went. It moved slowly at first, but soon you could see it start to accelerate. The rockets were unbelievably bright. I had the biggest goose bumps on my arms and neck. Suddenly the crowd roared as loud as when Dale Earnhardt takes the lead at Talladega—people screaming, hands in the air, American flags waving, it was awesome—just *awesome*. Completely caught up in the excitement, I found myself waving and cheering too.

The guy with the camera, his eye planted in the rubber boot of the viewfinder, hollered at me and said, "You think that was good? Wait till the sound gets here."

"What?" I said, forgetting that we were miles away, and it takes a while for the sound to travel that far. Then I realized. There was no sound. I was so engrossed in the visual, I forgot about the sound.

"If it was daylight," he said, "you could see the sound coming across the water; it causes these little ripples. A few more seconds. Get ready."

I waited and all of a sudden, *it hit*. "Oh my God," I hollered out loud. It didn't matter—nobody could hear me above the strange wall of sound. It was the ungodliest sound I had ever heard. Not like a jet: a roar, a rumble, and a series of very rapid, nonstop explosions all rolled into one. It was spooky. Unnatural. And it was *loud*. It was so loud, you could actually feel it. It made your clothes move. As the shuttle went up and up into the black sky, I remembered my binoculars around my neck. I was so engrossed, I forgot I had them. I put them to my eyes and I could clearly see the shuttle roll over onto its back (a maneuver that allows the antennas to point toward earth). After a few minutes, I watched the booster rockets fall away as the shuttle roared away into the night. Soon all was quiet. I was still watching through the binoculars, but it got harder to see anything.

Everyone was like me. *Stunned*. The huge smoke cloud drifted off to the right of the launch pad, which was still lighted, and the trail that led up the night sky was starting to drift apart. Then a strange thing happened. Starting with a low moaning sound, a subtle mumble started to grow. It soon turned to a roar as the thousands who were gathered there began talking to complete strangers about what the hell they just saw. I looked back up at the perfectly clear sky, dotted with stars, and I could see the traces of the trail from the huge white cloud on the launch pad go in a long sweeping arc into the black sky and simply disappear there. Soon, another round of roaring cheers went up. I'll never forget it. Everyone cheering, screaming, and clapping. What an experience. It was worth the trip. I thought, *They should tape this crowd and give it to the astronauts. They would be so proud.*

Driving back, the traffic was the same as when a race was over. Bumper to bumper. I didn't mind as my mind kept playing over and over what I had just seen. It was almost like a dream. Did I really see that? I spent the next day telling everyone how the shock waves moved my shirt, and about the sounds and the smoke. Nobody cared, but I kept mumbling to myself all day.

☙

That weekend was the Rolex 24 at Daytona. It started at night and ran from 8:10 p.m. to 8:10 p.m. the next night. With the credentials I had, I could go anywhere, so I spent the early part of the night on Pit Lane. I watched the start and after about

Standing on Pit Lane just before the start of the Rolex 24 Hour.

twenty laps of the race, I went to my motel where the sound of the cars could still be heard.

I woke up the next morning to the same sound that put me to sleep—the race cars. They were still going. I went to the track and got my coffee from the maintenance building. There were a lot of races coming up and the big job we had was changing Victory Circle signage from race to race. Most of the signs we could use from last year but we had to make a few new ones. An example: Friday morning, Victory Circle had to have the Time Trial sponsor on it—at noon it changed to a Race sponsor. Saturday morning it was another Time Trial sponsor, then a new Race sponsor. Sunday it was the Race sponsor again. Lots of changing signs. They were all stored in a large shed right by Victory Circle, so changing them was not too bad.

One of the fixtures at Daytona was Charlie, a tall, lanky black man about sixty-five or seventy years old, with short, curly white hair. His face was drawn, his eyes were wide with reddish streaks, and you could always see his large white teeth because he was always smiling. A lifetime friend of Bill France, he worked at the track doing, well, actually, I never really knew. He was just there doing all sorts of menial things. Charlie never moved very fast and was always willing to talk, which we did often. We got along great. I really liked Charlie. After the twenty-four-hour race was over Charlie and I were talking about, in his words, "Friggin' stupid, souvenir-hungry race junk collectin' assholes." What brought on this rage happened after the Rolex 24 Hour Race.

We were watching two middle-aged guys rolling a well-used race tire across the parking lot in front of the sign shop when he said, "What the hell do ya think they gonna do with it when they get that goddamned tire home? It's gonna be in the goddamned garage takin' up space for ten years. They won't do a goddamned thing with it, but them souvenir huntin' idiots gotta have it."

I laughed hard—the expression on his face was so serious. Then I said, "Charlie. Come over here; I got something to show you." I started walking to the shop, pointing over by the wall. "I wanna show ya something," I said again as I walked.

"Are you crazy, boy? I ain't gonna walk clear the hell over yonder. You walk over there and bring back whatever you gotta show me. I ain't movin'."

I said, "Get the hell off your dead ass and get the hell movin'." He climbed to his feet, mumbling some obscenities. We walked slowly to the shop.

As always, Charlie was hunched over a little and walked with a pronounced limp; with the one-size-too-big maintenance uniform he had on, he sort of slithered along. When we got to the shop, I pointed: There, lying against the wall was a race-worn section of a fiberglass front fender from one of the race cars that crashed during the race the night before. It was covered with rubber and brake dust, and the best part was that it had decals all over it. The one that set it off was the decal that read: ROLEX 24 at Daytona 1998. "Look," I said with great excitement, "It still has the rear view mirror on it. I got it out of the back of a crash rescue truck this morning."

Charlie straightened up, his eyes round as paper plates, and took two steps back. It was like he had just seen the devil himself. He slowly raised his right hand and with a shaky finger he pointed at me. "Jesus Christ. You're one of them damned Northern, junk collectin' idiots!" I looked at Charlie, who was now shaking his head and mumbling, "Christ Ah'mighty. I seen it all. I *seen it all.*" I laughed so hard that I almost got sick. Charlie turned and walked out the door waving a hand in little circles over his head and mumbling. For the next few days, every time I saw Charlie, he would shuffle slowly by shaking his head and mumbling under his breath, "Damn Northerners come down here" then it would trail off. I couldn't get the rest of what he was saying but he would look back as he walked away and he would have a great big grin. Charlie was great.

☙

The Daytona 500 ran on February 15, and this was the year Dale Earnhardt won. It was his first ever Daytona 500 win—after nineteen tries—and his last at the 500. I look back and think, "I was there." It was something to see.

For the race, Dick gave me a seat in the top row of the front grandstand. I was sitting alongside another friend of Dick's, a guy from California who built Motocross tracks. He was there to start construction of the Motocross track that would go in the Tri-Oval grass for Bike Week. I can't believe they do that. The grass in the Tri-Oval of Daytona is put in by a turf company and taken care of like a golf course would be. You walk on the Tri-Oval grass; you don't drive. Period. The only motorized vehicle allowed on the grass is a lawn mower. Then during Bike Week, three weeks after the

Mine. All Mine! A "souvenir" from the Rolex 24 at Daytona.

500, hundreds of truckloads of dirt are brought in and a Motocross track appears. So much work. After it's over, it's all cleaned up and the pristine Tri-Oval grass is back to its beautiful green.

I was getting to know Jack and Glenn better. In the shop one day, Glenn told us that he taught martial arts in his spare time. He turned to Jack and said, "Here, I'll show you a way to protect yourself." He gave Jack a black magic marker with the top off. "Hold it like it's a knife and come at me." Jack held the marker like he was holding. Glenn said, "Put your fist around it and raise it over your head and stab me." Jack raised his hand and came at Glenn. In a tenth of a second, there was a black dot on Jack's sweatshirt, right on his heart. I didn't even see it happen. Glenn had grabbed Jack's wrist and spun him around so fast that Jack had no chance. If it had been a real knife, Jack would have been dead.

"Can you do that again, in slow motion?" I asked. "I couldn't tell what happened.

Jack Lane's drawing of A.J. Foyt that he got autographed for me while A.J. was at Daytona.

Glenn showed me the maneuver in slow motion. It was so smooth it looked choreographed! But after seeing it performed, I still couldn't do it. I didn't even try.

That weekend, Jack brought in some of his paintings. They were just incredible. He showed me a pencil drawing he did in 1979 of A.J. Foyt at Indy, putting on his helmet. I was in shock. I had to have it. It was an incredible drawing. A.J. was a racing legend and one of my heroes. Jack couldn't decide if he wanted to part with it, but he finally sold it to me weeks later, after I got back home. As we talked on the phone about shipping the painting, Jack said, "Hey. A.J.'s here at Daytona testing tomorrow. Want me to get it signed?" Hell yeah! That autographed painting now hangs on the wall in my shop and is one of my prized possessions.

On my last day at Daytona, the garage doors were open and the sun was blazing. My job was done here and I couldn't wait to get home. Thought of it every day! I was talking with one of the managers of the track when the familiar gold Caddy pulled up. "Oh no," I said, with my teeth clenched so he couldn't read my lips.

Jack and Glenn looked at me and said, "Oh-oh."

"I'm outta here tomorrow," I said. "Whatever he needs, you guys are gonna to do it. Don't laugh at me."

The president of the track walked up and approached me. Not knowing what to expect, I smiled and stood there in the door opening. I said, "Hello, sir. How are you?" He didn't answer, but shyly shuffled up to me with his head down and slowly brought his right fist around in a big wide circle and gently punched me in the left shoulder. I didn't know what to do. I didn't say anything.

He then looked up with a smile on his face said, "Tony. Ya hit a home run." I couldn't speak. Not waiting for an answer, he turned and walked out the door. I stood there silently. I didn't know what to do. Then, not turning around but waving over his head, he shouted, "Thank you." We stood there watching him get in the Caddy. He never looked back. He pulled the door shut and he drove away. I looked back to the guys and they were frozen in disbelief.

I told the track manager what happened, and he said, "He never does that sort of thing."

"Wow." I felt good. That was quite a show of appreciation and the type of man

With Jack Lane (left) and Glenn Morris (right).

he was, I knew it came from the heart.

The surprises were not over. Jack and Glenn said, "Wait a minute. Come over here." I walked over to where they were standing by the layout table. They pulled out a beautiful black jacket that had tan suede sleeves and the embroidered Daytona logo on the front. They gave me the jacket for a job well done and starting them off on a new career. Glenn and Jack were both shaking my hand at the same time and thanking me for coming down. That did it. I could not hold back the tears. Jack and Glenn are great friends to this day. It was hard to leave after all.

⁂

After saying good-bye to Dick, Bonnie, Glenn and Jack, and Charlie, I fired up the rental car and headed south to the Orlando Airport. My wife, my mother, and others always annoy me by saying, "Oh. You're so talented. We can't believe the things you do. Oh my God, how good this is or how good that is." I always say back, "I don't want to hear that crap. If I was so damned talented, I'd be rich." Well, you know what? While driving along Alligator Alley and looking back at the past month and my experiences, I realized I was wrong. I am rich.

Every year, to this day, in February around Daytona time the phone in my shop rings. All the voice says is, "Hey Vickio. Listen." Then the person holds the phone up and I can hear race cars testing at the speedway. Yup. It's Glenn. Harassing me no end.

As the plane took off, I watched the ground get further away. In a few hours, I'd be home. I couldn't wait to see Harriett, Beth, and Mark. Of course the snow would be there, but I didn't care. A month away from home was too much. *I won't even get a day off as there will be so many people after me for signs I haven't finished yet.* Working in my own shop was going to feel good, though. Besides, I had to put some of the practices to work that I taught Glenn and Jack while I was at Daytona.

On the plane, sitting next to me reading a newspaper, was a guy about fifty years old wearing a blue suit. Looking straight at the paper, he said, "I see here in the paper that Earnhardt finally won his first Daytona 500. Were you down there for the race?"

I turned from looking out the window. I looked at the man for a second, then I smiled and said, "Let me tell you a story."

We Face the Walls

Almost a year after my trip to Talladega with the Michigan crew—a job that was supposed to be my last in Alabama—I got a phone call out of the blue. Talladega was calling with a completely different request. Seems they'd hired yet another sign company, this one in Atlanta, to do the grass painting and they figured that was in good hands. However, a new marketing twist at Talladega had produced a new theme—"Big and Bold"—and they wanted this new logo all over the racetrack. They wanted everything from 4'×8' posters to signs that were in the two-hundred-square-foot range. Mike McWilliams wanted me to do the signs. They also wanted some lettering on the retaining walls. They asked me to come down for two weeks before the races. Of course, I said yes.

I decided to use Alumalite for the panels. This is a great material, made of two sheets of aluminum with a quarter-inch plastic core. Very rigid and light. I could do the signs in my shop over the winter and then put them in a truck and take them down to the speedway prior to the spring race. I wanted to make pounce patterns over the winter for the retaining wall lettering, but Talladega didn't have artwork yet. To solve this, I decided to box up my thirty-inch plotter, computer, scanner, and printer and take them with me. I would set them up in an office in the sign shop at the maintenance building. I worked on the "Big and Bold" signs in my shop during the winter. With the signs finished, it was time to get ready to go back to Talladega.

I needed help, and Bob Carson—the friend I took to Talladega on my last trip—couldn't make it. Luckily, I have more sign painter friends and potential helpers. A few years ago, Steve Hughey, owner of Hughey Signs in Corning, New York, came to my shop when it was in Ithaca to see my new computerized Gerber Vinyl cutter. I was one of the first in the area to have one and he wanted to see it work. We soon became very good friends. One day, on the golf course, Steve brought along this pathetic-looking excuse for a human (that's what I jokingly called him) by the name of Larry Orr. Actually, he fit right in as he was as pathetic as the rest of us! He also owned a sign shop? His was in Lindley, New York. Then through acquaintances, I met Bob Timmerman, who owned Sunshine Signs in Dryden, New York. Needless to say, Steve, Bob, Larry, and I all became best of friends. Did you see the word *golf* a few lines back? We are all addicted to the game. For many years the four of us met once a week at a different course and proceeded to tear each other up with verbal abuse and slurs.

Steve and Larry agreed to join me on my next Talladega adventure. At the time, Steve had a helper (who later opened his own sign shop; there's a lot of demand) named Brad Daudlin. He was about twenty-three years old at the time, average build, and he was addicted to the sign business. Brad was eager to learn anything he could about sign making, and he had one of the best teachers in Steve. Brad lived in Beaver Dams, New York, and he joined our circle of friends. Brad drove an old brown Ford pickup truck that reminded me of the truck Britten Banners had used to get the cardboard to Talladega. He wanted so much to go on this trip that I said, "You haul the signs down for me and you can stay two weeks and help us. How's that?" He went crazy. We loaded his truck with the signs and away he went, front wheels damn near off the ground. Brad left a couple of days before we did as he had a hell of a load in the truck and wanted to take his time. Steve, Larry, and I decided to take my wife's Ford Explorer. All of my computer stuff and our sign kits fit right in it.

We arrived at the track about two in the afternoon and greeted Mike and the gang. It was like I had never left. We parked at the sign shop in the maintenance building and started to unload my equipment. Brad was already there waiting for us. He had no trouble going down and made better time than he anticipated. He had all the signs unloaded and stacked against the sign shop wall at the speedway. Inside the office we set up all the computer equipment. We were ready for this new challenge, whatever it was. Officially we started work the next morning, but getting the plotter and computer set up on Sunday gave us a head start.

On Monday we were at the track by 7 a.m. We went into the war room, where Mike and a few other guys were already planning the day. Today, Mike wanted to start putting up the "Big and Bold" signs. Looking straight at me, he said, "The track maintenance men will put them up. I have other plans for you."

Having the maintenance men putting up our signs was a relief. "I have other plans for you," wasn't.

"I want you to go for a ride with me so I can show you where we want new logos painted." I got in his new GMC pickup and we headed for the racetrack. We were going to look at sign locations on the retaining walls that are around the entire 2.66-mile oval. I started to think that not painting the grass was going to be a letdown. Painting logos on the retaining walls, even though I'd never done it before, sounded like a bore. I was curious to see what Mike wanted done, hoping against hope it was not going to be boring. Man, did I get my wish . . . as in "be careful what you wish for."

Mike and I drove through the familiar tunnel and up the grade to the infield of the huge speedway. As we came up out of the tunnel, I turned to look out the rear window of the truck at the track between Turns 3 and 4. Like I've said before, it doesn't matter how many times I've seen this view, it gives me goose bumps up and down my arms. You can't take a picture of it, and you can't see it on TV. You have to see it in person to get the full effect of that steep banking.

Larry Orr checking signs at Talladega sign shop.

"Holy shit, what a sight," I said to Mike. "I know I say that every time I come here."

He just smiled and said in his low Southern voice, "Yeah, you better look at it. You're gonna see a lot of it. From the top." We drove onto the track near Pit In, just off of Turn 4. We turned left and headed to the start/finish line.

Mike slowed the truck down and stopped and we got out. He pointed to the start/finish line and said, "It needs painting. They want a black and white checker board line."

"OK," I said and thought, *All hand and knee work. This is not going to be good on the back.* I smiled to myself. *I'll let Larry and Steve paint it.*

Then he pointed to the retaining wall to the right of the start/finish line. "We are going to need four Talladega logos. One here, one in Turn 1, one on the Back Straight, and one in Turn 4. I don't have exact locations yet or the artwork, but it will be here by tomorrow."

"That's fine," I said.

We got back in the truck and drove around the track on the apron (the flat part of the track inside the banking) to Turn 1. We again stopped and got out. I looked up at the banking. All I could think of saying was, "Holy Christ." I'd seen the banking from a distance when we were on the Tri-Oval painting the grass. I'd even driven on it at speed, but to stand at the bottom of the banking and look up at it was scary.

Mike looked at me. "Go on up and see how it feels. When you get to the top, grab the fence." He meant the catch fence, which is on top of the concrete retaining wall. "When you start to come back down, remember, don't turn around. Come back down backward, the same way you went up, until you get used to it. Take it slow."

From where I was standing, the catch fence was five stories up. I'm petrified of heights. (You've heard that one before, but it's still true.) "I'm scared of heights. I don't know if I can go up there."

"Ya better git used to it," he said. "That's where you're gonna be workin'."

I turned toward the bank. It was like looking at an asphalt wall. I walked up the slightly elevated apron of the track, which was about six feet wide, to the actual start of the 34-degree banking. From the apron to the start of the banking there was a sharp transition. It is not a gradual change. Cars sometimes lose control when they get down to the bottom of the banking and run a tire off on that apron. Now I could see why.

I stepped onto the banking and started to go up. I found myself walking on the balls of my feet with my hands out in front of me actually touching the track. It was like climbing an invisible ladder. By the time I got to the top, the backs of my legs were burning. I was breathing hard and my forehead was starting to sweat. Man, was I out of shape. At the top, the concrete retaining wall was right above my head. I stood slowly while reaching up and over the retaining wall, sticking my fingers through the catch fence, and grabbing on like it was a matter of life and death. I was sure that no one could just stand up here without holding onto the fence. I slowly turned my head and looked toward the infield.

"Oh my God." I said out loud. "What a view."

Mike hollered up, "Whaddaya think?"

"Holy shit," I hollered back down.

"You better get used to it. That's where you're going to be painting tomorrow."

I was thinking to myself, *I don't know how I can do it. I can't do it.*

"Come on down—backwards," Mike hollered. I turned my back and slowly let go of the fence and grabbed the top of the concrete wall. With my left hand on the track surface, I slowly backed down the banking, the same way I went up.

Back at the shop, Steve, Larry, and Brad were sorting the "Big & Bold" signs so the maintenance men could install them. I told them of the banking I was just on. "You guys are not going to friggin' believe it. I don't know how the hell we are going to work up there. I mean it. I'm not kidding. I don't know how we are going to do it. Wait till you see the view from up there," I said. They couldn't wait to go out to the track and try walking up the banking.

Mike had a list of smaller directional signs he needed. I started to design them on the computer and cut the vinyl lettering. As I worked, I was mumbling to myself about the banking. Larry, Brad, and Steve applied the vinyl to the signs. We were in full production. One good thing about bringing other sign guys with me was I didn't have to baby-sit them. They know what to do.

The vinyl graphics age was not in full swing yet. For small signs, I used computer-generated vinyl. For larger signs, we painted them.

One thing I forgot to mention, Larry and I brought our wives with us. This would be the last time they traveled with us. They did not like being away from home so long. Harriett worked at the time, converting court stenographer notes for attorneys. She brought her computer with her and the track gave her an office and Internet connection so she could keep up with her clients. When her work was done, she would go tour the area around Talladega with Sally, Larry's wife.

The next day Mike had the artwork for the retaining walls. I looked at the Talladega logo and my first impression was, *I don't like it. It will not fit right on the walls.* It was a curved type logo with long slashes on the Ls. It will be too small. I drew it to scale on the computer and showed Mike. He agreed and said, "Can you come up with something I can show them?" He was referring to the marketing people.

"I'll make a drawing for you."

"Thanks! See what you can come up with," he said as he was walking out the door. I turned to the computer screen and went to work. I drew a TALLADEGA that was straight across with the letters stretched to make it longer. The two Ls dropped below the letters and went all the way under the rest of the letters, fading to a point. At each end of Talladega were two slashes that were used in the new "Big & Bold" logo. For the final drawing, I used most of the slashes and style of the new logo, but straightened out the word *Talladega*. I printed their logo and mine to show the comparison of how they would look on the wall. The concrete retaining wall at Talladega was forty-four inches high and eight inches thick. The logo they wanted, if held to the proportion of their drawing, would have been only sixty inches long. You would never see it on television. The new logo that I drew was sixty-eight *feet* long. They chose mine. Since we were doing four of these, we needed a pounce pattern.

We got started at 7:00 a.m. the next morning, excited to tackle our first wall job. We chose the Front Straight logo as our starting point. It would be the easiest. I did the layout on the computer and sent it to the plotter. The plotter had a pen in it that drew the layout on a roll of thirty-inch-wide paper. The layout was then printed in ten-foot strips, each half the width of a section, which we taped together lengthwise. Once the layout was printed, placed on a large metal table in the shop and—using an electro pounce machine—holes were created along the pen lines on the paper. I hated doing this job, so I just said, "Here it is boys! Have at it!" *Aahhhhhh.* To be the boss! Sometimes it makes life good.

With the punching finished, we packed up our paint, patterns, chalk lines, and tape, put everything in the back of the John Deere Gator, and headed for the track. Mike was to meet us out there. We gathered in front of the wall on the Front Stretch, where the track was not banked as steeply as the turns. The banking here was only about 12 degrees (which is what some tracks have in their corners). Steve and Brad had coffee in hand. I stood there looking around at the size of the Front Straight. This place was huge. I looked to my right, and standing by the Gator was Larry, stuffing his stupid pipe with tobacco. You can always tell if he's been around . . . ashes all over the place. *You should see my truck.* At least, he'd never get lost. To find him, we just followed the ash trail.

After the placement of the logo was set, Mike gave us one word of warning: "One thing before you start. *Don't get a drop of paint on the racetrack.* Especially when you're working on the banks. I don't want a streak of paint running down the banking." He turned and walked to his truck.

I understood. The track surface is treated like it's made of gold. Better.

We looked at each other and I said, "Well, let's get at it." The first step was to locate where the logo was to go on the wall. This is extremely important. Television dictated placement. The paintings had to be seen.

We taped our first pattern section to the Front Straight wall. The wall had been painted white and was ready for our artistic touch. Talladega Superspeedway has a group of guys that do nothing else but paint. They paint the retaining walls white. They paint the sluice pipes and concrete drains white. They paint everything white. It's unbelievable how much white paint they go through at this track.

The next step was to pounce our pattern on the wall. This was one messy job, involving a bag of charcoal dust almost as fine as talcum powder that had to be tapped against the paper hard enough to force the dust through the tiny holes in the pattern. I didn't want to pounce, nobody wanted to pounce. It was a dirty, dirty job. But then Larry Orr said, "I'll pounce it." That secured his job for the next six years. He became known as "Pounce Man." He was actually a pounce machine. With that stupid pipe positioned at just the right angle in his mouth, he would bend over and walk down the wall, slamming, banging, and rubbing the bag on the pattern as he went. Bang, bang, bang, swirl, swirl, swirl. It was like watching John Henry. Remember him? Johnny Cash would sing, "You know that he was a steel drivin' man, Lord God, John Henry was a steel drivin' man." John Henry had to compete against the steam drill. They hadn't invented a machine yet to challenge the Pounce Man. Larry was like John Henry, a legend.

The farther Larry moved down the pattern, the more dust he made. He totally disappeared into the black charcoal dust cloud. When Larry walked back out of the charcoal cloud, it was the signal that it was time to paint. He was always covered in charcoal dust.

After the pouncing was finished we carefully rolled the pattern up from right to left. This way when you go to the next site, you set a centerline, measure a certain distance left and you have your starting point. Tape the pattern down and roll it out. Doing it the same way every time eliminated mistakes and made things a lot easier.

Thinking of what Mike said about paint on the track, I sent one of the guys for cardboard. I didn't want to take a chance of spilling paint on my first wall job. The pattern turned out good on the wall. This was where Larry brought up a good idea that we use to this day.

While working on a job in Corning, painting designs on a concrete walkway over a river, he'd discovered something that was just the ticket for rough surfaces: a thing called a pad painter. It had a red plastic handle with a flat bit set at a slight angle and a 1.5"×2.5" bristly pad that slipped over the flat part. You laid the pad flat on the paint in a tray, getting some paint to soak into the foam, and then just pulled a stroke (that is, a line) down your pattern. It put a perfect line on the wall. When we go to Lowe's to get them, we buy the store out. That's the only place that carried our favorite brand (Shur-Line Pad Painters). As all of us were sign painters, it didn't take long to knock

Getting ready to paint the Start/Finish line along the Front Straight at Talladega.

off a sixty-eight-foot-long Talladega logo on the Front Straight wall. Two of us outlined and two guys with rollers filled in right behind us.

That day we finished two logos—one on the Front Straight and the other on the Back Straight. The next day we would attack the high banks of Turn 1 and Turn 2. We drove around the bottom of the track to look at where we would be working the next day. I stopped the truck in Turn 1 and got out. Everyone else got out and we all looked up at the wall. . . Five stories up. "Holy shit," they all said at once.

"I can't wait, I have to go up and see what it's like to paint up there," Steve said.

"Me too," "Me too," came the response from the others.

"You bums think you are in shape? Try it." I told them what Mike told me about how to go up and come back down. They all started up the 34-degree banking at once. I followed. We got to the top and grabbed onto the catch fence. I didn't mention it before, but the retaining wall wasn't vertical, it was perpendicular to the track which meant it angles over you. It was not like standing and painting a wall in your house.

Once the guys were up there, the questions started.

"How is the pattern going to stay on?"

"How the hell are we going to paint up here?"

"Oh my God."

"This is going to be an experience."

We were all mumbling to each other—no one was listening to anyone, just talking. We started back down with looks of wonderment on our faces . . . wondering what the hell we were going to do tomorrow. I must have said "Holy shit" thirty times from the track back to the motel. That's all I could say. The next day was going to be an experience.

 # High Wallers

We pulled into the track at 7 a.m. as usual. This day was going to be memorable. I don't know who came up with the name, but from that day on we would be known as "High Wallers": members of a small, select group of brave sign artists. The four of us weren't alone—others around the country also qualify for this honor. They challenged the high banks of famous racetracks: Daytona, Bristol, Talladega . . . Risking injury or even death to apply their skill so others may enjoy.

We went right to the shop and picked up the John Deere Gator, which was loaded with all the paint and supplies we would need. Steve Hughey and I jumped on the Gator and took off toward the infield, not waiting for Larry Orr and Brad Daudlin who followed in Brad's truck. Larry was just lighting his stupid pipe as we sped by.

Steve Hughey looking for paint in the handiest "tool" we had—a John Deere Gator!

He just gave us a dumbfounded look as if to say, "What the hell is the hurry?" Steve and I had been parked just off the asphalt on the grass between Turns 1 and 2 for five minutes before Brad and Larry pulled in behind us. From the back of the Gator I grabbed a quart can of One-Shot Red lettering paint, a black plastic paint tray, two Shur-Line Pad Painters, and four foam brushes and threw them in the plastic tray. Steve had a quart of black Chromatic lettering paint and another tray. Larry grabbed the roll of pounce patterns.

"Well, this is it, guys," I hollered. "Let's go." We were all so anxious to get to work on this new venture that no one answered. We just took off up the 34-degree banking of Turn 1 at the Talladega Superspeedway.

It must have looked like the California gold rush as we made a mad scramble to the top of the five-story-high bank, where we all grabbed onto the fence as if our lives depended on it. With a one-handed death grip we took a minute to catch our breath. "That was one hell of a walk," Steve said, huffing and puffing (Yes. He was a smoker). We were all breathing hard as the hike up the banking showed us how out of shape we were. I was at the right end of the line. I looked down the wall at the rest of my painting friends clinging to the catch fence. I had to smile: we looked like monkeys hanging from the jungle canopy in Africa. We were turned around toward the infield. All of us were hanging onto the fence with our right hands and our heads were turning back and forth surveying the unbelievable view of the speedway. No one made a sound as we all looked around. It was breathtaking in more ways than one. Very few race fans have seen, or will ever see, Talladega Superspeedway from this location. We hung there for about five minutes, each of us silent and lost in our own thoughts. Now it was time to try to get used to our new environment . . . working sideways. That 34-degree angle does throw you off a bit.

"Well boys, let's get some work done. Just be careful. This sure as hell isn't going to be easy," I hollered. "Larry. Got the pattern?" He was standing next to Brad who was on my left.

I looked down the line and Larry was holding the roll of paper up as he shouted, "Got it, boss. Let's find the center line of this logo and get this pattern pounced."

Our enthusiasm faded as we suddenly realized that no one wanted to let go of the fence. I said, as I slowly released my death grip, "We better start getting used to this. We have a lot of work to do up here and we better figure this out."

To anyone watching, we had to look like a bunch of clowns. We worked together to find the centerline of that logo on the wall. It took twice as long as usual because everyone was getting used to standing, let alone walking, on the 34-degree banking. Just turning around was a challenge. All of us were very uncomfortable working at this angle—especially being five stories in the air. We bumped into each other and constantly panic-grabbed at the catch fence or the top of the concrete wall to stabilize ourselves. God forbid if someone's face was in the way. If it was, you found yourself grabbing an ear or a handful of hair or someone's lip.

The funny thing was that eventually you would find yourself face-to-face with someone you thought was your friend. You see, no one wanted to let go of the catch fence to walk around anyone else. We were all nestled up against the retaining wall

An example of Pounce patterns on the high walls. Bob Timmerman visited us on a later trip to Talladega and helped out.

afraid to let go. We just stared each other down until one of us would let go. The one that let go just stood still and the guy holding onto the fence slowly went between him and the retaining wall, going hand over hand along the fence. As soon as he went by, the other guy would lunge upward and grab on again. It was a sight. I wish someone had a video of us. It's funny to think about, but it was also dangerous working up there. Just a week earlier, a worker at that track had slipped and fallen down the banking, breaking a leg.

We finally found the center line of where the logo was to go and accomplished the first manual task: getting the first ten-foot section of the pattern rolled out along the wall.

"OK. Who's got the tape?" I called. "We need the tape."

Everyone looked at everyone else. No one had the tape.

"Oh shit," I yelled. "Who was in charge of the tape?" I figured if I put the blame on someone else right away, I wouldn't have to go down and get it. It was not the trip down that was the trouble. It was the dreadful walk back up. Steve, Larry, and Brad looked at each other, all blaming one another, knowing one of them had to go down.

I secretly grinned. *Ahh. Being the boss.* Since Brad was the youngest, I said, "Brad, would you go down and get the tape?"

Brad, not saying a word, started down the banking. He was standing almost straight up, sort of shuffling down sideways. His right foot was sliding ahead of the left, hopping down the banking with his arms stretched out to the sides for balance like he was walking on a tightrope. For only his second time on the high banks, he was going down pretty fast. Actually, he was quite impressive. We all watched in awe. He was quite impressive . . . until. In his sideways shuffle, he stepped on the lower lane white line that was painted on the track. In a split second he went down. Damned good thing he was near the bottom. He rolled once and on the second roll he popped straight up and stood there at the apron of the track. He looked up at us and waved his right arm around in a large circle and hollered, "I'm OK, man." He walked to the Gator.

"That had to hurt," Steve said.

Brad grabbed two rolls of one-inch 3M masking tape and started back up. I'll tell you what. After a few times of forgetting something, you make damn sure you bring everything up the first time. No one ever forgot the tape again. Also, another lesson for the day. Don't step on the white lines.

We found out another inconvenience about working on the wall. Being in a turn, the wall had a slight curve. This made it necessary to tape the pattern down a lot more often than on the flat. Also, the wall was 90 degrees to the track (so the wall is actually at a 68-degree angle to the world), and the pattern wanted to hang away from the wall.

"Hey, Orr," I hollered. (Why am I always hollering?) "Get that pounce bag ready." He was carrying it in a black pouch on his belt. He pulled the pounce bag out and, to get the absolute perfect consistency, he banged it a few times on his hand. Puffs of black charcoal dust engulfed his hand. At the same instant, a puff of white smoke shot up from his stupid pipe signaling that the pounce bag was ready. As we all watched, Larry started walking down the pattern pouncing like a man possessed. While bending over with his right hand holding the top of the retaining wall, he pounced the pattern with his left hand. We were hanging off the catch fence like ripe fruit, as Larry (the Pounce Man) disappeared into a cloud of black charcoal dust.

"Man, can that guy pounce," Steve said.

"Yeah, he's a pouncin' fool," I said back.

When Larry emerged from the cloud, we rolled the pattern up and for the first time we were ready to paint on the high banks. Just then I heard a noise. A vehicle of some sort was coming around the outside of the track. At Talladega (and Daytona), a one-lane road ran just outside the track and about level with the retaining wall. It went around the entire track at the top of the banking.

Those days it was used for emergency vehicles to get access to any part of the track fast, but that wasn't why they built it. The road was built for heavy dozers. That's right, large bulldozers and other heavy equipment. When they were building the track, the banking was designed with such a steep angle that there was no way to just drive the asphalt pavers, dump trucks, and rollers around the corners. Instead, they positioned huge dozers with specially built arms holding large cables on the road above the track. These cables were attached to the heavy equipment. As the asphalt trucks and the rest moved along, so did the dozers—thus holding them in place. It was a huge and dangerous undertaking. There are photos in the Motorsports Hall of

Fame in Talladega, next to the speedway, showing the construction.

Now, like I said, the road is used for emergency access vehicles. There was a special High Bank Rescue Team at Talladega. They were trained to repel over the wall if a car crashed on the high banks, get hung up in the catch fence, or stayed up on the banking. There were slots (two-foot squares) cut in the catch fence at intervals around the corners so the rescue team could get through to the track.

We all stood up—still clutching the catch fence—and looked through the chain link to see a white van approaching. As it got closer, it slowed down and stopped. We heard doors opening and about six people got out and walked toward the catch fence. They were twenty feet or so to the left of us. They came up to the fence and we could hear them talking. When they saw the banking all you could hear was Ohhhs and Ahhhhs, Oh my Gods, and a few Holy shits. Then one of them said, "Hey look over there." They saw us.

They all ran over and with fingers sticking through the fence they all started talking to each other:

"Oh my God, look at them."

"What are they doing?"

"How did they get out there?"

One woman said, "How do they dare do that?"

The weird part was, all they had to do was ask us and we would have told them. We were only three feet from them. But we were just like animals in a zoo. Now I know how the monkeys feel. They were talking among themselves, pointing at us, like we couldn't hear or understand them. It was really weird. We later found out that it was a tour van from the Motorsports Hall of Fame. It had a regular run and would come by every couple of hours.

When we went back to the shop for lunch, I made a sign that read "Please don't feed the Sign Painters." We would attach it on the fence where we were working, facing toward the road. Now when the van stopped the people would laugh and come over to where we were working and talk with us. Some would take pictures. That added some fun to the day.

As I painted, I only put a small amount of paint in the tray just in case it spilled. "Don't get a drop of paint on the track," Mike had ordered. If we did spill any, we could clean it up with rags before anyone saw us. Each guy had to hold his own tray while he painted. There was no place to set a tray down. Painting on the high banks was really tough—one hand holding the tray while brushing paint on with the other. This was harder than you think. While concentrating on painting a straight line the paint tray would slowly start to tip and soon you would feel paint running down your thumb. Also, you didn't have any hands left to hold onto the wall. That first day on the high banks was a real learning experience.

A big problem, we found, was locating a place to store the gallon of paint. I'd just thought we could put it on top of the wall, between the concrete wall and fence. We found that the wall was angled too much and the catch fence was too tight to the wall leaving no room to wedge the gallon of paint between the concrete and the wire. Every time we needed more paint in the trays, we had to go down and get it. Doing

Steve Hughey, Brad Daudlin, Larry Orr, and Tony Vickio on the High Banks of Talladega.

that all day took a toll on a person.

One good thing that did come from going up and down all day was that we discovered a new way of walking up the banking. This is what we came up with. As we stood at the bottom of the banking, we would pick a spot on the wall where we wanted to be. We would drive down the track a hundred feet or so and park. We then walked from that point up the banking, at an angle toward the spot where we wanted to be. It meant a longer walk but at a lesser angle that was much easier on the legs. This was the same way a mountain goat goes up a mountain. They don't climb straight up, so why should we? We had finally graduated to the intelligence of a mountain goat. Up and down, up and down, all day long.

By late afternoon, I couldn't feel my legs. "Let's get back to the shop and do some more small signs for a change of pace," I said.

That night, we went to Lowe's. The way the wall angled over us at the top of the banking, we had to kneel to paint. This meant a quick trip for knee pads. We were learning.

The next day we were back on the high banks by 7:30 a.m. We were surprised to find ourselves more at ease going up and working on the banks this time. The more time we spent up there, the more things became natural. It was a beautiful day. The sun was bright and a slight breeze was blowing over the wall and swirling around us. It was quiet. We had been working for about three hours and consumed with our painting to the point that we were not talking at all. The only sound was the music from the radio. *Yes, it was that same radio I had when the bug landed on the projector years ago at Watkins Glen.* We listened to an oldies station from Anniston, and the woman DJ was asking for requests. I got on the cell phone and called her. She was really interested when I told her that we were from Watkins Glen, New York, and what we are doing down here. In a little while, she came back on the radio. We all stopped work and listened. She said, "This song was requested by the boys from Watkins Glen, New York. They are down here painting signs at the Talladega Superspeedway." Being at the track and around the racing crowd, I had requested "Hot Rod Lincoln," by Commander Cody, one of my favorite songs.

When the song started playing, I stopped painting and turned with my back to the wall. I slowly slid down into a sitting position, leaning back against the wall, and sang along with the song. I get goose bumps every time I hear that song. Years ago, my brother, Chip, and my cousin Johnny Vickio had a band called "Jacobs Ladder." Johnny would sing that song for me. This was good.

When the song was over, I happened to look way off into the distance toward the Tri-Oval grass. I noticed someone walking on the grass. I wondered who it was. It was too far to see who it was, but I could tell it was a man. The painting was going well and my song was over, so I decided to go down and get on our John Deere Gator and take a ride over and see who was out there.

As I was halfway down the banking, I turned a hollered to the guys, "I'll be right back. Keep painting."

It took a while as a Gator only runs at about 25 mph, tops, but I finally got there and I saw a guy out on the grass with a tape, measuring and sticking flags in the ground. Another man was standing off to the side with another tape. I got off the Gator and introduced myself to the second man. The first guy had an intent look on his face. I didn't want to bother him, so I stood back a little. *How the heck is he laying this out? No patterns, no horizontal or vertical marks for a grid. I don't get it.* He finally put a flag in the ground and stopped his work. He walked over and we shook hands and introduced ourselves and started to swap stories. We talked for fifteen minutes. His name was Allan Jones, from Atlanta. I remember his name, because it was the same as a past Formula 1 driver that won a race at Watkins Glen in 1980.

I asked him what method of layout he was using. I had never seen it before. He smiled and I could see that he was a little hesitant to tell me. He thought for a second and said, "I'll show you an easy way I found to lay out large logos."

I listened and as I got more and more details, I smiled. "Wow. That's awesome," I said in a low voice. "Well, I've got to get back or the guys will kill me. Man, I really appreciate the information. Thanks a lot."

"What are you doing?" he asked.

I turned around and pointed over to Turn 2 where the guys are painting. They looked like ants, they were so far away. "We are putting logos on the retaining walls," I said.

"That don't look easy," he said.

"It's different," I admitted.

We shook hands, and with my newfound knowledge, I jumped on the Gator and headed back to the guys. When I got back, I had bugs on my teeth from smiling so much while driving with no windshield. "Where the hell have you been?" the guys asked. "You'll do anything to get out of work."

"You wouldn't believe what I just learned," I said. "I'll tell you about it later. Let's get this wall done."

At 7:00 a.m. Wednesday morning, we stood on the Front Straight. Steve had his truck on the track (a Toyota with a cap on the back). He walked up to me. "Hey, boss?" He always called me that when we are on a job. "Can I take a lap in my truck?" I looked around. There was no one here yet.

"Sure," I said.

Harriett and Larry's wife (Sally, called Sal) were with us on this trip and Steve talked them into going along for the ride. He asked me if I wanted to go, too.

"Are you nuts?" I said. "I'm not riding with you."

He ran to the truck and jumped in. Away they went. He could only get 100 mph on the high banks. Harriett loved it. I don't think Sal saw a thing. She was petrified. Steve came back around and stopped on the Front Straight. He got out of the truck. "Oh my God! That was a blast, man," he said, all smiles. "Thanks for letting me do that, Boss. I didn't know if we were allowed to do that or not."

"You stupid ass," I said. "How the hell do I know if it's OK? I'm just a sign painter." He stared at me with a dumb look on his face and started to laugh. We all started laughing.

After Steve's hot lap, the women took the Explorer and left to tour the countryside. We got in our trucks and headed for the next logo location, which was in Turn

Painting the lines at Talladega; I'm glad it wasn't my job to walk all those miles!

4. We parked our vehicles about fifty yards from where the logo was going and goat-walked up the banking.

We'd been working about an hour when way off in the distance I could hear a sound like a paint sprayer. I looked toward the Tri-Oval, where Alan was yesterday, but there was no one there. The sound didn't go away. I looked around to my right as that sound was bugging me. I wanted to see what it was. If there is one thing I do know it is the sound of a gas-powered paint sprayer. *Where is it? It's not in the infield anywhere.* I looked to my right and way down the track (on the racing surface), just entering Turn 3 and coming toward us, were two, no, more like three men with some kind of machine. They were walking up on the outside lane about a car width from the retaining wall. We all stopped painting and watched as they got closer. I couldn't believe it. They had a gas-powered paint spraying machine on wheels. I knew that sound anywhere.

"What the hell are they doing?" I said out loud. In unison, we all stood up and grabbed the catch fence. We started talking at once trying to guess what the hell they were doing.

I'll be damned. As they got closer, I could see they were painting the white lines on the track. The track had three lanes, plus a shoulder at the bottom—two rows of white dash lines for the lanes and a solid one for the shoulder. These guys had to walk three laps around this 2.66 mile track spraying the lines. The banking was so steep they needed two big, muscular guys walking above the machine, holding ropes attached to the machine to keep it from sliding down the banking. The machine was a three-wheeled sprayer, but the unique thing was, the engine and five-gallon pail of paint were angled to match the banking. It looked weird. The third man guided the wheeled paint machine and painted over the old lines. He stopped when he got to us. He was about forty-five years old and wore a white T-shirt and checkered shorts. He had a thick gold chain around his neck and on his wrist. His reddish hair was a mass of short, wiry curls surrounding a bald spot.

"What the hell are you guys doing?" he said.

"What the hell are you doing?" I said.

He laughed. "Puttin' stripes down, man. Puttin' stripes down."

"Hell, you got a lotta' walkin' to do," I said.

He smiled and stuck his right hand up in the air with the index finger pointing up and twirled it in a circular motion three times (reminding me of my signals to Raymond), then pointed it straight ahead. In one motion, the engine revved up and all three guys took off at the exact same time. You had to see it to believe it. Watching them walk off, paint machine purring away on the high banks, was a sight. It had never occurred to me to wonder how they painted those lines, but a truck would not stay on the banks going that slow any more than the paving machines they'd used to build the track.

By late Thursday the logos were done, and except for a few small signs that might come into the sign shop, we were finished with the walls. Friday we would clean up the small sign orders in the shop. Saturday would be the time to enjoy the races.

Talladega Race Time

Bob, Larry, Steve, and I were at the track early as usual on Saturday. The women were back on the road sight-seeing. Today was the Busch Race. Man, did it feel good not to have to worry about cars sliding through the grass and making us work late into the night to repaint for the Sunday race. Of course, I didn't feel good about the chance of cars hitting the wall, either—those logos would be nasty to repaint and they were more of a target than the grass was. The usual sellout crowd was coming in.

By 6:45 a.m. we were in the war room at the Maintenance Office. Yup, cookies, doughnuts, and cakes, all supplied by the food vendors at the track. One hand

Larry and Steve in the NASCAR Garage on race morning.

washes the other. When they need something from maintenance, they get taken care of. When maintenance guys get hungry, they get fed. Once you are on the inside, it is pretty neat. If you get hungry during the day, just go to a hospitality tent and eat. The food in Alabama was good—but man, was it fattening.

In the NASCAR Garage.

We were drinking coffee while talking to Mike and the boys. The NASCAR garage opened at 7 a.m. We had a lot of time to kill before the Busch race at 2 p.m. We all moved out to the closest pickup truck. Mike took his spot at the back, so he could put his foot on the bumper. The rest of us shuffled for position along the sides. It got a little tense before we were all nestled in around the box of the truck.

Elbows on the box, coffee in hand, I just happened to look to my right—and did a double take. There, standing by the sign shop all by themselves were Sal and Harriett, both staring at us. By the look I was getting, I could tell what they were thinking: "What are you two idiots doing leaving us here by ourselves?" I turned back wondering if they saw me look. I looked at Larry. He was oblivious. I sort of jerked my head up and over my right shoulder in their direction and, like a ventriloquist, talking with my lips stretched tight and not moving I said, "Hey. They're looking at us." I shook my head in their direction a couple more times.

Larry looked over and said, "Ah. They caught me. We better go see what they want." We took our elbows off the truck and walked over to them.

"What are you two idiots doing?" they both said in unison. "Don't leave us here by ourselves."

"I told you that's what they were thinking," I whispered to Larry.

"When does the race start?" Sal asked.

"About six hours," I said.

"What the hell are we going to do for six hours?" they both screamed at once.

"We're going to the garage. We will meet you here later," I said. Away we went, leaving them to amuse themselves however they could. (They went shopping).

Any NASCAR fan would kill for a NASCAR garage pass—that's one of the most sought-after credentials in motorsports. They are not for sale; the only way to get one was to have it issued to you by NASCAR. We were lucky enough to know the right people. We had also been around racing long enough to know how to use the pass: go in, look all around and soak up the atmosphere, talk to some guys so we're part of the action, take a few pictures—and leave. We don't muck around and make nuisances of ourselves. We spent an hour or so in there watching all sorts of things. Engine changes are always fun to watch. When we'd seen enough, we headed back to the sign shop where the women were waiting for us.

The Busch race had its share of wrecks. One car ran through the grass forcing Allan Jones, from Atlanta, to work late that afternoon. What concerned me was the car that hit the wall right at one of the Talladega logos between Turns 3 and 4. As soon as the race was over, we were at the sign shop gathering the supplies to fix the damage. Mike came over and asked how many logos got hit.

"Just one," I said.

"You're lucky," he said. "Tim will be out there to do the white." Tim was the track painter. We didn't have to paint any of the white on the walls. Tim and his crew would do that for us. We just had to take care of the logos. We got out to the damaged logo and went up to take a closer look. *Wow*, I thought to myself.

I had never seen a hit up close before. On TV it looked like the wreck was over in a second. On the high banks, I stood by the wall and looked off toward Turn 3 to see where the skid marks started. Way, way, way over there. I couldn't believe the distance that the car had traveled. I could see the start of the slide, maybe a thousand feet or more away. The two tire marks did a lazy twist and came up the banking and struck the wall about two hundred feet from the logo. Then the marks continued down the wall, crossed the logo, and stopped maybe two hundred feet past it, and then drifted back down the banking to the grass. The concrete wall where the impact took place was gouged and scraped. A big black rubber mark was left on the wall. It would be Tim's job to repair the wall up to our Pepsi logo.

As it turned out, repairing the logo didn't take as long as I'd feared. We had fixed our first hit. We thought the hit had been huge, but that just shows how little we knew.

Sunday morning, Harriett and Sal joined us for the race. "Where are we going to watch the race?" Harriett asked. I had managed to get them the same credentials that we had.

"I think we will go down inside Turn 1 by the infield wall. It is as close to the track as you can get," I said with a certain amount of authority. This was where the

Brad Daudlin, Larry Orr, and Steve Hughey on the high banks repairing a hit. Tim, the track painter, is to the right and top of the photo. He was painting the wall white where the car first hit.

jet blowers, wreckers, ambulances, and pace car parked. It was beyond the spectator fence, right on the edge of the track. "It's right down from the Tri-Oval, near the start/finish," I told her. "Let's go on the track and out to the Tri-Oval and watch the pre-race show and the driver introductions."

With our all-access maintenance credentials, we could go anywhere, even onto the track. We were standing with all the VIPs, watching the show right on the track surface at the start/finish line. I noticed this guy next to me in a suit, but paid no attention to him. When he walked away I looked and said, "That was Dan Marino" (future hall-of-fame Miami Dolphins quarterback). You never know who you might see at a NASCAR race.

When the show was over, a brand new John Deere tractor towed a stage into place. (John Deere was a track sponsor.) A bus pulled up right in front of us and the NASCAR drivers started piling out. I got some good photos as the driver introductions began. All the drivers paraded right past us as they were introduced to the crowd. After the introductions were over, we walked down the track toward our spot inside Turn 1.

We unlocked the gate at the fence—a rare privilege, but Mike trusted me with a master key. (That way I didn't have to call security every time I needed a gate unlocked when we were working. The only rule was "make sure the gate gets locked behind you"!) The people lined up there just looked at us wishing they could come along.

Left to right: Larry Orr, Harriett Vickio, Sally Orr, and Brad Daudlin on track for pre-race ceremonies.

We walked in and there was Buster Comfort, the pace car driver. I went over to him, shook his hand, and shot the bull for a minute. Over by the jet dryer, ready to blow the track clean if it was needed, was Jimmy Elkins. He worked in maintenance and had become a good friend of mine. Standing by Jimmy was my cousin Ernie Thurston. He had just started his new job at Daytona Speedway, heading up track safety for ISC. We gave each other a hug—Italians hug, you know—Mafia style. We all mingled around as the excitement was growing and the race was about to start.

What a view. You could see the whole Tri-Oval, with the start/finish off to the right. We turned around and there was the Turn 1 Jumbotron (a huge TV showing the race for the Turn 1 grandstands). What a spot to watch from.

The sound of the cars, this close, hurt. The race was going smoothly. When Dale Earnhardt got the lead, the 150,000 fans roared. The sound of the crowd is something that has to be experienced. I can't describe it. It temporarily drowned out the sound of the cars. As the race went on we heard the horrendous sound of metal grinding concrete. We looked right and in the Tri-Oval were Dale Earnhardt and Bill Elliott, who had both slammed the wall hard. They were sliding right toward us, maybe a quarter mile away. Dale was sliding on his side. Bill's car was on fire and they were hooked together. The flames were going into Dale's car. More cars wrecked . . . it was the Big One, and it was headed right for us. It was like they were in slow motion. As they got closer we could see that they were not slowing down much. *How the hell can they slide that far?* I thought as I watched them coming closer.

They slid right by us maybe twenty feet away and came to a stop. I got a little nervous about getting hit with debris as there was no catch fence where we were standing. I could feel the heat from the fire in Elliott's car—we were that close. No one was seriously hurt. Dale had some burns. The thing I remember the most was the sound of the cars hitting the wall. It was scary and awesome at the same time!

As soon as the race ended, we all went right out of the slot in the wall that the

A major crash at the Tri-Oval in 1998. The "Big One" happened right in front of us. I took this photo without a telephoto lens! Bill Elliott's car was on fire when it stopped. We could feel the heat. Dale Earnhardt is walking from his car in the background.

pace car used to get on the track. We drove around Turns 1 and 2, riding with Ernie, to the end of the Back Straight where there was a gate to the outside of the track. The guards were opening the gate by the time we got there. We were back at the Maintenance Office before the winner went to Victory Lane.

We stayed for the party after the race, but by then Harriett and Sal were ready to get out of Dodge. At dawn the next morning, we drove north toward Chattanooga, Tennessee, on our long ride home.

Pace Car Rides

I don't really know how it started, but I have been driving the pace car at Watkins Glen International for more than twenty years. My racing background helped. My personality? Being able to get along with people was definitely a factor. Along with pacing races, the job turned into giving VIP rides around the circuit on race weekends. I would have never guessed in a million years the people I would meet giving these pace car rides—presidents of large companies, CEOs, business owners. The rides were reserved for the sponsors of races, team owners, and famous people who serve as grand marshal for the races. I wish I'd kept a record of all the people I have had in the pace car.

One of the most memorable was a small gray-haired woman. She was about seventy years old. Two other women got into the back seat and she, with some help from a man standing by, plopped into the front seat of the bright red pace car. What caught my attention was the glass in her left hand. As she sat down I could hear a tinkle tinkle. It was ice cubes sloshing around in what looked like iced tea. Knowing only VIPs were riding, I wondered, *Who is this? Ah. It doesn't matter.* I smiled as I watched her adjust herself as the man outside tried to attach her seat belt. Finally she was set and the door slammed shut. She said, "Well, let's go."

We have different pace cars every year. That year we had a brand new 1998 Ford Thunderbird Super Coupe with five-speed manual transmission. The car was fast and man, did it handle well. These rides weren't just a cruise around the track. They were fast and exciting—especially through the turns. As I drove around the 3.4-mile road course I explained the racing line and the reason for the brake marker locations. All this was interesting to most riders who have never been out on the track before but the woman in the front seat just sat there silent.

As I drove down the Back Straight, she broke her silence. "Sir. Could I bother you for a minute? Could I please ask you something?"

"Sure," I said. "What is it?"

In a shaky voice, she asked, "Sir, how long have you been doing this?"

I glanced over at her as we were flying down the Back Straight and in a very serious tone I said, "Actually, Ma'am, today is my first day on this job. This is my first

In the Ford pace car waiting to give VIPs a ride around Watkins Glen International.

time on the track."

    She stiffened straight up and grabbed the dash with her right hand. At the same time spilled some of the drink on the floor. She screamed, "Oh My *God*." The two women in the back started laughing as they must have known (or were hoping) I was joking. When we drove into the pits and stopped, one of the marketing people opened her door and helped her get out. She motioned me to come around the car, and I did, a little cautiously. I thought she was going to holler at me! She gave me a big hug and said, "That was the most fun I have had in years. Fabulous. Thank you."

I went on with the rest of the rides and when we were done I parked the car and went into the Press Tower to watch the start of the race. One of the marketing people came up to me and said, "Hey, Mrs. Wick wants you come down to her suite."

"What the hell are you talking about? I'm not going anywhere. The race is starting. I want to watch it here."

"Remember the older lady you gave a ride to? She spilled her drink? She wants you at their suite. You better go—she owns Zippo Lighters. I have a golf cart and I'll take you down."

I got in the cart, wondering, *What does she want?*

We pulled up to the suites and the golf cart stopped. "Here you are. Suite B," the marketing guy said.

"You're going in with me," I said. "I'm not going in there alone!"

"I've got to get back to the Press Tower. Call me when you want a ride back." Off he went.

I really didn't want to go in there. I didn't know a soul and these people were, I must say, way out of my league. I walked up to the guard at the door and flashed my track ID badge. He opened the door and I nervously walked in. Of course everyone turned to see who was coming in. I immediately heard, "Tony."

I looked over at a table near the bar and there was the lady that rode with me. I walked over and she stood up and said in a loud voice so all could hear, "This is Tony, the pace car driver."

I nodded (this was so embarrassing) and sheepishly gave a halfhearted wave and sat down next to Harriett Wick. From that day on, Harriett and I were friends. Zippo sponsored the vintage race at the Glen and every year when the WGI marketing people went to Bradford, Pennsylvania, to renew the contract, they would come and tell me that Harriett's first request was to have Tony in their suite.

Over the years I have become great friends with most of the Zippo people. They are all awesome. I've mentioned George Duke, who got me into the Skip Barber driving school. Former Zippo president Mike Schuler and his wife, Diane, are great people too. Mike is addicted to racing and he is quite good at it. Diane is a horse person. She has a beautiful stable at their home in Bradford. I carved a sign for the stable that said "Donerail Farm." Donerail is the name of her grandfather's horse that won the Kentucky Derby in 1938.

Back when he was running Zippo, Mike gave me a call on Saturday during a race weekend. He said Zippo wanted to sponsor a car that was racing in a three-hour endurance race on Sunday. The car was a Prototype "Spice" car.

"Tony, can you make me a couple of large Zippo decals to put on a car for the endurance race on Sunday? We want to sponsor the car. I know it's late, but can you help? The race starts at 10 a.m. tomorrow so be at The Glen at 9 a.m. We can put Zippo decals on the top of the rear fenders. There is room there for about a four-foot long decal on top of each rear fender."

I made the decals that night. The next morning I got to the track at nine o'clock as promised. As I walked down Pit Lane with the decals, I saw Mike running toward me waving his arms as if to say "Come here, come here." Just then I heard the race cars' engines fire up. I ran toward him and as I got closer, he hollered, "I made a mistake. They start at nine, not ten." We stood there as the cars left the grid and pulled onto the track. "Damn. I wanted Zippo on that car." Mike said.

Dejected, we slowly walked back to the Press Tower. I carried with me the roll of large decals that would have gone on the rear fenders. Mike was silently shaking his head when he suddenly stopped in his tracks. I took two more steps before I stopped and looked back at him. He looked at me with eyes wide and said, "Hey. It's a three-hour race and they have to change drivers twice. It's in the rules. When they do their pit stops, we can put one decal on one fender on the first stop and do the other one on the second stop. What do you think?"

I stared at him and said, "You're nuts. We can't do that. These are four feet long." I thought about it for a few seconds. "I don't know. I'll need a hand. It sounds crazy but I don't think they will let us do it anyway." After some excited talk, the Pit Marshal gave the OK. I couldn't believe it.

The biggest concern the Pit Marshal had was related to the refueling. We had to wait until after the refueling was done before we could go over the wall and we could only work on the car as the driver change took place. It didn't give us much time. We didn't worry about getting bubbles in the decal or even worry about getting it on perfectly straight. After all, no one was going to see it very close.

Standing behind the crew on Pit Lane I was surprisingly nervous. *I now know how a tire changer feels*, I thought to myself. I looked around and thought, *This is in-*

The newly labeled Zippo car.

sane and also embarrassing. We're going to look like fools out there. Especially if the wind catches the decal wrong and sticks it to itself before I can get it on the fender. Every crew member, even from other teams, were looking at us thinking, "What the hell are these idiots doing?"

The crew chief told the crew what we planned to do so we wouldn't get run over. They all gave us the same weird look. At the first pit stop, the car was refueled and as the driver change was going on, Mike and I jumped (or more like rolled) over the pit wall. We didn't have time to apply the four-foot long strip of vinyl properly. We just had to get it stuck on the fender more or less straight. Mike was on one end of the four-foot decal, I was on the other. I looked at him and nodded my head to give the signal to lay the decal on the fender. Together we laid it down. It stuck. I quickly rubbed it down with a plastic squeegee and we rolled back over the pit wall.

During this strange Pit Lane event, the track announcer spotted us from his perch high in the Press Tower and was suddenly talking about the unbelievable sight that he was watching on Pit Lane. The crowd that was in sight of us was going wild. No one had ever seen anything like it. Come to think of it, neither had I. This had to be a first in racing history. Lettering a race car . . . during the race. On the next stop, with about an hour to go in the race, we did the same thing on the left rear fender. An hour later the race was over. I know it's hard to believe, but the Zippo car *won*. In a victory lane interview they were talking about the lettering of the car during the race. Mike, who was on the victory lane podium representing Zippo, said, "As you have seen, Zippo has a new race strategy. We wait until the race starts and when we see who's leading the race, we letter that car." Everyone roared with laughter. That was the first (and the last) time I have lettered a car while the race was going on—one for the racing record books!

Back to Work

About a year after we got home from painting the high walls at Talladega, I was working in my shop when the phone rang. I found the portable on a work table under some papers and picked it up. "Vickio Signs."

"Hi there, this is Donna." I recognized the voice instantly—Donna Price, Mike McWilliams's secretary at Talladega.

"Hi, Donna, how're you doin'?" I said.

In her best Southern voice she said, "Well, I'm doin' just fine. How are y'all doin'?"

"We're workin' away, as usual."

"Mike wanted me to call ya. We have a ton of wall logos to paint and he wants you down here two weeks before the race. Let me know how many rooms you will need, and we'll see you then."

"Great. I'll call you tomorrow with the info. Thanks and see ya later."

I smiled as I hung up the phone. It is so nice to work with people who totally trust you to get the job done. Mike McWilliams, the general manager at Talladega, doesn't ask the price, how I'm going to do the job, or how many men I'm bringing. He tells me the job and from there on in he trusts me to get the job done and never bothers me again.

I got on the phone and called Larry Orr (of Orr Signs) and told him of the new gig. He said he was in. I needed one more guy, and I remembered my friend Steve Tinker saying awhile back, "Take me on one of your trips to Talladega. I'll kill to go. I'll do anything."

So I called Steve. He went crazy. I finally had to hang up on him. He called right back, blasting out of the phone with "Are you kidding me, man?"

"You're going to have to work and work hard."

"I will do anything, man. Holy Christ, I can't believe it. I'll get my vacation scheduled today."

I hung up and went back to work, grinning and thinking how one phone call could make someone so happy. It made me feel really good. I'd known Steve most of my life. We rode the same school bus when we were kids. As a matter of fact, you could say I saved his life on a snowy night back in the 1970s.

❧

Back in the 1970s, we had real snowstorms in upstate New York. Everyone had snowmobiles and rode the crap out of them. Steve lived in Townsend, which was just west of the racetrack and about five miles from my house. One night in 1976, around seven o'clock, Don Romeo stopped by my parents' house where I was working on my Yamaha snowmobile in the garage. Headlights shone through the small window in the door, so I looked out—and there was Don with his four-wheel-drive pickup towing a trailer with his snowmobile on it. He had a bright red Rupp sled. My Yamaha was ready to go, so we decided to ride to Pappy's—a bar in Monterey, New York, west of the racetrack and about five miles from Steve's house. (Pappy's Bar got about the lowest temperatures and biggest snowfalls in the state.)

We unloaded Don's sled from the trailer as the snow started to fall again. There was already a good foot on the ground and the clouds looked like they were going to offer up a lot more. Don and I went into the garage and put our suits on. By the time we walked back out the door, Don's sled had collected an inch of new snow. We talked for a minute about not going as the snow was starting to come down a little heavier. But then, the challenge of facing danger took over and we headed out.

It wasn't too cold so the snow was wet and heavy. A couple of pulls on the starter cord and my twin cylinder 340cc Yamaha came to life. The headlight was dim at first, but after the engine revved up it got brighter and pierced the heavy snowflakes. The engine pumped out smoke (gas mixed with oil) for the first fifty feet I rode but then the smoke diminished. I led Don south past my house to a shrub-filled field where a trail ran along the hedgerow that paralleled the railroad tracks. The grass had been packed down but even with a foot of snow we could still see the trail which led through the goldenrod before winding around some small pine trees. We rode through the hedgerow at the back of the field and into another field. The second field was a pasture—flat as glass. With no obstacles, we opened the sleds up to 60 mph and crossed the field side-by-side. Reaching the other, we slowed and snaked through some small trees. In the next field, we turned to the right and zipped through a gap in a rusty old wire fence that led to a farmer's crossing of the railroad tracks. We crossed the tracks carefully and then went down a twelve-foot bank and across a wide ditch with about six inches of water in the bottom. It had not frozen yet, so we splashed through and continued our ride up an eight-foot bank to another field, headed west to the racetrack.

The swirling snow continued to fall and had started to pile up so deep the snowmobiles were getting bogged down. It was also getting colder by the minute. Don and I crossed the racetrack property and stopped at the far end of the track near Townsend. It was now snowing like hell. Our headlights penetrated only twenty feet through the heavy snowflakes. As we discussed what to do, another inch of snow built up on the hoods of the sleds. We decided to head back. We had to take turns breaking a path through the thick snow so we didn't burn up a drive belt.

When we left the racetrack, we decided to ride County Route 16 instead of the trail we'd come up on, even though the snowplows hadn't been through. The snow was coming down at an unbelievable rate and the wind was blowing from the west, at our backs. We were going about 15 mph and the snow was passing us: a full-blown blizzard. We could not see fifteen feet ahead. Don was breaking the trail, and we had slowed down to about ten miles per hour. With the snow swirling up from Don's sled, the beam from my headlight looked like a solid wall, so I turned it off. Don, seeing my light disappear, twisted on his seat and looked back at me. I waved to him to keep going. I could barely see Don's taillight through the snow. With my headlight off I could see a little better, but visibility was steadily getting worse. My helmet shield kept fogging up making matters even worse. I flipped it open but the snow was so heavy I couldn't keep my eyes open. I wiped the inside of the shield with my wet, snowy glove and flipped it down halfway.

Just as I was flipping it down, out of the corner of my eye, I spotted a dark form. It was maybe ten feet from my sled, right at the edge of visibility. If it had been one more foot to the right I wouldn't have seen it. What the hell was that? It looked like a dark shadow of a small tree. I thought it couldn't be a tree; we were on Route 16, a paved county road. Knowing we were *in the road*, there definitely was something back there that shouldn't be.

I traveled another fifty feet down the road before I decided to go back and see what it was. I couldn't stop thinking about it. I turned my headlight on, and when Don saw my light turn away, he stopped.

He looked over his right shoulder and through the snowfall, but he no longer could see me. Not knowing that I had seen something, he also turned around—not an easy chore with the snow more than two feet deep and getting deeper. I drove my snowmobile back up the road following my own tracks but saw nothing. I stopped and looked over my left shoulder and could see the faint glow of Don's headlight approaching. His headlight looked like a dim candle in a heavy fog. I was a little nervous about getting stranded out here as there were not many houses nearby. The shield on my helmet kept fogging over so I flipped it open and wiped the inside again with my wet glove. While it was open, I squinted and looked into the falling snow. I heard Don's sled laboring as he came up behind me. Looking back to where the road should be, I saw it. There. A dark form in the snow, barely moving. Sure as hell wasn't a tree. I squeezed the throttle with my thumb, not waiting for Don, and rode toward the form.

About ten feet away I made out the form of a human, bent over and barely walking in deep snow. I got off the sled and approached the guy, who didn't even know I was there. In this blizzard, he was disoriented and totally exhausted. I grabbed his shoulder and he turned. His face was snow-covered, but I saw it was Steve Tinker.

"Steve. Steve. Come this way," I said, motioning with my hand. Just then Don pulled up. Steve didn't know where he was or in what direction he was going. We got him to my sled and sat him on the seat. We headed to my house as it was closer than Steve's. It was tough riding in two feet of snow, especially with two on a sled—a strain both on my arms and on the sled. Don led the way breaking the trail. I was breathing so hard my shield was fogged over to the point I had to flip it up and ride with my head down, just peeking under the open shield. It was snowing so hard the snowplows weren't out.

We finally pulled into the driveway and helped Steve into the house. My parents were worried sick—they could see it was a real blizzard and worried about their kid and his friend being out in it. Once Steve got revived enough to talk, he told us his truck got stuck. He got out thinking he could walk home—but the storm came up faster than he expected. After a snow plow finally passed by, Don drove Steve home with the help of his four-wheel-drive truck. I don't know if I saved Steve's life or not, but I don't think he would have made it without someone coming by.

After Steve hung up the phone, still thanking me for the inviting him on the trip, I thought, *Now he owes me twice! Once for saving his life and now for taking him to Talladega!*

In Talladega, we would be painting wall logos, so I would need my computer and plotter to make patterns. Steve agreed to drive, so when the time came, we loaded all our gear into his Chevy pickup, which had a cap on the back, picked up Larry on the way and headed south.

We rolled right along, but not fifty miles down the road, just into Pennsylvania, we hit a deer. We were all excited, talking and drinking coffee when suddenly a deer came out of nowhere. The brakes slammed on and coffee went flying as we hit the deer square on. It got spun around but kept going—heading off into the field at a full run. In the dark, we pulled over and got out to inspect the truck. No damage to the truck or, apparently, to the deer. We all climbed back in the truck. I said to the guys, "I hope this isn't an omen."

TALLADEGA

Painting and Repainting

We drove non-stop. Taking turns behind the wheel, we made it to Talladega in great time. When we pulled into the motel at 11 a.m., I smiled as it was almost like being home.

"Now. Who are ya all with?" the guy behind the desk asked.

"We have reservations from Talladega Superspeedway," I said.

He punched the computer keyboard looking for our reservation. He was about thirty years old, five-foot-three and about that big around. He wore black pants with sharp creases running up the legs. When he turned around, I could see the same sharp creases up the backside as well. His long-sleeved white shirt was buttoned tight at the cuffs. He had buttoned the top button of his shirt even though he wasn't wearing a tie. I don't know how he had gotten it buttoned as the shirt was so tight around his fat neck I was surprised he could breathe. I moved a little to the right so I wasn't directly in front of him. If his top button ever broke loose, it would go right through somebody's forehead. "Wow. You guys are here for a long time," he said, finding our reservations.

"Yeah, I know," I said in a not-too-excited voice. I looked over at Steve and he was all giddy and grinning. I just shook my head and thought, *Oh, God.* Yup, he was itching to get to the track. I signed the papers and we got the keys and headed out the door into the bright Alabama sun.

Steve and Larry went to their room and I went to mine, which was right next door. We were on the second floor as the guy at the desk told us the ground floor rooms were for travelers. I was the boss so I got my own room. We unpacked and met out on the balcony.

"What do you guys want to do?" (Like I didn't know.)

Steve almost screamed, "Christ, let's go to the damned track, man. What the hell do you think we wanna do?" Larry and I looked at each other and laughed.

"OK, let's go see Mike," I said. Steve was so excited already, I couldn't wait to take him through the tunnel and see the expression on his face when he saw the banking for the first time. To be quite honest with you, I couldn't wait to see it again myself.

We pulled off I-20 and onto Speedway Blvd. Off in the distance, to our left, I could see the main grandstands—and it gave me the usual excited feeling. It's funny how the sight of a certain object can trigger memory after memory. In about five seconds I relived all the experiences I'd had at the speedway to that point.

We traveled past the Talladega Airport which was just off Turn 2. (I looked way back in to see if any planes were in there. I love planes.) A little further down the road, on the right, was the Talladega Short Track, a quarter-mile dirt (actually red clay) track.

"Do they run Modifieds there?" Steve asked.

"They run Late Models—and they would run circles around a Modified."

"Bullshit," Steve snapped back with a cocky smirk. You see, he worked with a Modified team back home and he thought Modifieds were king of the dirt tracks.

I let out a little sarcastic laugh. "You wait till you see those guys run, buddy. You're gonna shit."

Finally, we drove by the deli; I wondered if the same women were working and if they had any apple pie. We didn't stop but took the next left turn and reached the main gate to the track. We drove down Thirty Lane and stopped at the security shed. The guard remembered me and welcomed us back to the speedway. When I had first come to Talladega, this security guard hadn't been very friendly. After I got to know him, we got along great. As we drove through the tunnel, I told Steve, who was driving, "Blow the horn."

All three of us were smiling as we came out of the tunnel and into the bright sunlight heading to the infield. I told Steve to slow down and stop.

"Steve, look back there."

He looked back, as Larry and I did, and there it was—the most awesome sight imaginable: the high banks between Turns 3 and 4. "Jesus Christ. What the hell. I can't believe it. This is awesome," Steve was yelling.

"I know," I said in a real quiet voice, feeling the goosebumps. "We're back."

We drove around the infield for half an hour, Larry and I showing Steve the garage area, the gates, and how to access the track. We went to the infield, where the Harley Davidson test track (about as wide as a sidewalk) wound all over the place. It had every kind of surface variation built into sections of it. Bikes run on it twelve hours a day. You have to keep your eyes open all the time when driving around the infield of the track.

"While we are out here, let's take a lap," I said.

It was Sunday and no one was out here except us. I looked over at Steve, who was driving and suddenly he had a wild look on his face. Away we went with Steve driving. Until you get to go out on the high banks and drive on them, you cannot understand what it feels like no matter what anyone says. I can't tell you what it is really like. Sorry. You have to do it yourself. There just aren't any words that I know of that can do it justice.

I told Steve, "Get it up to at least seventy before you go up on the high banks. He gripped the wheel, leaning forward in the seat with his chin inches from his hands. With a scary-strange look on his face, he mashed the gas pedal. I suddenly thought to myself, *Why the hell didn't I get out before I told him to do this?* We completed a lap and I told him, "Pull it down on the apron and into the pits. There will be more time later to do laps." *Later when I won't be in the truck*. Reluctantly, he pulled down and we entered Pit Lane.

We headed for the Maintenance Office and the sign shop and pulled into the familiar overhang in front of the sign shop.

"Let's go see the boys," I said.

We walked into the Maintenance Office and there at her desk was Donna. Donna Elkins Price was blonde and had the best Southern accent you will ever hear. She stood up and said cheerfully, "Hi y'all. It's so good to have y'all down here. Did ya have a good trip? Have ya seen Mike yet?"

"Yeah, it was a long drive. We haven't seen anyone yet. We were out on the track showing Steve the place," I said.

Just then I heard a voice from the next office. "Hey. Who is that I hear out there?"

I walked over to the doorway to another office and there at his desk was Pete Woodard. Pete was in charge of all the equipment used at the track—and believe me there was a lot of it. He stood up and we all shook hands. Pete was retired and worked part time at the track. He is a great guy with a great dry sense of humor.

"While you're here, you might as well sign out a Gator," he said.

"Make sure it's a diesel and a six-wheeler."

"They're brand new, just delivered. Take your pick."

Donna must have called Mike as he soon strolled into Pete's office. "Hey, Mike," I said. "How're you doing?"

"I've been workin' like a dawg," he said. "Good to have you here. There's a ton of work for ya." After everyone was introduced, Mike pulled me aside. "Tony, come with me. Got some logos to show ya."

I told the guys I'd be right back and walked out the door with Mike. We went to his office, got a stack of drawings, and went out to his truck. We rode around the track as he pointed out the locations of the new logos on the retaining walls. I marked the drawings (location is very important). We got back to the shop and as I got out of the truck, Mike said, "You gotch'er work cut out for ya."

"I guess so," I said, while thinking, *Holy shit. This is going to be tough.* I walked over to Larry and Steve, who were standing in front of the sign shop, and said, "We are in deep shit. We have a ton of work to do."

"Good, that's what we're here for," was Larry's response.

"I'm ready for whatever it takes," said Steve. "I'll do anything, man."

I said, "Let's get the plotter and computer set up. We officially don't start until tomorrow, but it will be good to get things set up so we can come in tomorrow morning and start right off." After we set up and tested everything, we headed to the motel and supper.

The next morning we were at the track at 7 a.m. I went to my office and grabbed the first piece of artwork. It was for Pepsi. The next one was for the speedway's brand-new website: www.talladegasuperspeedway.com. I looked at Larry and said, "Oh my God. Couldn't they come up with something shorter like 'tss.com'? This thing is going to be a mile long and they want three of them," I said in a disgusted voice.

We spent the day making pounce patterns. Not a glamorous job but it had to be done. Tomorrow we would repair some logo hits left over from the last race. This would be good practice for Steve and give him some experience working on the walls. Steve was a mechanical engineer and not a painter, but he would be able to do fill-in work on the repairs. Besides, I had to give him something to do just to shut him up. He was so excited about being here he wouldn't keep quiet.

The next morning I went to the Maintenance Office to see Donna. She gave me a Talladega Superspeedway credit card and a master key, so we wouldn't have to bother anyone with getting materials at Lowe's or opening the many gates around the track. It was a great feeling to be trusted. We went to the sign shop and loaded the truck with pounce patterns and the Gator with paint. I looked at Larry and said, nodding toward Steve, "I know what we are going to do with him. Let's put him on the Die-Hard 500 logo on the Back Straight that Jeff Gordon hit last year. He can touch that up." Larry nodded his head between puffs on his stupid pipe, and we headed through the tunnel and onto the track. And yeah, we blew the horn.

The logo was at the end of the Back Straight, so we drove around Turns 1 and 2 on the apron. I hollered from the Gator to Steve who was in his truck and told him to stay on the apron. Steve started yelling, "I wanna go up on the banking. I wanna go up on the banking."

"*No!*" I said, "You shithead, there's going to be enough time to do laps. Just follow me."

We stopped on the Back Straight and I showed Steve what I wanted done to the DieHard logo. Jeff Gordon gave it a hell of a hit the year before, and it was really

Inspecting a hit on the back straight wall, damage from Jeff Gordon's crash from last year's race.

damaged. "I will do all the outline work and then you get the roller and do the fill-in," I told Steve.

"OK, let's get going," he said in an excited voice.

We started painting the logos on the retaining walls. There were more of them than ever before. So many, that what happened during this year's races would put us to the supreme test.

After I painted the outline, Steve Tinker finished up the repaint of the Jeff Gordon hit.

 How Many Hits?

We painted retaining wall logos all week—twelve, so far. At last count the retaining walls around the speedway held a total of thirty-three logos. This included the walls on the inside of the track on the Back Straight and at Pit In and Pit Out. When I first went to Talladega in 1992, we had a total of three wall paintings and they all said the same word: "Talladega." How things have changed.

TV time is *big money* and retaining walls are almost impossible to hide from TV. If you notice while watching a race, the camera shots are sometimes so close to the cars that you miss what's going on in the rest of the field. That's because the network shooting the race does not want to let billboards or other signs that are not paying for

Steve Tinker (left) and Larry Orr (right) Repairing a hard hit.

TV agreements get any free air time. This was a big deal. I have sat in meetings with sponsors, ad companies, and track marketing people going over tape after tape of past races to pick spots to put logos or signs where the cameras can't avoid shooting. When you see a sign or retaining wall lettering at a racetrack, it just didn't happen to be placed there. Much work and thought went into choosing the location. Pricing also varied—the sponsors paid a premium for a TV-accessible location.

The Information Superhighway on the Back Straight. Wouldn't just www.tss.com have been easier?

It was early Wednesday morning and the sun was just showing over the distant mountain range. We stood on the Front Straight drinking coffee and talking about the day's schedule. I decided to do the three "www.talladegasuperspeedway.com" logos first. I wanted to get those big logos done so we agreed to work into the night. We ended up using the truck and the Gator headlights to finish the lettering. In the future, on the request sheet (a list of equipment and materials I request before arriving for the racetrack to supply), I decided I was going to call for a Light Plant. You never know when you will have to work at night to get things done. Pit In, Pit Out, and the inside of the Back Straight were the locations chosen for the "www.talladegasuperspeedway.com" logos. One good thing, they were all on the flat. I said to Larry, "Christ almighty, why didn't they just make it www.talladegasuperspeedwaylocatedintalladegaalabamajustoffofroutei20betweenalantaandbirmingham.com?" Oh well, we just kept painting.

I couldn't believe how these walls were filling up with logos, but it looked really good. Then a thought came to mind. Not a good thought—a real scary thought that put goose bumps on the back of my neck. I turned to Larry. "You know something? With all these new logos and ARCA racing this weekend, no matter where they hit, they are going to hit a logo." Any logo that got damaged on Friday or Saturday had to be repainted to look new for the Sunday race. Before, there were only a few logos and the chance of somebody hitting one was slim, but now. . . *Holy Shit!* "I think we created a monster that can bite us."

Steve said, "Ah, they won't wreck."

"It's ARCA, you idiot," said Larry. "They even wreck on their way to the track." ARCA—which stands for Automobile Racing Club of America—is a series made up of 70 percent new and upcoming racers trying to get into the NASCAR Truck, the Nationwide series, or the Sprint Cup series. So 70 percent had little experience and drove used cars while only 30 percent were experienced drivers with good equipment. Add this together and you got . . . *wrecks!*

"Maybe they'll all wreck into the grass and the grass guys will have to do all the work repairing damage," Steve said.

No sense worrying about it, I thought to myself. We just kept painting on into the night and got a ton of work done.

Left to right: Me, Steve Tinker and Larry Orr painting at night with the aid of truck headlights!

༄

The next day was Thursday. There was a scheduled test that day so cars would be using the track, and that meant . . . We couldn't work! We had a day off. Larry and I had only one thought in mind. *Golf.* We were addicted to the stupid game—so addicted, we'd brought our clubs to Alabama. We convinced Steve to bring his clubs, too just in case we got the chance to play. Alabama has some of the most beautiful golf courses in the country, and with our day off, we headed out to play on one of them. Robert Trent Jones Trail course was not too far from our motel. Jones was a world-famous golf course designer. The courses down in Alabama are so beautiful that at times while you are out on a course, you have to stop, get out of the cart and just look around. It was that awesome!

We had a great day playing golf, being away from the track and enjoying the beautiful Alabama sun.

On Friday, we got all of our work done early giving us time to watch practice and qualifying rounds. We took Steve to our special spot to watch practice—with the rescue crew inside Turn 2, right by the track.

All the maintenance guys do a pool on Friday and naturally we wanted in on it. "What's the pool for? The winner of the race?" I asked.

"No. This is a special pool," the guy said to me. Then everyone laughed at us. They knew those thirty-three logos on the retaining walls were a big fat target. The pool was for how many logos would get hit on Saturday. In the past the record was three. We hoped it wouldn't get broken, as we'd have to fix them starting Saturday afternoon right after the race—and that would cut into beer time! Fixing three would take some work but that would be acceptable. I didn't get in the pool. I didn't want to jinx myself.

Saturday's Busch race went badly. Wreck after wreck. I could see two hits from where I was but I knew there were many more wrecks. After the race, Steve and Larry went back to the Maintenance Shop for the official tally. Mike and I went out and checked the track and the logos. The more we drove around the track, the more carnage we could see. *This can't be happening. I'm counting hits and I just ran out of fingers.* The grand total was thirteen. I was stunned. My head was spinning and I wanted to puke.

When we got back to the shop, I looked at Larry and I said, "Let's get the hell moving. There are thirteen goddamn logo hits."

He said, "Are you shittin' me?"

"Where the hell is Steve?" I asked.

Larry looked around and said, "I dunno."

Larry and I got the Gator, which we loaded with all colors of paint, rollers, pad

With the credentials we had we could go anywhere at Talladega. We watched the Nationwide race with the fire and rescue crew stationed in turn 2.

painters, and thinner. It reminded me of my past encounters as a fireman. The whistle blows and you take off to fight fires. This time, we were fighting time. We had thirteen logos to fix and they all had to be done by ten o'clock Sunday morning when the live TV comes on. The walls had to be ready.

We saw Steve walking by as we took off in the Gator. "Follow us," I hollered in his direction. "Meet us on the Front Straight."

I looked back as we sped up and could see him running for his truck. I thought, *Man, he doesn't know what he has gotten himself into.* We buzzed through the crowd like driving through a Wal-Mart parking lot during a Christmas Day Sale. We went down through the tunnel (blew the horn on the Gator; sounded like one of those air horn cans) and up the other side and into the infield. The infield was nothing but a mass of traffic. We took some shortcuts and ended up at a gate near the Infield Hospital. We drove by the heliport concrete pad and to a gate near the track surface. I got out of the Gator and walked through the crowd and in a very macho way pulled out my master key. I sort of held it up while twisting it and letting the sun reflect off of it. I was letting everyone know, *I have a key.* I unlocked the gate. Larry pulled the Gator through and closed the gate and locked it. "Oh shit," I said out loud. "I gotta wait for Steve." About five minutes later he showed up.

We drove out Pit In, turned left and drove onto the Tri-Oval and stopped. Immediately it wasn't hard to see the carnage! "The Carnage. Oh, the Humanity." I screamed.

We all got out and stood there staring at the Front Straight wall. Some fool hit the wall at the Tri-Oval area and rode the wall all the way to Turn 1. In the process, he took out about five logos while leaving black tire marks across everything. We got back in the Gator and did a track inspection. We then checked our paint colors and supplies and thanked God we were in good shape. Thankfully, we could count on the track painting crew to paint all the white around the logos.

"Well, let's get the high banks first while it's still light. I don't want to be up there in the dark," I said to the guys. We all got our paint, pads, and rollers, and like ants we attacked the high banks.

 # Under Attack

We worked late into the night—later than I'd ever worked before at Talladega. We had no choice. We had no food, no beer, no nothing except work. Thank God the weather was good and the track's paint crew was out there with us doing the white on the concrete retaining walls, or we wouldn't have had a chance of finishing by 10 a.m. Sunday. The repair painting was going great. The logos were already there, just damaged, so we could skip the whole time-eating pounce pattern step. Larry and I sailed right along doing the new outlines and Steve followed us filling in the color. We were moving fast! And the track maintenance crew brought out a light plant so we weren't stuck with headlights. That was a great help.

A light plant is a gas-powered lighting system towed on two wheels behind a truck. It had a mast with a cluster of four very high-output lights that pivots to stand straight up when the plant is stationary. Once the mast was upright, you cranked a handle and the mast extended up to about twenty feet. Fire up the engine and generator and hit the light switch. In a few minutes (it took time for the mercury vapor to warm up) the lights would start to flicker with a dull glow. After they warmed up it was suddenly almost daylight.

The maintenance crew even left a man with the light plant to move it along for us as we painted. Around midnight, the dew was starting to come out. I learned years ago while doing grass signs, when the dew comes out . . . *stop*. When the dew came it was like a rainstorm had just passed through. I told the guys, "We aren't going to get done tonight. We got a lot done and we only have a little more to do in the morning. Let's pack up and get back to the shop."

Back at the shop we reloaded the Gator with everything we would need in the morning. Our plan was to be back before sunup and get moving on the remaining repairs. Tomorrow was race day. I had never, in all the years working at racetracks, had to work on race day. It was not a good feeling. I figured an hour and a half of work in the morning and we would be finished. We headed to the motel for some well-deserved food and sleep.

On race day morning the pressure is at its best, or should I say worst. Race day was different. You can feel race day. The security was different—more intense. The fans were different. Emergency crews were already hard at work when we arrived making their tours and checking everything. Jet blowers were running to clear the remaining dampness and any debris off the track. Helicopters were flying all over and pre-race ceremonies were preparing for the 180,000 screaming fans that would soon be in place. The whole place was buzzing: A city born right before our eyes.

We had arrived so early that we climbed the high banks at Turn 1 in almost complete darkness. For now, the city (the camping area on the infield of the racetrack) was dead quiet. No one was awake yet from the partying the night before. Up on top of the banking we looked around at the infield. It was just light enough to see the mass of motor homes and tents—everyone packed in so tight that it looked like a shaggy carpet. The campfires had burned themselves out hours ago, but the smoke still lingered lying low, just over the tops of the motor homes.

"Some of those poor bastards won't even see the race today after partying all night," I told Steve.

We quietly started to work, going faster than I expected. By 7 a.m., we only had one more logo to fix—the Winston logo. We walked up the banking in Turn 2 and stood there for a minute to catch our breath. The Alabama sun was just peeking over Cheaha Mountain. I although thought of my friend Billy Swinford every time I saw that mountain. Billy had named his construction company Cheaha Construction after the mountain.

It was quiet as could be and the air was cool. Without looking around at the campers I could tell that some of them were now awake. How could I tell? I could smell bacon cooking. Oh man, did that make me hungry. Breakfast aromas floated through the air toward us. "Man. Isn't this something? Half an hour and we can eat," I told the guys.

"I can't wait a half hour," Steve said.

"So paint faster and we can be done in fifteen minutes!"

Steve looked at me with a growling frown, but he rolled paint a little faster after that.

Almost done. The sun was now shining brightly. I picked up a few things while Steve finished some color fills. We were home free. Man, was I relieved. It had gone really well even though I hated the thought of working on race day. I bent over to pick up my mat (a padded cushion I had custom-made by my friend Mike Wells of Welco Interiors in Ithaca about twenty years ago. I use it to kneel on.) Suddenly, out of the clear blue, I head a subtle hissing sound. Then, a second later, a loud *splat*.

I looked around and yelled, "What the hell was that?"

Larry looked over and said, "What?"

"Take that stupid pipe out of your mouth and maybe you could hear something," I said.

There it was again. I looked over at Larry and now he was looking around too. Steve hadn't heard it. Just then, something hit the catch fence about six feet up. I looked up just in time to see the water flying straight through the fence. It was like a spray from a garden hose. Stuck in the fence were the remnants of a blue balloon.

We were under a water balloon attack! I hollered to Steve and Larry, "Those assholes are shooting water balloons at us. Try to see where they are coming from." Larry and Steve jumped up and started looking off into the campers in the infield to try to see where the balloons were coming from. We were up on the banking in Turn 2. The campers were at least two hundred yards across the track from us, so we knew they must be using giant slingshots, which are illegal at the track.

A giant slingshot was made from surgical tube rubber. Two guys stood about three feet apart, each holding the end of a surgical rubber tube. The third man grabbed the center of the tube, which had a pocket to hold the water balloon. Loading a water balloon into the pocket, the third man grabbed the tube with both hands and walked backward while the two guys up front strained to hold the ends of the tube. The puller backed up maybe fifteen to twenty feet, until the tube was at its maximum stretch, then he aimed and let go. Some of those things could shoot a thousand feet. If we got hit, it would hurt. We were under a merciless, unrelenting attack. Time to call for backup!

I had my binoculars with me, but they were in the Gator. Larry went down the banking and got them. I told Steve to keep painting. We watched for incoming balloons. Before I tried to find the idiots, I got on my track radio and called Security. I said, "Security. This is Ninety." (That was my radio number). "We are painting the retaining wall in Turn 2 up on the banking and we are under a water balloon attack. Can you get someone out here before we get hit? They are getting closer." A woman quickly came on the radio. "Security to Ninety. Can you see where they are coming from? We need a location."

Splat, another one hit the track, just off to our left, leaving a long, wet trail up the banking. "Christ, that was close!"

"Those bastards," Steve hollered. That time I could see the arc of the balloon and I followed the line back into the mass of tents and campers.

Searching with my binoculars, I found the launch site. I called Security back and said, "I found 'em. They're in the campground inside Turn 2, between two motor homes. There's a yellow rental truck right behind them. They are three rows in, east of the Tunnel Road, just to the right of the Tunnel sign."

The woman at the Security Headquarters came back on the radio and said something that prompted me to say to Larry, "She didn't just say that, did she?"

What she'd said was, "We have a helicopter in the air watching traffic. I will direct him to your area and when he is over the shooters, let me know and I will tell him to hover over the site. Our troopers will have a reference point and we will surround them. Keep them in sight and let me know if they move."

I laughed out loud. "Holy shit," I said. "You guys won't believe what's happening." I told them what the dispatcher said, and just then we heard the chopper. "Hope he's got some hellfire missiles," I said.

We looked up and there it was. It hovered over us at about five hundred feet waiting for me to tell the dispatcher where it should go. Just as I looked at the shooters, they launched another balloon. *Splat* on the track about twenty feet away. The shooters were too busy shooting to pay any attention to the chopper. Helicopter noise at a track on race day was common. There were police, TV, and medical helicopters in the air all the time—and besides, those guys looked like they were still drunk.

I watched them through my binoculars as they staggered around, bumping into each other and tried to load a new balloon. A small crowd had gathered to cheer them on. I relayed directions to Security who directed the chopper closer to the shooters. As it hovered overhead, another balloon came in. Sooner or later, they would get a lucky shot and hit one of us. I looked through the binoculars and saw three troopers running through the crowd, not fifty feet from the shooters. I told the dispatcher to tell them to go one row to their right because they were between a blue and white motor home with an awning and a yellow Ryder rental truck. Some of the shooters' buddies, who were gathered around cheering them on, spotted the troopers and hollered at the guys to run. It was too late. I watched as they were cuffed and taken away. The crowd cheered. One of the troopers looked my way and waved. I called Security and thanked everyone.

I stood up by the catch fence and said, "Man. That was just like a war movie! We were under a mortar attack and we brought in air cover and then ground troops attacked and got 'em. Sign painters, water balloons, troopers, and choppers—only at Talladega." I looked up at the chopper and with both arms stretched out waved my hands back and forth. The chopper hovered for a second and then banked sharply over to the left and flew away. I looked back at the chopper flying away and saluted, thinking *He must've been a pilot in Nam.*

We high-fived each other. We'd survived the attack and lived to paint another day—and it was only 8 a.m. I said, "Let's eat and get ready to watch the race."

As we walked down the banking we were actually hearing cheers from the infield campers. I gave a victory wave and walked to the Gator already loaded with wet brushes, empty paint cans, and thinner rags. We all climbed in and away we went down the Back Straight to the crossing gate by Turn 3. As we were driving down the Back Straight, I said to Steve, "Just think, in a couple of hours Dale Earnhardt will be driving right in our tire tracks."

Steve's eyes glazed over and with a look of pure awe. "Cool, man."

⁂

Back in the war room at the Maintenance Office, we told Mike McWilliams and the rest of the crew about the latest adventure. They were all still laughing—they'd listened to the whole thing on their radios as it unfolded.

"If you'd worked harder last night," Mike said smiling, "you wouldn't have gotten in that mess."

I looked at him and said, "You nut. Where's the coffee?"

We ended up watching the race from the top of the new Allison Grandstands on the Back Straight. They were dedicated that week to Donnie, Davey, and Bobby Allison. We did the signs for their reserved seats and the scissors that were used to cut the ribbon. We were way up on top, where the spotters stand, just behind the fans' seats. I was standing at the end of an aisle, all the way to the top, when I saw four guys trudging up the stairs not five rows down from me. "Hey," I hollered at them. "You're not allowed in these stands."

The lead guy's head snapped up with "What the hell did you say?" written all over his face. Then with a shocked look he hollered, "Vickio!" It was Charlie Trickler, a great friend of mine from Waterloo, New York, He'd come down with some friends to watch the race. More than 180,000 people in the stands and his tickets led him up the aisle to the seats right below me! He walked up to within twenty feet of me.

The race was great. Earnhardt won! On Monday, we were ready to head home. Driving home, all we could do was talk. Steve had a great time. He had had such a good time that he'd flown his wife down on Friday to watch the race with him. Larry and I had one of the best trips to Talladega we'd ever had. Yes, we worked our asses off, but it only added to the spice. Although I've tried to describe things that happened on these adventures, no description actually matched being there with some good old buddies. Man, this trip was fun.

Highwaller Shoes

The garage door in my sign shop was open on a hot summer day in July 1999 when the phone broke the silence. "Vickio Signs," I said. "I can't hear you, could you talk louder?" I added, carrying the cordless phone toward the wall-mounted TV to turn down the sound. I reached up while holding the phone to my ear with my shoulder to turn the volume down. I couldn't find the damned remote so I actually had to turn the volume down manually. *There. Now I can hear.*

In that low, slow Southern voice, the general manager of Talladega Superspeedway said, "Hey Tony. Mike McWilliams here."

"Hi Mike, how're you doing?"

"I'm workin' like a dawg." I smiled at his classic answer. We talked for a minute and then he said, "How would you like to come down here for a week in August?" Talladega had two NASCAR Winston Cup races in 1999. The first, in April, was the DieHard 500. The second race wasn't until October, the Winston 500. "We have so much work that you won't be able to get it done when you come down for two weeks in October."

"Sure, what do we have to do?"

"We have a ton of logos to put on the walls. There are a lot of them. A media company will be here to go over the layouts and the placement of them with you." I told him I would be bringing one man with me and he told me to be there the twelfth of July.

Oh great, I thought—and not in a good way. I hate being right out in the sun. *Alabama in July. Oh God. Wall painting,* he said. I started to make a list of what I needed to bring. My computer and plotter were the big items. The paint and other materials I could get down there. There was a big sign supply house in Birmingham and the track had an account there. The track also supplied a man to travel to Birmingham when we need something. One more thing I needed . . . somebody to go with me.

I got on the phone and called Larry Orr. He went on the last trip—and besides, I don't want to pounce. "Hey Larry, want to go to Talladega?"

"The race isn't until October," he said.

I told him the story, trying not to sound like I was holding my breath. I was afraid he would say no! There was no way I could go to a track to do the work I do without Larry Orr, Steve Hughey, or Bob Timmerman! They all had tremendous experience and we all got along great! There was no shortage of people who wanted to go on these trips, but I don't have time to do on-the-job training!

"I'd love to go!" he said. So in July, four days before my birthday, we were once again headed south in my Chevy shop truck.

We pulled into the track and looked around, and all our friends greeted us. Most of them said, "What the hell are you doing here? The race isn't till October."

In the Maintenance Office we were talking to Mike about the job when I remembered we didn't have a place to stay yet. "Mike, where are we staying?" I asked.

"Oh," he said, "The track owns some houses on the other side of Speedway Blvd. You can stay in one of those—no one is in them until the races."

We got in our truck and followed Mike. When he turned in through a gated

A house owned by the speedway. This is where Larry and I stayed.

entrance to a beautiful, huge house, I said to Larry, "This can't be it." Just then, Mike stopped and got out of his truck. "Oh my God." I said.

Larry and I looked at each other with our eyes bugging out and said, at the same time, *"Wow."*

I never got around to counting how many rooms it had, but it was *big*. It had a beautiful sun porch where we spent our free time at night watching TV. Most wonderful of all, it had central air. It was July and it was *hot*. We got settled in and the next morning we were up before sunup. (We always start early.) I opened the door to the carport and it was still dark, but I was hit with the same heat blast as you get when you open the oven to check on the Thanksgiving turkey. "Holy shit. This is not good," I hollered.

"Holy Christ" came out of Larry's mouth at the same time.

I couldn't believe all the heat and the humidity *before* the sun rose. *This is not going to be good.* We stopped at the familiar deli, where the girls looked at us like they were thinking, "What the hell are you doing here? The race isn't till October." We told them we had a lot of new logos to paint as we headed to the back of the store and looked for a Styrofoam cooler. We found one and loaded it up with Gatorade and Ice. We were ready.

At the track, Mike filled us in on the new logos. At 9 a.m., Mike called me to over to the Main Office and introduced me to several people from an ad agency and some marketing people from the track. In a conference room, we spent an hour watching tapes of past races. Their job was to time the seconds (not minutes) each part of the retaining wall was on TV. The amount of TV time determined the value of a spot on the wall. This finished, we were ready to make our patterns and go paint.

Outside, the heat was unbelievable. I can stand cold, but heat is my enemy. During the week, we worked on the high banks from daybreak until about 11 a.m. Then it was time to retreat to the air-conditioned sign shop. We drank gallons of Gatorade while the sweat dripped off our eyebrows and onto the insides of our sunglasses. Out on the asphalt you could look down the Back Straight and see heat waves like in the desert. I swear that on the Back Straight I saw a camel walking in the shimmering heat waves coming off of the track. This was insane.

When the sun dipped below the retaining wall at about 3:30 p.m., we would go back out and work on the Back Straight where the wall was now in the shade. That meant that from the neck down we were in the shade; our faces were still burning. One day, as we were painting away, we heard a clanging sound coming from the Front Straight grandstands. It had been dead quiet out on the track until that sound. I got my binoculars out of the truck and looked over at the Front Straight grandstands, where I saw six guys working among the aluminum seats.

"That must be like working in a microwave oven," I said to Larry. Come to find out, they were painting the grandstand seats. They had to cover everything with plastic, tape it all down, then sandblast and paint the seats. I didn't feel so bad for myself after watching those guys.

The following day we were working in the air-conditioned shop when I went out to the truck and pulled a bag from behind the seat. I carried it back into the shop where Larry said, "What the hell is that?"

Slowly, with a sly grin, I pulled out the contents of the bag.

Larry, laughing now, said, "What the hell are those?"

"The *shoes,* man. These are *the shoes.*"

When Mike called me at my shop to ask me to come down, I got a crazy idea to build a pair of shoes that would let me walk up the 34-degree banking standing straight up. I talked to my friend Ken Coates, owner of Inlet Glass and Mirror in Ithaca, we agreed to help me build them. We cut wood bases for the soles and glued on a rubber tread type sole from some old sandals. Then we fabricated adjustable

The original highwaller shoes.

supports using aluminum side braces. Ken stuck a small plastic level on the side just for show. On top was another plywood platform that my sneakers would sit on. Now we needed to attach them to my sneakers. Mike Wells (another friend, who owned Welco Upholstery & Awning, also in Ithaca) made Velcro straps that hooked to the plywood shoe mount and I could pull tight over my sneakers.

"Let's take the Gator out to Turn 4," I said to Larry, "and test these bad boys." He grabbed his camera and away we went.

He kept saying over and over, "Oh, my God. I can't stand it. You gotta be kiddin'."

When we reached the center between Turns 3 and 4, I backed up the Gator to the banking so I could sit on the tailgate and put the shoes on. The shoes needed to be on banking when I stood up as I'd fall over forward for sure on flat ground. While I sat on the tailgate strapping the highwaller shoes on, Larry laughed uncontrollably while sucking on his stupid pipe at the same time. Looking at Larry, I motioned him to get the camera up to his eye. I wanted photographic proof of the success of my latest invention. "Stop your goddamned laughing," I said. "This is serious." He only laughed harder. "Are you ready?" I hollered.

"Oh, my God. Hurry," he said. "I don't know how long I can stand up. I can't stop laughing." he said.

I slowly stood straight up from the tailgate of the Gator and looked up the banking. The shoes were set at 34 degrees, the same as the banking. I felt like Neil Armstrong. "One small step for man. One giant leap for mankind." I heard Larry's camera

Standing on the highwallers on the Talladega Superspeedway banking.

click. I looked over and he was laughing so hard, spit was flying out of his mouth and running down the side of his stupid pipe.

    I took two steps up the banking. Just then, my ankles started to wobble and I lost my balance. Falling back, I tried to take a long step backward so I could sit, or more like fall, back on the tailgate. Too late. I tumbled into the back of the Gator full force. My feet went up as I was on my back in the back of the Gator. I slid to the back of the box and stopped with a loud thud. For a minute I couldn't get up. I hollered, "Did ya

Falling into the back of the Gator as the shoes failed.

get it? Did ya get it?" I rolled to my left and put two hands on the side of the box. I pulled myself up and looked over the side.

Larry was lying on his side on the apron of the racetrack. He was laughing so hard that he was curled up in the fetal position. It wasn't like a laugh; it was more like uncontrollable screaming. He sounded like a girl. He was jerking around and he clearly couldn't catch his breath. All he kept saying between screams was, "Oh my God. Oh God."

I pulled myself to the tailgate and sat on the edge. I was laughing so hard, mostly at Larry, I couldn't move. If anyone had seen us, they would have called Security. I got the shoes off and threw them in the Gator and hollered to Larry, "Did you get it? Did you get the shots?"

He kept hollering, "Oh my God. I can't stand it. I'm going to throw up." We rode back to the shop laughing all the way. Larry laughed so hard, I thought he was going to pass out.

When we got back to the shop Mike was standing outside. We showed the shoes to Mike. He then had to show them to everyone else. They loved them and asked how they worked. Larry broke into uncontrollable laughter again. I told them they needed some work. I said, "The first test failed. After analyzing the data and onboard telemetry I have detected a severe lateral destabilization problem." Everyone liked the shoes so much it prompted a phone call to me the next day. It was from the International Motorsports Hall of Fame. They had to have them. My highwaller shoes now reside in a glass case, along with Larry's photos and a story, in the Hall of Fame in Talladega, Alabama. If you ever visit the place, you will see them.

Induction of the "highwaller" shoes into the International Motorsports Hall of Fame in Talladega, Alabama.

☙

I was at home one night about a year after my highwaller shoes were put in the Hall of Fame and I got a call from Mike McWilliams. He was in Houston at the NASA facility where NASCAR had debuted their latest IMAX film. (Houston Space Center has one of the largest IMAX theaters.) Mike said after the movie, there had been a dinner and a reception for all the NASCAR people. "A friend came up to me and said, 'Hey. You gotta come in here and see something. You're not going to believe it.'" Mike told me they went into the reception hall and there on a pedestal were *"your damned shoes."* It seemed that NASCAR wanted to decorate the Hall with some objects from the Motorsports Hall of Fame for the showing that night and my highwaller shoes were among the items.

☙

At noon after the shoe debacle we went to the deli for more Gatorade. We were sitting at a table having lunch when the door opened and in came the six guys I'd seen working on the grandstands. The boss was a big guy, around 300 pounds, and most of them had blue coveralls on. When they walked in, one little guy stood out from the others; he was about five-foot-five and 105 pounds, and was hunched over slightly. His hair was dark and uncombed and stuck out in all directions from under his dirty blue hat. He had on a dark green pair of coveralls that were a size too big for him. The coveralls looked funny when he walked as the pant legs dragged on the floor hiding his shoes. His skin looked burned black. Was he that dirty? Was it a tan? No, it wasn't a tan. It was beyond a tan. He was actually all wrinkled, skin drawn up tight and it wasn't a brown tan . . . he really was burned black. I've never seen anyone so tanned and still be alive. He was jittery, never standing still. I think his skin was burned down enough to expose all of his raw nerve endings. But the thing that stood out the most was his eyes. They were wide open, white and huge. The look of pure fright was in them. We never saw him blink. His eyes were always moving, darting from left to right, like he felt someone was going to sneak up on him at any minute and stab him in the back. Larry immediately dubbed him "Cinderman."

I said, "He looks like one of those big old wooden matchsticks. You light it, hold it between your fingers, and let it burn down the length of the match. When the flame dies out, the wood match stick is all black, bent and twisted with the head of the burned out match sticking up at the top." This was Cinderman.

Larry said, "You know why he has the scared look? He doesn't want to go back to the grandstands."

The men got plastic water bottles and walked out through the door following the boss. As they were driving away, we found ourselves feeling sorry for the little guy. We saw him a couple of times after that, then he was gone. We can speculate that he quit or just disintegrated into a pile of black dust somewhere in Row 23 of the Moss-Thornton Grandstand.

Larry and I finished our week's work and had gotten a good jump on the upcoming race. I was glad to get the hell out of Talladega. Don't get me wrong, I love Alabama, but not in the summer. It was way too hot for me even with an air-conditioned mansion to stay in. We returned in October to finish the work we'd started. Like Mike had said, there had been too much to do in just one trip.

Painting Big

By the middle of winter I'd been busy at Watkins Glen for months and hadn't thought about any work at other tracks, except for one snowy winter day when I was looking through a box of photos from Talladega and Daytona. "Man, there are a ton of memories in this box," I thought.

I had been traveling south to work at Talladega for eight years, usually twice a year for the spring and fall races. Now, I got a strong feeling that my traveling race-track work was coming to an end. Big business had taken over and I expected to be replaced at some point by larger sign companies.

∽

The phone kept ringing as I walked over to the wall phone and picked it up. "Vickio signs," I said into the portable handset. I walked over to the overhead door and looked out the window at the snow falling.

"Hello Tony? It's Donna."

I'd recognize Donna's southern accent anywhere. I quickly straightened up and walked back toward my desk. "Donna. How are you?" I said as my heart jumped. *It may be another job.*

Donna said, "Hey Tony, Mike wants to talk to you. Hang on and I will put him on."

After a few seconds I heard, "Hey Tony, how ya doin'?"

"How are *you* doin'?"

"I'm workin' like a dawg. I got a job for ya. We built a new 25,000-seat grandstand on the Back Straight and we need some work done. Not on the grandstand, we already had another sign company do the signs for that. I want you to put the Talladega logo on the backside of the grandstand—on the blacktop area between the grandstand and ticket booths. I want to be able to see it from the helicopter or blimp. I want it big. What do you think?" Pause. "Nobody down here wants to touch it," he added, meaning those big-business sign shops that had crowded me out.

"Sure we can do it," I said, "but it will take four guys. When do you need it?"

"For the next race in April. We've got a lot of time but I wanted to give you a heads-up. I'll have Donna get the rooms and I'll see ya when you get here."

"I'll be there two weeks before the race," I said.

I hung up the phone and immediately jumped in the air, arms flailing, and screaming. *"Yeahhhhh!! We're back!"* I got right on the phone and called my two main men, Steve Hughey and Larry Orr, and told them the news. They were as excited as I was. Back to Talladega, and for a large job.

I needed a fourth man but I hadn't picked one yet. The more I studied this job, the more complicated it got. Mike gave me the exact dimensions of the asphalt where the logo needed to go. Leaving some edge distance, the logo would be 126 feet long and about 70 feet high. This would be an 8,820-square-foot sign, painted on asphalt. I'd never painted on asphalt before. Larry had painted on asphalt once doing a job for Corning, Inc.

"I used latex paint and it worked really well," he said. That problem was solved but there were other problems to overcome.

The Talladega Superspeedway logo was a hard one to lay out. The top of the lettering is straight across but from there on, everything was on an arc. "Talladega" is flat on top but curved on the bottom. "Superspeedway" is curved on both top and bottom. Long, tapering curved slashes separate the words and trace the bottom of the logo. After the speedway sent me the artwork, I struggled to figure out how to lay it all out. Suddenly, the light bulb went on: we could triangulate it! That was the secret I learned from Allan Jones, the grass painter I met while I painted the walls on the high banks. He told me he could lay out a huge sign with no pattern and no grid on the ground—just a couple of measuring tapes and some flags.

The triangulation system worked this way: About 6 feet above where the logo was to go, you drive two pins (actually large spikes) into the asphalt about 130 feet apart, centered where the logo would go and parallel with the top of the logo. Fasten a 200-foot measuring tape to each pin. Call the pin on the left "A" and the one on the right "B." Your layout sheet has two columns of measurements, labeled "A" and "B," with numbers 1, 2, 3, and so on down the side. For example, the "T" in Talladega has eight points, defined by numbers 1–8 on the layout sheet. To place the top left of the "T," I would say, "'A': 10 feet 5 inches and 'B': 118 feet 4 inches." The guys working each pin stretch out their tapes to the measurements. In this case, the one on the "A" pin holds his thumb on 10 feet 5 inches, and the one on the "B" pin does the same on 118 feet 4 inches. They walk together and hold the tapes so their thumbs touch, forming a triangle with the pins. Then they lower the point to the ground. I put a mark there, or have a fourth guy do it. Every part of the layout has its two numbers on the sheet—which sounds simple, but gets complex quickly when you have to deal with a curve . . . and the Talladega logo is almost nothing but curves. When I saw the final layout sheet I almost fainted. It was eighteen pages long and almost six hundred measurements. I took it and made two copies. I wasn't going to lose it.

I'd wanted to invite Steve Tinker as our fourth, but he couldn't go this time. He did pitch in with AutoCAD—he's a real expert—and made the layout for us to use with the triangulation. All we needed was one more man. Steve and Larry are experienced sign men and have been with me to Talladega many times. What I needed was someone who wanted to work—and to go to the best NASCAR race on the circuit and have a time he would never forget. It was a job for a young guy as he was going to be the grunt man. He would do the jobs us old guys can't do anymore.

One night, Harriett and I had been shooting pool at the Rambling Brook Inn in Montour Falls, New York, in a winter league we belonged to. There we saw Mike Dean—a guy who'd been bugging me about going to Talladega. Harriett said, "Why don't you ask him to go? I'm sure he can do the work and he would really enjoy it."

"I don't know," I said. "I really don't know him very well. I'll think about it."

Well, Mike and I got talking, and when I hinted about a trip, he went crazy. "I'll do anything, Tony. Whatever you need, I'll do it. Please take me. I've never been to a race. *Please.* I'll work my ass off." Mike was about twenty-five years old, and he was strong. He convinced me he would do anything we asked. We had our number four.

⁂

What a feeling when we pulled our trucks into the speedway. Steve and Larry and I were back home. Mike was in awe. It reminded me of my first time there. After we got all the equipment hooked up in the sign shop (I had brought my computer again, thank God), we went out with Mike McWilliams to see where the logo was to go behind the new grandstand. The grandstand was huge: twenty-five thousand seats. The asphalt was new and jet black. This huge asphalt area behind the new grandstand would be our new canvas.

Mike left us there and I said to Steve and Larry, "Well, here it is. Man, this is awesome. Just for the hell of it, let's check the dimensions they gave us before we go eat. I want to make sure we are OK so I can sleep tonight. I don't want to be thinking the measurements are wrong all night."

Steve said, "Come on. Let's go. They aren't wrong. You had them measure it and they did. Let's eat."

"I don't know. It'll only take a minute."

While holding the reel, I handed Steve the dumb end of the tape and told him to go to the other side of the asphalt. Mike grabbed the tape right out of his hand and ran over to where I'd pointed.

Steve and I looked at each other and smiled. "See?" I said.

The tape was running out so fast, you would have thought I had a three-hundred-pound blue marlin on the other end. Thinking about it, Steve would have taken five minutes to get there. He's getting *old,* you know.

Mike knelt down and held his end of the tape on the edge of the asphalt. He waved his hand over his head to signal he was set. I put mine end down and I looked at the measurement. My eyeballs almost bugged out of their sockets. I looked up to see if Mike was on the edge of the asphalt and—waving my hand signaling to go farther—I hollered, "Are you on the edge? Go all the way to the edge of the asphalt. To the edge."

He hollered back, and it put goose bumps down my spine: "I am on the edge of the asphalt." He was pointing down, moving his hand up and down.

It was about this time I almost shit my pants. I jumped straight up and screamed, "Are you shittin' me?"

Larry came walking over with that stupid pipe sticking out of his mouth. Slowly he put his hand up and held the bowl and took it out of his mouth and said, "What?"

The strangest thing happened. I tried to holler something and gasp for breath at the same exact time. I almost exploded. I finally got some coordination back and screamed, "I don't friggin' believe it. Steve. Get the goddamned drawing out of the truck."

Steve brought the drawing back and it confirmed my worst fear. The dimensions the track gave me were *wrong*. *Wrong!!* I looked up and hollered, "NOOOoooooo!" You've seen it in a movie where the guy is kneeling down and he looks up at the camera above his head and the camera draws back as he screams "NOOOooooo." That was me. Everyone gathered around me and looked at the drawing. The logo was too big by four feet. Remember those eighteen pages of coordinates? Toilet paper. A job I had all planned out, layout done thanks to Steve Tinker, suddenly it was turning into a nightmare. I was stunned. My mind was whirling. This was not a small painting like we've done on the retaining walls. This was *huge*.

Back at the sign shop, I fired up my computer. *Thank God I brought it with me.* I almost had left it home—after all, Steve had done my layout already. I don't know why I brought it but thank God I did. Now I needed it and my college classes that I took at Corning Community College for AutoCAD were going to come into play. I silently thanked Claude Sullivan, the CEO of Watkins Glen International, who'd sent me to AutoCAD class years ago. I didn't even want to go to the motel that night. I wanted to work on the layout. The guys talked me into getting some sleep.

They kept asking, "Are you sure you know what you're doing?"

I kept saying, "I wish Steve was here." I didn't sleep well that night.

☙

I got to the track by 7 a.m. the next morning and sat down to get reacquainted with AutoCAD. It had been years since I'd used this very sophisticated program, and it took me a couple of hours to get the hang of it. I told the guys, "Go do something. Show Mike the area. I'm going to be here all day." Once I got into the program, I was sailing. I was done with the new coordinates by 3 p.m. When the guys came back, I was smiling. When they saw me smiling, they were noticeably relieved.

I turned to Larry. "Are you sure you used latex on the asphalt you painted?"

"Yup. It worked really well."

We went to see Donna in the Maintenance Office. "Hey, Donna. Where does the track get the white latex you use around here?"

"We use Gower Paints," she said. "They're just down the road. They'll mix whatever you want. We have an account there."

I turned to the guys and said, "Let's get the paint today and we can start the job tomorrow." Away we went.

Gower Paints was about fifteen miles from the track. I thought it was a paint supply house. Not so. It turned out to be a family-owned paint *factory*. They make their own paint from scratch. We walked in and there was this 250-pound guy behind a counter. He said in a deep Southern tone, "Hep ya?"

I bored him with the whole story to the point that he was almost ready to give me the paint just to get me to shut up. I told him I needed this shade of blue (I handed him an inch-square sample), black, white, and Rubine Red (Talladega is very fussy on the right red color and I had a color chip for it also). Try to find Rubine Red in latex.

The man behind the counter yelled, "Dad!" Out came a frail-looking old man, and the counter guy said, "Dad, these gentlemen need this red matched."

He handed over the color chip and the old man looked up at me and said, "I can match anythin'." He turned, and walked back into the plant, still looking at the color chip. He hollered back without turning, "How much ya need?" I told him my estimated gallons; the Rubine Red was about forty-five gallons. The counter guy said, "Once he figures the red, we can get you whatever ya want. We deliver to the track." We loaded up about sixty gallons of white and headed back to the track.

Steve said, "Hope this shit is good."

"We'll find out tomorrow," I said.

On the way back to the track, we stopped at Lowe's for supplies. We stocked up on rollers, handle extensions, paint trays, and everything else we were likely to need.

⁂

The next morning, we were ready to get started. Here we were. Four guys from the North, standing on a huge section of asphalt sipping on our coffee and watching the sun rising over the beautiful mountains. Mike was ready to go. I appreciated his energy. Steve and Larry, just by being here, gave me confidence that the job would be done right. I trusted those guys.

This logo would be right behind the new grandstand, so fans coming from the ticket booths would walk over the painting. That was problem number one. We couldn't paint this like a grass painting. Because people will be right on top of the painting, the edges have to be straight and crisp. I love *crisp*. At supper last night, we'd agreed to use one-inch 3M Tape to make our edges. This was a big problem. Have you ever put masking tape on asphalt? The paint will seep right under the gaps. This is where Mike came in.

"Hey, Mike," I said. "Remember when you said you'd do anything to come here? Well, do I have a job for you." On the Lowe's run, we'd picked up a pair of the best knee pads you ever saw. I held the pads out to Mike and said, "Yours."

"No problem, boss," he said, taking them with a happy, ignorant smile.

The three of them were looking at me for a hint of what to do next.

"You guys ready?" I asked.

Mike was first to answer: "Hell yeah. Whaddaya want me to do?"

I thought to myself, *You're about to find out.*

 # We Paint the Asphalt

As we stood on the asphalt behind the Allison Grandstand, the sun was just clearing Cheaha Mountain. I took a sip from my coffee. "Well, I guess the first step is to clean the surface," I said. The guys knew this wasn't like sweeping the floor in your house. For one thing, your floor is smooth. This was asphalt. Your living room floor is maybe a few hundred square feet. This was more than eight thousand. We all stood there for a second and looked at each other. Then I pulled out my two-way radio, clicked the talk button, and said, "Tony to Jimmy . . . Tony to Jimmy."

"Tony. Whatcha need, man?"

"Hey Jimmy. I need the jet blower over here behind the Allison Grandstand. I gotta clean the asphalt. We're starting to paint the logo this mornin'."

"Get a broom," Jimmy said. "Nah. I'll be there in a half hour. Have to fuel the jet up first."

The jet blower—built for rain cleanup on NASCAR tracks—was an honest-to-God jet turbine engine mounted horizontally on the back of a heavy-duty pickup truck. With a special-built, tapered nozzle pointing down and outward, this thing put out a blast of hot air that was unbelievable. When the turbine was running, the jet blast from the nozzle removed any debris from the racing surface. You would not find a single grain of sand on the track after the jet blower went by. The sound was deafening—just like standing next to a jet plane as its engines wound up for takeoff.

"He'll be here in half an hour. Let's move the trucks over there so they don't get sandblasted," I said to Steve.

After moving the pickup I went to the back and got a hammer and two large spikes to set the pins. After we got them into the asphalt, we put empty trash barrels over them so Jimmy wouldn't run over them with the jet blower. Just then I heard a truck coming.

"Thar she blows," Steve hollered.

I showed Jimmy where we needed the surface cleaned. He rolled up the window and put his ear protectors on. The jet turbine started with a low whine and ramped up to a roar. Steve and Larry and Mike and I all ran to the other side of the fence with our hands over our ears.

Jimmy only needed to make two quick passes. As the jet blower wound down, Jimmy rolled his window down and hollered over the whistling of the turbine, "Is that OK?"

I didn't answer, just gave a thumbs-up. Jimmy waved and drove off. I turned and looked at the guys and said to Mike, who'd never heard a jet blower before, "It's clean." Then I hollered to everyone, "Make sure your shoes are clean before you go on the surface. I don't want any sand making the paint peel up."

My plan was to paint a white background, in the shape of the logo, six inches larger than the logo. That would give us a bright background to contrast with the logo's blue outlines and black Ls. Plus, two good coats of the white latex paint would fill many of the voids in the asphalt, smoothing it out and making it easier to tape. It turned out to have an extra, unplanned benefit. We were ten times cooler working on the white surface than we would have been standing or kneeling on the black asphalt.

Larry and Steve were holding the two tapes. I had the brand new eighteen-page layout book and turned to page one. It was a solid mass of numbers. Mike quietly stood by. "What do you want me to do?" he asked. "I'll do whatever you want. I'm ready."

"Nothing yet. Your job is coming up." Larry, Steve, and I gave Mike sinister smiles. We all knew the job I had planned for him.

I hollered out the first orders. "Larry. You are 'A.' Steve. You're 'B.' Don't forget who the hell you are. It will screw up everything if you idiots screw up. Got it?"

The layout before we started painting.

They hollered back at once, "Yeah. Yeah. We got it. What was I again? HaHaHa."

"Yeah. You'll think it's funny when I kill ya," I said. "I'm only going to holler 'A' 60 feet, 'B' 120 feet and so on. You find your number and go to the spot where the tapes cross. Remember who the hell you are. This is damned important. No mistakes. OK? Here we go." I hollered out the first coordinates, then marked the spot where the tapes crossed with white chalk. The first few numbers were awkward but after about five or six readings we got the hang of handling the tapes and, amazingly, we were sailing right along.

With the border layout finished, I turned to Mike and with a devilish smile I said, "Now, Mike. It's show time. You're next."

Mike was excited to help. "Great! What do you want, man?"

I might have been a little paranoid about getting perfectly straight and clean lines on the asphalt surface. But we'd tried pad painters like the ones we used on the retaining walls, as well as paint rollers and stiff brushes. Nothing got results as good as taping the entire edge did. We used tape to get the straight edge and the crispness that I wanted. I knew this meant a lot of extra work, but I was sure the results would be worth it.

Steve Hughey, Mike Dean (foreground), and Larry Orr. Mike and Larry are taking coordinates from Steve and plotting layout points.

We chalk-lined between the points so we could see the edge while rolling the tape out. We got the first roll of masking tape out and put it down between the first two points. Being too lazy to bend over, we walked on the tape to press it down into the valleys in the asphalt. Now Mike started to pay for his trip. He knelt down on his brand new Lowe's kneepads and with a new, round rivet brush (an inch-wide wood-handled brush with short, stiff bristles) started burnishing the tape—rubbing it down to the asphalt. We stopped him at three feet.

"Let's test it," I said.

Larry had a paint tray with some white latex paint in it. He rolled along the tape for a foot and we all stood back and waited five minutes for the paint to tack up. It didn't take any long as sun on the asphalt created a lot of heat. I bent down and took the end of the tape and peeled it up. If this failed we would have a major problem. I held my breath. RRrrrriiipppp. *"Perfect!"* I screamed. Since the tape system worked, I knew the rest of the logo would go great.

We outlined the border with chalk, taped the edges and then waited for Mike to finish burnishing the tape. You don't realize how big almost nine thousand square feet is until you have to paint it, and I could see right away that this project was going to need two coats of white. It took a lot of paint to fill the little voids in the asphalt, and even then the first coat didn't provide the pure white that I wanted. We wouldn't have to double-coat the entire white area, though. Where the letters were going we only needed one coat. "If we are lucky we can get both coats of white on today," I told the guys. "Then we will have all day tomorrow to lay out the logo."

☙

The next day, bright and early, we started the logo layout. The background white looked great. We started with the word *Talladega* which gave us practice before we had to do the long curving slashes. Those slashes looked like they would be really hard to get right. Once we finished the *Talladega* layout, we tackled the slashes. They

Mike Dean filling in the "L";

took many points to plot because of their curves. It was a good thing that we had the grandstand right behind us. I sent Larry up to the top and from there he could look down, see if there were any lines in the arcs that had a flat spot or looked bad, and tell us what to fix. The logo took a full twelve-hour day to lay out and tape. Mike worked away on the tape, unspooling miles of it. Larry invented the "ORR" (named for himself, naturally): a mop handle with a modified tape dispenser attached to the end so he didn't have to creep; he just walked along and the tape was down. While we worked, the big guy from Gower delivered the colored paint. The old man had been true to his word—the Rubine Red was matched perfectly.

Steve, Larry, and I started painting with long-handled paint rollers. We painted and painted. Mike, with his miles of taping finished, helped us paint. Thank goodness the weather stayed perfect.

From start to finish the whole job took four days. Painting the logo required 120 gallons of Gower paint (the absolute best latex I had ever used), 20 paint rollers, and more than 50 rolls of masking tape. A few other sign men might argue against the tape method for this type of job (it was *very* time-consuming), but the end result was worth the effort. When we stood on the painting, it looked like it was printed on the asphalt. Of course, Mike might never walk again!

∽

The next day, we wanted to get pictures of the sign. We tried to do it from the top of the grandstands but that didn't do it justice. You couldn't get the whole painting in the shot. Mike McWilliams said they had a contractor on the grounds with a

Steve Hughey took this shot from a 120-foot man lift. (Those bugs around the "E" in Talladega are Larry, Mike, and me walking on the logo.)

120-foot man lift. He agreed to bring his lift over to our painting in an hour. When it arrived, I immediately said, "I'm not getting in that thing. Somebody else do it."

"I'll do it," Steve said. "Lemme get my camera."

I couldn't even look over the side of the grandstand, let alone go up in a 120-foot man lift. Steve got some great pictures.

For the rest of the trip, we just enjoyed the races. Mike had the time of his life. I was proud of the job we'd just finished. Everyone at the speedway was ecstatic. It took a lot of good people to do a job like that. Larry, Steve, and Mike should be as proud as I am. And even though Steve Tinker wasn't there, he was also part of the job—the new layout would have been a hell of a lot harder to do from scratch without his original to work from.

During the time we were in Talladega, I had a chance to meet Dave Gentile, the future general manager of the new Chicagoland Speedway in Joliet, Illinois. Chicagoland was still being built. Dave was at Talladega observing what it took to put on

Me, Larry Orr, and Mike Dean. (Steve Hughey is taking the picture.)

a race. We talked about sign painting and the possibility of my going out there when the track opened. I didn't think much more about it as the construction was still going on. My next goal was to watch my man Dale Earnhardt win the 500. He did. It would be his last win at Talladega.

After we got home, anyone who got near Mike risked losing an ear from his nonstop storytelling. He had been a rookie, but bringing him along had been a great decision. Years later, in July 2005, I got a cell phone call from Mike. I could hear the excitement in is voice. "Tony. Guess where I am?" he said.

"How the hell do I know?"

"I'm on my cell phone and I'm standing right on our Talladega logo. I'm standing right on it."

"Are you shittin' me?"

Mike told me he'd been driving his tractor-trailer from Texas on I-20 east of Birmingham, which ran right by the speedway. "I had to stop in," he said. "I drove the truck to the Security Building and told them who I was and that I had helped paint the logo behind the Allison Grandstands. I wanted to drive out and see our logo. They let me. It looks as good as the day we painted it! I just wanted to let you know."

I almost had tears in my eyes. Mike's experience sure stuck with him. I'm so glad that I took him along.

 ## This Bud's for You

    Watkins Glen International, four miles from my house, was really growing. Mattman had retired and Tim Coleman became general manager. I'd known Tim a long time. He was a great guy to work for and I counted him as another one of my good friends. We got along great and he wasn't afraid to work. He actually jumped in and helped me at the track when I needed it.

    As the track adding new events and sponsors, it opened up more work opportunities for me. One of the big projects that year was the addition of a tall water tank at the end of the Back Straight and the entrance to the Inner Loop. The water tank would be in a camera shot at the Inner Loop every lap. Remember the value of signage in a TV shot? Well this tank had value. Budweiser grabbed it up and wanted it painted Budweiser Red with a big white BUD lettered on it. I went up to the track and looked at the tank and said, "I don't know. It's not that I can't letter it, but I'm so damned scared of heights I don't know if I can go up that high." The tank was ten feet across and thirty feet tall. "I really don't think I can do it. I might have to pass on this one." I stood at the base of the tank and started getting a little light-headed just looking up at the thing. I had to look away.

    I turned to watch a construction workers bolt the base of the tank to a large concrete pad. I walked over to a guy kneeling down on the concrete. He was putting a large nut onto a bolt that would secure the tank to the concrete pad. Six of those large bolts would hold the tank in place.

    The construction worker was about 280 pounds and as he knelt over the bolt, it was hard to avoid the sight of his butt crack. *Oh God. That is disgusting,* I thought as I quickly walked around in front of him. He had an unlit cigar sticking out of his mouth and a four-day growth on his face. The scratched-up old orange hard hat he was wearing had a faded American flag on the right side and a nude blonde on the left. (She was in the sort of pose used for nose art on a WWII B-17 bomber, and you could tell the picture was cut out of a Playboy magazine with a pair of scissors and glued to the helmet.)

    "Hey," I said. "This thing isn't going fall over anytime soon, is it?"

    He just glanced up with the look of, "What the hell do you think, you dumb shithead?" He bit down harder on his cigar and went back to turning the huge bolt with his fat fingers. He didn't say a word. I stood there for a few seconds.

"OK," I said, and walked away, not looking back. I didn't want to see that butt crack again!

I really did not want to do this job! But . . . I figured that if I turned it down, someone else would be hired and the "big" jobs might go to them from now on. I did own a sign business! Signs are what I was expected to do, and I had always strived to do my best. Turning down this job was just not me.

I agreed to do the job even though it would be a huge challenge for me. Not only a big, vertical painting, but the height factor! I had a 1973 Chevy sign crane truck that had an extendable boom that would go up forty-five feet. It could be used as a sign crane or a bucket truck. On the end of the boom I could attach a one-man bucket. Man, was that thing scary. The bucket (cobbled together by someone who had the truck before me) was made of angle iron, and two bolts attached it to a U-shaped channel iron piece that wrapped around the sides of the bucket. This allowed the bucket to pivot and stay upright as the boom went up or down.

The boom consisted of three sections of pipe that slid into each other. To extend the boom, I grabbed hold of a switch on the bucket's crude control panel, and the electric motor would come to life. With a snap, the cable drum would start turning and wind up a cable, making the boom start moving outward. Actually, it was more like jerking outward. It would grind and creak and bang. When the bucket was up at about a 45-degree angle and out about thirty-five feet (I never took it to its forty-five-foot max), a hell of a bow could be seen looking back down the boom. The weight of the bucket and its occupant bent the boom down.

Then, to make matters worse, the boom-up and boom-down was operated from a toggle switch. If you clicked the switch to down, the boom would instantly drop. For a split second, you would be weightless. Sometimes your feet would be off the floor of the bucket. When you stopped the boom, whether it was going up or down, it would bounce for a while. The wrong toggle movement and it was like you were on the end of a catapult. If you weren't expecting it, you could be shot right out of the bucket! The truck served its purpose, but at the same time, it scared the hell out of me.

When I got the job to paint the water tank Budweiser Red and letter it, I hired a friend and put him in the bucket for the first part. I didn't want to get in that damned thing one second sooner than I had to, so I operated the boom and bucket from the bed of the truck while he spread on the red paint that I'd carefully ordered to Budweiser specs. But after a few days, it was my turn! I had to letter the damned thing. This was a very scary job even though all it said was *BUD* (running vertically with the "B" on top). The total lettering was about twenty-five feet tall. It didn't take that long to do, but the height and the bouncing bucket made it less than fun. Looking back, I don't know how I did it. I would never get in that bucket today.

This tank was on TV more than any sign at the track.

With the Bud tank finished, I settled into the everyday task of running my local sign shop. Some days, while working on mundane sign jobs, my mind would wander back to some of the experiences that I have written about, and I wondered, *When, if ever, will I get the chance to go somewhere to work again?*

All I heard while playing golf with Steve, Larry, and Bob was, "When are we going somewhere? Have you heard from any of the tracks?"

"Haven't heard a thing," I had to reply. "I honestly feel we are done. We sure had a good time while it lasted." They all agreed and for the next few holes we'd reminisce and laugh over some of the stories. Then slowly we all were silent lost in our own thoughts about our past adventures.

I never knew when one of the tracks would call.

 # Startling Sights

On one of my wistful days, I was in my shop working on a sign for a local deli. It was middle of June and the weather was beautiful. I had the overhead door open and the birds were chirping away in the sixty-foot pine trees outside.

I heard the phone ring. Picking up the receiver, I heard one of the voices I'd hoped most to hear. It was Dick Hahne from Daytona Speedway.

"Tony. Can you come down for the Pepsi 400?"

Absolutely, I thought. "I'm not going to do the month thing again," I told him right off the bat. "That's too long."

He laughed. "A week. Just a week."

"OK. A week."

Jack Lane had broken his wrist, so Dick wanted me to come down to help Glenn Morris get ready for the Pepsi 400. Not a lot of work probably, but Dick wanted me there just in case. Besides, you never know what projects people will suddenly come up with at Daytona. The 2000 Pepsi 400 was going to be a night race. I really wanted to see a NASCAR race at night.

Watkins Glen International wanted me to take the new Mustang pace car down to show a presence there. I said OK and away I went.

My previous month-long trip to Daytona had been in January and February—a great time to visit Florida. This time I would be there in late June. It was going to be hot.

I was happy to see Jack and Glenn again. They were both doing fine in the sign shop. We quickly got busy preparing for the upcoming race. The first job we had to do was create and install new directional signs for the tram system. The tram would run from the distant outfield parking lots to the grandstands. With those new trams, Daytona started to look more like Disney World! Making the signs in the air-conditioned shop was great. When it came time to put them up . . . God, was it *hot!* Sweat dripped off my eyebrows and behind my Serengetis. *I'm not used to this.* If I put the cordless drill on the ground to get a sign into position, by the time I reached down to pick it up it would be so damn hot I had to drop it. I quickly learned to put tools in the shade.

One hot day, I was working alone installing a tram sign outside the track along the Back Straight. Suddenly I heard a plane flying low—and not your basic passenger bus serving the nearby Daytona airport. *No, this was different!* My head snapped from left to right and up and down. *I don't want to miss it. Where is it?* I dropped everything on the ground and spun around toward the airport, just off to my left, trying to spot the plane. *Where the hell is it?*

I'm a World War II aircraft nut, and I could recognize that twelve-cylinder Rolls-Royce Merlin engine anywhere. *That sound was so distinctive.* In a flash, rising up at a 40-degree angle from behind the trees and shrubs that hid the runway was a bright silver plane. The beautiful P-51D Mustang flew up and over the fence at the end of the runway.

I stopped everything. Even my breathing. My mouth was wide open as I tore off my Serengetis. I wanted to see the natural beauty of the plane without the aid of sunglasses. With my eyes squinting from the reflection of the sun off the fuselage, I watched as the landing gear retracted under the wings. I noticed one side retracted slower than the other. The wheels tucked up into the wings, and I could see the wheel cover doors slowly shut making the underside of the wing shiny and smooth. The plane leveled off at about three hundred feet, tipped its wings, and did a slow, looping right turn. It flew a full circle around the racetrack and came back directly over me. I almost fell over backward as I watched it go over. *Oh my God. So beautiful.* The P-51 is my all-time favorite aircraft; I couldn't believe there was one flying right above my head.

To fly over Daytona Speedway and Florida on a perfect sunny day—I was envious. The plane was polished aluminum with a red flair around the nose. I could almost see the rivets in the skin. It shone so bright that at times, with the sun reflecting off the fuselage, I couldn't look directly at it. If flew low enough that I could see the pilot sitting under the glistening clear canopy. He had a white shirt on and was wearing sunglasses. I could see the light green headset he had and how it folded down the brown hat he wore tight to his head. Oh, how I wanted to be him.

For a second, I imagined I was in the cockpit and at the controls. What a view the pilot must have. After a loop around the track, the Mustang flew directly away from me. Then he put the power on. Man. The sound of that Merlin put goose bumps on my arms. He headed straight east and pointed the nose at a 30-degree angle and climbed off into the cloudless blue sky. I stood there motionless until he was just a silver dot. When I got back to the shop, I told Glenn of the P-51 I saw take off.

"Oh yeah," he said. "That's Jack Roush. He flies that thing a lot." Come to find out, Jack Roush, a NASCAR team owner, had the largest collection of WWII Merlin engines in the world. I watched for him every day, and he didn't let me down. I would stop what I was doing and watch until he was a speck in the sky. Yeah, people who saw me standing there looking straight up while holding my sunglasses down to my side for a couple of minutes must have thought I was nuts. I didn't care. I already knew I was nuts.

I was staying right across Speedway Blvd. from the track, in a new motel on Bill France Drive. Right down the street was a Hooters. One night after work I decided to go there for wings. I heard they have good wings, among other things. It was about eleven o'clock on a Tuesday night and the place was empty—just one guy at the bar and another couple at a table. Over by the window was a tall, round table with three stools around it. I sat there facing the window, where I could watch traffic and see the Daytona grandstands. Behind me was a four-foot wooden divider, with more tables behind it. I was eating my wings and sipping on a Bud. I must have been there an hour when someone sitting behind me on the other side of the divider hollered at me: "Hey buddy. Want some wings?" I jumped as I hadn't heard anyone come in.

I was turning around, I said, "No, I just finished some. Thanks anyway." When I looked, there on the table was a tray of about a thousand wings. It was huge. The guy that asked me if I wanted wings was Dale Jarrett, a NASCAR driver. Next to him was Robert Yates, an owner, and two other guys. I thanked them as I was just getting up to leave. Looking back on it, I should have stayed.

☙

I had never been to a NASCAR night race. I was excited. On race day, I always dressed in tan Docker slacks, white sneakers, and a golf-type shirt that today had the Daytona logo embroidered on the front. My track two-way radio was on my belt with the wire running up to my earpiece and another one to the mouthpiece clipped to the opened front part of my shirt. Oh yeah, I had on my Serengeti sunglasses, too. I headed over to Pit Lane to check out the race cars.

I wandered down pit road to get a closer look at the cars. Of course, I cared the most about getting near Dale Earnhardt's car. Good thing I had my camera! I was able to get a photo of Dale by his car and Dale with his son Dale Jr.

I was standing there minding my own business, looking cool, when I saw two black Ford Crown Vics coming down the right side of Pit Lane right alongside the race cars. They were moving pretty fast for the conditions. I stepped out onto the Tri-Oval grass as the cars came to a screeching halt right in front of me. The cars hadn't even stopped yet when the back doors flew open and two men in black suits and dark sunglass jumped from the still-moving cars. They jogged alongside, shoulders bouncing and arms bending like spaghetti, the way an overweight, middle-aged, sweat-soaked has-been-wannabe-again jock runs after he slows down after missing a pass in a touch football game. You know the moves I'm talking about. I call it the Big Deal Bounce. Anyway these guys jumped out and do the Big Deal Bounce. It was comical, to me anyway. "Oh My God. Who the hell are these idiots?"

As they got themselves stopped, they both put their right hands in the left inside breast of their suit coats, letting everyone know they are packing. I thought to myself, *You assholes. Why would anyone carry a gun here?* These guys clearly watched way too much television. Another guy in the front seat got out and held the back door open. Not five feet from me, George W. Bush stepped out of the car. He was governor of

Dale Earnhardt, Jr. (left) and Dale Earnhardt, Sr. before the race.

I took this photo of Dale Earnhardt, Sr. on Pit Lane before the race.

Gov. George W. Bush behind Victory Circle at Daytona.

Texas and the Republican nominee for President of the United States. What a commotion. He had come to Talladega to serve as the race's Grand Marshal.

The agents surrounding Gov. Bush checked everywhere. They checked the crew's Pit Boxes, looked under the race cars with mirrors, and checked everyone's ID. For some reason, they never checked me. I honestly think they thought I was working undercover. The whole area near Gov. Bush was locked down.

Suddenly, a panic arose. A stage was needed Gov. Bush to stand on to do the opening ceremonies. The stands were packed and the race cars were on Pit Lane. Five minutes to opening ceremonies and they wanted a stage. Dick, who was standing near me, called two maintenance men over to him. They got on their blue Kawasaki Mule and raced across the track to the gate in the Turn 3 wall.

Members of the maintenance crew unbolted the guardrail gate so they could get out and locate the stage, which was in the hospitality area right behind the main grandstand. This was not an easy job. When the track went hot (has cars on the track) guardrails and large steel beams were bolted in place to seal off the gate. Now the guys had to frantically unbolt everything. It was like watching a cartoon.

I guess they thought Gov. Bush was so short people wouldn't see him. In a few minutes, the Kawasaki Mule blasted through the gate and onto the track. Two maintenance men on the back held a 6'×6' stage at a 45-degree angle. A huge cheer rose from the fans in the grandstands. Two more maintenance guys picked up the plywood stage (which was covered with well-worn green Astroturf) and set it in front of

Gov. Bush. Another guy quickly set up a microphone stand on the stage. Two minutes to go. Gov. Bush got up on the stage along with a couple of Secret Service guys who stood off to each side. One of them adjusted the microphone height.

After watching the agents do all the security checks earlier, looking in toolboxes and under cars and checking bags and ID, I leaned over to one of the Secret Service agents standing next to the stage and with a smirking smile I said, "I didn't see anybody check under the stage. Did you?" I thought it was a good question. He leaned his head over to listen to me and then, after I said that, he stood straight up. Hands clasped behind his back, sunglasses shining in the sun and a mean, annoyed look on his face, and not looking back at me, he walked away into the crowd. Now I'm convinced they were here for show purposes only. Then I got thinking. *Shit. I didn't look under the stage either.* I moved away.

What the hell. I'm here so I might as well get on TV (maybe Harriett will see me). I walked over behind Gov. Bush and stood there. I was actually in front of the Secret Service guys, who formed a line around the stage. The way I was dressed, radio and all, I must have fooled them. Sure enough, you could see me on TV with Gov. Bush when he said, "Gentlemen, start your engines."

Some of my friends saw it! I have a tape of the race that my cousin Duffy sent to me. It looked like I was guarding Gov. Bush. All that fuss, pandemonium, and activity, and then—with the same fury as they arrived—they were gone. Gov. Bush did his photo op and disappeared. It was finally time for the race!

At 7 p.m. it was still 85 degrees. The humidity was unbearable. None of that mattered because watching a race under the lights was fantastic. I watched the race from inside of Turn 2 with the rescue trucks. What a spot. I loved night racing.

Unfortunately, I had been at the track since 6 a.m. and with Dale not in contention (although he did finish 8th), I was ready for it to be over. My cousin Ernie Thurston (who worked at Daytona) and I were both tired and hot. When the checkered flag fell, I headed to the hotel."

On Monday, it was time to I started my drive home. Glenn and I had worked great together. He had come a long way and I was really proud of him. I was proud that I had a hand in his future.

 We Play the Game

The phone rang with the news of a job at the Talladega Superspeedway in October 2000 to work on the high banks. Steve Hughey was on the list to go on the next trip with me so I called him up. Not only were we going to Talladega, but my complaining to Mike (Talladega's general manager) meant we didn't have to suffer that nineteen-hour highway trek. No more driving! They were flying us down. I got excited telling Steve how we were flying to Talladega. I got Steve's normal, excited answer, "Cool."

As I mentioned earlier, golf had turned into an obsession for me, as well as for a bunch of my friends. We couldn't stop playing the stupid game. Steve, Larry, and I shot within a stroke of each other. Bob's handicap was within a few strokes of ours. We played a dollar a hole and $5 for the winner of the front nine. Same for the back nine. Here we were, four sign company owners, meeting once a week and playing golf. In the days of cutthroat businesses and companies just not speaking to each other, we played golf. I guess the four of us were different. That was why I have three good guys I can call on at any time to go with me on a trip to work anywhere in the country. It was a rare friendship. *Although don't get me wrong, it was vicious out there on the fairways!*

Years earlier I had gone shopping with Harriet at the local mall and had seen a sign: Golf Club Traveling Bags. I had to have one. That bag sat on a shelf in my shop collecting dust for years. I told Steve about the bag. "You gotta go to Dick's and get one," I said. He went over and got one and we were all set. I knew we would work hard at Talladega, but I hoped we might get a day to play golf in Alabama. Just one day was all I could ask for.

We got on the plane at the Elmira Airport Sunday morning and flew to Pittsburgh, where we connected on our way to Atlanta. We collected our bags and golf clubs we got our rental car and drove ninety miles west on I-20 to Anniston, Alabama. We arrived at our hotel near Talladega at 2 p.m. We had been formulating a plan since we landed: sign in quick and then head straight for the nearest golf course. We didn't have to be at the track until the next morning. The guy at the motel desk recommended a golf course in Gadsden, so we headed over there. We drove up to the club house—it looked like something out of a golf magazine! We stopped, looked at each other. "Holy shit. I don't know if we should go in there," I said. This place was gorgeous. We shoot in the 95 to 110 range and didn't want to make fools out of ourselves.

We walked into the clubhouse and just stared. High cathedral ceilings, dining halls, and a large pro shop. We walked up to the young man at the desk and were greeted with that good old Southern hospitality. "Where you all from? Don't recall seeing you fellas here before," he said. We told him our story and he handed us the key to a golf cart. Then he said, "Number 1 is just down that path," pointing over his right shoulder out the window and to a paved cart path that wound down a hill and into some big green bushes. Then he apologized. "I screwed up your green fees. I charged you $2 extra for the GPS on the cart. Is that OK?"

"GPS?" I said. *What do we need global positioning for on a golf course?* I thought.

He explained that the carts had GPS units with TV screens that would show you where you were on the course. Your cart would show up as a white dot moving around a full-color map of the course, and the unit talk would talk to you. If you were playing too fast, he explained, it would tell you to slow down and enjoy the scenery—and if you're too slow, to speed up. This was too much. "When you pull up to your ball on the fairway, park alongside it and look at the screen. It will show you distances, within a foot, to the front of the green, the back of the green, to the pin, and where the hazards are on your screen." This was even *more* too much. *We' will be spoiled beyond imagination when we play back home,* I thought. *Hell, some courses we play at home don't even have roofs on the golf carts.*

So off we went, and it was amazing. Many times while playing, we had to stop the cart and get out as we just looked in awe at the scenery. It was that gorgeous.

Well, on the way back to the motel, we kept saying that if we didn't get to play again while we were down here, we didn't really care. This one time was unbelievable. And we wouldn't have believed it, but we hadn't seen *anything* yet.

At the track we worked our asses off. Nothing real hard, but lots of small stuff. When we told Mike about our adventure on Sunday, he said, "You think that was something? You oughta see the Winston 500 Golf Tournament they have on Wednesday."

"The Winston 500 Golf Tournament? What the hell is that? I didn't know they had such a thing," I said. The tournament was an event prior to the race to put media, dignitaries, and a few of the drivers together in a relaxed atmosphere. Some of the drivers had a hell of a golf game. The golf tournament was by invitation only so it is not something anyone could go to.

Before I could control my brain and mouth, I blurted, "How do we get in?"

Mike smiled and said, "Ya can't. It's for the media and drivers only." I didn't think we would be able to play but the thought of playing just came out. It was something to think about. As Mike walked out the door, without turning around, he shouted, "I'll see what I can do."

"Cool," Steve said. We figured there was no way Mike could get us in, plus, we had work to do.

Shifting Gears • 305

❦

The week of the race, both Steve and I forgot about the golf tournament. We had not made it back to a course to play again, and we were pretty well done with all the little signs that had piled up when Mike walked into the shop first thing Tuesday morning.

"Hey, boys. How're the signs goin? Ya gettin' caught up?"

"We're in good shape," I said. "Unless some nut—not you, Mike—comes up with some last-minute crap."

Then Mike floored us. "I talked to two of the marketing guys about the golf tournament, and they decided to give up their spots so you guys could play." I jumped up, eyes as wide open as when I saw that P-51 in Florida. Then I said in my best, most perfectly punctuated Northern accent, "You are kidding me."

Steve said, "Cool."

We high-fived each other and thanked Mike about ten times before he could get out the door. "Be at the clubhouse at seven-thirty. Here are the directions." He tossed a paper on the table. "They'll be expecting you," he said as he walked out the door. Here we were, on the clock, and Mike gave us a day off to go play out our wildest dreams. Mike is quite a guy.

It was 7:15 a.m. when we pulled into a gated housing development. "You sure this is right?" I asked Steve, who was the navigator.

"This is it," he said, as we drove down a winding road lined with homes worth half a million or a million bucks. They were beautiful. Most of them were brick with manicured lawns and a BMW or Mercedes SUV in front of the garage. I excitedly pointed to a black Turbo Porsche in one garage and Steve pointed to a yellow Hummer across the street.

We came to another gate and drove out of the residential area and down a beautiful paved road that wound through the woods. The view opened out on the most elegant country club I had ever seen. We looked at each other and said, "Oh my God" at the same time. Half a dozen cars were in the lot as we pulled in. We were early. We parked but before we could get out of the car, two golf carts rolled up. Two young guys dressed in white shirts and tan shorts got out of the golf carts and one of them said, "We'll take your clubs, sir." I opened the trunk and they put our clubs into the racks on the back of the carts. He must have noticed that mine still had some northern dirt on them. "We will clean your clubs," one of them said, "and they will be in your cart." They asked our names as we got into the golf carts and were chauffeured to the clubhouse. "Your cart will be over there (pointing down a paved path, with about forty carts all lined up in two rows) when you come out. Just look above the windshield. Your names will be on the carts." Steve and I thanked them. We looked at each other and walked toward the clubhouse.

I whispered to Steve, "Should we have tipped them? I saw it in a movie once."

"We will when we come back out."

We walked through the front doors—ten feet high with stained glass windows—

entered a dimly lit carpeted hall. It was lined on both sides with golf art mounted in huge gold ornamental frames. I felt like we were walking on hallowed ground. At the end of the hall we saw a table that had been set up with three men in white shirts and black slacks sitting behind it. A little sign said, "Registration."

"Mornin', boys. How's y'all doin' today?" the first guy asked with a huge smile. Not giving us a chance to answer, he said, "OK. What's your name and affiliation?" I told him our names and that we were from Talladega Speedway. He said, "Oh, you're the guys from New York that the track sent over. Fill out this form and go over there and get your shirt."

We filled out the form and went to the end of the table where another guy said, "What size y'all wearin'?" He handed us our shirts. The shirts were beautiful—white golf shirts with the Winston 500 Golf Tournament logo embroidered on the front and on the right sleeve. We walked out to the car and we put them on in the parking lot. We threw our old shirts in the car and walked back to the clubhouse, then stood around waiting. "Man, we are out of place here," I said, "but you know . . . who the hell cares?"

Steve said, "Yeah, man. I can't wait to play."

We looked around and everyone had handmade Rive Gauche shoes and Rolex watches. I looked down and thought, *Hey. My sneakers aren't even a year old yet.*

The guy that signed us in caught my attention and crooked his finger to motion me over to the table. He said, "You guys got such a high handicap" *we know, just don't say it so loud* "that we are pairing you with Matt and Greg to make your foursome. That's them over there. Why doncha go over and meet 'em."

We walked over and introduced ourselves. Matt was a small, slender guy, about twenty-eight years old. Greg was a heavier guy about the same age. We hit it off right away. They said they were TV sportscasters on a sports channel operating out of Huntsville, Alabama. After talking a little golf, we were sure that they could *play* golf. This was going to be *fun*.

Ring, ring, ring went a bell. Everyone quieted down to a dull roar. We all went to the tables in the dining hall and sat down for the pre-tournament press conference. The waiters were dressed in black pants, white shirts, and black bow ties. The waitresses wore short black skirts and white shirts. This was too high-class for us. We felt uncomfortable at first. As we sat at our table watching what was going on, we saw media sitting with some of the drivers doing interviews. We wanted to play golf but had to be patient. When the press conference finished, coffee and pastries were served . . . and then it was time to play. Outside we walked down the rows looking for our cart. We saw Jimmy Spencer, one of the competitive drivers, sitting in his cart already. I'd raced with Jimmy in the NASCAR Modified Series years ago, so when I saw we were both wearing the same Zippo watch I stopped and compared watches. Steve and I found are car and, sure enough, our clubs were all strapped in already. We fired up the motor and followed the other carts down a paved path and into the woods. Back in New York, we are accustomed to loud gas-powered carts. These brand new electric carts were really quiet. This was heaven. The weather was perfect. It was sunny and warm.

We drove the beautiful, almost silent electric golf cart down a winding paved road to the third tee (the foursomes start on different holes). Steve and I looked at each other and broke out in uncontrollable laughter. "Do you believe what the hell we are doing? Just look at this place," I said.

"Look at this cart," Steve said. "Brand new. A TV monitor on the dash, showing a full color GPS display of the course and that white dot moving along is us. Oh my God. I can't believe it." If anyone had heard us they would have thought we were nuts. We drove past some of the most beautiful fairways you can imagine to get to Hole 3.

At the third tee, we met up with Matt and Greg, the other half of our foursome. "Let's set up an order of teeing off," Matt said, "and we can keep it through the whole eighteen. Why don't you guys tee off first and we will back you up."

I pointed the handle of my driver at Steve and said, "OK, Steve, you go first."

"No, you go first," he said.

"I'm the boss down here, you go first."

"All right, you're the boss." Steve sighed as he hung his head down. Holding the handle end of my driver to my mouth, like it's a microphone, I said, "Ladies and gentlemen, we are ready to tee off for the world famous Winston 500 Golf Tournament in Talladega, Alabama. First on the tee will be Steve Hughey from Corning, New York." Steve looked at me as he pulled his driver from his bag on the back of the cart. I could see by his expression he was thinking, *Shut the hell up, you stupid shit.*"

Steve slowly stepped up to the tee box. As any golfer will tell you—that first tee shot is intimidating! Everyone was watching you and the pressure to do it right was the only thing on your mind. Steve set up, took a long, slow backswing, and swung the mighty club hard. A loud crack, and he hit a good one. "It's in the fairway," I whispered into my microphone.

I got into the tee box. I was sweaty and nervous. *Why?* I thought. This is a fun tournament. Just have fun. I hit a shorter one but in the fairway. There. I felt better now.

Then it was Matt's turn. He set up like a pro. He stood back, behind the ball, looking at the spot on the fairway he wanted the ball to land. He walked up to the ball. He took a long, round backswing and with a loud crack, the ball went up in a straight arc and almost out of sight. Steve and I looked at each other, confirming Matt was not a normal player. "Christ almighty," I said out loud, "what a friggin' drive. That was awesome." He hit the ball twice as far as Steve. We were playing "best ball," which meant that all four of us hit a shot and then we picked the best shot and marked it. From there, all four of us hit our next shot from the location of the best ball. Every shot, even putting, we'd swing from the same spot and then pick the best one and play from there. Steve shook his head. "We are playing our second shot from places we've never been before even after our second shot." We finished the first hole with a birdie. We all high-fived each other, got into our carts, and moved on to the next hole.

Heading to the hole, Steve and I had a newfound confidence. These guys would carry us. They were good. This took some of the pressure off.

Just as we were teeing up on our second hole, we heard a cart coming down the path. We looked up and it was a young girl driving the beer cart. As it stopped, we saw it wasn't a beer cart, it was a whole *bar* cart. This thing had a special-built stretch golf cart with a full bar on it—more stuff than in the actual bar I hang out at back home. Anything you wanted, she could make it. Steve didn't drink, so he got a Pepsi. It was only about 9:30 a.m. and I wanted to be around to remember the eighteenth hole, so I got a Pepsi also. Matt and Greg had beer. On every other hole, one of these carts appeared. No charge for anything—it was part of the tournament. *You could easily get into trouble out here,* I thought.

It was something just to watch Matt play. It was like watching Tiger Woods. The eighth hole was a long Par 5. Matt teed off, and we all played from where his shot landed. On the second shot, he hit a three wood and the ball landed on the green. He hit his three wood off of the fairway longer than I hit with my driver. We used that shot, of course. From there, he nailed a forty-foot putt for an eagle.

Steve and I were getting embarrassed as they hadn't used one of our shots yet. By the rules you have to use at least one drive from each player in the round. I don't remember what hole it was, but it was a dogleg to the left, Par 4. I hit a ball in the fairway—not very far, but in the middle so it would easy to use, and I figured that was mine. Steve hit his a little longer but into the fairway sand trap. Matt overshot, sending the ball past the dogleg and into the rough across the fairway, and Greg hooked one into the woods.

"We'll pick up Greg's ball on the way up the fairway," I said.

"No you won't," he said with a laugh. "Copperheads in there." Growing up in Watkins Glen, There were no poisonous snakes around when we played golf in upstate New York. I never went after another ball in the woods in Alabama.

"Hey. We finally get to use my ball," I said as we pulled up to it. I was really proud.

"Yeah. Finally," Steve said.

My smile went away when I saw Matt motioning to us to come over across the fairway, to the sand trap. I looked at him with my arm in the air pointing my finger down at my ball. Again he waved his hand to come over. I pointed to my ball and mouthed the words (you can't shout on a golf course) so Matt could read my lips, "Not my ball?" Matt waved us to come over to the sand trap again. Steve looked at me and shrugged. We picked up my ball and drove over to Matt. "Shit," I said to Steve, "I thought we would use my ball for sure."

We got to Matt and he said, "I know you were in the fairway, but it was a long shot in. The GPS says we are 146 yards out from the ball in the trap. Let's shoot out of the sand."

Steve said, "I can't shoot out of the sand that far. Christ, it's damn near 150 yards."

"I can't do that either," I said. "Why can't we shoot yours from the rough? You are way up there," I said to Matt, pointing up the fairway about fifty yards.

"You don't know what the rough is like down here," Matt said. "You wouldn't be able to get it out. This grass will grab your club like a vise. You'd break your wrist trying to hit it out of there unless you're Tiger." Matt laughed, then he said to Steve,

"Get the club you would use to hit 150 yards."

Steve went back to the cart and put his sand wedge back in the bag. He'd been planning to just hit the ball out of the sand and onto the fairway, maybe thirty yards, but now he pulled a 6 iron out and walked to the edge of the trap. By the look on his face you could tell he didn't want to hit this shot.

"Now get in there and I'll give you a quick lesson," Matt said.

Steve stepped down into the sand trap and stood there, hands at his sides, holding the club in his right hand like it was a cane. Matt was facing Steve. He knelt down on both knees in the sand.

"What the hell you doin'?" I said.

Matt looked up and said, "I'm giving Steve a quick lesson on bunker shots. Pay attention, you're next." Bending his head down and leaning over, he grabbed Steve's shoes, one with each hand, and wiggled them back and forth to set them deep in the sand. "You want your feet planted firmly in the sand," he said, wiggling Steve's shoes back and forth a little more. Steve's shoes were deep in the sand. Now Matt drew a line with his finger just behind the ball in the sand. Steve gave me a sad dog look and then looked back at the ball and then back at me. He didn't have to say anything. I knew what he was thinking: "I can't do this. This is going to be embarrassing. Just let me hit my sand wedge."

Matt told Steve, "Pay attention. You can do this. Now use the same swing you would use to hit the ball 150 yards if it was in the fairway. Just hit it right here." He

Steve Hughey and I participating in the Winston 500 Golf Tournament thanks to our friends at Talladega Speedway.

pointed at the line. Matt stood up, bending over and brushing the sand off his knees. Then he backed up away from Steve and stood in the sand with his hands on his hips.

We waited a few seconds for the foursome ahead of us to clear off the green. Steve, bending over to address the ball, did his normal backswing. He swung with all his might. *Whack.* The ball went up in a nice long, slow-motion arc. I hollered, not knowing if it would be long enough to make the green, "Nice shot, man."

"That's it. Good shot. I said you could do it," Matt said. At least it was out of the sand. All four pairs of eyes were on the ball as it reached the peak of the arc and started to come down. "You might get to the green," Matt added. Plop. Right on the edge of the green. We jumped and hollered as Steve climbed out of the sand. He was happy to be on the green from the sand. We high-fived as Steve turned to look at the green and where his ball was.

"Wait a minute. It's still rolling. You caught the slope, it's still rolling," Matt said excitedly. We watched as the ball slowly rolled to the right in a long, slow arc. After about twenty yards . . . it *disappeared.*

"Oh my God," Greg shouted. We all looked at Steve, and then back at each other. Matt—with his mouth open and eyes bugging out—hollered, "Oh My God. . . . "

The foursome ahead of us saw it and were waving back and yelling, "Hell of a shot . . . it's *in!*" A hundred and forty-six yards from the sand trap and in for an eagle. That was the shot of the day. (I was also happy I didn't have to take my shot out of the sand!)

After the first nine, we went in for lunch and then headed back out for the second nine holes. No more eagles, but we, I should say Matt and Greg, played well. For the entire eighteen holes, my driver was used twice, and two of my putts.

We rode back to the clubhouse talking of the fabulous day on the golf course.

Golfing was over—now it was time for supper. What a meal. While we ate, they handed everyone a beautiful plaque with Winston 500 Golf Tournament and a picture taken of your foursome with Miss Winston on one of the holes. The prizes were awesome. We thought for sure we would place (a top three finish) as we shot a 59. That was 13 under par! We didn't even place. Two teams tied for third and we finished fourth—out of twenty foursomes. It didn't really matter. The time we had that day was unbelievable. We met two great guys, Greg and Matt, and for the track to get us into the closed-entry tournament made it even more special.

Back at the track the next morning, we thanked Mike for one of the best times we ever had at Talladega. He just smiled and said, "You got anything to do?"

"We've got one more wall logo and then we're caught up."

I'll tell you, it was things like this that showed the class of friends you really have. Man. We were in good company.

 # Racing Southern Style

The next day, Jimmy Elkins, the maintenance foreman and jet blower driver, came over. "Ya busy?" he asked.

"No, whatcha need, Jimmy??"

"I need my race car lettered."

"You got a race car? What is it?"

"A Super Late Model. We're racin' Saturday night across the street. I don't drive it—my brother-in-law drives it."

"Let's go over and measure it up and tomorrow night," I said. "I will come to your house and letter it. Got any beer?"

Jimmy Elkins' car at the Talladega Short Track.

Thursday night we went over at Jimmy's garage so I could letter his car. Next to Sprint Cars, Super Late Models are some of the fastest dirt cars in the country. *I wanted to drive it!* Instead, we drank beer as I lettered the car. When I finished, we stood in the opening of the overhead door, just outside the shop, talking and looking back at the race car. It was 10:30 p.m. but still hot. Outside the shop, I could see a large dirt bank off toward the right side of Jimmy's house. I did a double take while sipping my cold can of Budweiser.

"Hey," I said, pointing my can toward the bank, "What the hell is that?"

Sticking out of the bank were two doors. It looked like a big box truck had driven into the dirt bank at a hundred miles per hour and all that was visible were the two rear doors. Jimmy laughed. "That's my tornado shelter."

"You're shittin' me."

"Nope, right by the house, it's stocked with some stuff and we've used it a couple of times. I took the back of an old box truck and buried it in the bank."

We walked over and Jimmy opened the doors. We looked inside . . . scary! Just thinking about living where a tornado was part of your life—I wouldn't like that. I finished my beer and Steve and I got ready to go to the motel. Jimmy invited us to the face. "Saturday night," he said. " It's right across from the speedway. You know where it is. I will have you signed in as my crew members. Come in the back way and sign in at the Pit Shack. I'll see you in the pits. You'll find us, just walk around."

"We'll be there," I said. "I wish I had my driving suit and helmet." Jimmy laughed. I was serious.

☙

Saturday night was a warm and humid, so humid it was hard for a Northerner to breathe. The sign out front of the track said "TALLADEGA SHORT TRACK." In smaller lettering it promised that we'd be seeing racing in "Southern Style." What was that, we wondered? After we signed in, Steve and I found ourselves following some other guys toward the glow of the lights just over the hill that ringed the 1/3-mile red clay oval. The dark dirt road led to the center of the Back Straight of Talladega Short Track. Some cars on the track were doing slow laps, running in the mud, packing down the surface. We walked right up to the edge of the track. "Holy shit, it's *red*," I hollered. Red clay. We learned the hard way that once red clay gets on your shoes or pants, it was there forever. It was like a dye. Finding a break in traffic, some of the guys dashed across the track to the infield. It was clear that no one was going to let us cross, so we waited for an opening—and ran.

"Don't slip," I said. "These idiots will run right over ya."

We got across the track and into the center of the dirt oval, where the pits were located. We wandered around the pits looking for Jimmy.

"Oh look. Over there. It's Red Farmer." Red was in his eighties, one of the oldest drivers in the country. He was on the helicopter with Davey Allison when it crashed at Talladega and was killed. "He's racing tonight," I told Steve. There were young girls with their babies . . . in the pits. *Is that a beer can on the roof of that car they are working*

I loved the tagline on the Talladega Short Track sign! "Dirt track in southern style."

on? We walked closer—yup, it was. We finally found Jimmy's car.

"Hey, ya made it," Jimmy hollered. "There's beer in the back of the truck if you want some."

"Naw. That's all right. I'll have one later."

We walked all over looking at the cars. There were some Street Stocks that were absolutely scary. Then there were the Super Late Models. These things were beautiful. Sleek, lightweight, and *fast!* They carry $30,000 motors that rip the eardrums right out of your head. We couldn't wait to see these guys race.

We heard some of the big boys fire their engines up and drive out onto the track for practice. Jimmy told us to get up on the roof of the truck to watch.

He had a van built like a bread truck that hauled the race car trailer. Inside the truck he had a generator, an air compressor, and other tools. The rest of the space was filled with every type of race car part—all in one big pile. A ladder from an old motor home went up the back of the truck, just off to the right of the back door. On the roof was a plywood platform in an angled iron frame. It had a railing built of inch-square tube iron about thirty inches high that went around the entire platform when the van was parked, but folded down for road travel. The platform was about seven feet wide and twelve feet long.

Before we went up, Jimmy said, "Go over on the Back Straight. You can get a close view of these suckers coming out of Turn 2."

We walked past some of the worst-looking Street Stocks you can imagine as we headed toward Turn 2. On the inside of Turn 2 and down the Back Straight was an eighteen-inch concrete wall—about as high as my knee. Jimmy was right when he said *close*. You could stand with your foot resting on the concrete wall and the cars raced by at 80 mph with their left front wheel not six inches from your toes. I mean *six inches*. I could feel the exhaust as a hard puff on my pant leg for the split second the car passed. I could look right into the driver's eyes as he flew past. It was *total insanity!* You'd be safer in the car racing than you were standing by that wall. I watched two of the big boys fly past—because I couldn't move quick enough to get the hell away from that spot before the second one came by. I decided to retreat to the safety of the roof of the truck. There were twelve-year-old kids standing right at the short wall. The sign at the gate said it all. Racing "Southern Style" indeed.

I have to say one thing. They did have food. We got talking to the woman who was running the food stand and we told her where we were from and that we were painting signs at Talladega Speedway. We found out she owned the short track. From that day on we were welcome there any time. We ordered two hot dogs and a Pepsi each, and ate our hot dogs while walking back to the truck. They were delicious.

We climbed the ladder to the platform and joined about ten people already up there. We found a spot by the railing that looked out over toward Turn 2. What a view we had from up there! The track was short and from on top of Jimmy's truck we could see the whole thing.

The Super Late Models were so fast. Through the corners and partway down the straight, they would pick the inside left tire a foot off the ground and hold it there. The power these things had was amazing. The sound! Eardrum-ripping, eye-squint-

Turn 2 at Talladega Short Track.

ing, drool-out-the-corner-of-the-mouth sound. Awesome. Those engines screamed for mercy. I wanted to be out there. I watched the cars go round and round, I suddenly started to get this strange feeling. My heart was beating faster and my breath was short. I don't know what came over me, but I was suddenly sweating a little. I thought it might have been the hot dogs.

I glanced over to Steve, who was facing the other way watching cars go down the Front Straight. I was going to say something to him but I couldn't. *It'll go away,* I thought. *I shouldn't have eaten that second hot dog. Wow.* Looking back to the track, I watched the cars sliding through Turns 1 and 2. *That's strange.* The sound of the cars was starting to fade. I quickly placed my two hands on the square tube railing around the platform, and on this warm Southern night, I suddenly felt cold. I felt slightly faint and my palms were sweating. I was getting a little nervous. I looked around at the other people on the platform. No one was looking at me. They were talking and pointing to cars on the track. I could see their mouths moving but I could barely hear them—they sounded far away. Just as I looked toward Steve to tell him I was getting down and I didn't feel good, I saw a dark gray fog rolling in from across the track just off on the other side of Turn 2. It engulfed the dirt road that we'd walked in on.

As I watched, the fog slowly covered Turn 2. It quietly drifted across the track at the Back Straight and it was drifting for us. Everything was soon engulfed, and I felt like I was starting to float.

I drifted into the past. In my head, it was 1972, and I was at Weedsport Speedway in the last lap of the feature race. Jim Gabriel and I were coming through Turns 3 and 4 to the checker, foot to the floor, in a four-wheel drift! I was inches from his bumper. Suddenly his car bobbled! It was just a twitch, but I couldn't help it—I tapped his bumper and spun him around! As his car spun to the inside of the track, almost in slow motion, I went to the right side of his spinning car and I won the race!

The crowd was booing and screaming as they took the victory photos. In the pits, Jim and I talked about what happened. He didn't admit that he'd bobbled for a split second, but he wasn't that mad either, as we knew what really happened. When you are an inch from someone's bumper with your foot to the floor, one little blip by the guy in front of you and you are going to touch him! We were friends after that. He even bought a race car from me later.

The next thing I knew, Steve grabbed my shoulder shaking me back to reality. It took a while to figure out what he was saying: "Hey, Vickio. Let's get another hot dog."

"Yeah. . . . Let's go get a dog and a Coke," I said with a smile. (Yeah, Coke. For some reason, this is about the only time I remember seeing Coke instead of Pepsi at a track.)

We got down from the platform, and I was a little sad that I was not out there on the track. This is why I never go to a short track anymore to watch a race. I haven't been back to Rolling Wheels, Weedsport, Canandaigua, or Dundee since I quit dirt racing. It's like putting a shot of choice bourbon in front of a reformed alcoholic. Put a race car in front of me and I am weak. I'll break. I'm not that strong. As we wandered through the pits the smell of Wolf's Head gear oil, racing fuel, hot engines, and tire rubber filled the air. *Aaahhhh. The smells of racing.* Then suddenly, the aroma of a perfectly cooked racetrack hot dogs drifted across our path. We made a right turn and followed the smell right to the food stand. We had a couple more track dogs that night as we experienced dirt track racing Southern Style.

∽

Steve and I were back on the high banks the next day finishing up the wall logos. Once we climbed up on the banking, there was nowhere to sit or rest. If we sat on the track, we would likely slide down the banking. Plus, the track was usually quite hot. Since necessity is the mother of invention, I felt inspired to invent the HWPHSS-RP—the "High Waller Portable Horizontal Stabilization Safety and Relaxation Platform." I had Jimmy Elkins weld up some square tubing to make a frame that would hang on the retaining wall and support a horizontal two-by-eight just above the track surface—something nice and level to hold our paint and supplies and give us a place to sit. It took a little effort to get it up there each day, but man, was it worth it. As we moved along the wall working on a logo, we just slid the HWPHSSRP along the wall with us. Getting it down was easy: just unhook it from the wall and let it slide down the track. We did have to make sure nothing was in the way as it got going about 100 mph by the time it hit the bottom.

As we stood on the 34-degree banking, Steve said something that made me think. "Hey, Famous. How much longer do you think we can do this? My legs won't take many more years of this banking."

"I know what you mean," I said. "My legs and back are about done. I don't know, man."

As Steve and I flew back to Watkins Glen, I stared out the window of the Boeing 727 watching the puffy globs of clouds drifting by far below us. I couldn't get Steve's words out of my mind. How much longer could we do this? I had never thought about it before. *NASCAR was getting bigger all the time,* I thought. I guess we had to enjoy what we did as long as we could, because the handwriting was on the wall. I was not big enough to take on all the tracks. That would be a gigantic chore. I thought, *I'm happy we had the chance to do all the things we've done so far.*

As I was walked from the plane to meet Harriett, I wondered if I would ever get called to work at Talladega or any other track again. I got a sad feeling. I've made a lot of good friends around the country. I thought of my friends from Talladega. Larry Johnson, Mike McWilliams, Andy McWilliams, Donna Price, Pete Woodard, Jimmy Elkins, Sarge, and the rest of the boys. When would I see them again?

 # We Paint for Dale

Despite my worries in October, by April, Steve Hughey and I were once again headed back to Talladega. We were a little down thinking of Dale Earnhardt. He had won so many great races at Talladega. He had been killed in an accident at the 2001 Daytona 500 only two months earlier.

Our plane landed at the Atlanta Airport Sunday afternoon at about one-thirty, and we waited for our golf clubs to come out of the hole in the wall and onto the belt in the baggage area. When we spotted both travel bags, we grabbed them like they were filled with $100 bills. We hurried out of the airport and half ran (we were getting old) to our Chevy Monte Carlo rental car. I put on my Serengeti glasses and fired up the car. The same thing was on each of our minds. *Golf.*

It was Sunday afternoon and we were going to play golf. We headed for the motel to argue with the fat guy about our rooms. (They'd been screwed up for the past five years, and we didn't expect any improvement—and weren't surprised.) Then, we headed straight to the Silver Lakes Golf Course on the edge of Talladega National Forest between Anniston and Gadsden where we played until it got dark. It was the most beautiful course I had ever seen. We went back to the motel with huge smiles on our faces. If we hadn't been getting paid, the golf would have been worth the trip down here.

I love being in Talladega in April. The International Race of Champions (IROC) cars were there along with ARCA, the Busch Series, and the Winston Cup cars. It was awesome. The wall lettering for this trip consisted of repairing some damage left over from the October race and the addition of a few new logos.

Once again, after three hours on the high banks, Steve hollered over and said, "Hey boss. How much longer do you think we can do this, Famous? My legs are shot."

"No shit," I hollered back. You have no idea how hard it is to work up on top of the banking for three hours. We were fighting gravity every second. One misstep and either of us could get hurt. Worse, we might spill paint on the track! Fall down the banking, break a leg, but whatever you do . . . *"Don't spill paint on the track!"* Mike McWilliams's words run through my brain to this day. It's like I was brainwashed.

"We better enjoy every minute while we can," I said. "Someday they will find a sign company down here to do this, and we will be done. This may be our last trip."

On the Tuesday before race weekend, we had finished all our work. We'd never wrapped up that early! The only thing we were thinking now was *more golf*. In the war room—the Maintenance Office where the coffee and doughnuts are—We ran into Mike McWilliams. "How's it goin', boys?" he said.

"You're all set, Mike," I said as I poured a nice hot black coffee. "Everything went pretty fast. We've been doing this so long, I think we're finally getting the hang of it. Anything else you want done? Need any help anywhere?"

"Nope. You guys just enjoy yourselves." Mike is the one of the best managers I know.

Steve and I got our coffee and went outside into the warm Alabama sun. "Let's go see the IROC cars test for a while," I said. "Then we'll go play golf this afternoon."

"Yeah, man."

We got in our John Deere Gator and drove toward the sound of race engines warming up. We headed for the tunnel to the infield. At the bottom of the tunnel I blew the horn. I couldn't help myself. We got to the IROC garage and parked the Gator by the gate. We walked in and there, standing by a race car and talking to the crewmen, were Dick Trickle and Dave Marcis, NASCAR Winston Cup drivers.

We walked around and looked at the cars. Inside the garage, I saw an old friend. He saw me and waved. "Let's go see Jay, I said to Steve. Jay Signore was the owner

My friend Jay Signore (founder of the IROC Series) and me at Talladega.

and founder of the IROC Series. I first met Jay years ago at Watkins Glen. Matter of fact, it was the race that J. D. McDuffie was killed at the Glen. Jay and I would run into each other about once a year at a Talladega. We talked for a while and I told him I missed the IROC cars at the Glen since the series moved to another track (about ten years back). He did, too.

"Jay," I said, "do you mind if I go in the garage and get some pictures?"

"The garage is yours, Tony. Good seeing you guys."

After taking some photos, we hopped on the Gator and flew to the Maintenance Office, where we jumped in the rental car and headed for a golf course. It was another perfect day for playing golf.

Not much happened on Wednesday. We arrived at the Warm Room bright and early Thursday morning. It was full of maintenance guys. Jimmy Elkins sat on the overstuffed couch. Sarge stood by the wall, and Pete was leaning on the door casing at the entrance to Donna's office. Mike McWilliams sat on a tall director's folding chair near a wall. A few other maintenance guys are also sitting around. We walked in and everyone said, "Mornin'."

Steve and I got our fresh coffee and looked through the two huge trays of doughnuts and cookies. I picked out a nice fat glazed doughnut. It was race week, and Americrown, the catering company of NASCAR, was taking care of us in its usual fine style. On the way to the track. Steve and I had talked about how good it felt to be done so early and to have more time to play golf. A local sign company was doing all the small signs so we were not bothered with the menial tasks. We planned to play golf again at 1 p.m. We felt good. (Actually, we also felt a little guilty.)

Mike slowly got up and walked toward his office. He turned as he was walking and said, "Hey, Tony. Come in here a minute."

I looked at Steve and said, "Oh-oh. This is not good." I followed Mike into the office, holding my half-devoured glazed doughnut down to my side. In my mind I was thinking, *This is* not *going to be good. Mike has come up with something. Usually when he does, it's something* big. I had a feeling that we would not be playing golf that afternoon. I followed Mike into the office and shut the door.

"Hey, Tony. I've been thinkin'. All the other tracks have done some sort of tribute to Dale and I just realized we don't have anything."

Oh-oh. Not good, I thought again. *If Mike's got an idea, it won't be easy to do.* I know Mike.

"You know the bank on the outside of Turns 3 and 4, just left of the tunnel?"

My mouth was full of doughnut, so I just nodded my head.

"Well, I thought of painting a huge '3' on the grass so the fans coming in would see it. It has to be big enough to see it from I-20. Maybe we could make it as large as the whole hill." *What is this we?* I thought. "What would you charge me to do it? I know it's the last minute and I'm sorry about that, but I think we need something," Mike said.

I thought for a minute. You see, Dale was my man. I saw the many wins he had at Talladega. I saw his first Daytona 500 win. I had a chance to meet him once at Watkins Glen—and that's a story in itself.

⁂

I had been working in my shop one day when I got a call from the track. They said there was going to be a Busch Beer commercial filmed at the track and the company doing the commercial wanted an experienced person familiar with the track to drive the camera car. Of course I said, "hell yeah!"

After I hung up I had visions of driving a NASCAR race car on the track. I arrived early next morning and met the producer. He took me out to the car we were going to use that afternoon. There it was! A nice, shiny NASCAR stock car! Well, no. There sat a drab brown 1998 Lincoln Continental, about as far from NASCAR as you can get. The camera crew attached a large aluminum lattice across the hood and down the right side of the car beside the front tire to hold the camera. I almost went home.

That afternoon they were ready for the on-track filming. I got in and saw a large monitor mounted on the passenger-side dashboard. Another monitor was mounted behind the passenger seat so the people in back could see it. The producer got in front and two Anheuser-Busch people climbed into the backseat. We did three slow laps and the filming was over!

They asked me to stay on for the next two days as an adviser. The third day Dale and his wife showed up. He did his talk and then announced he had thirty minutes, before he had to get to the airport, to sign things and take photos. I had a beautiful photo my friend Jack Eckert took at Watkins Glen. Dale signed it. He loved the photo enough to call his wife over and look at it. Jack sent him a copy later. Dale was an inspiration to me. He never gave up. I will miss his racing forever.

⁂

"Whaddaya think?" Mike said again.

I snapped out of my trance and said, "Well, Mike, we have a couple of problems."

"I figured we would. If you can't do it, that's OK. It's just a thought," Mike said.

I looked at Mike and said, "One problem is the grass." (No need to explain that. Mike knew the only way to mow it is by hand with Weed Eaters because the banking was so steep.) "The second one is the '3.' It is trademarked or copyrighted. You'll have to have somebody in Marketing get permission from Richard Childress—Dale's team owner—and get the exact artwork. The third problem is I don't have enough men. I only have Steve here with me and he's only half a man."

Mike laughed. "I'll get the grass cut, get Marketing to get permission for the art and you can have two or three of our painters. Whatever you need, you'll have it. How's that? Now. How much ya chargin' me?"

I thought for a minute. I already had my computer with me which I needed to design the layout. *The "3" would be large enough to use the triangulation system. The grass was getting cut, and I have help.* I asked Mike, "You buyin' the paint?"

"We'll have the paint," Mike said. "Just tell me what ya need."

"Dale was a great driver and I will miss him. Racing will never be the same. I'll do it. It won't cost anything extra." Steve and I got an hourly rate when we worked.

"Thanks, Tony." Mike said. We walked out into the war room. Steve was sitting on the overstuffed couch.

"Get up, you fool," I said. "We got work to do."

Steve loved it when I volunteered him for things. We walked out the door into the bright Alabama sun, and Steve said, "Do I dare ask?"

"No."

I got the artwork for the "3" late Thursday morning. Steve and I went out and measured the bank. We thought it was hard working on the track banking. This was worse. It was 30 degrees, 4 degrees less steep than the track surface, but it was grass. To make it more interesting, a 30 mph wind was blowing. I got the layout done fast and Steve and I headed out to the bank to start plotting our points.

If at all possible, I wanted to get the first coat of white on that day. The two track painters arrived with the airless sprayer and the five-gallon pails of black, white, and red paint. I heard the sound of an engine screaming around the track. The bank we were working on was on the outside of the track, right between Turns 3 and 4. I walked (that is, climbed) up the bank to the access road that ran around the top of the banking just outside the safety fence. I walked near the fence as a yellow car went by. Busch practice was going on. The car was going so fast I could only see that it was yellow. I had my camera and tried to photograph it. I took about twelve pictures before I could get it. I went back to work on the banking.

Dale's number consisted of a white 3 with a red outline on a black background. We only had two days to finish it, so we were forced to paint a different color while

Working on the "3" layout.

Spraying the second coat of white on the "3" layout.

From left to right: Sue Williams, me, Tim Johnson, Jamey Popham and Steve Hughey. The guys in white shirts are part of the Talladega painting crew.

the first one was still wet. The track guys helping me had to hold the hose up as I painted so it wouldn't drag through the wet paint. Sometimes we had to stand in the wet white paint to finish the fill-in. When we walked off the logo we left white tracks. I didn't worry because I made sure we walked in an area that would eventually be painted black, thus covering our tracks. The wind blew hard. When the sprayer kicked up some grass chunks, they would fly up the grass banking and across the safety road, through the safety fence into the infield parking area. We had to be careful these chunks didn't fly across the track when a car was testing.

Friday was a nice day. No wind. We were making good progress. The track painters normally only paint the concrete pillars, drainpipes, and retaining walls at the speedway. One of the track painters asked, "Tony, do you think I could do a little fill-in?"

"Why not," I said. "Just be real careful. You screw up and I'll kill ya."

They had a ball. We finished that afternoon and everyone was happy. We all had fun painting.

When I thought about it later, I was proud of being so good they could slap a last-minute job on us and we could get it done. The next day, a picture of us painting the "3" appeared on the front page of the *Birmingham News*. Steve and I watched the races from the spotter's stand on the new Allison Grandstand. I really missed Dale. The race was not the same.

We said our good-byes Sunday after the race and headed for the motel. Our flight was Monday morning. On the plane we had some good stories to reminisce about. Steve mumbled once again, "How much longer can we do this?"

Painting New Walls

It was 2 p.m. on a hot Thursday late in June 2001 when I'd returned to my shop after playing golf with Larry, Steve, and Bob. *Man, it's hot,* I thought as I walked into my cool, dark shop. *Don't open the overhead door. It would let the heat in.*

I flipped the lights on and walked over to my answering machine. Yup. The tiny red light was blinking. First message was Frank Dudgeon of Frank's Disposal wanting to know when I could letter a new truck. *Man, I'm glad it's a new one.* I hate that smell when I have to do some lettering on an old garbage truck. They always have juice dripping out the back. When I accidentally step in the slime, I have to frantically rub my shoe on the dry floor trying to get it off before it soaked through the sole. Aaargh. Not to mention the smell! I figured I'd call Frank right back as he was a good friend. A salesman was the next one jabbering about something as I pushed the Delete button. Then there was an interesting message.

"Hello, Tony? I met you at Talladega last year. You probably don't remember me. My name is Dave Gentile. I'm the new general manager of Chicagoland Speedway. Could you give me a call? I have some questions that maybe you could answer."

I thought, *I hope this call is for a job. But he probably just wants information.*

I did remember meeting Dave at Talladega last year. I grabbed the portable phone off the wall and dialed the number he'd left. Dave said that had seen my work at Talladega while he was down there, and Mike McWilliams had some good things to say about me. The Chicagoland inaugural race was coming up in July, and Dave wanted me to come out and paint the Tropicana 400 logos on the retaining walls. It was short notice, but I happily said yes.

Dave sent me the dimensions of the retaining wall. (I had him check them twice.) I also got the artwork for the Tropicana 400 sent overnight to me from a graphic artist in California.

I needed a helper, so I called Larry Orr—mainly to shut him up from his constant whining on how he'd missed the last Talladega job! We did one pounce pattern for the Tropicana 400 (we were to paint four of those) and another pounce pattern for www.chicagolandspeedway.com (they wanted one of these). There wasn't much lead time so we had to hurry with the patterns. I didn't have time to ship my equipment out there. Larry and I made the pounce patterns in my shop and we rolled them up and put them in our golf bags for shipping.

Our plane tickets arrived by FedEx that week and two days later we were on a plane heading for Chicago. Believe it or not, this was Larry's first time on a plane. I didn't want him to be nervous, so I told him, "If we start to go down, do what you have to do to get near a window. Keep looking at the ground, and keep your eyes open. Just before we hit the ground, jump straight up. You will actually stop and the plane will disintegrate around you and you will simply walk away."

He just stared at me with a dumb look like he was thinking, "you stupid bastard." I thought about it and figured that if I ever really tried it, the headlines would probably read, "One Man Killed In Plane Crash, 120 Survive." The story would explain that just as the plane hit, this guy unbuckled his seat belt, pushed his way to a window, and just as the plane hit the ground, he jumped straight up and was killed instantly. Hey, I still think it's worth a try if the plane is really going down. What have you got to lose?

Landing at O'Hare in Chicago, we found our rental car, a nice maroon Chevy Impala, and headed for Joliet, Illinois. It was only 2 p.m. when we checked in at the hotel, so we headed for the track. Normally, we would have headed for a golf course, but this was a totally new venture; I wanted to find the track so we didn't waste time looking for it tomorrow. Chicagoland Speedway was brand new then, and the Tropicana 400 was its very first race. When we pulled up to the main gate of the racetrack there wasn't a soul around and the gate was locked. I found that strange. A week before the inaugural race and no work was going on? We drove around and found another gate on the back of the track that was open. We drove in. Ah, there was the tunnel to the infield. We drove over to it. *Wow.* Now this was a *tunnel.* It was large enough for two tractor-trailers side by side, and had two sidewalks for pedestrians. As I drove through, I thought of the small one-lane tunnel at Talladega. I blew the horn.

The gate to the pits was wide open so we drove out onto Pit Lane. I still couldn't believe there wasn't a soul around. Then we saw why the gate was open. There were guys out in the Tri-Oval there starting the grass painting. I said to Larry, "Hey. That's Duane out there." (Duane was from Missouri Turf Paint. They did lots of grass paintings, and I got to know all of them over the years.)

I waved as we drove out Pit Lane. He looked up but didn't recognize me as we were a good distance away. I headed out onto the track. We made a slow lap and I said, "It's early. Let's go on the Back Straight and pounce a Tropicana 400 pattern on the wall. I have the track map showing where the logo is to go. It's too late to find a golf course, so we might as well get a jump on things. We will be ahead tomorrow."

"It's all right by me. We have nothing else to do." Larry said between puffs on his stupid pipe.

We stopped on the Back Straight and I got the track map out of my briefcase. "They want one right in the center of the Back Straight."

It was too long to measure so we drove to the exit of Turn 2, at the start of the Back Straight. With both of our doors open, the radio on, we idled down the Back Straight. We were counting Safety Fence poles. We stopped at the entrance of Turn 3:

fifty-eight poles. I put the car in reverse (too lazy to turn around) and backed up. We counted poles and stopped at twenty-nine. "The center of the back straight," I said.

I shut the car off, flipped the key to Accessory, and turned the radio up high. Larry and I got out of the car and opened the trunk. We grabbed the rolled-up pounce pattern out of the golf bag and started to unroll it on the track. "There is the center mark. Tape it right between those two poles," I told Larry, pointing up to the two safety fence poles on top of the concrete wall.

Larry taped the top of the pattern to the top of the concrete wall and let the pattern fall flat against the wall. As I watched the paper drift downward, I held my breath until it stopped—one inch from the asphalt.

I hollered, "*It fits.* Dave measured it right."

We rolled out the rest of the patterns, four in all, and Larry (the pounce man) got his prized pounce bag out of the trunk and began pouncing the pattern. I stood there leaning on the wall and watching Larry disappear into his charcoal dust cloud.

As I stood there looking around I thought, *This is strange.* Except for Duane and his helper, who were working on the grass painting, there wasn't a soul there. It was a week before the race and there was not a soul around. I reached down to my right side where I always carry my two-way radio (I had Bob Brown program it with Chicagoland frequencies before I left) and felt a little uneasy as it wasn't there. I remembered I left my radios home as the track insisted they had radios here waiting for me when I arrived. Against my better judgment, I succumbed to my desire to travel light and listened to them. I was going to call out on it and see if anyone answered. *Oh well. We'll get this pattern on and go back to the motel,* I thought. Larry was walking back up the track after pouncing the 130-foot pattern. As we rolled it up, I thought of my radio again. *Wish I had brought it with me.* After all those years working at racetracks, I know that a radio was a critical tool. I felt uncomfortable without it. I felt naked.

I looked up at the sky while holding the rolled-up pattern as Larry taped it closed. I said, "Looks like it might rain tonight. Think it will wash the pattern off?"

"Naw. I had it rain on the charcoal before. It will stay."

"Yeah," said, "It stayed on in Talladega with the dew that was on it. That was like a rainstorm. Don't think we'll have enough time to do another one. They want four of 'em. Let's go eat."

Larry threw the pattern and the pounce bag in the trunk and slammed it shut. "I thought I saw a Red Lobster near the motel. Let's go there," I said with my mouth watering.

"I don't care where we go," Larry said.

We drove around Turn 4 and pulled onto Pit Lane. "Duane's gone," I said to Larry. I drove up Pit Lane to the slot in the wall and turned left to go out the gate—then hit the brakes. The abrupt stop threw Larry forward almost slamming his stupid pipe into the dash—he smacked his hand on the dash just in time to stop before the pipe got stuffed down his throat.

"Christ," Larry said. "The gate is closed."

"No shit. Get out and open it. It has to be false locked. Duane saw us go in," I said.

At the Watkins Glen track, we false locked gates all the time. (False locking is when the gate is chained shut and the padlock is placed around the chain, but not fully closed. The U-shaped hook is moved to the closing position but not pushed down and locked. At a glance, it looked like it was locked—but wasn't.) Larry fumbled with the lock while I leaned my head out the window and hollered, "Come on. I'm hungry."

With the look of horror on his face, Larry held the lock and with his head turned 180 degrees around. He looked right at me. With the radio playing, I couldn't hear him but I could read his lips: *"It's locked."*

I waved to him to get in the car. "There must be a gate open," I said. "We just have to find it. We had to find one to get in. Duane wouldn't leave us in here. Why didn't I bring my radio?"

We drove all around the entire track checking every gate and we came to the realization that we were *trapped*. We were like rats in a cage. We went back to the main gate and got out of the car. We stood at the ten-foot fence with our fingers through it holding on, looking like prisoners peering out at the rest of the world. I walked back to the car and turned on the headlights *Maybe someone will see us,* I thought hopefully. It was dead quiet. Not a soul around. It would be different if we were outside the track, but we were on the inside. I said in a stern voice to Larry, "See what I mean about radios? You always have to have one at a track. I shouldn't have listened to them. We wouldn't be in this mess."

"They probably don't have theirs turned on anyway," Larry said. "Somebody eventually has to go by."

An hour went. The sun was dropping rapidly on the horizon. It was dusk. Suddenly, off in the distance, I spotted a car driving across the infield. We both started jumping up and down, waving our arms and hollering, "Hey. Hey. Over here. Over here." We looked just like shipwrecked cast-a-ways stranded on an island when a plane suddenly flew by overhead. The car kept right on going down into the tunnel. "We're going to be sleeping in the damned car," I said.

I looked away just as Larry hollered, "A truck! There's a truck."

We started hollering and waving again. I jumped in the car and started blowing the horn and flashing the lights. The truck stopped.

"He saw us," I said as the truck headed our way. The guy got out and walked to the fence. "Hey. Glad you saw us," I said. "We got locked in. Do you have a key?"

"No. And I don't know anyone who does. There's nobody here. Do you know anyone you can call?"

"I've got Dave Gentile's number," I said, "but it is for his office here and nobody's there. See if you can find a sheriff. He can contact somebody." The guy got back in his truck and drove off.

A half hour went by and up through the tunnel came a sheriff's car. It was dark now. We explained the situation and I could see that he was trying not break out in laughter.

He drove off and in ten minutes a car pulled in. It was Dave. He got out of the car and said, "Hi, Tony. How ya doin'?"

"Great. We just feel like we are in jail."

Come to find out, we were right—Duane finished the grass he was working on and forgot we were on the Back Straight. He left and locked the gate behind him. Now that we were out from behind bars, we were too relieved to be furious, so we all had a good laugh.

The Inaugural Race

We got back to the track at 7 a.m. Painting at a new track was a whole different feeling. The new and unfamiliar surroundings and the new people created a sense of excitement mixed with a little uneasiness.

Larry and I drove to the infield and parked near a fenced-in area where maintenance machinery was stored. As we walked by, Dave Gentile drove out of the compound with a Kawasaki Mule pulling a trailer filled with white paint and a sprayer. "Hey Dave," I called out. "What're ya doin'? Where ya headed?"

Dave was about forty years old, average build, with brown hair. He stopped and said in an excited voice (it was his first race as general manager), "I'm headed out to do some touchup on the retaining wall."

"Get the hell off that thing," I said. "That's what we're here for. You must have more important things to do than paint the wall."

"Thanks, Tony." Dave said as he headed off at a brisk pace.

"He's got to slow down," Larry said.

Larry and I were in great shape on this job. We were working with a graphics company from California who had worked with other tracks out west; the artwork was perfect. They got everything scaled to the right size, and that helped me a lot. We had our patterns with us and we threw them in the Mule and headed out to find the flaws in the white paint on the wall. It only took us an hour to fix everything. We touched up the wall, and then commandeered the Mule as our own.

Since the first logo layout went well, it was time to lay out the rest of the Tropicana logos. We settled into our normal routine of pouncing patterns and painting. When you were out there painting, your mind wandered. Mine wandered around aimlessly for ten minutes, then somehow settled on *golf*. "Golf!" I hollered to Larry.

"We gotta play golf once before we leave," he said back.

Having great patterns, the right colors for the logos, and only 12 degrees of banking (compared to the 34 degrees at Talladega) we really sailed along. NASCAR had stopped allowing test days at a track before the race, so we had the track all to ourselves for the week we were there. To play golf, we had to get our work done first, so we painted like automated machines. We had a goal. Thursday was Golf day.

Painting the retaining wall at the start/finish line at Chicagoland Speedway.

Larry and I took turns painting the retaining wall at the start/finish line.

On Wednesday, we painted the start/finish line and a small Tropicana logo on the retaining wall at the finish line, right under the Starter's Stand. This logo was a last-minute request. We would have done it with the computer in vinyl if we'd known about it before we came down. We hand-painted it, but it was no problem getting the work done in one day.

We finished at about 3 p.m. and asked Dave if he needed help on anything. We knew it was the first race at a brand new track, and we figured we could help with anything he needed. We did a few small errands and finished up by 4 p.m. That night Dave took us to dinner with his wife and some of the crew from the track. It was a lot of fun. A new place, new people, but the same type of work. We felt at home—and most of all, we had met new friends.

Thursday morning we headed to the golf course. Dave gave us directions and we traveled down the famous Route 66 and then turned down a side road. In the distance, we saw Joliet State Prison, where the Blues Brothers did a scene in their movie. We stopped and got out of the car, looked at the place for three seconds, jumped back in the car, and took off. We had to get to the golf course.

We pulled in to the clubhouse and got our clubs out of the car and walked in. We couldn't play a twosome so the course teamed us up with two retired attorneys. They knew the course well— in their thirty years of golf, this was the only course that they had ever played on! That was hard to believe. Of course, it *was* a lawyer that told us that.

The most striking feature of this course was that it was *dead flat*. Standing on any hole on the course, you could look around and see the entire course. The only bumps were where they had dug a pond and piled up the dirt. If these guys ever saw the courses we played on at home, they would be in awe over the landscape. We had a great time anyway, and on the way back to the motel we talked about the new track and what we could do on Friday.

☙

On Friday, we looked for something to do at the track. We didn't find anything until noon.

"Hey, Tony. Cm'ere a minute," Dave hollered.

I immediately got the same feeling that I got every time Mike McWilliams called me by name at Talladega. *Not good.* We pulled the Mule up to where Dave and some guy in a gray suit were standing. "Hi Dave. Whaddaya need?" I said.

Dave introduced the man in the suit, who said, "I think we need a second website logo on the Front Straight wall right near the Starter's Bridge. The one you did on the inside wall looked so good that we'd like another one."

"We can do that," I said. "There is one thing, Dave. Can you get me a light plant? I think we will be working late."

 # Work and Play

We drove onto the track riding our trusty Kawasaki Mule and took a lap to do a last-minute check on the Tropicana Logos. Just as we exited Turn 2, I noticed two men trying to sweep something off the track with large brooms. It looked like they'd washed about ten feet of the track surface. As we got closer I could smell what it was. It wasn't water. It was gasoline. They'd had a couple of five-gallon cans of gas in the back of a Mule and somehow the cans fell onto the track. I immediately pulled my radio off my belt and keyed. I hollered into the radio. "Emergency. Emergency. I need a fire truck on the Back Straight. We need water. We have gasoline on the track surface." Good thing I'd finally gotten my track radio.

"We are on our way," was the quick response from the track fire crew.

Gas is a killer to asphalt. It eats asphalt. Spilling gas on the track was like a medical emergency. I jumped from the Mule and hollered at the guys to stop brushing it. They were making it worse—pushing the gas into the asphalt. The fire truck pulled up within minutes and they started spraying the spill toward the inside of the track and the grass. Working at racetracks had taught me that the track surface is treated like gold, only better. This was brand new asphalt, and my call averted a major disaster—those two guys weren't going to call anyone. They were afraid they would get in real trouble if anyone knew what happened. But people would know soon enough, and repaving two days before a race is almost impossible.

As we left the scene, I noticed Stan Alexander—the engineer for NASCAR (out of Daytona Speedway)—racing toward it in his car. I'm sure he'd heard the radio transmissions, and the track surface was in his hands. We drove around the track to the Front Straight, where the maintenance crew had positioned a light plant on the inside of the track surface near the start/finish line.

While we were putting the pattern on the wall, Stan pulled up to our location. Stan was a very quiet person. For him to say something to me was not normal. He rolled down the window and I walked over the driver's side of his light blue Buick.

Placing both hands on the top of the door, I leaned down. "Hi, Stan."

"Thank you so much for your quick action," he said. "You saved the track. Thanks again."

Standing in front of a wall painting at Chicagoland.

"Thank you, Stan," I said. "I learned from all the harping that Mike McWilliams did about not spilling anything on the track, especially gas and paint." He smiled, and then he drove off. That felt good.

We started pouncing the pattern on the wall in daylight but we wound up painting into the night to get that big logo finished. Luckily for us, it was very warm and calm that evening. We didn't mind the extra work, as we had nowhere to go anyway.

The next day started off with a bang. "Hey Tony. Could you come here for a minute?" Dave hollered.

"Oh no. Not good," I whispered to Larry.

We walked over to Dave and he said, "Sorry Tony, but I have one more job for you." I looked at Larry, thinking, *They want* more *www's*. "The FAA is here for an inspection as we have a heliport and a makeshift control tower, Dave continued. "They want the three concrete heliport pads numbered. It was Federal law, but they hadn't put the numbers on the pads when they built them. Can you do it?"

"Sure, Dave. But I want the FAA to show us exactly what they want. I don't want to make a mistake with this," I said.

Just outside Turn 3 the track had three 20'×20' concrete pads for the helicopters. We had to paint a six-foot number on each of them. We would make a freehand layout, draw the numbers on with a grease pencil, and just paint them black. NASCAR practice was about over when we started, and all the choppers were supposed to be gone by 5 p.m. We finished pad 1 and pad 3, but a chopper was still sitting on pad 2. Finally I called Dave and said, "Dave. We've been here for half an hour. Could you get this thing moved? Even if they just move it over to one of the other pads, it would be great."

"They're calling the pilot," he said. "It's Rusty's chopper."

I said to Larry, "That figures." I knew Rusty Wallace is always stopping to talk! Some reporter must have spotted him, and he talked forever. An hour later, Rusty and the pilot showed up. "Sorry, guys. Thanks for waiting," Rusty said as he walked by.

"GGGgggrrrrrrr," I answered politely.

We jumped on the pad as soon as the chopper was twenty feet above us. We quickly painted the number 2 on the concrete.

"There. We're finished with everything. Let's go up on top of the tower and check out our logos. I want to see how they look," I said to Larry.

We headed for the back of the grandstand and the tower, where they'd put in a couple of elevators—but nothing like the death trap that was at Talladega years earlier. Here, we walked into a lobby under the grandstand and the elevators were similar to what you'd find a large, high-end hotel. A woman wearing a red uniform operated the controls for people with the appropriate credentials, which happily included us. We rode up to the top floor, which was the Race Control section of the tower. I carefully stepped out. I didn't like the height, but I wanted to see the work we had done. As we looked over the handrail I got my normal feeling of being pulled over the side. While looking, I heard an electric saw close by. Someone was cutting a board. I looked over to my left and there were two men working on a temporary wooden camera platform. I was already turning back to look at the logos below when what I had seen suddenly registered. I did a double take.

"Holy shit," I said to Larry. I hit him on the shoulder and said, "Follow me." We walked over to the two guys cutting the boards and I hollered, "Hey. That's not right. You cut it too short."

The two men gave us a mean look. The guy on the left was my cousin Eddy Menio. He lived in Watkins Glen too. Eddy did a lot of work for different racing series,

Larry Orr fixing a hit at Chicagoland.

building camera platforms and installed scaffolding for major television networks. When he saw me, his eyes widened and he said, "What the hell are you doin' here?" We caught up for a while and then Larry and I finally headed back to the elevator.

☙

    Saturday was the NASCAR Busch Series race. It was a good race—just two hits on the retaining wall, and they took us only an hour to repair. On Saturday night, we planned to go to the World of Outlaw (WoO) race at the new dirt track nearby. Larry was excited. He had never seen a WoO Sprint Car race.
    A WoO Sprint Car has a classic shape that has been around since the 1930s. They are a larger version of the 3/4 Midget I raced at Watkins Glen. The front tires are smaller (the inside tire is not on the ground that much) and the rear tires are huge, especially the right rear tire. Like the Midget car I raced, they are an open-wheel race car consisting of a tubular chassis with a fiberglass body with a huge wing above the roll cage that holds the car to the track and gives tremendous down force, allowing super-fast cornering. A race-ready Sprint Car weighs about 1,600 pounds and is powered by an alcohol-burning 400 cubic inch V8 engine that pumps out 850 horsepower. In action, these cars are in an almost constant slide around a half-mile track, sometimes lifting both front wheels in the air going down the straight.
    That evening, Dave drove Larry and me over to the dirt track in a van. He through the gate and around the track to the backside where the pits were. To our right was Steve Kinser, twenty-time World of Outlaw Champion. Across the road was the Dude—Danny Lasoski, the guy who drove Tony Stewart's car for him. Tony was standing there talking to Danny. Then we saw Slammin' Sammy Swindell and Jac Haudenschild (who is also known as the Wild Child). We didn't know what to look at first. Then suddenly we heard the roar of engines of the cars out for practice. Just off the Back Straight was a line of concrete Jersey barriers. Lined up along the barriers to watch practice were the car owners and crews. We walked over to watch practice. *Holy shit!!* The cars were running about three feet from the barrier, going full bore—about 110 mph—down the Back Straight.
    Larry and I leaned on the concrete wall and looked up toward Turn 4. The cars came around the corner in a broad slide headed right at the concrete wall. At the last second, each car would snap forward and fly down the straight. Those alcohol-burning monsters were turning about 8,000 rpm as they went by us. The dust hit us with the force of a shotgun blast. Now we knew why most of the crewmen had goggles on. The sound was incredible. Imagine tipping your head sideways, dangling fishing line with tiny fish hooks into your ear and then yanking your damned eardrum right out of your head! This was exactly what it felt like when one of those cars went by at speed.
    The view was so good there we stayed anyway and watched with our hands over our ears for the whole session. Man, did we have a great time. We headed to the motel with ears ringing. I was looking forward to tomorrow's NASCAR race.

Chicagoland Race Day

We got to the track before daylight on race day, July 15, 2001, and drank coffee in the office. Dave saw us and called us over. "Go in and see the secretary and get an elevator sticker on your credentials. You are watching the race from the Chicagoland Speedway suite and you'll need a special sticker to use the elevator today."

"Thanks, Dave" I said. Larry and I looked at each other and smiled. Ahhh, the perks. This time we weren't hung over like we were at Talladega.

Near race time we headed to the elevator. We rode up with President Mike Helton of NASCAR and legendary driver Darryl Waltrip. "Hey, Tony," Mike said. "I see they got you out here, too?"

"Yeah, Mike," I said. "It's a lot smaller than Talladega." Mike had been president of Talladega when I first went there in '92.

"It sure is," Mike said. "Good to see you here. They got the best."

My chest puffed out a little and my face felt warm. We got off at the top. Mike and Darryl went to Race Control, and Larry and I turned right and headed to the suite.

There were a lot of people talking, eating, and drinking as we walked into the back of the Chicagoland Suite. We didn't know anyone there but someone said, "Help yourself to anything you want and grab two seats right down in front before someone else takes 'em."

"Thanks!"

We grabbed some water and picked two seats down in front. We were right next to the huge glass windows. It was a little scary at first—we were about twelve stories up, and the windows slanted forward, making me feel like I was going to fall out. *What a view.* We looked at each other and just shook our heads and smiled.

From our seats we could see every inch of the track. It was fantastic. I looked down into the grandstands to my right and thought, *How the hell did we get to this level where we have the best credentials, accommodations, food, flying all over the country, and sitting in suites to watch a NASCAR race.* I peered way down at the crowd and thought, *Look at those mere mortals. I'm ruined.* After what we'd become accustomed to, I felt we could never sit in a grandstand again.

Larry Orr in the Chicagoland Speedway suite on race day.

"It was a good race and we had fun in the suite meeting new people and finally relaxing. Looking out at our artwork made me proud even though out of the thousands of people in the grandstands, only a handful would actually wonder how that lettering got there.

Kevin Harvick won the inaugural NASCAR Winston Cup race at Chicagoland. Although I enjoy watching NASCAR races still, I do not have a favorite driver since Dale Earnhardt was killed at Daytona. I was lucky to have been at the tracks when he won some of his best races. Today I root for drivers who are aggressive and can't be intimidated—*or the guy I have in the NASCAR pool at Maria's Tavern that week!*

When the race ended we went out to the balcony on the back of the suite. There we talked with Dave, who thanked us for coming to help with the race. It was a really hot day, around 98 degrees and humid. The victory lane celebration was just starting. To celebrate the inaugural race, that track had mounted air cannons in Victory Lane and all across the top of the suites to blow red, white, and blue confetti over the grandstands as the fireworks went off. Suddenly, we heard the air cannons shoot. There was a loud whoosh from the nearest cannon on the roof and the confetti (paper cut to about an inch wide and two inches long) rained down all over us and the 80,000 people in the grandstands. There must have been tons of the stuff—it got so thick it was hard to see people in the grandstand. The confetti was in our hair and sticking to our sweaty faces. I even had some on my lip like a mustache.

A man came running toward us, hollering, "Dave. Dave. We got trouble."

Dave said, "What the hell's the matter?"

"All the air conditioners for the suites have quit. Some of the main circuit breakers blew, which made *all* the power go out." Dave got on the radio and called all the maintenance people to the roof of the suites.

Tagging after Dave, we climbed to the roof of the suites to look at the line of huge air conditioning units. The trouble was instantly clear. The air cannons. No one had thought about half a ton of confetti getting sucked up by the intake vents of the air conditioners. But when the confetti hit them, they all overheated and started blowing circuit breakers all over the place. We began pulling handfuls of the red, white, and blue confetti off the air intake screens and throwing the stuff in the air, where the slight breeze could blow it over the roof to the grandstands below. It was fun, and the vents were soon clear enough to make it safe to flip the circuit breakers open again.

With this crisis over, it was time for Larry and me to say good-bye to everyone. The week had gone by so fast. Dave Gentile was a great guy. As Larry and I walked to our car, we had to turn and look one more time at the back of the huge grandstands, maybe just to remind ourselves how lucky we are. On the drive to the motel, Larry was all excited about flying again. It was his second time and he was ready. We hit the sack early as our flight was at 8 a.m.

We had a nice flight home. We landed in Elmira to find Harriett and Sal (Larry's wife) waiting for us. We all hugged and went our separate ways. The strange part about this track work was that I never know when I would be called to travel to some far-off place. I had no contract with anyone, just a reputation of being able to paint anything and getting the job done on time. When they needed me they would call. It might have been a strange way to do business, but I liked the surprises.

 # Peeling Vinyl

I was sitting in my chair, staring at the computer monitor, hard at work. I was swamped with signs for the upcoming NASCAR Race at Watkins Glen. The race was three weeks away and the work orders kept coming in.

The phone rang and I thought, *Oh, no. Not more track signs.* But to my surprise, it was not the track. It was Peter White from Britten Banners in Michigan, the company I did the grass job for in Talladega. They wanted me to do an install for them at Watkins Glen. At first, I was hesitant as the race was not far off and I didn't need more work, but it was close, and how much work could it be? Figuring it was banners he wanted installed, I said, "Yeah. I'll help you out."

Peter laughed and said, "I need an estimate from you on the install. It's *huge.*"

"How huge? How the hell big is the banner?"

"It isn't a banner."

Immediately I knew my *big mouth* had gotten me in trouble once again. "Not a banner? What the hell is it?"

"It's the Press Tower windows," Peter said. "You know those large windows on the second floor, the ones that run across the front of the building?" He went on to explain that the art on the windows was a two-way film that was applied by an Arizona company. From the outside, it says "SIRIUS" and shows a dog logo on the end for SIRIUS Satellite Radio. From the inside, you can see through it. The whole thing had to be removed as SIRIUS had changed their colors to white and blue and they wanted new film on the glass.

I told Peter that I would look at it, emphasizing how short the time was. I went to the track and got in a man lift—*I still don't like heights but a good man lift makes me feel safer; at least this one wasn't homemade!*—and peeled some of the vinyl off the window to see how hard it would be to get the old film off the glass. With the sun shining on the windows, it was still hard to peel the film, but it did come off. I called Peter back and told him I would do the job, for a highly inflated rate (because of the height) and he said to go for it. He told me the vinyl would have to go on the glass panels in two pieces as the glass was larger than they could make the film.

Well, here was a new challenge. I would have to remove old window two-way

This was a huge window film. Applying large sheets of vinyl is hard enough, then you add doing it from a man lift!

film and apply new, perforated see-through vinyl film to the Press Tower windows. The row had seven windows that measured 120 inches high by 96 inches wide, and another eight widows that measured 120 inches high by 59 inches wide. That added up to almost a thousand square feet of glass. This meant working two stories up in a man lift, in the wind, with huge sheets of adhesive film that I'd never worked with before. What really made me nervous was working with a man lift within six inches of the huge plates of glass. One mistake on the controls and it could be a disaster.

This was not a job for the faint-hearted. I got on the phone to my old racetrack helper, Larry Orr, and told him the story—and he was ready to help out. The track had recently rented a brand-new two-man man lift. It was a dream to operate. The controls were precise and made it possible to work close to the glass without the bucket jerking and threatening to smash into the glass. We were lucky as it was hot both days that we spent removing the old film. That old film cost $92,000 (labor not included) and when we were done, it lay in a pile on the ground. FedEx delivered the new film and Larry and I struggled with the first window. If you put any stress on the film, we found that it would stretch. The first piece hung down as we rubbed from top to bottom, sticking the film to the glass. When we went to put the second piece on, we found that letting the film hang down, the weight of the film allowed it to stretch a little and the mating piece would not line up. We ruined the first piece. I called Britten Banners in a panic and they overnighted new pieces. Finally we got the hang of applying the film.

By Friday afternoon we had finished the job. The cars were practicing while we were working on the Press Tower, so we had a great view whenever we could look away from the film. We went home very satisfied with the job. I told Larry, "Another one for the record books." The Press Tower looked great.

Early Saturday morning the phone rang at my house. I looked at the clock. It was half past six. My good friend Steve Ely, race director at Watkins Glen, was on the other end of the line.

"Hey, Toneman. You better get up here quick. The NASCAR Scorers are in the Press Tower and they don't like looking through the film. You gotta take it down. *Now.*"

"Yeah, right, Ely," I said. You're shittin' me. What do you really want?"

"I'm not shittin' ya. I'm standing right here with the NASCAR Official and it has to come off. You better get here as fast as you can. The race starts at noon and it has to be off. Rudy is bringing the man lift over now and he will help you."

I hung up and called Larry, who couldn't believe what I was telling him. He would head out as soon as he got dressed. I got to the track and met the NASCAR official and Tim Coleman, the general manager, at the Press Tower. I told them that I wasn't touching a thing until I got permission from Britten Banners and SIRIUS Satellite Radio. The cell phones were blazing. The final word was given.

Rudy and I started peeling the film from the windows. It hadn't been on the glass twenty-four hours yet, so it came off fairly easy. Larry showed up and we took turns peeling the huge sheets of vinyl off the glass. It was kind of funny removing the film.

On a man lift peeling off the window film that we had put on about fourteen hours earlier.

From the outside, with the film on, I couldn't see in. As we peeled the film off, there were all of these people staring at us from inside the Press Tower. This was unbelievable. A job this big and it didn't stay up twenty-four hours. But yes, I did get paid.

Stepping into History

In 2004, Tim Coleman, general manager of Watkins Glen International, visited my shop to bring me artwork for a sign. As he cracked open a cold Budweiser—just stole from my refrigerator—I asked, "Why do you always bring me artwork in the late afternoon? Just in time for a beer? Grab me one."

He laughed and said, "They just laid more work on us." He was referring to International Speedway Corporation, which owned the track. "We now are in charge of Nazareth. We are going down to look things over. There's a NASCAR Busch race coming up."

"Wow. Do they need sign work?"

"Yeah. I'm sure they will. The girl they had working there quit. They have a hell of a sign shop. I'm sure you'll be going down."

Nazareth was the home of the Andrettis. Nazareth Speedway was one of the oldest racetracks in the country—almost a hundred years old. Racing started there in 1910. It started as a dirt track and after many changes and updates, it was paved in 1987. I was excited to go to this historic track.

Months later, Tim called and said they needed a lot of retaining wall lettering before the Busch race. It would take a week, and I'd need help. I called Larry Orr, who was (as usual) ready to travel. Tim provided artwork and I trusted his dimensions of the retaining wall. Tim's been around long enough to know the importance of getting dimensions right when we letter something. He also knew that if the numbers were wrong, I would kill him. Larry and I made the pounce patterns and we were ready for a new adventure.

We piled into my Dodge Dakota pickup truck, and three and a half hours later we pulled into Nazareth, Pennsylvania, passing some huge cement plants that were in the middle of town. As we drove down a road near one of the old plants, the grandstands of the speedway loomed in the distance.

"Look at that. The track is right in town," I said.

We drove by two locked gates to the speedway and headed to our hotel. After we checked in, we headed back toward the track, where we saw a diner on the corner of a four-lane road. We pulled into a parking lot.

"Is this the lot for the diner or for that building back there?" I said to Larry.

"The sign says Da Vinci's. I guess it's a pizza joint. Let's go in the diner." Wrong choice. To put it mildly, the food sucked. We had mashed potatoes and gravy but I think the potatoes were concrete from one of those plants we saw. We stopped at a deli and got Rolaids.

The next morning we found an open gate and pulled into the Nazareth Speedway. No one was in the small guard shack. "Timmy has gotta be here someplace," I said to Larry. "Let's drive around until we find him." We dove all over the place looking for the general manager. Everything was locked. Finally, we saw Tim standing by a building, talking to a short, stocky, balding man. We stopped and got out.

"Who the hell sent you here?" Tim said.

"You did!"

We all shook hands and Tim introduced us to Gino Pfautz. Gino was the caretaker of the speedway. He lived in an apartment over the top of one of the maintenance buildings. Gino was hard to forget once you met him. He claimed to know all the NASCAR and Indy Car people, from Roger Penske and Bill France down to all the crew members. (Later, he came up to Watkins Glen for an Indy Car race. I walked around with him—and I'll be damned if he didn't know everyone *and* they all knew him.)

Tim said, "That's the sign shop down there on the end." He pointed toward the fence that ran along the main road that went by the track. We drove down and went inside. It was a small shop, maybe 16'x24', with a large work table and a bench along the far wall. It had a vinyl plotter, a Gerber Edge (a thermal printer that prints on fifteen-inch-wide adhesive vinyl), and a computer at a desk on the end of the bench:

On the track at Nazareth Speedway.

Tim Coleman asked "Can you repair this?" The Front Straight wall was in bad shape.

a typical vinyl shop. In an adjoining building was a large double-bay shop where they worked on billboards. It was full of old billboard panels.

Tim, Larry, and I got into Tim's truck and drove through the tunnel to the infield. From there we went out the pit gate and onto the track. (That time, I managed to keep my hand off the horn button.)

"Wow. This place is small. It's nothing like Talladega or Watkins," I said to Tim.

"Yeah. Nothing like The Glen."

We rode around and looked at where the lettering on the retaining walls was to go. We stopped at the start/finish line and got out of the truck. Tim said, "This wasn't in the contract, but can you fix up the lettering a little? It'll be on TV."

"Holy shit!" I peeled a piece of hanging paint off the wall and picked it apart, finding at least six layers of color where it had been repainted over and over. "Christ," I said. "You'll have to get somebody out here to clean the old paint that we take off the wall off the track. Maybe the jet blower will work."

"We'll get the track cleaned," Tim said. "You paint."

"It won't be 100 percent," I said, "but it will look better than this." It had been neglected so long, it was pathetic. I figured it needed to look decent, because only two more races were going to be held here. Then, after almost a hundred years of racing, the track was officially closing for good.

The next day Tim helped us by coating out some of the old lettering on the walls where we were going to paint the new logos. I think he felt sorry for the start/finish line mess. Larry and I started our routine of pouncing patterns and lettering the logos

Painted this in Turn 4 in the afternoon.

Next morning, we had to repaint the wall after a hit by Ed Carpenter.

on the wall. This was our first day there, and at 7 p.m., we decided to call it quits. As we drove to the motel, Larry said, "Where are we going to eat?"

We were stopped at a stop sign and the diner we ate at last night was on our left. I said, "We sure as hell aren't eating there."

Larry said, "Let's try the place out back. We can get a pizza."

I pulled into the parking lot and there were no cars at Da Vinci's. We went in anyway. It was an old house that was converted into an Italian restaurant. You would never know it from outside. Each room had tables and there was a small bar to the right. After looking at the menu for pizza, we decided to get a spaghetti dinner instead. The food was the best I had eaten in a long time. The meat sauce was fantastic. The homemade bread was great. We told everyone from the track about what we

Grass painting at Nazareth.

found and from that day on, we all ate there every night. One night there were eighteen of us at one table that they had set up for us.

Along with the wall lettering, we had to do a grass painting. It was the NASCAR Busch Series logo. It would be a small logo, only twenty-six feet high and twenty-eight feet long. We were going to use a layout method that we had never used on grass. For the standard logos—the Busch Series, NASCAR, Craftsman Truck, NASCAR.COM—NASCAR had made huge pounce patterns they shipped from track to track. The pattern they sent for the Busch logo was a 26'×36' piece of heavy clear plastic with two-inch holes cut along the lines of the logo. We spread the pattern on the grass and walked along the lines, spraying the holes with marking paint. This worked really well for a small painting. NASCAR also made a series of these patterns to lay out large grass painting. After we sprayed the holes, we rolled up the pattern and put it back in the fifty-five-gallon plastic drum to be shipped to the next track on the schedule. Then we went to the maintenance building to get our paint and sprayer. The paint was there all right, but we couldn't find the sprayer.

It turned out that Gino was using the only sprayer the track had. It was on a Kawasaki Mule and he was spraying the lines in the fields to lay out the camping spaces. This meant we had no sprayer. Off we headed to a rental shop to get one. The shop had several airless sprayers but only had one that was working. It was an ugly thing and not very big. Lucky the logo was small, so we took it. We finished our painting without incident. Even though it was a small painting, it was a tough job. The logo had oval slashes, many colors, and some small lettering. We made sure that it looked good when we finished.

On May 23, 2004, we watched the last Busch race ever to be held at Nazareth. Martin Truex, Jr. won the Goulds Pumps/ITT Industries 200. The next day we headed home. I wondered if we would go back for the IRL Indy Car event. That night we headed for Da Vinci's for another great Italian meal. After a good night's rest, we drove back to Watkins Glen.

 # Wild Ride

A few months after the Busch race, Larry and I were called back to Nazareth Speedway for the IRL Indy Car Race. This would be the last race at the famous Nazareth Speedway. A racetrack which had started almost a hundred years ago was closing its doors forever. There was so much history at Nazareth. Our job was to coat out the NASCAR Goodyear logos on the retaining walls and paint the Indy Car Series sponsor Firestone logos in their place. We also had to do a grass painting of the Indy Car Series logo.

It was standard racetrack work and it went well until Wednesday, the day I'd scheduled to do the grass painting. When I arrived at the track, I was informed that I couldn't paint that day after all. Roger Penske had, at the last minute, arranged for his VIPs to take Indy Car rides in special built, full-blown two-seat Indy cars. That meant painting Thursday and working around scheduled practice. I would have to lay out the painting early Thursday morning, do some painting at lunch hour and finish after practice was over at 5 p.m. It would make for a long day. I was not happy.

Two-seat Indy Cars. That caught my attention. I went over and watched the crew from the Indy Car ride team set up the cars. These were real Indy Cars—capable of 200 mph—stretched to add another seat right behind the driver. As I stood there I got talking (I always do) to some of the crew. I found out that Michael Andretti was driving one in the morning session, and Davey Hamilton would take over for the afternoon session. Sarah Fisher was driving the other car. I'd always wanted to meet Sarah. I loved watching her race. She started in Sprint Cars and worked up to Indy Cars. She had won the pole at Texas Speedway with speeds over 220 mph, the first woman to win an Indy Car pole position. Erin Jones (now Erin Smith), director of communications at Watkins Glen, came by to talk to the Indy Car people. I couldn't stand it any longer. I had to get a ride in an Indy Car.

I cornered Erin and cried about what a strain this Indy Car thing was going to cause me. I put on my best story, and said, "The least they could do is get me a ride with Sarah Fisher."

After a while, Erin came up to me and said, "Go see that lady at the table and sign all the papers. It is not guaranteed, but if they have time at the end of the last session, you can go."

"*Yes!* Thank you, Erin!" Erin is a great person who always treated me so well. I filled out a ton of paperwork, and then I went into the tent that was set up to change clothes—even a passenger needed a complete fire suit, right down to the shoes. These two-seater Indy cars ran on methanol and drivers and riders had to have protection from fire.

I sat on Pit Wall for three hours anxiously waiting my turn. Finally a man walked over and said, "You ready?"

I jumped up and said, "Hell yeah." We went over and he put a fireproof hood on me. Then he fitted me with a helmet. I put the fireproof gloves on, left one first, and I was ready.

"Here comes your car," the man said. It was Davey Hamilton.

"Can I wait for Sarah?" I asked.

He gave me a surprised look, then leaned into the cockpit and told Davey what I said. Davey looked at me and threw both arms up in the air as to say, "The hell with ya."

Sarah pulled in behind him. The crew helped me into the very tight cockpit, right behind Sarah. It took a while for them to buckle me in, but then seconds later we were driving down Pit Lane in an Indy Car.

Pit Lane entered the track between Turns 1 and 2. Sarah picked up speed down the Back Straight. The engine, not six inches from my back, was screaming. No earplugs. It hurt. Coming down the Front Straight, I could just see past Sarah's helmet.

Two-seater Indy Car ride with Sarah Fisher.

The Turn 1 concrete wall came up fast. From my racing experience, I figured I knew approximately where she was going to brake—but she didn't. For a split second I thought it was all over. She didn't even lift off the throttle, let alone hit the brake. Through Turn 1 flat out. Almost 2.9 lateral G's in the corner. I honestly couldn't move and couldn't breathe going through a corner. We did three laps and averaged about 145 mph on the one-mile Nazareth Speedway. When I got out, all I could do was thank the people that were with the ride. It was the most awesome ride you can imagine.

On August 29, 2004, Dan Wheldon won the Firestone Indy 225 ending Nazareth's racing history. This was the first time I had seen an Indy Car race at Nazareth. Unless you have been there to see it for yourself, it is hard to imagine how fast cars go on such a short track! I guess an Indy race was a fitting end to the 100 year history of Nazareth Speedway. In those 100 years, Nazareth had gone from running jalopy's on a dirt track to hosting a premier Indy Racing event. Unbeknown to me at the time, racing at Nazareth wasn't the only thing ending that day. This trip marked the end of my travels to do sign work at race tracks other than Watkins Glen. Two historic "old timers" done at the same time!!

 Déjà Vu

Except for the work at Watkins Glen, my racetrack jobs have all but disappeared. I hadn't been back to Talladega since painting the "3" for Dale on the grass bank. Larry Orr regretted turning down that last trip to Talladega, and calls to whine every now and then. I'm sad myself. I really missed the people at Talladega. They were a great bunch. Donna and I stayed in touch over e-mail and she kept me informed on breaking news. Not that there was anything for me to do.

Technology had replaced sign painters in many areas where we were once in demand. Billboards are mostly digital printed wraps now. Even some lettering on the concrete pit walls had gone the high-tech vinyl route. The old-timers like me and my buddies were being replaced by robots. Oh, well. My commercial shop work continued to keep me busy.

And I loved working in my shop. It was so crowded with stuff (it's practically a museum) that sometimes I noticed things I hadn't noticed before. Sitting in there, my mind often wandered to the tales in this book. I would find myself staring at the computer screen and daydreaming of past adventures. To be honest, I couldn't believe we did all those things. I missed the adventure of the traveling, the people I met and most of all confronting the awesome challenges that came out of nowhere and yet somehow we figured out how to accomplish a seemingly impossible task.

A year after my ride at Nazareth, for instance, I was working on a display banner for the Corning Museum of Glass at Watkins Glen International. It was Wine Fest weekend and the track had a lot of displays, but now—around 5 p.m. on a Friday—almost everyone was gone. I drove out of the garage area and noticed the Two-Seat Indy Car trailer over in the paddock area. The car was on jack stands and three men were working on it. I drove over to the trailer and stopped.

I watched them work on the car from my truck when I noticed them struggling with a side panel. I got out and asked if they needed a hand. They were changing an engine. I stayed until dark helping them. That night we went to Seneca Lodge for a beer. That was when I found out that the two guys working on the car owned the Indy Car Ride. Jeff Sinden and Scott Jasek instantly became my new friends. After talking, they remembered me from Nazareth. The next night was my birthday. Scott

With good friends (from left to right): Jeff Sinden, me, Travis Cobb and Scott Jasek with one their Indy Racing Experience two seat Indy cars.

and Jeff took Harriett and me to Seneca Lodge for supper to celebrate my birthday. Some of my friends from the track were there, and we had a blast.

That year I did get a ride with Davey Hamilton at Watkins Glen in an Indy Car. Davey wanted to film the track with his digital recorder and needed someone to ride and take the movie. Scott hollered at me and said, "Get suited up." I rode with Davey on a slow lap, filming the track. We pulled in and I was ready to get out, when Scott says, "Stay in." He motioned to Davey to go back out. We did a fast lap.

༄

Scott called me the other day on the cell phone. He said, "Hey, Tony. We are driving to Kansas and we were talking about you. Do you know what day it is?"

"No."

He hollered, "It's our first anniversary." It had been a year since we'd first met. We all laughed and after I hung up, I thought of the good times we'd had. It was great to have friends like that. Our personalities just clicked. It was like I had known Scott Jasek all my life.

༄

I was at Watkins Glen International in 2006 preparing to do a grass painting for the NASCAR race that AMD sponsored. Steve Hughey had moved to Florida,

Craig Gardner trying his hand on a grass painting at Watkins Glen.

so I called on Larry Orr once again to help me. The AMD logo was only thirty-five feet long and not too complicated. We made the pattern and I called my friend Craig Gardner to help also. Craig worked for NYSEG (New York State Electric and Gas) and loved racing, so I thought it would be fun for him to give us a hand. Craig mowed the grass and he and Larry laid down the pattern while I lined up the airless sprayer. Believe it or not, there was not one to be found in a hundred-mile radius. Rental places told me they were too much work to clean and they didn't get much call for them anymore. I went to a Sherwin Williams dealer and purchased my very own airless sprayer. I'd been using them since 1992, but this was the first time I actually owned one. I couldn't wait to use it.

The site for the grass painting was at the top of the Esses, in an area where the camera would pick it up almost every lap. As Craig mowed and Larry got the pattern rolled out, I hooked up the hose to the spray gun's brand-new shiny chrome gun handle. I didn't really want to use my new sprayer—I didn't want to get paint on it. As I screwed the wand extension to the gun handle, my mind slipped back to the very first time I used a paint sprayer at Talladega Superspeedway in Alabama. Then I thought of all the other paintings—including the one that almost killed me right here at Watkins Glen. I realized that this would be the first time I sprayed a grass painting here since that fateful day. *Not going to let that happen again,* I thought to myself.

Two Toyota track trucks pulled up breaking the silence. Tim Coleman, the general manager, and Andy Logenberger, the marketing manager, got out of one and Steve Ely, the race director, got out of the other. Tim walked up to me and said, "Hey

Covered in paint as the gun was shipped with no hose gasket.

Vickio. Gonna shoot yourself in the finger again?"

I laughed, partly because that was just what I was thinking about when they drove up. "Hell no. I'm more careful now and this gun is brand spanking new."

By the time Larry and Craig finished setting up, Tim, Andy, and Steve had left. *Good,* I thought, as I didn't need anyone hounding me. I was thinking about Tim's comment about shooting myself in the finger again as the paint ran through the lines and I pulled the trigger of that brand new chrome spray gun.

Instantly, there was a white flash. I let off the trigger and dropped the gun to the ground. The taste of white latex paint was in my mouth and paint was in my eyes. *This cannot be happening!* my mind screamed.

"What the hell happened?" Larry hollered.

I could see a little now and—still spitting paint—I walked to my truck where I had a bottle of drinking water. I took a slug to rinse my mouth out. Craig and Larry were rolling with laughter. Just then, Steve drove by and stopped. Now three of them were rolling with laughter. What else could I do? I rolled with laughter right along with them. Of course Tim drove up. Now the whole group was rolling with laughter. None of us could believe it. My luck with spray guns at this track was not good! After inspection, I found that the brand new gun had a defect. A seal had been left out at the factory. Luckily, I had a spare handle assembly and I used that to do the painting. *Paint washes off,* I thought. *At least I didn't shoot myself in the finger again!*

As I finally got the painting under way, the steady drone of the airless sprayer let my wander a little. Steve Hughey's words came back into my head. I remembered him saying as we were working on the high banks at Talladega, "Hey, Boss. I wonder how much longer we can do this?"

Those words made me feel sad, as I sprayed the white latex on the grass. While I was spraying paint, I thought back to 1972, when I was in that dingy gas station watching Bob Shaw pinstripe Don Romeo's Corvette and then he handed me the pin striping brush. That chance meeting started me on a path that led me to adventures all over the country. Now, here I am, back at where it all started—painting at Watkins Glen.

Then I thought about all the good times my friends Steve, Larry, and Bob had at Talladega, Daytona, Chicago, and Nazareth. I thought of all the people I had met along the way. Many had turned into great friends. I thought of all the stress when things went bad. How I handled it, I don't really know. I don't think I could work on the High Banks like I used to. I thought of the exhilaration when things went well. It was like an adrenalin rush I got when I won a race. I have looked at jobs we have done a year later and wondered, "How the hell did we do that!" I honestly can't believe we did some of those paintings. Larry always said, when I talked about some impossible job we did, "Famous! We forget who we are!" I smile and say, "Yeah. I guess we do."

☙

Among the many joys of my life that have threaded silently through these tales is the renovation of my own '65 Vette—the Glen Green one that became my dream car the instant I saw it at Shiny's gas station. Over the years, I worked on it off and on—with much help from friends, including a steady supply of now-unobtainable parts from Mike Fendt—a parts manager at a Chevrolet Dealership in Syracuse, New York—and Phil Husted of Phil's Body Shop in Elmira, New York, who specialized in Corvettes.

I remember the first time Phil looked it over. He got down on his knees and looked under the fender to check out how the flares were put on, then got up and said, "You're outta luck, man. The only right way to fix the fenders is to put new front fenders and rear quarter panels on. You aren't going to find any originals. They are long gone. I love working with fiberglass. I'd love to do this, but I don't have the right

My friend Mark Johnson doing the dirty job of stripping the paint off the Vette!

Fender flares removed and new fenders are ready to install (new fender on the roof).

My dream car!

parts. Find someone else."

"Come upstairs," I said. I pulled the folding stairs down from the ceiling and we climbed up into the attic. He stopped dead in his tracks. There, lined up in a row, were six Original GM Parts boxes. In them were front fender panels, the rear quarter panels, bonding strips and a complete side exhaust with covers.

He almost had a heart attack. He was fondling the pieces and mumbling something. Finally he got up and said, "I'll do it. I will take a long time, as I'm retired—and I want this car perfect." That week, my friend Scotty (Carl Scott) hauled the Body to Elmira and the start of the restoration.

When we were about done, Mike Wells, owner of Welco Interiors in Ithaca, came over and installed the Al Knoch interior (leather seats, carpet, and door panels). Ken Coates, owner of Inlet Glass & Mirror in Ithaca, came by and installed the glass. All the glass was tinted (it was an option in '65) and is the original glass that was in the car. Scott and Greg, owners of Freeman Communications, installed the complete new wiring harness. The engine went to Ithaca, NY where good friend Rich Seeley, owner of Rich's Garage and a race car engine builder, built a replica 327 Corvette engine for me. (It has the sweetest sound at 6,500 rpm!) We hooked the battery up, turned the key, and everything worked. And it's kept on working for the past ten years.

Wait a second. . . .

I just had to get up and look in the Corvette room to see if the car was there, and this was not just a dream. It's there. If you have never restored a car, there's no describing the effort it takes to do it right. Some Corvette collectors can't believe I drive this car, but on a sunny day, I will take it out and drive around town. (The longest drive I have been with it is a trip to Elmira, twenty-two miles away.) I haven't even spun the tires. It has never seen rain. As a matter of fact, I have never washed it. I dust it and use McGuire's wax and detailer on it. This car is not a Trailer Queen; I do drive it. But reverently, in celebration of a life well and truly lived.

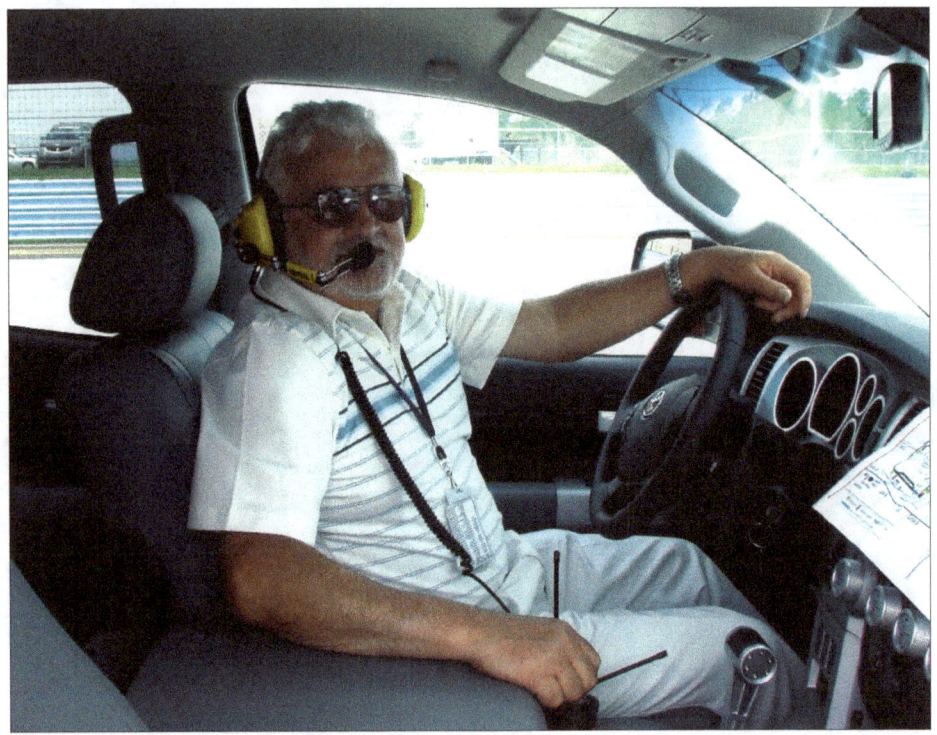

The NASCAR pace car driver did not show up so I stepped in to do the duties for a NASCAR Bush North race at Watkins Glen.

Victory Lap

I hope you enjoyed reading this book as much as I enjoyed living it!

Since 2006, when Lap 57 ended, I have kept busy with my sign business, Vickio Signs. I occasionally do work at Watkins Glen International, but I have not worked at any other race tracks since. I did travel back to Talladega for a visit in 2010. I took my two good friends, Gordon Dennis and Jack Eckert with me. It was nice to introduce them to all my good friends in Alabama.

I still give VIP Pace Car rides at The Glen. It almost satisfies my "need for speed." I do not go to short track races in my area as it would be like putting a shot of whiskey in front of a reformed alcoholic!

These days, Harriett and I love spending time with our granddaughter, Rachel. Harriett gets Rachel a fishing license once a year and we take her fishing. Rachel also loves camp fires in our back yard *(and so do Harriett and I!)*

Another thing that keeps me busy is Spirit of Schuyler, the charity Harriett and I founded. (Schuyler is the county we live in.) Spirit of Schuyler is a volunteer organization dedicated to helping improve the quality of life in Schuyler County. We assist county organizations in providing financial assistance for Schuyler County residents in times of emergency. The charity is supported by the generous donations of Schuyler residents and sponsors from around the country.

I want to thank my publisher, Gordon Cooper, and editors Hillary Powers and Bonnie Romeo for turning my mass of words into a readable book. Thanks also to Fred Wickham and the late Bill Bauman who were responsible for shooting the beautiful back cover. A special thanks to my daughter Beth for helping keep this venture moving forward.

Finally, a special "Thank You" to my family—and the many friends around the country—for their support, and a big thanks to all those "special guys" that got me through all of those racing years!

Painting the Start/Finish at Watkins Glen International with my granddaughter, Rachel Vickio, and my daughter, Beth Vicko Howard. I retired after 50 years in the business that I loved. I am truly blessed to have so many memories.

Index

A

Acid Indigestion 10, 11, 13, 166
Alexander, Stan 332, 333
Allen, "Wee" Willie 40
Allison, Bobby 272
Allison, Davey 272, 312, 349, 350, 353
Allison, Donnie 272
Americrown 319
Andretti, Mario 70, 83, 89, 343
Andretti, Michael 149, 343, 349
ARCA racing 265, 266, 317
Argetsinger, Cameron 1, 2, 13
Avery, Dan 138

B

Bodine, Geoff 153
Bovaird, Ed 13, 14
Brett Bodine 81, 89, 90
Britten Banners 156, 158, 160, 191, 228, 339, 340, 341
Britten, Paul 156, 160, 163, 164, 191
Buick LeSabre 59
Bush, George W. 299, 301, 302

C

Camaro 10, 157, 168, 169
Camden, John 50
Canandaigua Speedway 34, 36, 38, 39, 40, 52, 66, 73, 315
Cape Canaveral 218, 219
Carson, Bob 132, 157, 158, 159, 160, 161, 162, 163, 181, 182, 183, 184, 185, 187, 188, 189, 190, 191, 192, 193, 194, 195, 197, 198, 199, 200, 201, 202, 203, 204, 227
Cheaha Mountain 270, 287
Cherock, John 20, 26, 28, 30
Chevelle 19, 20, 23, 38, 40, 49, 50, 51, 52, 54, 72, 168, 169
Chevy 7, 19, 26, 33, 50, 58, 78, 82, 105, 112, 119, 157, 258, 275, 295, 317, 325
Chicagoland Speedway 87, 292, 324, 325, 326, 330, 333, 334, 336, 337
Childress, Richard 320
Ciprich, Chuck 16, 17, 18, 19, 20, 21, 24, 27, 28, 29, 32, 33, 41, 78, 82

Citroën 22, 23
Coates, Ken 86, 93, 132, 157, 276, 358
Cobb, Travis 353
Coleman, Tim 124, 294, 341, 343, 344, 345, 354, 355, 356
Comfort, Buster 248
Cornell University 87
Corning Community College 130, 285
Corning Enterprises 87, 129
Corning Glass Works 87
Crouch, Henrietta "Aunt Lega" 157, 172

D

Darlington Speedway 87
Daudlin, Brad 228, 230, 231, 235, 236, 237, 238, 240, 247, 248
Daytona International Speedway 12, 87, 94, 96, 98, 105, 106, 107, 112, 196, 200, 205, 206, 207, 208, 210, 211, 214, 215, 217, 219, 220, 221, 222, 224, 226, 235, 238, 248, 282, 297, 298, 299, 301, 302, 317, 319, 332, 356
Dean, Mike 284, 285, 286, 287, 288, 289, 290, 291, 292, 293
DeDominick, Robbie 20
Dempster, Keith 131, 132, 134
DeMunn, Holley 20, 39
Dennis, Gordon 361
DeSarno, Junior 13
DieHard 500 95, 122, 156, 157, 184, 185, 187, 262, 274
Dodge Charger 7
Donohue, Mark 10
Dudgeon, Frank 324
Duke, George 134, 149, 150, 151, 155, 175, 252
Dundee Speedway 16, 17, 23, 25, 26, 36, 37, 38, 42, 52, 315

E

Earnhardt, Dale 191, 220, 222, 248, 249, 272, 292, 299, 300, 317, 319, 320, 321, 323, 337
Earnhardt, Dale Jr. 299, 300
Eckert, Jack 133, 134, 153, 155, 320, 361
Economaki, Chris 18
Elkins, Jimmy 248, 287, 288, 311, 312, 313, 314, 316, 319
Elliott, Bill 249
Ellison, Johnny 132
Ely, Steve 43, 44, 124, 341, 354
Evans, Richie 84
Evans, Roy 36

F

Farmer, Red 312
Fendt, Mike 356
Ferrari 69, 135, 136, 137
Fisher, Sarah 172, 349, 350, 351
Five Mile Point Speedway 36, 58, 60, 61, 62, 63, 65, 66, 74
Ford 5, 13, 16, 18, 50, 78, 99, 100, 109, 110, 134, 139, 140, 158, 159, 160, 161, 191, 205, 228, 250, 251, 299
Ford Thunderbird Super Coupe 95, 102, 110, 111, 122, 123, 250
Foyt, A.J. 83, 224
France, Bill 94, 96, 200, 217, 221, 299, 344
France Kennedy, Lisa 217
Franzese, Chris 10, 11
Freeman, Greg 135, 140, 141, 143, 144, 146, 358
Freeman, Scott 135, 140, 141, 143, 144, 146, 358

G

Gabriel, Jim 315
Gardner, Craig 354, 355, 356
Gentile, Dave 292, 324, 326, 327, 329, 331, 333, 335, 337, 338
Gordon, Jeff 83, 149, 172, 262, 263
Gower Paint 285, 286, 291
Green, Bill 70, 151
GT-40 13

H

Hahne, Dick 38, 47, 94, 103, 104, 105, 107, 200, 201, 206, 207, 210, 211, 213, 215, 216, 217, 222, 226, 297, 301, 318
Haight, Bob 26, 28
Hamilton, Davey 349, 350, 353
Harvick, Kevin 337
Haudenschild, Jac 335
Helton, Mike 122, 336
Hidden Valley 2
Highwaller shoes 277, 279, 280
Hill, Graham 45, 47, 48, 69, 70, 106
Homestead-Miami Speedway 87
Hromada, Missy 159, 162, 182, 184, 191
Hughey, Steve viii, ix, 126, 227, 228, 229, 230, 231, 233, 235, 236, 237, 238, 240, 242, 244, 247, 275, 283, 284, 285, 286, 287, 288, 289, 291, 292, 303, 304, 305, 306, 307, 308, 309, 310, 312, 315, 316, 317, 318, 319, 320, 321, 322, 323, 324, 353, 356
Hunt, James 70
Hurd, Gary 38, 39
Hurd, Larry 44
Husted, Phil 356

I

International Speedway Corporation 87, 94, 132, 248, 343
IRL Indy 348, 349
IRL Indy Racing League 348, 349
IROC 88, 317, 318, 319
Irvan, Ernie 122

J

Jackson, Paul 9
Jackson's Dragway 9
Jarrett, Dale 299
Jarvis, Jim 75, 76, 77
Jasek, Scott 352, 353
Javelin 53, 54
John Deere Gator 162, 186, 196, 200, 201, 231, 235, 241, 318
Johnson, Larry 98, 100, 102, 103, 104, 105, 106, 107, 162, 316
Johnson, Mark 357
Johnson, Tim 322
Jones, Allan 241, 246, 283
Jones Smith, Erin 349, 350

K

Kansas Speedway 87
Kendall, Tommy 153
Kent, George 81, 83, 84
Kerbein, Gary viii
Kings Dragway 8, 9, 10, 13
Kinser, Steve 335
Kohler, John 134, 135, 136, 137

L

Labonte, Terry 172
LaDue Benjamin, Michelle xi, 124
Lane, Cal 93
Lane, Jack 213, 215, 216, 217, 218, 219, 223, 225, 297
Lasoski, Danny 335
Late Model 18, 24, 25, 29, 36, 38, 49, 50, 52, 53, 72, 76, 168, 311
Lurcock, John "Shiny" 12, 13, 14, 356

M

Macy, Bill 132
Macy, Harry 132

Marcis, Dave 318
Maria's Tavern 132, 157, 158, 337
Marion, Dale 78, 79, 80, 81, 82, 83, 84, 85, 89, 92, 170
Marlin, Sterling 75
Martinsville Speedway 87
Matusicky, Betsy 146
Matusicky, Matt "Mattman" 94, 96, 124, 129, 139, 140, 145, 146, 147, 148
Matwiejow, Joe 49, 51, 52, 53, 55, 56, 57, 58, 60, 63, 64, 65, 89, 92
McDuffie, J.D. 152, 154, 319
McWilliams, Andy 191, 316
McWilliams, Mike 162, 183, 186, 196, 197, 199, 200, 227, 228, 229, 230, 231, 232, 233, 255, 272, 274, 275, 279, 280, 282, 284, 291, 304, 305, 310, 316, 317, 318, 319, 320, 321, 324, 331, 333
Meehan, Bill 20, 59
Melon, Chris 47
Menio, Ed 3
Menio, Eddy 55, 56, 57, 59, 60, 132, 334
Messinger, Keith 86
Michigan International Speedway 87
Midget Racing 131, 132, 133, 134, 175, 335
Milliken, Bill 3
Mitchell, Walt 33, 40
Modified 16, 17, 18, 24, 32, 40, 78, 79, 81, 82, 83, 84, 89, 131, 138, 168, 170, 260, 306
Monterey Jacks 59
Montour Falls ix, 7, 13, 17, 20, 24, 94, 157, 210, 284
Morris, Glenn 213, 214, 215, 216, 217, 218, 219, 223, 224, 225, 226, 297, 298, 302
Morrow's Junkyard 59
Mosport International Speedway 135, 136, 137, 175
Motorsports Hall of Fame 238, 239, 279, 280

N

NASCAR 78, 79, 84, 89, 92, 94, 96, 122, 125, 129, 132, 138, 139, 151, 152, 154, 157, 164, 170, 184, 191, 195, 200, 207, 212, 217, 244, 245, 246, 247, 266, 274, 280, 284, 287, 297, 298, 299, 306, 316, 318, 319, 320, 329, 332, 333, 335, 336, 339, 341, 343, 344, 347, 348, 349, 353, 360
Nazareth Speedway 177, 343, 344, 347, 348, 349, 351, 352, 356
Nicholson, John viii
North Carolina Speedway 98

O

Oldsmobile 442 7
Olevnik, Bob 20, 26, 27, 30, 39
O'Malley, J.J. 134
Orcutt, David 'Butch' 208, 209

Orr, Larry viii, ix, 126, 227, 228, 229, 230, 231, 232, 235, 236, 237, 238, 240, 242, 244, 245, 246, 247, 248, 255, 258, 259, 261, 262, 264, 265, 266, 267, 268, 269, 270, 271, 273, 274, 275, 276, 277, 279, 281, 283, 284, 285, 286, 287, 288, 289, 290, 291, 292, 296, 303, 324, 325, 326, 327, 329, 330, 333, 334, 335, 336, 337, 338, 340, 341, 343, 344, 345, 347, 349, 352, 354, 356

Orr, Sally 231, 242, 245, 246, 248, 249, 338

P

Pappy's bar 59
Penske, Roger 10, 344, 349
Pfautz, Gino 344, 348
Popham, Jamey 322
Price, Donna 255, 261, 262, 282, 283, 285, 316, 319, 352

R

Richmond International Speedway 87
Rolling Wheels Raceway 17, 25, 26, 27, 28, 36, 51, 52, 55, 58, 61, 63, 73, 77, 78, 168, 315
Romeo, Don viii, ix, 17, 20, 24, 26, 27, 30, 32, 34, 35, 42, 50, 55, 61, 63, 64, 65, 66, 73, 82, 84, 129, 209, 256, 257, 258, 356
Root, Jimmy 14
Rudy, Maurice 125, 126, 139, 140, 148
Russell, John 88, 128, 129

S

Sargent, David 'Sarge' 197, 316, 319
Saunders, John 129, 132, 140, 146
Scheckter, Jody 70, 71
Schmidt, Knute 87
Schuler, Diane 252
Schuler, Mike 149, 252, 253, 254
Schweitz, Jerry 75
Scott, Carl "Scotty" 358
Seely, Rich 157
Shangri-La Speedway 78, 80, 89, 93
Shaw, Bob 42
Shepard Niles ix, 7, 13, 17, 19, 24, 68, 86
Signore, Jay 318, 319
Sinden, Jeff 352, 353
Skip Barber Driving School 149, 150, 151, 152, 175, 208, 252
Smalley, Frank 42
Smalley, Lester 22
Smith, Gary 135, 136

Smith, Jay 20
Snow, Denny 20, 24, 25, 26, 27, 28, 34, 157
Space Shuttle 218, 219
Spencer, Jimmy 81, 89, 90, 306
Spirit of Schuyler 361, 372
Sprint Car 52, 53, 56, 131, 208, 335
Stewart, Jackie 70
Stewart, Tony 83, 335
Sullivan, Claude 129, 130, 285
Swindell, Slammin' Sammy 335
Swinford, Billy 99, 100, 113, 114, 121, 122, 195, 196, 270

T

Talladega Speedway ix, 87, 94, 95, 96, 98, 99, 103, 104, 106, 109, 110, 115, 118, 119, 120, 122, 123, 124, 125, 156, 157, 158, 161, 164, 172, 176, 177, 178, 183, 191, 197, 199, 200, 201, 202, 204, 207, 211, 212, 215, 220, 227, 228, 229, 231, 232, 233, 235, 236, 238, 239, 240, 241, 242, 244, 246, 255, 258, 259, 260, 262, 264, 267, 269, 272, 273, 274, 278, 279, 280, 281, 282, 283, 284, 286, 290, 291, 292, 293, 301, 303, 306, 307, 309, 310, 311, 312, 313, 314, 316, 317, 318, 319, 322, 324, 325, 326, 329, 331, 334, 336, 339, 345, 352, 354, 356, 361
Taney, Dennis 34
Tantallo, Dominic 39
Ten Limited Tavern 71
Thurston, Ernie 122, 196, 248, 249, 302
Timmerman, Bob viii, 227, 237, 275
Tinker, Steve ix, 19, 49, 255, 257, 258, 259, 260, 261, 263, 264, 266, 267, 269, 270, 271, 272, 283, 285, 292
Tioga Speedway 78
Toyota 209, 242, 354
Trickle, Dick 318
Trickler, Charlie 54, 75, 273
Troyer, Maynard 92
Truex, Martin Jr. 348

V

Vickio, Beth 77, 86, 124, 172, 207, 226, 361
Vickio, Faith 16
Vickio, Harriett vii, 86, 124, 144, 145, 150, 156, 158, 172, 204, 205, 206, 207, 208, 209, 210, 226, 231, 242, 245, 246, 248, 249, 284, 302, 316, 338, 353, 361
Vickio, Johnny 241
Vickio, Kathy 8, 17, 19, 25, 26, 30, 44, 45, 48, 63, 65, 66, 73, 74, 75, 76, 77, 86, 92, 93, 172
Vickio, Mark 17, 21, 25, 77, 131, 168, 172, 226
Vickio, Nick "Chip" 1, 3, 4, 5, 6, 165, 241

Vickio, Nick "Dad" 1, 4, 5, 6, 7, 18, 19, 20, 26, 50, 51, 58, 60, 172
Vickio, Rachel 172, 361
Vickio, Rachel "Mom" 1, 6, 26, 43, 60, 172, 226

W

Wallace, Rusty 334
Waltrip, Darryl 336
Watkins Glen International xi, 4, 6, 7, 61, 87, 94, 107, 124, 128, 131, 132, 138, 139, 148, 149, 154, 250, 251, 285, 294, 297, 343, 352, 353, 361, 362
Watkins Salt Company 51
Waugh, Al 44
Weedsport Speedway 36, 39, 52, 62, 72, 73, 76, 172, 315
Wells, Mike 86, 157, 270, 277, 358
Wheldon, Dan 351
White, Peter 339
White's Hollow 2, 8
Wick, Harriett 250, 251, 252
Williams, Jeff 20, 26, 27, 28, 29, 34
Williams, Kirk 20, 30, 59, 60, 61
Williams, Sue 322
Winston 500 Golf Tournament 304, 306, 307, 309, 310
Woodard, Pete 261, 316
Wood, Mike 20
World Famous iii, 71, 372
World of Outlaw (WoO) 335

Y

Yates, Robert 299
Yip, Teddy 71

Z

Zippo 134, 135, 137, 138, 149, 155, 175, 252, 253, 254, 306

Other books by Preston Woods Publishing

Watkins Glen Tour Guide
by Gordon D. Cooper
Filled with hundreds of full color photos and maps, Watkins Glen Tour Guide provides a photo-rich history of the village of Watkins Glen, N.Y. and the surrounding area. Five self-guided tours cover Watkins Glen State Park, the Finger Lakes Trail, the original road race course that brought racing to the village, a historic walk through downtown and the dozens of wineries on the south end of Seneca Lake. (320 pages) **$29.95**

Schuyler County Days Bygone
by Barbara H. Bell
Schuyler County's longest-serving historian has opened her extensive archives to share the stories and photos that detail the history of New York's smallest county. The legend of the Seneca Lake monster, horse rustling, pioneer living, salt mining, gold mining, winemaking, and the origins of many of the settlements in Schuyler County are a sampling of the topics that appear in Bell's fifth book on local history. (338 pages) **$23.95**

Seneca Sunrise: The Life and Times of Frederick Davis, Jr.
by Frank W. Steber
Frank Steber lovingly re-creates the life of Frederick Davis, Jr., who in the late 1800s made a large impact on the small town that is now Watkins Glen, N.Y. Davis's accomplishments and his life have been all but forgotten, but Seneca Sunrise will allow you to travel back to the time before cars, vaccines, running water and electricity to witness how the character of a man helped shape a town. (128 pages) **$12.00**

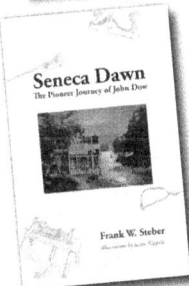

Seneca Dawn: The Pioneer Journey of John Dow
by Frank W. Steber
Frank Steber imagines the journey of one of the Finger Lakes region's first pioneers, John Dow, who traveled from Connecticut to the head of Seneca Lake in the late 1700s. After apprenticing with a cabinet maker and spinning wheel maker in Connecticut, young John takes his skills to the frontier of western New York. Travel along as he pursues his dream of carving a new life out of the wilderness. (128 pages) **$12.00**

Seneca Hope: The Life and Landscapes of James Hope
by Frank W. Steber
In 1872, landscape painter James Hope moved from Castleton, Vermont to Watkins, N.Y. – a small village on the southern end of Seneca Lake – where he spent the last 20 years of his life capturing the beauties of the glen on canvas. To bring this artist to life, author Frank Steber imagines Hope's life from his days in Castleton, to his studio portrait in New York, N.Y. and finally to his life in Watkins Glen. (128 pages) **$15.00**

Order your copies now at **www.prestonwoods.com**

About the Author

Tony Vickio

Tony Vickio was born and raised in Watkins Glen, N.Y. He developed a passion for sign painting at an early age and is the owner of the "World Famous" Vickio Signs in Watkins Glen. Tony's sign work has been published in SignCraft magazine and he has worked with many high-profile clients from around the world in the racing community. In 2011, Tony was awarded the Schuyler County Chamber of Commerce Community Spirit Award for his leadership and excellence in philanthropy and humanitarianism efforts in creating and growing the Spirit of Schuyler, a local non-profit organization that he and his family began. Spirit of Schuyler continues to significantly impact his community, improving the quality of life for Schuyler County residents in times of need. Tony never planned to be an author. *Shifting Gears: Tales of Pistons, Paint cans, and Personalities* — based on his adventures in the racing and painting worlds — is his first book.

Contact the Author

Do you have feedback on the contents of this book or questions for the author? You can send the author a message at www.prestonwoods.com/shiftinggears/author

www.ingramcontent.com/pod-product-compliance
Lightning Source LLC
Chambersburg PA
CBHW071853290426
44110CB00013B/1124